Teaching Secondary Physical Education

Preparing Adolescents to Be Active for Life

Cathrine Himberg, PhD

Gayle E. Hutchinson, EdD

John M. Roussell, PhD

California State University, Chico

Human Kinetics

Library of Congress Cataloging-in-Publication Data

Himberg, Cathrine, 1965-
    Teaching secondary physical education : preparing adolescents to be
active for life / Cathrine Himberg, Gayle E. Hutchinson, John Mathieu
Roussell.
            p. ; cm.
Includes bibliographical references and index.
    ISBN 0-88011-939-X (hard cover)
    1. Physical education and training--Study and teaching
(Secondary)--United States.
    [DNLM: 1. Physical Education and Training--Adolescence. 2.
Teaching--methods. QT 255 H657t 2003] I. Hutchinson, Gayle. II.
Roussell, John Mathieu, 1961- III. Title.
    GV365.H56 2003
    613.7´071´2--dc21   2002009439

ISBN: 0-88011-939-X

Acquisitions Editor: Bonnie Pettifor; **Developmental Editor:** Myles Schrag; **Assistant Editor:** Jennifer L. Davis, Kathleen Bernard; **Copyeditor:** Bob Replinger; **Proofreader:** Erin Cler; **Indexer:** Betty Frizéll; **Permission Manager:** Dalene Reeder; **Graphic Designer:** Fred Starbird; **Graphic Artist:** Angela K. Snyder; **Photo Manager:** Leslie A. Woodrum; **Cover Designer:** Jack W. Davis; **Photographer (cover):** Leslie A. Woodrum; **Photographer (interior):** Leslie A. Woodrum; **Art Manager:** Kelly Hendren; **Illustrators:** Tom Roberts, Roberto Sabas; **Illustrators (Mac):** Kristin A. Darling, Angela K. Snyder; **Printer:** Edwards.

Printed in the United States of America   10 9 8 7 6 5 4 3 2 1

Human Kinetics
Web site: www.HumanKinetics.com
United States: Human Kinetics, P.O. Box 5076, Champaign, IL 61825-5076
800-747-4457
e-mail: humank@hkusa.com

Canada: Human Kinetics, 475 Devonshire Road Unit 100, Windsor, ON N8Y 2L5
800-465-7301 (in Canada only)
e-mail: orders@hkcanada.com

Europe: Human Kinetics, 107 Bradford Road, Stanningley, Leeds LS28 6AT, United Kingdom
+44 (0) 113 255 5665
e-mail: hk@hkeurope.com

Australia: Human Kinetics, 57A Price Avenue, Lower Mitcham, South Australia 5062
08 8277 1555
e-mail: liahka@senet.com.au

New Zealand: Human Kinetics, P.O. Box 105-231, Auckland Central
09-523-3462
e-mail: hkp@ihug.co.nz

We dedicate this book to all individuals who, for good reasons, hated public school physical education, and to the teachers who are working hard to make physical education a positive and beneficial experience for *all* students.

Contents

Preface

Every individual matters.
Every individual has a role to play.
Every individual makes a difference.
And we have a choice:
What sort of difference do we want to make?

— Jane Goodall

As we were working on our last chapter revisions for this book, the January 2002 issue of the *Journal of Teaching Physical Education* came out. We were thrilled to see that it included an article by Dr. Charles B. Corbin, an internationally recognized researcher and professor at Arizona State University. Although we had heard him express the ideas before, seeing them in print was exciting and encouraging. The article seemed to be a call for our book because it expressed the philosophy that we promote: Physical education teachers must help students become physically active for the rest of their lives.

If you ask physical educators in the United States to identify the main purpose of physical education, many of them would have trouble finding a clear, specific answer. When we ask this question of colleagues, students, and friends, we receive a variety of answers, including developing motor skills, understanding concepts, becoming responsible human beings, attaining fitness, learning social skills, practicing sport literacy, having fun, and taking a break from academic classes. Most of these goals are appropriate for the physical education setting, but only if they support the main purpose of guiding students toward a lifetime of physical activity. We agree with Corbin (2002) that it's time for physical education to respond to the concerns about physical inactivity and the related health and wellness issues. We must focus our public school physical education programs on promoting physical activity in any way we can.

Of course, our profession faces many real and perceived barriers to achieving this goal. These include ineffective teaching, poor or inadequate planning, large class sizes, limited equipment, and inadequate facilities. Poor programs result in excessive student absenteeism and marginalization, as well as less than favorable public relations with students, teachers, parents, and administrators (Locke 1992). We have witnessed many poor programs during our careers, and we have heard countless stories of inappropriate practices from students, teachers, and parents. We believe it is time to make a positive change in physical education programs, and we need your help to make it happen. We can overcome these barriers only if current and future teachers do all they can to teach physical education with the purpose of preparing students to be active for the rest of their lives.

We wrote *Teaching Secondary Physical Education: Preparing Adolescents to Be Active for Life* to challenge you to improve secondary physical education programs and to help you focus on helping students develop the skills and knowledge they need to become active for the rest of their lives. We do this by introducing you to appropriate physical education practices that engage secondary school students. Using what we call the Diamond Conceptual Framework, we examine several areas—the adolescent, the teacher, the curriculum, the setting, and the journey—to help you teach physical education effectively.

How did *we* arrive at the conclusion that physical education curricula need to focus on helping students become physically active for the rest of their lives? Well, it just made sense! Although people have known about the health benefits of physical activity for a long time, we have seen a negative trend in physical activity participation and obesity rates in our society over the last three decades. As this book goes to print, the numbers show that more than 45 million U.S. adults are obese, and the percentage of overweight children and adolescents has more than doubled to 8 million in the last 20 years. In addition, more than 60% of adults are not active enough to reap health benefits (U.S. Department of Health and Human Services 2000 and 2002). There is no longer any question that obesity and inactivity are related. Sufficient amounts of regular physical activity can help with more than obesity levels, as the surgeon general's report on physical activity and health (U.S. Department of Health and Human Services 1996) shows. It reviews the benefits of regular participation in physical activity and suggests that if people would just get off the couch and participate in moderate physical activity for 30 minutes each day, they would improve their health significantly. Moderate daily physical activity could postpone or completely prevent major diseases such as certain forms of cancer, high blood pressure, cardiovascular disease, osteoporosis, and diabetes. Why, then, are so few adults physically active? When we observe young children in our society, we see plenty of physical activity. But a dramatic drop in activity levels occurs during adolescence. Could it have something to do with the fact that enrollment in daily physical education drops at about that age (National Association for Sport and Physical Education [NASPE] 2002)? Are we discouraging children from becoming active by offering opportunities only to the athletically gifted? Are we failing to teach our children what they need to know and do to be active outside school and for the rest of their lives?

Why, during this time of recognition of the benefits of physical activity, are many states eliminating physical education programs or giving PE credit for band, drivers' education, and athletics (NASPE 2002)? When this happens, the message we give the public is that we're not teaching anything in our physical education classes that is worthwhile for *all* students to learn. And for many secondary school physical education programs, that is sadly the truth. Students aren't learning the things that will help them become active for the rest of their lives. Some programs even discourage students from being active by using inappropriate teaching practices. A student who associates physical activity only with physical and emotional pain because she was punished with push-ups and sit-ups, was chosen last for teams, was out first in elimination games, and was embarrassed in front

of the class by failing the pull-up test may be tough to convince that physical activity can be enjoyable.

We'd be the first to say that inappropriate physical education can be more harmful than no physical education at all. But we are completely convinced that *we* can make a difference and that *you* can make a difference! The image of secondary school physical education must change! The excellent teachers in our nation have to publicize the great things they're doing. Many are already doing just that (Condon and Collier 2002; McCracken 2001). New teachers entering the field must have a purpose for physical education that answers the national concern about physical inactivity. They must know how to teach for that purpose using effective and appropriate practices, and they should constantly reflect on what they do so that they can continue to learn and grow.

How to Use This Book

We wrote this book for future and current physical education teachers because, after years of searching, we could not find a book that addressed all the important issues that we cover in our physical education teacher education courses and professional development workshops. What follows is an overview of the contents and unique features of the text.

The Diamond Conceptual Framework, explained in chapter 1, is an innovative way to conceptualize the progression of focused physical education experiences for preschool through grade 12. The framework centers on the outcome of having educated students who are likely to be physically active for the rest of their lives. We refer to the Diamond Conceptual Framework throughout the book to help you understand how to apply it to all aspects of teaching physical education.

We consider this book an interactive text. Several features of the book are designed to help you gain greater understanding from your reading experience. Let's start with some of the more distinctive features.

Diamond Icon

We have used a diamond icon in the margin of the text in most chapters. This will help you understand and focus on the purpose of physical education. We hope that seeing the icon will help you remember the ideas of the Diamond Conceptual Framework and understand the direct connection between certain issues in those chapters and teaching secondary physical education with the purpose of helping students become active for life. In other words, the icon appears in places where we want you to think about big-picture questions such as "Why is this important?" and "How does this help me guide students in the process of becoming active for the rest of their lives?"

Real-Life Scenarios

We start each chapter with a real-life scenario that relates to the issues we explore in the chapter. The scenarios set the stage for you to understand that what follows relates directly to what you may have to deal with when you teach. In each chapter the physical educators who appear in the opening scenario resurface later. These real-life situations are meant to encourage issue-oriented discussions as you learn more about the issues at hand. We hope the scenarios also help you realize that others deal with real-life situations similar to those you may experience.

"Your Turn" Questions

As you're reading each chapter you will come across boxes labeled "Your Turn." Listed will be a few questions that we encourage you to think about when you read the text. When you discuss the chapters in class, your professor or instructor will probably ask these or similar questions. Thinking about the questions before you come to class will enable you to share your experiences or solutions with the rest of the class.

T 'n T Boxes

In chapter 2 we introduce a philosophy for using technology in the physical education classroom. Throughout the remaining chapters of the book we have inserted T 'n T (Tools and Techniques) boxes designed to help you use technology to continue learning or to teach your students. Some of these boxes contain ideas about using instructional technology to reach your learning objectives. Other T 'n T boxes refer you to technology resources.

Chapter-Opening Quotes

Quotations from famous and not-so-famous people open each chapter. We feel that the ideas expressed summarize the importance of what follows. Although many of these quotations were not uttered in the context of physical education, the universal values and truths they express apply to physical education taught with a purpose. The ideas remind us that what we teach in our physical education programs extends far beyond a particular class period.

Student Learning Objectives

Learning objectives highlight the key issues or ideas in each chapter. The learning objectives identify the focus of each chapter and the most important topics. When you study for exams by reviewing the chapters, the learning objectives will guide you to the most important information.

Key Terms and Phrases

At the start of each chapter we provide a list of key terms and phrases that help you understand issues raised in that chapter. They are listed in the order that they appear in the text.

Chapter Summary and "Checking for Understanding" Questions

We conclude each chapter with a summary and questions that help you check your understanding of the issues, concepts, and key terms discussed. You can use these questions to help you review the chapter. The questions are congruent with the learning objectives and key terms at the beginning of each chapter.

Reflection and Discussion Questions

Each chapter ending includes questions designed to make you think, solve problems, and synthesize information to determine viable solutions to posed dilemmas. Reflection is a critical piece of teaching. We hope that you will make it a daily habit.

References and Suggested Readings

At the end of each chapter is a list of references used in creating the subject matter for that chapter plus suggested additional articles and books that we think are helpful. We suggest that you consult these sources if you want to learn more about a particular topic. By placing the list at the end of each chapter rather than at the end of the book, we make it easier for you to find topic-specific information.

Overview of the Book

This text is divided into six parts, each named for a vital aspect of the profession that teachers and soon-to-be teachers should strive to understand. Each of these parts introduces and explains important issues that face physical education teachers. We start by presenting you with the challenge of teaching physical education in a new century, and we end with an invitation to join us on the wonderful journey that our profession offers. Here is a part-by-part synopsis of the book:

Part I: The Challenge

We call the first part of the book "The Challenge" because we think the book will challenge you to start thinking differently about secondary physical education and your role as a promoter of lifelong activity. As mentioned earlier, we begin by presenting our philosophy in chapter 1. We explain how we arrived at the conclusion that the main purpose of physical education should be to guide students in the process of becoming physically active for the rest of their lives. In the first chapter we define how we use the words *skills* and *concepts* throughout the book. We also introduce the "guiding lights" for our profession and the GET ACTIVE FOR LIFE factors, which summarize the determinants for physical activity in youth. We explain how this information provides the backbone for our Diamond Conceptual Framework for physical education.

In chapter 2, we introduce the concept of technology and provide a guideline to use when you want to know how to include technology effectively in your physical education program. We address the purpose for implementing instructional technology and explain how that purpose should center on meeting your established goals and objectives. We introduce the GOT-IT model, which addresses a series of questions that can help you avoid adopting expensive and ineffective technology. We explore ways of using technology to help in teaching, class management, assessment, atypical class contexts, and motivating students to continue being active.

In chapter 3, we further explore the determinants for physical activity in youth. We explain why the focus of physical education programs should be physical activity, not physical fitness. In discussing the concept of lifetime activities, we give you a few questions to focus on when deciding which activities and sports to include in a physical education curriculum. The challenge is this: "Will you create and teach physical education classes that will help students become active for the rest of their lives?" The remainder of the book helps you get to the point where you can say "Yes!" to that challenge.

Part II: The Adolescent

To understand the process of teaching and learning, we must understand the students we work with. In secondary physical education, we typically work with students between the ages of 11 and 18. This age range is the era of life known as adolescence. Chapter 4 examines the growth and development of adolescents, paying special attention to growth, maturation, and puberty. We describe self-concept along with six essential components necessary for developing positive self-concept. Other considerations like nutrition, eating disorders, and drug abuse are also discussed. After completing chapter 4, you will have a broad overview of how adolescents grow and develop, how they form positive self-concept, and how behavioral and chemical factors can affect their development.

Physiology and environmental factors affecting student growth do not in themselves explain adolescent complexity. We need to look at cognitive development as it relates to student learning. In chapter 5, we examine how adolescents learn. We discuss the process of learning and each person's unique learning path. Through information about brain development, IQ, multiple intelligences, motor learning, and metacognition, we paint a picture of student diversity.

Diversity includes students with disabilities. In chapter 6, we discuss how teachers work with students with disabilities. An overview of federal legislation and a description of individualized education plans are part of the discussion. We describe multiple types of disabilities and disease. This chapter will help you in teaching students with disabilities in your classes. It will also guide you toward making your classroom more inclusive for all students.

Now that we understand adolescents further, we are ready to take a close look at ourselves as teachers in part III.

Part III: The Teacher

In this section we concentrate on what the teacher can do to teach secondary physical education in a way that will help all students become physically active for life. We explore the teaching methods we think are most important to becoming an effective and reflective teacher. In chapter 7, we introduce the concept of inclusion teaching and discuss issues of quantity and quality of practice in learning important skills and concepts. Chapter 8 presents a variety of teaching styles for physical education in this section. To become an effective teacher who can accommodate learners with a variety of learning styles, you need to be able to use a variety of teaching styles. We have modified Mosston and Ashworth's (1994, 2001) spectrum of teaching styles in this chapter by infusing the inclusion concept into each style.

All the information and skills concerning effective teaching will not go very far if the environment where students are learning is not positive and safe. Chapter 9 guides you with strategies for creating a positive learning environment. You will learn the difference between harassment and violence. You will examine closely your biases and prejudices toward students using the self-fulfilling prophecy cycle. From there, we describe in detail protocols for establishing positive learning environments.

Part IV: The Curriculum

Designing a curriculum that is aligned with your philosophy of physical education is important if you want to reach your goals. In this section we explore issues related to curriculum design, and we look at value orientations and curriculum models. In chapter 10, we also tell you which curriculum model we embrace and which we think can work with the Diamond Conceptual Framework for physical education. We introduce you to lesson and unit planning and explain each important part of a lesson and unit plan. We help you understand how to write objectives that are attainable in the time frame that you set. In chapter 11, we explain the purpose of and ideas for safe and effective warm-ups that don't waste valuable

time. Then we explain why assessment is so critical to a program's success. We explore a variety of ways that you may assess your students' learning. Traditional assessment practices are presented, but chapter 12 encourages and focuses on alternative and authentic assessment. We end this section (chapter 13) with a variety of ideas for what to do when you encounter unexpected situations. We encourage you to be prepared for the unexpected and to explore ways that "plan B" days can be valuable learning days for your students.

Part V: The Setting

Teaching involves more than just working with students. You must consider the culture of the setting in which you work. We begin in chapter 14 by looking at this through the challenges and roles of the teacher-coach. Here, we ask you to reflect on your biography and why you chose to become a physical education teacher. You will also explore the power of socialization in your career choices. We point out that many teachers want to become coaches first and physical educators second. One of the realities of teaching and coaching is that teachers must make decisions about where to commit their time. Each role could be a full-time responsibility. We offer strategies for dealing with the challenges of role conflict and point out the numerous roles that teachers are expected to perform while working in public schools.

In chapter 15, we explore legal issues associated with teaching physical education with the help of real-world case studies involving claims of negligence on behalf of students who were injured during physical education class. With the prevalence of lawsuits in society today, physical education teachers need to be aware of liabilities associated with their profession. We discuss the most common areas associated with lawsuits and physical education. By addressing areas linked to design, delivery, procedures, and practices in physical education programs, we offer suggestions that can minimize possibilities for dangerous and legal liability for the physical education teacher. Other areas concerning legal risks are explored to encourage a commonsense approach to teaching safe physical education based on professional standards and guidelines.

We move on, in chapter 16, to present areas associated with creativity and design in developing effective and positive physical education environments. First, we describe a general approach to addressing, designing, and implementing a new way of thinking and acting to make designing for change realistic and attainable. We offer suggestions that range from relatively simple designs for equipment and facility management to long-term, high-commitment designs for community access, involvement, and partnerships with your program. Also included at the end of this chapter is a way to design strong communication mechanisms for promoting the success of your program and partnerships.

Part VI: The Journey

The last section of the text focuses on the remaining information you need so that you can accept the challenge in part I: teaching secondary physical education with the purpose of helping students become active for the rest of their lives. It is not enough for physical educators simply to teach their classes. They must serve as effective teachers first and as advocates of their programs second. In chapter 17, we examine strategies for becoming a teacher leader and working to create positive change in physical education. We hope that the strategies presented will motivate you to take on an active leadership role among your colleagues.

In the last chapter, we present an overview of typical career development for a physical educator. We explain the importance of continued professional development after you graduate from college with your teaching credential. Your journey has just begun. We give you ideas for how you can make sure to travel in the right direction by becoming a critical consumer of professional development information and continue to learn for the rest of your career. We challenge you to set out on the journey of the excellent teacher—one who stays up-to-date, continues to improve, and always keeps in mind the main purpose of physical education.

We hope that you enjoy reading this text, and we encourage you to become a teacher who will make a positive difference in the lives of your students!

References

Condon, R., and C. Collier. 2002. Student choice makes a difference in physical education. *Journal of Physical Education, Recreation and Dance* 73(2):26-30.

Corbin, C. 2002. Physical activity for everyone: What every physical educator should know about promoting lifelong physical activity. *Journal of Teaching Physical Education* 21:128-144.

Locke, L. 1992. Changing secondary school physical education. *Quest* 44:361-372.

McCracken, B. 2001. *It's not just gym anymore.* Champaign, IL: Human Kinetics.

Mosston, M., and S. Ashworth. 1994. *Teaching physical education.* 4th ed. New York: Macmillan.

Mosston, M., and S. Ashworth. 2001. *Teaching physical education.* 5th ed. San Francisco: Benjamin/Cummings.

National Association for Sport and Physical Education (NASPE). 2002, 2001. *Shape of the nation report: Status of physical education in the USA.* Reston, VA: NASPE Publications.

U.S. Department of Health and Human Services. 1996. *Physical activity and health: A report of the surgeon general.* Atlanta: U.S. Department of Health and Human Services, Centers for Disease Control and Prevention, National Center for Chronic Disease Prevention and Health Promotion.

U.S. Department of Health and Human Services. 2000. *Healthy people 2010: National health promotion and disease objectives.* Washington, DC: U.S. Government Printing Office.

U.S. Department of Health and Human Services. 2002. "Physical Activity and Good Nutrition: Essential Elements to Prevent Chronic Diseases and Obesity—At a Glance." Available: **www.cdc.gov/nccdphp/dnpa/dnpaaag.htm**.

Acknowledgments

We would like to express our thanks and gratitude to a few people who were instrumental in helping us get this book completed. Scott Wikgren: thank you for being excited about our ideas in the first place, and for recognizing the importance of this text! Bonnie Pettifor, our acquisitions editor: thank you for giving us that first real "push" to make the book a priority in our very busy lives. It took awhile to get it completed, but you were understanding and helped us work around our teaching loads of eight courses per year. Your feedback was very helpful in our continued conceptualization of what the final product would look like, and your encouragement was greatly appreciated! Myles Schrag, our developmental editor: thank you for your ability to see the big picture and ask the right questions that kept us moving forward. Your attention to detail and knowledge of our field were critical. Without your help and ability to understand our sometimes unorthodox ideas for the book, the result would not be the same! Jennifer Davis, our assistant editor: thank you for your diligent and detailed work in the final stages of writing and production. Les Woodrum, you are a great photographer. We had a lot of fun working with you! Thanks also to the talented production staff who made this book look so good: Fred Starbird, who designed it, and Angela Snyder, who laid it out. Our model teachers and students at Bidwell Junior High School, Chico High School, the Alternative Transition Center of Chico Unified School District, and California State University, Chico: thank you for helping make this book look its best! Your positive attitudes and flexibility made it an enjoyable experience. Linda Allen and Corina Peruzzi, we want to especially thank you for helping to organize the photo shoots. Your attention to detail helped things run so much more smoothly.

Thanks also go to our colleagues, Craig Buschner, Peggy Gray, and Rebecca Lytle, who continually encouraged us to press on. And last, but definitely *not* least: Joakim, Stian, and Linda, thank you for all your support and patience, and for understanding that *we* didn't even know what "almost done" meant. Our free time is now yours!

Part 1

The Challenge

Chapter **1**

The Main Purpose of Physical Education

> Unless someone like you
> Cares a whole awful lot
> Nothing is going to get better
> It's not.
>
> — *Dr. Seuss (from* The Lorax*)*

obin, a student in the physical education teacher education program at Action University, was watching the movie *Clueless* with her 12-year-old sister. "I can't believe how they portray physical education in this movie. Standing in long lines, getting one turn to practice the skill, that's not PE!" Robin said, irritated at the negative image coming from the TV screen. Their father popped his head in from the kitchen, where he was cleaning the floor. "That's just how *I* remember *gym class*," he said, knowing that Robin would be upset at his choice of words. He liked to tease her about her career choice, and usually referred to her major as *gym*. "Yeah, but Dad, things are changing," Robin replied. "We're learning how to do things right. I wish they would show examples of appropriate physical education in the movies and on TV." Her father laughed. "It's payback time," he said. "All those film and TV writers are remembering their experiences, and I'm sure it feels good for them to show gym class the way it was!" Robin thought about the discussion they had just had in her Philosophy of Physical Education class that morning. Maybe her father's observation was true. But how could this perpetuation of negative images of physical education stop? Maybe this was what her professor had tried so hard to get through to them in class. They had to learn how to teach appropriately and according to the national standards and guidelines in order to help students become active for the rest of their lives. She suddenly realized that, by becoming a physical education teacher, she would be accepting the challenge to help turn around the image problem of physical education.

◆ Learning Objectives

After reading this chapter thoroughly and discussing the issues in class, you should be able to

- explain what should be the main purpose of physical education,
- explain how this main purpose is congruent with the various national standards and guidelines for physical education,
- explain how we use the words *skills* and *concepts* in this book,
- list at least four national organizations that have written guidelines for physical education,
- describe the essence of the National Association for Sport and Physical Education (NASPE) standards,
- describe the key principles of the Centers for Disease Control and Prevention (CDC) *Guidelines for School and Community Programs to Promote Lifelong Physical Activity Among Young People,*
- explain the premise of NASPE's appropriate practices documents,
- list the GET ACTIVE FOR LIFE factors,
- for each GET ACTIVE FOR LIFE factor explain what teachers can do to help youth become physically active,
- explain the basic ideas of the Diamond Conceptual Framework, and
- explain the implications of the Diamond Conceptual Framework for physical education programs in middle and high school.

◆ Key Terms and Phrases

Skill
Concept
CDC
NASPE
National standards for physical education
GET ACTIVE FOR LIFE
National guidelines
Appropriate practices in physical education
Diamond Conceptual Framework

Almost all teachers have a philosophy about teaching. You can ask them what they believe teaching their subject is all about, and they will give you an answer colored by their education and experiences. This freedom to choose one's philosophy is a right, and the variations make life interesting. When it comes to physical education, however, we have a problem: The lack of teacher commitment to one main purpose of physical education has contributed to our profession's scattered mission and negative image. The way the popular media has portrayed our field through the years often leaves us in need of defending not only ourselves and our career choice but also our profession as a whole. So individuality and the assortment of physical education teaching philosophies can be problematic if we want to convince people that we are an important and needed profession. Professor Larry Locke (teacher educator and philosopher in physical education), at a NASPE keynote address in October 1995, compared our profession to the sinking *Titanic*. He said that several options are available to us if we want to save physical education, but that our best chance of surviving is to leave the sinking ship. In other words, we should abandon the traditional ways and embrace a new physical education philosophy described in our national standards and pointed out in our various guidelines. If we want to convince the public that physical education is important, maybe it is time to join those who have already left the sinking ship and are trying alternative approaches to save what they believe is an important field. These teachers implement developmentally appropriate physical education, continue to learn, attend workshops and conferences, read the professional journals, use the NASPE standards and their state's framework, and share with others what they know and have learned. These teachers are abandoning a sinking ship, but they are saving physical education.

In this chapter we will be introducing our philosophy of physical education. We believe that the main purpose of physical education is to guide children in the process of becoming physically active for the rest of their lives. This philosophy is aligned with the NASPE standards (NASPE 1995); the Council on Physical Education for Children (COPEC) and Middle and Secondary School Physical Education for Children (MASSPEC, 1995, 1998) documents on appropriate practices for physical education; the American Academy of Pediatrics (AAP 1987), the American Heart Association (AHA 2002), and the American College of Sports Medicine statements (ACSM 1988) on physical fitness and youth; the CDC guidelines (U.S. Department of Health and Human Services [USDHHS] 1997); and the surgeon general's report on physical activity (USDHHS 1996). Two prominent researchers, authors, and teacher educators, Charles Corbin and George Graham, have also expressed the need for reform in physical education, and they call for a focus on promoting lifetime participation in physical activity (Corbin 2002, and personal conversations with Graham).

Guiding youth in the process of becoming physically active for the rest of their lives is a journey to a destination that we can reach in many different ways. We believe, however, that the research on the factors that make people active has produced some unambiguous road signs that we should observe. The national standards and guidelines published by our leading health-related and activity-related organizations are based on this important research. In this chapter we will first describe these guidelines and standards. Then we will introduce the GET ACTIVE FOR LIFE factors that summarize the research on determinants for physical activity (we will present these factors briefly in this chapter and explore them further in chapter 3). Based on all this information, we have developed a conceptual framework for physical education that we call the Diamond Conceptual Framework. We will present this framework last and show you how we think it embraces all the important information we present in the other chapters in this book.

Before you read on, it is critical that you understand our broad definitions of the words *skill* and *concept*. We use both words in an inclusive fashion that takes in what we know is important in encouraging children and adolescents to become physically active for the rest of their lives. Traditionally when we think of skills, we think of someone who has the ability to do something well ("They've got skills"). We often think of physical movement when we use the word *skill* in physical education. In this book we use the word **skill** to include physical movement along with cognitive, social, and personal abilities. We include problem solving, critical thinking, acceptance, cooperation, and self-management skills such as goal setting, self-monitoring, program planning, and overcoming barriers (Corbin 2002).

Concept often refers to movement concepts or movement descriptors in physical education. The broad meaning of *concept* is "general idea or thought." Concepts are important, and we will use the word **concept** when discussing movement concepts and cognitive, social, and personal aspects of physical education such as fair play, diversity, equity, and democracy. Keep these broad definitions in mind as you read this book.

Our Guiding Lights

If you put 10 physical educators in a room and asked them a seemingly simple question such as "What is, or should be, the primary goal of physical education?", you would likely get a number of different answers. People enter the profession of teaching physical education for different reasons, and they have experienced a variety of physical education classes during their years as students in the school system. These factors influence how they feel about the purpose of physical education and thus what physical education should look like.

As a physical educator, you can explore many different value orientations and curriculum models before deciding what your program should look like. Models differ quite a bit (a selection of curriculum models are discussed in chapter 10). Whatever your choice, you should ensure that your program addresses the major concerns identified by the "guiding lights" of our profession—the standards and guidelines of various national health and physical activity-related organizations. One major concern is highlighted in standards, guidelines, reports, and position statements from NASPE, COPEC, MASSPEC, the American Academy of Pediatrics (AAP), the American Heart Association (AHA), the American College of Sports Medicine (ACSM), the Centers for Disease Control and Prevention (CDC), and the surgeon general, among others. The concern centers on the fact that too few adults are leading a physically active lifestyle and that physical activity levels drop dramatically during adolescence. For example, the **CDC** *Guidelines for School and Community Programs to Promote Lifelong Physical Activity Among Young People* (U.S. Department of Health and Human Services 1997) suggest ways to help young people get active and stay active (figure 1.1), and the **NASPE** content standards for physical education list as the primary goal of physical education to help students become physically educated, which includes "exhibit[ing] a physically active lifestyle" (NASPE 1995) (figure 1.2).

This book offers suggestions and strategies for addressing and implementing some of these standards and guidelines into your program. You, as a

---

The guidelines state that physical activity programs for young people are most likely to be effective when they

- emphasize enjoyable participation in physical activities that are easily done throughout life,
- offer a diverse range of noncompetitive and competitive activities appropriate for different ages and abilities,
- give young people the skills and confidence they need to be physically active, and
- promote physical activity through all components of a coordinated school health program and develop links between school and community programs.

Figure 1.1 Key principles for promoting physical activity.

A physically educated person

1. demonstrates competency in many movement forms and proficiency in a few movement forms,
2. applies movement concepts and principles to the learning and development of motor skills,
3. exhibits a physically active lifestyle,
4. achieves and maintains a health-enhancing level of physical fitness,
5. demonstrates responsible personal and social behavior in physical activity settings,
6. demonstrates understanding and respect for differences among people in physical activity settings, and
7. understands that physical activity provides opportunities for enjoyment, challenge, self-expression, and social interaction.

Figure 1.2 NASPE content standards in physical education.

Reprinted from *Moving Into the Future: National Standards for Physical Education* (1995) with permission from the National Association for Sport and Physical Education (NASPE), 1900 Association Drive, Reston, VA 20191-1599.

physical educator, have a responsibility to study these guidelines in depth. Therefore, we suggest that you obtain a copy of the standards and guidelines so that you can refer to and reflect on them. Some are available free on the Internet, and you can buy the others through the American Alliance for Health, Physical Education, Recreation and Dance (AAHPERD) Web site, at AAHPERD conferences, or in your university bookstore. Let's explore some of these documents a little further.

NASPE developed *Moving Into the Future: National Standards for Physical Education, A Guide to Content and Assessment* in 1995 to answer the nation's quest for educational standards in all areas. The movement to create standards began in the early 1990s, and progress continues today. "In effect, standards have become the cornerstone of the educational reform movement" (NASPE 1995, vi). The NASPE **national standards for physical education** answer the question "what should students know and be able to do?" as they progress through the grade levels and by the time they graduate from high school. For each step (every other grade level, K–12) an explanation, sample benchmarks, and assessment examples are presented for each of the seven content standards. For secondary school, 6th, 8th, 10th, and 12th grades are used. The standards are specific enough to outline the overall goals for your program yet general enough to allow you to include a variety of activities. The fact that the standards cover every other year of the K–12 curriculum allows flexibility regarding when you reach certain benchmarks. For example, you have two years to reach the benchmarks for grade 10. You can cover the relevant skills and concepts at any time in your 9th and 10th grade curriculum as long as you reach the benchmarks by the end of 10th grade. In table 1.1 we have selected, for each content standard, one or two sample benchmarks from 8th, 10th, or 12th grade, and we explain how they support the overall goal of physical education: guiding students in the process of becoming physically active for life. Later in this chapter we will go over the factors that influence people's activity levels. We have summarized them into an easy-to-

remember mnemonic phrase: **GET ACTIVE FOR LIFE.** After reading the rest of the chapter, it will be clear to you how the GET ACTIVE FOR LIFE factors, based on research of determinants for physical activity (covered in more depth in chapter 3), are the reasons we say that the standards support the goal to be active for life.

The CDC issued *Guidelines for School and Community Programs: Promoting Lifelong Physical Activity* in 1997. The **national guidelines,** aimed at teachers, coaches, administrators, parents, and community sports organizers, includes a section on how these groups can help youth become active and stay active. Table 1.2 presents the CDC's appeal to school and community programs and where in this book you can find more information about each area.

By writing these guidelines, the CDC makes it clear that it sees physical education teachers and coaches as major participants in the quest to help our youth become physically active. And it makes sense. All children go to school (except the small percentage who are home schooled, and even they are often taught physical education by professionals), and their physical education teachers have immense potential to influence their physical activity habits in regular physical education. The CDC guidelines are clear about how physical education teachers should and should not accomplish this (figure 1.1).

The U.S. Department of Health and Human Services has also published objectives for children and adolescents' physical activity and fitness. The document *Healthy People 2010 Physical Activity and Fitness Objectives Relevant for Children and Adolescents* calls for an increase in the proportion of children and adolescents who participate in moderate and vigorous physical activity. The text addresses physical education directly in three objectives: increased proportion of schools requiring daily physical education, increased proportion of students who participate in daily physical education, and increased proportion of adolescents who spend at least 50 percent of their physical education class time being physically active (USDHHS 2000).

Table 1.1   NASPE Content Standards, Sample Benchmarks, and Support of the Goal to Be Active for Life

NASPE standard	Sample benchmarks	How the standard supports the goal to be active for life
1. Demonstrates competency in many movement forms and proficiency in a few movement forms.	10th grade: The student uses a variety of clubs competently to play a round of golf. 12th grade: The student navigates a kayak skillfully and safely through white water.	People tend to participate in activities in which they feel they are competent. For example, a person is not likely to play much golf unless she has the basic skills, nor is she likely to get in a kayak and take it down rough waters without having learned the necessary skills.
2. Applies movement concepts and principles to the learning and development of motor skills.	8th grade: The student explains and demonstrates some game strategies involved in playing tennis doubles.	With knowledge of how to analyze and improve skills, students can work on furthering their competence by understanding and then practicing the skills.
3. Exhibits a physically active lifestyle.	10th grade: The student participates in health-enhancing activities that he can pursue in the community.	When taught how to be physically active in the community, people are more likely to participate in physical activities. Problem solving skills to overcome barriers (such as lack of time) help students carry activity into adulthood.
4. Achieves and maintains a health-enhancing level of physical fitness.	12th grade: The student uses the results of fitness assessments to guide changes in her personal program of physical activity.	Helping students set goals for physical activity levels and fitness, and teaching them the self-management skills needed to reach those goals, encourages them to develop positive habits that increase their likelihood of being physically active. Sufficient physical activity usually leads to physical fitness.
5. Demonstrates responsible personal and social behavior in physical activity settings.	8th grade: The student identifies positive and negative peer influences.	Peer influence is crucial during adolescence, including in the physical activity setting. Responsible behaviors translate to more enjoyment for all, and enjoyment encourages involvement in physical activities.
6. Demonstrates understanding and respect for differences among people in physical activity settings.	10th grade: The student enjoys the satisfaction of meeting and cooperating with others of diverse backgrounds during physical activity.	This aspect of physical activity provides yet another source of enjoyment and fulfillment in physical activities, which may increase people's activity levels.
7. Understands that physical activity provides opportunities for enjoyment, challenge, self-expression, and social interaction.	8th grade: The student feels satisfaction when engaging in physical activity. 12th grade: The student enjoys learning new activities.	Satisfaction comes with a feeling of success, and this leads to a feeling of competence, which strongly influences activity levels.

Reprinted from *Moving Into the Future: National Standards for Physical Education* (1995) with permission from the National Association for Sport and Physical Education (NASPE), 1900 Association Drive, Reston, VA 20191-1599.

Table 1.2 CDC's Appeal and Where to Learn More in This Text

Appeal from CDC to PE teachers and coaches	Where to learn more
Use your national standards (NASPE).	Chapters 1 and 6-13
Keep your students active during physical education.	Chapters 7 and 8
Emphasize activity and enjoyment over competition.	Chapters 1, 3, and 7-13
Help youth become competent in many motor and behavioral skills.	Chapters 1, 3, and 7-13
Refrain from using physical activity, such as doing push-ups or running laps, as punishment.	Chapters 7-9
Ensure that young people know safety rules and use appropriate protective clothing and equipment.	Chapters 7, 9, and 15
Involve families and community organizations in physical activity programs.	Chapters 1, 12, and 16

Reprinted from U.S. Department of Health and Human Services. 1996. *Physical activity and health: A report of the surgeon general.* Atlanta: U.S. Department of Health and Human Services, Centers for Disease Control and Prevention, National Center for Chronic Disease Prevention and Health Promotion.

Robin couldn't stop thinking about the episode with her father. She knew he was just teasing her, but the message from the movies and TV shows she had seen throughout her childhood and teen years, such as *Billy Madison, Clueless, Grease, The Princess Diaries, The Simpsons, Freaks and Geeks,* and *The Wonder Years,* all seemed to have a similar message: physical education is about bombardment, waiting in lines, embarrassment, and unfair competition. In her next Philosophy of Physical Education class she asked her professor some important questions. Robin had learned through other classes that research, governmental agencies, and national organizations concerned with health and wellness supported quality physical education. But there seemed to be a missing link. "We all know physical education is important," she said, "and we're not lacking support for that claim from research and all sorts of well-known organizations. How is it, then, that physical education is not mandatory at every school, for every grade? And why aren't physical education teachers held accountable for promoting physical activity?" The professor was impressed. He asked the class to form groups to discuss Robin's questions and then share their opinions with the whole class. Everyone had something to say. Most of the future teachers in the room felt that the answers to both questions related to a lack of public support for physical education. They also seemed to agree that this lack of support had something to do with people's experiences in PE. "That's exactly what my father said when we were discussing this a few days ago," Robin said. "He said he could understand the lack of support for PE from people who see it as wasted time in school because of how their PE classes were taught." The professor saw the opportunity to continue the discussion in the next class period. He left them with a new question and required them to come to the next class with a list of at least five possible answers. The question was "How can we, as physical educators, change the poor image of physical education so that parents and the public in general can justify supporting us and feel confident that we are doing our job in promoting physical activity among youth?"

Many other organizations that promote health and wellness have written statements or guidelines for programs that affect physical activity levels in youth. Among these is the ACSM, which in 1988 published an opinion statement (ACSM 1988) on physical fitness in children and youth that suggests these points:

- School physical education programs are an important part of the overall education process and should give increased emphasis to the development and maintenance of lifelong exercise habits and provide instruction about how to attain and maintain physical fitness.

- School programs also must focus on education and behavior change to encourage engagement in appropriate activities outside of class. Recreational and fun aspects of exercise should be emphasized.

The AHA is specific about what physical education programs should provide. Their strategic plan for physical activity states several recommendations for public policy to help establish standards for quality and quantity of physical education classes (AHA 2002):

- Require physical education in grades K–12
- Provide information on appropriate physical activity in physical education classes
- Integrate fitness testing into physical education programs that promote lifetime physical activity
- Promote lifestyle physical activities in physical education classes
- Encourage extracurricular activities that increase physical activity
- Use schools as community centers
- Provide sustained delivery of culturally and linguistically appropriate public messages to improve awareness, knowledge, motivation, and adherence to physical activity programs

The AHA is also specific about what behaviors youth should adopt and what they should know so that they can become physically active people. We have selected the ones that directly relate to teaching physical education. You can find the rest on AHA's Web site (**www.americanheart.org**) (AHA 2002):

- Learn to enjoy physical activity
- Learn to use self-management skills (such as goal setting, monitoring, barrier minimization) for maintaining active lifestyles
- Develop skills and learn how to participate in developmentally appropriate physical activities
- Engage in regular, moderately intense physical activity for at least 30 minutes daily
- Engage in vigorous physical activity that helps develop and maintain cardiorespiratory fitness three or more days per week, for at least 30 minutes per occasion

The American Academy of Pediatrics, in its 1987 statement "Physical Fitness and the Schools," gives a detailed description about what kinds of activities physical education programs should emphasize to help students become active for life (American Academy of Pediatrics Committees on Sports Medicine and School Health 1987):

- School programs should emphasize the so-called lifetime athletic activities such as cycling, swimming, and tennis. Schools should decrease time they devote to teaching the skills used in team sports such as football, basketball, and baseball.

- Physical fitness activities at school should promote a lifelong habit of aerobic exercise.

From the preceding excerpts you can see that our profession is guided by many organizations, all of which would like to see the same result—a more active population. Equally important to these various guidelines that prescribe *what* we should teach are the accepted guidelines for *how* we create positive physical education programs. We must know the nuts and bolts of how to create programs that promote participation in physical activity rather than discourage it. These guidelines are the NASPE documents on **appropriate practices in physical education,** developed separately for elementary school (by COPEC), middle school (by MASSPEC), and high school (also by MASSPEC). Both COPEC and MASSPEC promote appropriate practices in four main areas: curriculum guidelines, instruction, assessment, and support. For each category and subcategory, examples of both appropriate and inappropriate practices are presented. Table 1.3 represents the documents in a nutshell.

Your Turn ▶▶▶

With all these thoughtful and thorough documents to guide us, it is sad that we still have many programs at the secondary level in which teachers are simply rolling out the ball. Think about some of these questions before you read the next section:

◆ Why is it that some physical education teachers can get away with *not* teaching?

◆ How will you ensure that *you* do not become a teacher who just rolls out the ball?

◆ How would you convince a colleague that it is important to follow our guiding lights—the national standards and guidelines developed by a variety of major health, fitness, and wellness organizations?

◆ How will you, if needed, defend physical education to the public?

◆ How will you, if needed, achieve reasonable class sizes and reasonable budgets for resources so that you can implement a quality physical education program?

◆ How will you help your students become physically active for the rest of their lives?

GET ACTIVE FOR LIFE Factors

If we want people to be physically active as adults, we must consider a number of factors. Research has shown that most people need a variety of things to be just right if they are to plunge into the sea of physical activity. These include places to go to be active, programs that are interesting and convenient, sufficient time, good weather, adequate equipment, safe neighborhoods, and so forth (Pate et al. 1995; U.S. Department of Health and Human Services 1997; Sallis et al. 1992). Not all of these factors pertain directly to physical educators. Teachers cannot control the weather, of course, but they can teach their students strategies for being active in all kinds of weather. Teach-ers cannot alone provide safe neighborhoods, but they can work with other community members to have the city put in bike paths or have supervised open gym hours at local schools at night. Teachers cannot change the current socioeconomic status of their students, but they can start after-school activity programs or teach their students how to be active in the community without joining costly sports clubs. Teachers cannot limit the time students spend watching TV and playing video games, but they can educate parents and students on the importance of balancing activity and leisure activities, as well as give their students ideas on how to sneak activity into their sedentary activities, such as doing abdominal crunches or squats during TV commercials. You get the idea. The CDC guidelines for school and community programs encourage teachers to work with community recreational programs to offer more opportunities for all people to be active (USDHHS 1997). Many excellent teachers around the country are thinking outside the box when it comes to getting youth involved in physical activities outside regular school hours.

Some factors that influence people's activity levels relate directly to physical education. As an example, think about the activities you still enjoy. Chances are they are activities in which you are, or feel that you are, skillful. Your confidence in your level of competency in a skill is called self-efficacy, which has been shown to be a strong indicator of participation in physical activity (Sallis et al. 1992). Physical educators can assist in this area by helping students perceive themselves as competent in physical activities. Teachers should encourage positive physical self-esteem (Corbin 2002) and make sure that each student graduates from high school with the ability to "demonstrate competency in many movement forms and proficiency in a few movement forms" (NASPE 1995, 1). Research has shown that people's perception of their competence is as important as their actual competence when it comes to physical activity. This perception helps people decide whether they will become active people (Corbin 2002).

In many physical education programs today the mission of increasing actual skill competence and self-efficacy is impossible because of the way the

Table 1.3 Appropriate Practices for Middle School and High School "In a Nutshell"

Practice category	In a nutshell
Curriculum Guidelines:	
Program choices	Programs are based on national and state standards, as well as students' needs.
Locomotor, non-locomotor, and manipulative activities; refinement of skills	The major focus of class is learning skills. No rolling out the ball.
Physical fitness activities	Health-related fitness is incorporated into daily lessons. All areas are equally important. Student understanding and strategies to get fit for life are emphasized.
Knowledge	Students should learn how to use all that they learn for the rest of their lives.
Cooperative play; positive social behaviors	Cooperative behaviors are emphasized.
Variety	Students' needs and interests are considered, and a variety of activities offered.
Team and individual activities sport activities	A variety of activities are offered: in-line skating, aerobics, martial arts, yoga, team sports, weight training, and so on.
Rhythms and dance; dance	Dance is considered important, and a variety of dance forms are taught.
Aquatics	Focus is on teaching skills. No free swim.
Gymnastics	Skills taught are appropriate to confidence and ability levels of students. Educational gymnastics is emphasized in middle school.
Outdoor and challenge pursuits	A variety of activities focusing on problem solving and self-esteem development are offered. Creativity is used when facilities are lacking.
Instruction	
Success	Class allows success for everyone who tries.
Learning time	Practice time is sufficient for learning.
Learning environment	A positive climate is in place.
Feedback	Appropriate and specific feedback is given.
Inclusion	All students are included.

(continued)

Table 1.3 *(continued)*

Practice category	In a nutshell
Instruction *(cont.)*	
Forming groups	Students do not pick teams. Groups are formed with sensitivity to students' feelings.
Teaching styles	A variety of teaching styles are used.
Learning styles	Teacher accommodates a variety of learning styles.
Student choices	Teacher allows for student input and choices.
Individualization of instruction	Variations are used to accommodate all students' needs.
Warm-up	Only safe, activity-specific warm-up routines are used.
Assessment	
Role of assessment	Assessment is important and should be ongoing throughout the year.
Achievement	Assessment is based on goals and objectives. Criteria are clear, and grades are based on progress toward goals.
Physical fitness testing	Fitness tests are not used for determining grades. Personal goals and progress are emphasized.
Class atmosphere during assessment	Students are not put in the spotlight. Scores are kept private and reported confidentially.
Technique available for psychomotor, cognitive, and affective assessments	A variety of assessment tools that cover all domains of learning are used.
Outside-of-class assignments and activity assessments	Outside-of-class activities are considered important.
Interpretation of program to public	Assessment is used to communicate program status to the public. Physical education is promoted as an important subject.
Class attire	Safety and function are emphasized, but attire is not used for grade determination.
Support	
Class size	Physical education is treated the same as any other subject.
Scheduling	All schools should have daily physical education.

Table 1.3 *(continued)*

Practice category	In a nutshell
Support *(cont.)*	
Equipment	Developmentally appropriate equipment (considering size, skill level, age, and so on) is available for all students.
Facilities	Physical education has its own reserved, safe learning areas.
Substitution of credit	There should be no substitutions, waivers, or exemptions.
Technology	Appropriate technology is used in the curriculum.
Professional development	Teachers are encouraged to participate in professional development activities. Accommodation is made for their participation.
Administrative	Administrators view physical education as an integral part of the total school curriculum.
Home-school communication	Parents know what's going on in physical education through newsletters, parents' nights, and other avenues.

Data from Middle and Secondary School Physical Education for Children (MASSPEC). 1995. *Appropriate practices for middle school physical education.* National Association for Sport and Physical Education.

school year is divided into two- to four-week units. In this situation students rarely, if ever, have a chance to become competent or to increase their physical self-esteem, let alone gain proficiency in any activity. Another problem is the heavy focus on traditional team sports, such as baseball, softball, football, and basketball, which limits the appeal of physical activity to many students (figure 1.3). These and other factors we will discuss later are important in promoting lifelong physical activity. Physical education is the only place where (almost) all people have the opportunity to learn the skills and techniques, and develop positive attitudes and habits, that can help them be active throughout their lives (USDHHS 1997).

Many researchers have attempted to answer the question "What makes people active?" Numerous factors influence people's activity levels, including those mentioned earlier. They are generally categorized into four groups: biological, psychological, sociological, and environmental factors (Sallis et al. 1992). In chapter 3 we will discuss these determinants for physical activity in more detail. In this chapter we will take a quick look at them for the purpose of understanding how they can help you promote the main purpose of your physical education program: helping students become active for the rest of their lives. The mnemonic phrase GET ACTIVE FOR LIFE can help teachers and students remember most of the important factors that influence physical activity levels. Each letter in the phrase is the first letter of a word or sentence that describes a determinant for physical activity. Table 1.4 presents the GET ACTIVE FOR LIFE factors and includes a suggestion for how teachers can help address each factor. The rest of the chapters in this book will be useful in learning how to do just that, especially chapters 7, 8, and 9. Use the GET ACTIVE FOR LIFE phrase to help you remember the determinants for physical activity and understand your role as a physical educator. You hold the key that opens the door of opportunities and a lifetime of physical activity for your students.

Figure 1.3   Teachers should emphasize physical activities that their students can pursue for a lifetime.

Diamond Conceptual Framework

The GET ACTIVE FOR LIFE factors and the national standards and guidelines for our profession direct us to offer physical education programs that help students become physically active for life. But how can we do that in a way that allows for program individuality and uniqueness? How can we do that without devising *one* national physical education curriculum? We believe that answer lies in the **Diamond Conceptual Framework** for physical education. Bob Pangrazi, well-known professor, author, and researcher from Arizona State University, developed a hierarchical model of physical education. This model takes the shape of a diamond and suggests that we use a progressive, hierarchical curriculum in physical education that is articulated through the three main levels of schooling: elementary, middle, and high school (Cooper Institute 1999). Himberg later used their basic ideas of this model, saturated them with the research on physical activity through the GET ACTIVE FOR LIFE factors, infused the national guide-

lines and standards, and developed the Diamond Conceptual Framework.

The Main Idea

Regardless of what you feel are other important purposes of physical education, we hope that you agree that the main purpose is to guide children in the process of becoming physically active for the rest of their lives. You can agree with this statement without locking yourself into a particular curriculum model or a set of value orientations for physical education. In other words, many roads lead to the same destination: helping people become physically active. We can even have different reasons for why we believe physical activity is important. To reach this goal, however, you must address three main issues in every K–12 curriculum. First, just as a child learns to read by starting with the fundamentals of language and text, a student learning to be physically active must start with the fundamental concepts and skills related to movement. Second, if you want a student to be a reader for a lifetime, you'll be wise to introduce a variety of literature in his developing years. You hope that several categories will catch his interest

Table 1.4 GET ACTIVE FOR LIFE Factors and Suggestions for Teachers

Factors that influence activity in youth	How teachers can help
Goal setting	Help your students learn the self-management skills they need, such as goal setting and monitoring, to continue being active throughout their lives.
Enjoyment	Emphasize student enjoyment and interest when selecting activities for your curriculum. Create an enjoyable learning environment by using music and by helping all your students feel successful.
TV, video games, and computer games	Teach students strategies for how to balance their recreational time to allow for fun physical activities. Teach them how to sneak activity into their TV watching (for example, doing squats during commercials).
Attitudes	Keep your class environment positive. Reward effort. Make PE meaningful by catering to students' interests.
Confidence in abilities (self-efficacy)	Plan lessons with variations so that all students can feel successful. Use units of sufficient length so that students can become or feel competent in many activities and proficient in a few. Be an effective teacher and assess your students' progress.
Time and other perceived barriers	Teach students how to manage their time and minimize other perceived barriers to fit in physical activity. Teach them how to make physical activity fun (for example, making fitness dates with a friend) so that it becomes a priority in their busy lives. Teach them how to solve problems so that they can minimize barriers to physical activity throughout life.
Inclement weather	Teach students strategies for being active when the weather forces them inside.
Various perceived benefits	Help students experience the benefits of physical activity that are important to them, such as excitement and having fun, learning and improving skills, improving appearance, and increasing fitness.
Educated about how to be active	Teach students how they can be active in their community now and throughout their lives. Teach them the self-management and problem-solving skills they need to continue to participate in physical activity.

(continued)

Table 1.4 *(continued)*

Factors that influence activity in youth	How teachers can help
Family and peer influences	Involve the family unit in your curriculum. Organize activity days or nights, give physical activity homework that involves the family, and inform family members how they can help your students become more active. Use peer teaching and modeling, including celebrity peers and information about what they do as their physical activity.
Older—becoming less active as you age	Teach lifetime activities and strategies for how to be active throughout life. Emphasize realistic options and problem solving for the times when life gets in the way (that is, jobs, children, chores).
Recreational programs lacking	Encourage community activity programs to cater to all youth, not just elite athletes, or start your own recreational program at your school that caters to all students.
Lack of safe spaces in neighborhood	Teach strategies for being more active in safe places (home, school, church, and so on). Help students and their families organize to create more safe places to be active in the community.
Intrinsic motivation	Cater to your students' interests and provide choices. Make PE informational, meaningful, and fun. Emphasize individual task mastery, goal setting, and monitoring. Avoid comparing your students to each other.
Facility and equipment access	Work with your administrators and the community to keep school facilities open and equipment available at night. Teach students how to be active with limited space and equipment.
Economic status, culture, and gender	Be aware of economic and cultural factors that influence activity and encourage and teach strategies for increasing activity levels for all your students regardless of background.
	Teach activities that challenge and encompass the interests of both boys and girls. Consider factors such as muscle mass and motor-skill differences in adolescents when selecting units to teach.
	Be aware of how society influences the activity levels of girls and boys. Make an extra effort to motivate girls (they tend to be less active). Help them develop self-confidence in their abilities and offer them strategies to become more active by expanding their perceived and real opportunities.

and that he'll want to explore them further. Likewise, if you want someone to be physically active for a lifetime, you should introduce her to a variety of sports and physical activities in her developing years. You hope that she'll find two or more activities that she would like to concentrate on. You want her to develop the skills and concepts that will help her feel and be competent. Third, we know that if people are to become proficient in reading, they need to read a lot. We should provide them with options so that they will enjoy practicing their reading-related skills and comprehension. Likewise, it takes time to become proficient in the skills involved in a sport or physical activity. Most students cannot become proficient in two- to four-week units; they need more time. Providing them with choices will increase their motivation, enjoyment, and probably their likelihood to continue being active after they graduate from high school.

Here is how these ideas translate into a progressive physical education framework congruent with the NASPE standards and our other important national guidelines: To end up as physically active adults, children first need to learn the fundamental skills and concepts related to movement. In the elementary school years, physical education should focus on skills and concepts that the student can later transfer to specific sports and activities. Physical education should also develop skills in problem solving and self-management. In middle school, teachers should help students string these skills together to form and encourage participation in activities, sports, and games to help them further their skill development. At this level, teachers should introduce a variety of activities, most of which students can participate in for the rest of their lives. This is their time to sample the menu of the many wonderful lifetime activities that are available. If you have tasted all the items on the menu, you'll know which handful of dishes you are likely to order when you go to a particular restaurant. Likewise, if you have tried a variety of sports and physical activities, you know which ones you enjoy enough to put in the time and effort to become proficient. In high school you should get the opportunity to choose three to five activities each year and then develop proficiency and self-efficacy in these, along with problem-solving and self-management skills, so that you can improve your chances of becoming physically active for the rest of your life. Skill proficiency and self-efficacy lead to enjoyment. Together with self-management, problem-solving skills, and the other GET ACTIVE FOR LIFE factors, they lead to

participation in physical activities (Corbin 2002; Pate et al. 1995; Sallis et al. 1992).

Significance of the Diamond Shape

Traditionally, paradigms for skill and concept development use pyramid-shaped models. The Diamond Conceptual Framework, building on some of the basic ideas of Pangrazi's hierarchical model of physical education (Cooper Institute 1999), steps away from this tradition. Let's look at the significance of the shape from bottom to top. As you continue to read this paragraph, examine figure 1.4. The diamond starts with a point at the bottom and gradually widens. The shape signifies that we introduce only one or two skills and concepts to kindergartners when they first start school, and slowly begin to include more skills and concepts as our students learn. As we move up the shape of the diamond, we're moving through the elementary school years, when teachers gradually introduce more skills and concepts. The bottom part of the diamond, then, provides a picture of how we should gradually introduce skills and concepts in a progression, with one often building on the success of another. This is not to say that you should stick to one skill at a time. As you will see in chapter 7, motor learning research has shown that benefits are derived from mixing up skill practice. However, the point is that you don't bombard students with too many skills and concepts at a time, thus the gradual widening of the diamond as you progress through the elementary school years.

Reaching the middle of the diamond, the widest part illustrates the time when children have learned enough fundamental skills and concepts to enjoy being introduced to and participating in a variety of sports and activities. This should happen in middle school. The years represented by this middle section should be filled with exploration, or sampling the menu. As we move farther up and students enter high school, the shape of the diamond narrows again. This represents the need for a more narrow focus on mastering the problem-solving and self-management skills that may lead to a lifetime of participation in physical activity and for a more concentrated effort to become proficient and enhance self-efficacy in a few sports and activities. The key to achieving this focus is giving students choices. The diamond finishes with a point, which represents reaching the goal of becoming a physically educated person who will be active for life.

The shading that gives a three-dimensional look to the diamond shape represents the fact that the

NASPE standards, our other guiding lights, and the GET ACTIVE FOR LIFE factors should be the basis for physical education curricula. In other words, the main purpose of physical education—helping students become physically active for the rest of their lives—should guide anything and everything we do in physical education. Figure 1.4 is a graphic description of the Diamond Conceptual Framework.

Implications for Secondary Physical Education

The Diamond Conceptual Framework suggests that the ultimate purpose of physical education is to help children become physically active for the rest of their lives. Accomplishing this goal requires careful planning, articulation between the different levels (elementary, middle, and high school), and purposeful, effective, and reflective teaching.

During middle school the Diamond Conceptual Framework suggests that students should be able to sample the menu of physical activities and gain confidence and competence in many of those activities. The idea is that a physical activity is out there for everyone. But how many activities should a teacher introduce in a year? Motor-learning research tells us that if you use very short units, it is impossible to introduce an activity and let the students learn enough to realize if they like the activity or not (Schmidt 1991). Learning a skill takes time, and many great teachers who are concerned with skill development feel that units shorter than 4 weeks are too short. This means that a 36-week long program could offer about 9 samples from the menu in a year, or 27 for the entire middle school curriculum. For students to become competent enough in each activity that they have a fair chance to see if they enjoy it, the units should probably be longer than 4 weeks, or repeated. Even with longer or repeated units you can fit a large number of different activities into a middle school curriculum. Fifteen or 20 different sports and activities would provide quite a variety. The point is that students will benefit greatly from having the opportunity to become confident and competent in many of the activities. Traditional middle school curricula that focus on a few, mostly team-related sports, such as flag football, basketball, volleyball, softball, and track and field, and repeat those units each year, do not cut it. From what many secondary school curricula cover, it may seem to students that they can choose from only a few physical activities in life and if they don't like any of them, their only op-

tion is to become couch potatoes. If students can become competent in a variety of physical activities, chances are better that they will find two or three that they like well enough to continue, either in physical education or on their own.

That brings us to the high school level, where the Diamond Conceptual Framework suggests that students can choose activities or sports in which they can become proficient by the time they graduate. This level also emphasizes the independence that comes from mastering the self-management and problem-solving skills needed to ensure lifetime participation in physical activity. Corbin (2002) has used the following analogy to illustrate the logic in providing students with choices: "We know we can't teach every child to play every instrument in the band. Why do we think we can teach every child to play every sport?" We agree 100 percent and believe that when students explore their options in middle school they will likely make choices in high school based on experience, confidence in their ability, and enjoyment. This would narrow the focus and take students one step further toward becoming lifetime participants in physical activity.

Choice programs have been promoted by physical educators concerned with student motivation for a while now. And studies have found that providing students with choices makes it more likely to catch and hold their interest in an activity (Chen 1996). The self-direction and self-management involved in making choices are also seen as important factors in helping students become active for the rest of their lives (Lambert 1987). Many high schools today offer choice programs for their students. A choice program should enable students to focus on the activities they enjoy the most. This choice should be an individual one, not a class vote. The program could be set up as an elective system. The student's main subject for a certain period would be physical education, but within that period the student could choose from a number of activities and sports. Students would not always get their first choice, but if enough agreeable choices were provided, by the time they graduate from high school students would have successfully selected their first, second, and third choices at least once. Students should be permitted to select an activity two or three times. Some students take longer than others to become proficient in an activity, so allowing them to repeat their choices would provide them a fair opportunity. Over the course of their high school physical education, however, students should be required to choose at least three

National Standards and Guidelines

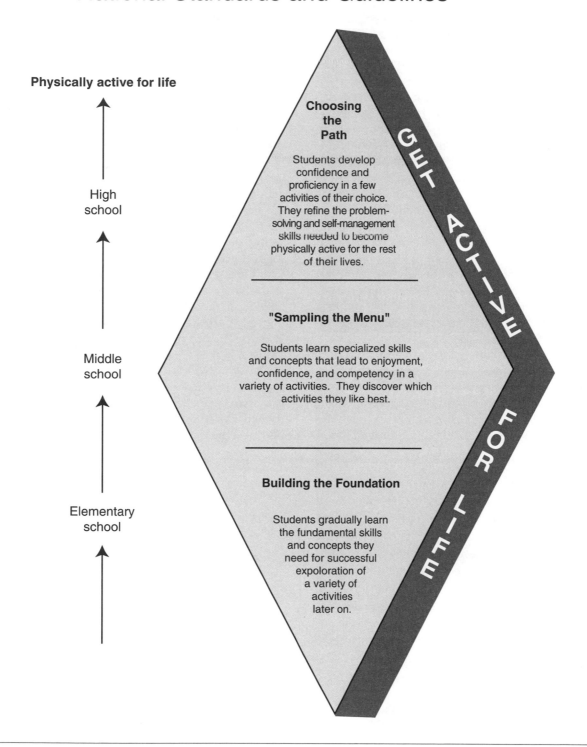

Physically active for life

High school

Middle school

Elementary school

Choosing the Path

Students develop confidence and proficiency in a few activities of their choice. They refine the problem-solving and self-management skills needed to become physically active for the rest of their lives.

"Sampling the Menu"

Students learn specialized skills and concepts that lead to enjoyment, confidence, and competency in a variety of activities. They discover which activities they like best.

Building the Foundation

Students gradually learn the fundamental skills and concepts they need for successful exploration of a variety of activities later on.

GET ACTIVE FOR LIFE

Figure 1.4 The Diamond Conceptual Framework for physical education. National standards and other guidelines, as well as the GET ACTIVE FOR LIFE factors, provide the backbone as students progress through curricula at each level toward the goal of becoming lifelong participants in physical activity.

different activities to ensure that they become "proficient in a few" (NASPE 1995). The choices offered should focus on lifetime, health-enhancing activities (we will discuss what this means in chapter 3).

Logistical issues will require your attention when you set up a choice program. Making a list of the teachers in your department, their sport and activity expertise, and the facilities available would be a good start. From there, the setup would involve the school's scheduling procedures, counseling, and other issues that would require involvement from teachers outside the department. Thorough preparation and justification by the physical education department are crucial. If you want things to change, you have to play an active part and do your homework. As with any other problem, if you think outside the box you may come up with a solution that will be agreeable for all involved. You can ask teachers from other schools how they have been able to provide their students with a choice program. Listservs and conferences are excellent places to go for such questions (see chapter 18). Obviously, schools will have different possibilities and needs when considering a choice program, but the key is to provide students with the opportunity to concentrate long enough on a few activities of their choice so that they can develop self-efficacy and proficiency. Therefore, units

in high school should be longer than those in middle school, probably as long as 8 to 12 weeks. When students choose the activity, their attitude toward a longer unit seems to be more favorable than it would be if they participated in an activity they did not choose (Condon & Collier 2002; Howard & Howard 1997; Thompson & Wankel 1980).

We believe you can use the Diamond Conceptual Framework to address the main concerns about the rapid decrease of participation in physical activity during adolescence and the prevalence of physical inactivity among adults. You can easily modify the framework to fit the needs of a state, school district, or particular school.

The Diamond Conceptual Framework can also be used with several of the curriculum models presented in chapter 10. As stated earlier, it is difficult for teachers and future professionals to agree on which curriculum models to use. But we believe that embracing a variety of curriculum models is acceptable as long as there is agreement that the primary purpose of physical education is to guide students in the process of becoming physically active and healthy for a lifetime, and as long as no more than two models are used at a time. If you frame your chosen curriculum models using the Diamond Conceptual Framework, you will be able to focus on the ultimate goal of physical education: helping students become physically active for life.

Robin and her class continued the discussion about what they, as physical education teachers, could do to change the image of physical education among the public. The class developed a top 10 list that they posted outside the physical education department office. Finding 10 items to put on the list was not difficult. The students used what they had learned in their classes. The only sticky point came when they were deciding the order of the items. "A top 10 list implies that number 1 is most important," said Robin, "and we're not agreeing on the order." The class saw her point. "Why don't we keep it as a top 10 list because it's fun to read, but include a statement saying that the order of the items is negotiable," suggested the professor. That's just what they did.

What teachers can do to change the image of PE:

10. Use the national standards and guidelines and our knowledge of children and adolescents when we develop our curriculum.

9. Use technology wisely in our classes and use it to educate parents and the public about what we do.

8. Create a positive class environment where everyone is included, to ensure students' perceived and actual success.

7. Teach for learning and use good assessment tools to guide us.

6. Reflect daily on our successes and needs for improvement.

5. Use only appropriate teaching practices. Avoid negative practices such as using exercise as punishment, having captains pick teams, and playing elimination games.

4. Always treat teaching as the most important part of the job. Other work-related responsibilities come second.

3. Emphasize enjoyment in every class.

2. Always promote the main purpose of physical education: helping students become active for life.

1. Continue to learn and develop as teachers for the rest of our careers.

Summary

The purpose of physical education should be to help students develop the skills and knowledge they need to become physically active for life. This purpose is in line with a variety of national standards and guidelines related to physical education, activity, and fitness. The guiding lights of our profession include the NASPE standards, the NASPE appropriate practices documents, the CDC guidelines for school and community programs, as well as various position statements from the AHA, the ACSM, and the AAP. These guidelines all state that physical education should help students become active for life, and some offer suggestions for how to accomplish that goal. Researchers have found that many different factors influence people's physical activity levels. The GET ACTIVE FOR LIFE mnemonic summarizes these points. For each GET ACTIVE FOR LIFE factor, teachers can do specific things to help youth become physically active for life. The national standards and guidelines and the GET ACTIVE FOR LIFE factors form the backbone of the Diamond Conceptual Framework. This framework suggests that students can learn to become active for life in physical education if they first learn fundamental skills and concepts (elementary school), then continue skill and concept learning while exploring movement opportunities (middle school), and ultimately use these skills and concepts to pursue proficiency in activities they choose (high school).

Checking for Understanding ▸▸▸

- What should be the main purpose of physical education?
- What do the words *skills* and *concepts* mean in this book?
- How is the main purpose of physical education congruent with the various national standards and guidelines for physical education?
- What are the guiding lights for our profession?
- What is the essence of the NASPE standards?
- What are the key principles of the CDC *Guidelines for School and Community Programs to Promote Lifelong Physical Activity Among Young People*?
- What is the premise of the NASPE's appropriate practices documents?
- What does self-efficacy mean, and why is it important?
- How many GET ACTIVE FOR LIFE factors can you list?
- With the GET ACTIVE FOR LIFE factors in front of you, can you explain what teachers can do to help youth become physically active for each factor?
- What are the basic ideas of the Diamond Conceptual Framework?
- What are the implications of the Diamond Conceptual Framework for middle and high school physical education?

For Reflection and Discussion ▶▶▶

- Which of the GET ACTIVE FOR LIFE factors do you feel limited your physical activity participation when you were an adolescent? What about now?

- Why is it important that teachers know and understand the GET ACTIVE FOR LIFE factors?

- How will you make sure you address the GET ACTIVE FOR LIFE factors when you teach?

- Did any of the GET ACTIVE FOR LIFE factors surprise you?

- How do you think using the Diamond Conceptual Framework can be helpful for physical educators?

- How can teachers at all levels help make sure that the upward progression represented in the Diamond Conceptual Framework occurs?

References

American Academy of Pediatrics Committees on Sports Medicine and School Health. 1987. Physical fitness and the schools. *Pediatrics* 80:449–450.

American College of Sports Medicine (ACSM). 1988. Physical fitness in children and youth. *Medicine and Science in Sports and Exercise* 20:422–423.

American Heart Association. 2002. Exercise (Physical Activity) and Children: AHA Scientific Position. [Online.] Available: **http://216.185.112.5/presenter.jhtml?identifier=4596** [May 28, 2002].

Chen, A. 1996. Student interest in activities in a secondary physical education curriculum: An analysis of student subjectivity. *Research Quarterly for Exercise and Sport*, 67 (4): 424–432.

Condon, R. and Collier, C. 2002. Student choice makes a difference in physical education. *Journal of Physical Education, Recreation and Dance*, 73:(2) 26–30.

The Cooper Institute for Aerobics Research. 1999. *FITNESSGRAM test administration manual*. Champaign, IL: Human Kinetics.

Corbin, C. 2002. Physical activity for everyone: What every physical educator should know about promoting lifelong physical activity. *Journal of Teaching Physical Education* 21:128–144.

Howard, B. and Howard, M. 1997. What a difference a choice makes! *Strategies*, 10(3): 16–20.

Lambert, L. 1987. Secondary school physical education problems: What can we do about them? *Journal of Physical Education, Recreation and Dance*, 57(2): 30–32

Middle and Secondary School Physical Education for Children (MASSPEC). 1998. *Appropriate practices for high school physical education*. National Association for Sport and Physical Education.

Middle and Secondary School Physical Education for Children (MASSPEC). 1995. *Appropriate practices for middle school physical education*. National Association for Sport and Physical Education.

National Association for Sport and Physical Education (NASPE). 1995. *Moving into the future: National standards for physical education, a guide to content and assessment*. St. Louis: Mosby.

Pate, R.R., Pratt, M., Blair, S.N., Haskell, W.L., Macera, C.A., Bouchard, C., Buchner, D., Ettinger, W., Heath, G.W., King, A.C., et al. 1995. Physical activity and public health. A recommendation from the Centers for Disease Control and Prevention and the American College of Sports Medicine. *Journal of the American Medical Association* 272:402–407.

Sallis, J., B. Simons-Morton, E. Stone, C. Corbin, L. Epstein, N. Faucette, R. Iannotti, J. Killen, R. Klesges, C. Petray, T. Rowland, and W. Taylor. 1992. Determinants of physical activity and interventions in youth. *Medicine and Science in Sports and Exercise* 24(6):S248–S257.

Schmidt, R. 1991. *Motor learning and performance*. Champaign, IL: Human Kinetics.

Thompson, C. and Wankel, L. 1980. The effects of perceived activity choice upon frequency of exercise behavior. *Journal of Applied Social Psychology*, 10 (5):436–443.

U.S. Department of Health and Human Services. 1996. *Physical activity and health: A report of the surgeon general.* Atlanta: U.S. Department of Health and Human Services, Centers for Disease Control and Prevention, National Center for Chronic Disease Prevention and Health Promotion.

U.S. Department of Health and Human Services. 1997. *Guidelines for schools and community programs to promote lifelong physical activity among young people.* Centers for Disease Control and Prevention.

U.S. Department of Health and Human Services. 2000. *Healthy People 2010: Understanding and Improving Health.* 2nd ed. Washington, DC: U.S. Government Printing Office.

Suggested Readings

Sallis, J., and K. Patrick. 1994. Physical activity guidelines for adolescents: Consensus statement. *Pediatric Exercise Science* 6:302–31.

2

Technology in Physical Education

> The future masters of technology will have to be lighthearted and intelligent. The machine easily masters the grim and the dumb.
>
> — *Marshall McLuhan*

Linda, a physical education teacher, requested and received video camera and editing equipment from funds earmarked for technology purchases. Upon receiving the equipment, she was notified that at the end of the school year she must report on how the technology improved her physical education curriculum. She realizes that the report must specifically describe how student learning outcomes and objectives have been met. The request causes her to reflect on how to implement the technology in a substantive way. Specifically, she considers how she can include video usage within her curriculum to produce observable evidence of improvement.

Learning Objectives

After reading this chapter thoroughly and discussing the issues in class, you should be able to

- explain major technological advances and applications in educational settings,
- explain some of the major hurdles in implementing technology into a sound physical education program,
- list and describe the GOT-IT model for implementing technology into your physical education program,
- describe the plusses and minuses with using technology in teaching physical education,
- explain concrete ways of using technology for setting up the learning environment,
- explain concrete ways of using technology for establishing rules and protocols,
- explain concrete ways of using technology for conducting assessment activities, and
- explain concrete ways of using technology for dealing with atypical class environments.

Key Terms and Phrases

Instructional technology
Instructional goals
Communication technologies
Instructional objectives
Instructional techniques
Digital media
Word application
Spreadsheet application
Presentation application
Database application
Heart rate monitors
World Wide Web

Teaching secondary physical education with the purpose of helping students develop the skills and knowledge they need to be active for the rest of their lives is a challenge. The various chapters in this book give you a solid foundation for becoming an effective and reflective teacher. Before you read on, however, we want you to be aware of some tools that can make reaching this goal a little easier. Using **instructional technology** in a variety of ways can be a great help if you know how to use it appropriately.

Many teachers use technology in their classrooms, but not all of them know how to use it in a way that benefits their students. Some embrace technology as if it will save the world from poor teaching. The fact is that much poor teaching is a result of ineffective uses of technology. Properly used, however, technology can be a wonderful tool for learning. For example, instructional technology can go a long way in helping you communicate to your students the expectations and **instructional goals** for your class. Technology can also play a significant role in creating a learning environment that communicates that learning, effort, and responsibility are not only expected but rewarded in your classes. The technologies and techniques we will describe in this chapter can be particularly rewarding to you because they will help you introduce, augment, and continuously reinforce your expectations for learning to your students throughout the year.

Teachers and students can also use instructional technology as an effective assessment mechanism. For example, teachers can record student movement and compare it with a recorded ideal modeling example. Advances in video and computer applications allow teachers access to powerful teaching tools that are relatively easy and inexpensive to use. Finally, instructional technology can help motivate students to become more aware of their learning process and goal achievement.

When discussing appropriate use of instructional technologies in a classroom environment, we must first distinguish between technology uses that directly aid in the teaching and learning process and technologies that aid in class management. Using a digital video camera to tape students so that they can analyze their movements would be an example of providing feedback that could have a positive effect on learning. The teacher could use the same video technology for capturing still pictures to aid students in proper return and storage of equipment. This would be an ex-ample of technology aiding classroom management. The distinction between learning process and management can be useful when analyzing how teachers normally use technology in their classes. In a typical classroom, teachers most often use technology in meeting classroom management needs (grade entering, material distribution, photocopying). On the actual teaching end, teachers spend little time and effort incorporating technology to augment learning. Technology examples in this book will include applications for both learning outcomes as well as management issues.

Adopting Technologies Into Educational Settings

Advances in consumer and mass media electronics have brought about a significant change in how we access information, how we entertain ourselves, and yes, how we learn. In the early days of mass media technologies, powerful broadcasting corporations dictated the types and delivery times of programs. Consumers had few choices about what they saw and how they saw it. **Communication technologies** such as the VCR and video rental business, cable and satellite systems delivering over 500 channels, and the Internet now offer many more options. Consumers of communication technology are now accustomed to having choices! These consumers are also more critical and less likely to stay with something that doesn't hold their interests.

In looking at producing communication and instructional materials, continued technology developments have also empowered individuals to produce, manufacture, and distribute personalized communication using common and inexpensive tools that were available only to a selected few 20 years ago. A look around the modern classroom makes it apparent that technological innovations have become a permanent fixture. This trend will surely continue to have an effect on our classrooms and the way we teach our classes. The lines between instructional material user and instructional material producer are less pronounced than ever before. Besides that, by the time a child reaches adolescence he or she will have spent more time interacting with communication technology than doing anything else, with the possible exception of sleeping. Teenage students have spent almost all their lives gathering information and entertainment from different technological media.

Technology offers the teacher an opportunity to present information in various forms (print, illustration, video, still photos, audio) that have proved to be beneficial in introducing and reinforcing information that addresses different learning styles among the students (see chapter 5 for information on how adolescents learn). Thus, an instructional curriculum that does not attempt to integrate technology runs the risk of not taking full advantage of learning opportunities for students. We should address the overall question of implementing technology into a curriculum by examining how we can include appropriate technologies and practices into a physical education instructional design. The result should be lessons that will hold the students' attention, introduce and reinforce concepts and skills, and aid in the successful completion of tasks.

Your Turn ▸▸▸

◆ Think back on your years in middle and high school. Which technologies were present in the school?

◆ In which classes was technology an integral part of the learning process?

◆ Describe how technologies have advanced in the schools since you graduated. Which technologies were used in physical education class?

◆ Which new technologies could be used in the physical education class?

◆ Select one technology and describe three ways you think it could be used in a learning setting.

Figure 2.1 Teachers need to make sure they use technology to do their job better, not just to say they use technology.

Figure 2.2   Teachers should devote significant time not just to planning and selecting suitable technologies, but also to implementing them for their students' sake.

Misconceptions About Instructional Technology

The questions physical education teachers may ask about using technology in their classes typically include the following:

- Which is the best technology to use?
- Am I teaching incorrectly if I don't have computers in my classroom?
- Is a video available that can teach this concept?
- How can I put my class on the Internet?

The problem with these questions is that embedded within them is a belief that implementing technology into a curriculum will magically transpose a mediocre learning environment into a superb one. Experiences in instructional technology adoptions have clearly established the problems associated with those beliefs. Before meaningful discussion about implementing technology into the classroom can occur, you should first address what you are hoping to accomplish. Teachers must have a solid understanding of their **instructional objectives** and student outcomes before attempt-

ing to decide which technologies can enhance the learning. Not being clear in your objectives will inevitably lead to technology choices that can undermine your teaching efforts, frustrate your students, and ultimately waste valuable time and resources (figure 2.1).

Technologies can enhance the likelihood that your students will master specific objectives under certain contexts. But this can only happen when teachers, with clearly definable learning objectives, devote a significant amount of time to the planning, selecting, producing, and implementing of suitable technologies that feature attributes that can help the learning of the particular objective (figure 2.2).

GOT-IT Model

When looking at instructional technology, teachers typically focus on the hardware (computer), software (PowerPoint application), and delivery system (projector). Part of the problem results from a misunderstanding of the term *technology*. Most people limit their view of technology to mechanical components such as wires, hard drives, and reboot buttons. Just as the idea of driving includes more than the wheels, engines, and steering devices of the car, technology embraces more than hardware and software. In instructional technology, process concepts that include issues of design and implementation make up an important but often overlooked part of the term *technology*.

Instructional technology should attempt to address all areas of the instruction design process. In everyday language this would include the following questions:

- What are the overall goals we hope to accomplish with our design?
- What specific objectives are we designing for our students to meet?
- What types of technologies will help us in our design?
- What types of instructional techniques can we use to make our design most effective?

By including goals, objectives, technologies, and instructional techniques into our design, a task we can more easily remember by taking the first letter of each word to produce the name GOT-IT, we end up with an instructional technology approach that emphasizes a systematic step-by-step focus on effectively and smoothly introducing technologies and **instructional techniques** into the curriculum. In typical instructional technology models, evaluation is the final step in the process. (For example, after completing all the steps you evaluate how effective your design choices were.) In the GOT-IT model the answers to each question (GOT-IT) make up your assessment. Thus assessment and evaluation are intertwined and considered vital throughout each step of the model. For the GOT-IT model (figure 2.3) to work, evaluation in the form of checks and signposts must be built into all phases. This design will result in continuous feedback that can provide valuable guidance for implementing technology.

Figure 2.3 In the GOT-IT model, technology usage is planned out ahead of time and continually evaluated for effectiveness.

As Linda starts to address the task of setting up her report, she realizes that apart from allowing students to borrow the camera to shoot each other participating in various drills during class, she has not used the technology in a concrete way to aid instruction. In addition, few students have even bothered to touch the camera. She realizes that she must be more creative at including the equipment as part of the learning experience. She reviews her lesson plans and tries to envision ways that video could be an active part of presenting information. She remembers the time in class when two of her students tried to emulate a move they saw on television the previous night when the star forward hit the winning basket on a turnaround shot. If Linda could have shown the move from the game on videotape to the students and had them break it down, she would have provided not only a useful learning experience but also encouragement to the students who were trying to get the move down. She returns to her lesson plans and attempts to identify other possibilities for including short video examples to augment her demonstrations and achieve the learning objectives.

Advantages of Using Technology

In looking at implementing technology into your curriculum using the GOT-IT model, certain advantages should become apparent. First, by investigating new experiences that you can add to your class activities, you acquire a frame of mind that addresses how you can reach your students in new and exciting ways. This way of thinking will also allow you to take into account how students may differ in learning styles, such as visual learners versus tactile learners (see chapter 5 for more on learning styles). You may see the possibility of providing alternative learning activities through technology. Students may also differ in what strategies and techniques motivate them to stay on task and self-monitor their progress. Different strategies, technologies, and media have been shown to be effective agents for motivating students in key learning areas. In addition, whether or not you end up adding technology to your existing curriculum, going through the decision-making process can provide you with insight into what you are teaching.

Finally, implementing technology into your curriculum can give you greater control over delivering content and concepts over numerous times and learning contexts. Pre-produced computer and video programs can present learning experiences in the same manner and context each time you use them. The video demonstration you show in one class will produce the same experience when you show it to another class. Teachers, on the other hand, are prone to variations each time they present in a live manner. VCRs and computers never have bad days. They come ready to stimulate, play, and review material. Turn them on and watch them go. Be aware, however, that ineffective materials will repeat the same mistakes each time you present them. Even inexperienced teachers know when the message is not reaching their students, and most will not ignore the reaction but adjust to it. The most advanced machines cannot do that. So much for machines replacing teachers.

Disadvantages of Using Technology

Although one of the goals of this book is to promote the use of effective instructional technology in your PE programs, you should be aware of certain limitations that arise when teachers began to implement instructional technology. You must consider the three key areas when adopting technology into your curriculum:

1. Cost
2. Time
3. Unrealistic expectations

Of course, we hope that the challenges of cost, time, and expectations do not cause you to abandon technological pursuits. Remember that people invest exorbitant money, time, and expectations in selecting a type of car and evaluating expensive options that come with it. They do this because they believe that the rewards associated with getting what they want (provided they know what they want) will in the end outweigh and justify the investment. You don't purchase every extra item the car manufacturer offers. An overall understanding and awareness of what you want and what you need to get around town guides you. Likewise, you should use the same understanding and awareness when implementing technology. A close examination of cost, time, and expectations will aid in that understanding and awareness.

Cost

First, in looking at cost limitations, you have to figure tying up resources for purchasing, using, and maintaining technology. In most teaching circumstances, trying to obtain additional resources for technology can strain an already stretched budget. Thus, in most cases this book will suggest sensible, low-cost approaches to including advantageous technological methods into teaching physical education. In addition, the cost of adding new technologies will always decline as the technology becomes more widespread. Finally, when looking at technological implementation efforts over a longer period, cost-saving benefits may become obvious. The software you bought this year may yield continuous long-term benefits for years to come. Ultimately, you will have to weigh the benefits to learning (return on investment) versus dollars spent. Obviously, the newest versions of computers or applications may add to the dollars you spend without necessarily affecting the learning. Any instructional technology decision should begin with these questions: Do I already have the necessary technology for meeting a learning objective? If not, is adapting what I already have a possible acceptable compromise? Finally, if not, will it be worth the cost to invest in new technology?

Time

A second potential negative is the amount of time required to become familiar with the new technology, re-create lessons that include the technology, and develop new instructional materials. In addition, you must factor in the time associated with conducting ongoing evaluation of the new process, including evaluations of the new design, the new materials generated, and the effectiveness of the technology. Although implementing technology can be time consuming, the result can be a physical education curriculum that is effective, enjoyable, and meaningful.

Unrealistic Expectations

The final disadvantage associated with technology implementation is the often unrealistic expectation people have about technology. This becomes evident when you meet a teacher who has never met a technology she did not like. We can trace part of these expectations to the slick marketing of technology that we see every day. Advertising fosters a belief that we can judge the worth of something by whether it exists on a computer, DVD disk, or Web site. These beliefs focus not on the learning but on the form of media that delivers the instruction. We may tend to make instructional technology decisions based not on the evidence of learning appropriateness but on claims presented and repeated through slick marketing. These marketing campaigns attempt to influence how you spend your resources. Being an aware consumer can go a long way in determining realistic goals and rewards for using technology.

Each of the remaining chapters in the book will have a technology and technique section, labeled T 'n T. These tips offer technology and technique possibilities related to particular aspects covered in a chapter. The T 'n T tips may not be the best or only solutions, but we believe that they can serve as a model for creativity when using technologies. To be successful with technology, you must be creative and have a plan that emphasizes a systematic design focusing on goals, objectives, technology, and instructional techniques (GOT-IT model). The resulting decisions will help you focus on goals and objectives first, which should be the number one criteria for determining what, if any, technology solutions will lead to a richer instructional physical education experience for your students.

In trying to come up with other uses for her equipment, Linda suddenly focused on another possibility for using video as a demonstration technique. Because she was spending so much time going over particular rules and regulations, she felt she could use the video to demonstrate correct procedures for getting and returning equipment. The instructional video would include her expectations for how things should be done. The students would be required to view the tape before the first class, and the tape would be always close by as a reminder if needed. In addition, she realized that a friend could take video stills from the tape and print them out as a reference for how various storage areas should look. She believed that the constant visual reminders would go a long way in helping her students get the message. In addition, they would be less likely to ignore her rules and protocols.

Using Technology to Help Establish an Effective Learning Environment

In keeping with our technology-as-a-tool concept, you want to find the best technology tools available to help you establish an effective learning environment. Remember from earlier in this chapter that the definition of technology involves more than just computers and high-tech gadgets. Finding technologies that can help you establish rules and protocols, use time wisely, and provide good cues and feedback will ultimately make you a more effective teacher.

Using Technology to Help Establish Rules and Protocols

You can easily apply technologies and techniques to your physical education classes to establish your rules and protocols. If your goal is to make sure that the students learn the rules and protocols quickly, it is wise to display visual reminders where students can refer to them often and

Purpose

To spend more time learning concepts and skills rather than class procedures

Technique

Bulletin board for visually displaying rules and protocols

Procedure

Step 1.   Prepare a list of protocols and rules you would like students to follow in your classroom.

Step 2.   Split your list in two based on your idea of necessary items versus ideal items.

Step 3.   Share your ideas with the class. Provide a rationale for why you feel the issues are important (i.e., safety regulations, school policies, management and care of class materials, and so on).

Step 4.   Encourage feedback from the students, and let them help you finalize the list of necessary and ideal items on the rules and protocol lists.

Step 5.   Break up the list into segments and assign groups or pairs of students to produce visuals representing each rule and protocol. For example, the group assigned the item on the protocol list to "leave equipment on the floor between the feet while the teacher gives instructions" would produce a drawing or picture of the correct behavior. Encourage students to create clear visuals. This assignment could be the first homework assignment of the year.

Step 6.   After collecting all of the visually displayed rules and protocols, prominently display all the items on a bulletin board in an area where students can see it during class.

Step 7.   If a student is not following a particular protocol or is breaking a rule, direct her to the bulletin board for immediate feedback and reflection.

with ease. Bulletin boards may not be on the cutting edge of instructional and communication technology, but they may be the best way to accomplish the goal. The number one goal is to make students aware of the rules and protocols for the class as quickly as possible. One reason that students may not follow rules and protocols is that they cannot remember them. Rules and protocols are typically not as relevant to the students as they are to the teacher. Students are not concerned with issues of class management, taking roll, and putting materials away properly. They may become more engaged, however, if they realized that spending less time on these tasks allows them more time to be active. If you are able to use concepts that include concrete visual reminders, students will be more aware of what you need them to do and why you want them to do it.

You can probably imagine other ways to present the rules and protocols visually to a class. One way would be to videotape examples of how students should observe rules and protocols. The problem is that the students would be able to see it only at the very beginning of the year. The retention of concepts presented in a video is short-lived without reinforcement. The bulletin board represents permanence. The rules and protocols can stay on the bulletin board day in and day out. They become an essential

Your Turn ▶▶▶

Come up with your own definition of instructional technology. Using your own definition, provide a rationale for why creating a bulletin board that uses limited technology could still be an excellent example of using instructional technology in a classroom.

part of the classroom and gym. Most important, if a student is confused, he can simply look at the bulletin board and find out what he should be doing.

You may be questioning the need for involving the students in the preparation and production of the visuals. After all, if you know what you want, why not create it yourself and simply display the same visuals each year? Most people learn best by doing. Although the quality of the visuals may vary from year to year or even within a particular semester, students could benefit by being assigned the creation of visuals for the purpose of demonstrating understanding of protocol concepts and practices. The visuals they create will provide you with instant feedback concerning their understanding of the rules and protocols. Students will also be more likely to follow guidelines that they had some part in creating (figure 2.4).

Figure 2.4 Students are more likely to understand rules when they understand their importance. Making a bulletin board to display the rules gives them this opportunity.

Using visuals may also be an effective way of conveying acceptable standards for storing and setting up equipment. Saying that the aerobic steps should "be returned to their proper space in the storage room" presents a potential for misunderstanding and misinterpreting. Whose standards are we talking about? Students who are unsure about the procedure can always refer to a picture prominently displayed in an appropriate place. Having equipment set up and returned properly may appear to be a small concern, but if you were to add up the time taken away from instruction to address or redo improper equipment use procedures, you would appreciate the significance of the issue (figure 2.5). A picture is worth not only a thousand words but also several valuable minutes.

Ultimately, if you engage your students in the process of developing rules and establishing protocols for the class, give them opportunities to create visuals that can augment the learning of rules and protocol, and display the visuals prominently where students can review them with minimal disruption, the students will have a clear understanding of what

Figure 2.5 Equipment properly stored can save a teacher lots of time and aggravation.

you expect of them. In addition, any student unsure of the rules or protocols can easily refer to this permanently displayed visual aid for assistance. You will not have to spend as much time addressing these problems, allowing more opportunity for active learning.

Computer Technology for Establishing Rules and Regulations

Although a bulletin board does not conjure up a high-tech image, it can be an important tool in augmenting your instruction. Pictures cut out of magazines, creative designs, painting, and crayons can allow you to include your students in the production of materials. Not having the latest computer and software (more often than not a reality in public schools) will not prevent you from creating instructional media that can get the point across. We cannot deny, however, that as we move further into a digital environment in society, computers are becoming the standard media production tool. Students at an early age now have computer skills in creating word documents, using **digital media** tools such as photo-enhancement software, operating and producing digital video products, and creating and manipulating graphic design and Web-based materials.

By following the procedures stated earlier for communicating rules and regulations, you can enhance the process by using digital photography and video in conjunction with a page-layout software ranging from a basic **word application** to complete professional graphic design software. By using digital video to capture the ideal setup and storage examples, you can copy and display the visuals in numerous ways.

You might store the video on computers and require students to view and review the rules and procedures. You could capture video stills and paste them into a word document that you could print and distribute to students as a handout for future reference. Finally, you could enlarge the same stills and use a graphic design software package to create posters for display in relevant spots as a constant reminder. One of the greatest advantages to working in digital format is that you can easily reproduce data to present in a variety of media. This advantage is valuable because your demonstrations and reminders need to be consistent. The picture in the poster is the same as the one in the handouts and the one in the segment of the instructional video piece. This consistency will go a long way in eliminating misunderstanding between your expectations and your students' awareness.

Using Computers to Help You Use Time Wisely

One of the major advantages of computers is their awesome ability to record, store, organize, and retrieve information in microseconds. Mohnsen (1998) pointed to database and spreadsheet software as being particularly valuable to physical education teachers (figure 2.6). Because of the sheer numbers associated with students in an average physical education class, a system that can easily manage students' attendance, grades, assignments, and miscellaneous information would obviously free the teacher to spend more time teaching and assessing students.

A typical computer database contains fields such as students' names, locker combination numbers,

As Linda continued to review her lesson plans for possible uses of video technology, it became apparent to her that she could use other technologies that she presently possessed more effectively in her teaching. She also wanted to be ahead of the game in creating next year's wish list for buying additional technology for her class. The computer in her office had only a standard bundled software package of applications, Microsoft Office, which included a word application, **spreadsheet application,** and **presentation application.** She was currently using only the word program for writing classroom instructions, cue sheets for skill-developing activities, and lesson plans. She could easily use the presentation program during teacher demonstrations to bring in pictures from the Internet to display proper body positioning for various physical activities. Although she could use the spreadsheet program to create an electronic grade book, she felt that she would gain little advantage for the investment of time required to learn a new program. But if she could identify additional benefits in conducting her class, she knew it would be worthwhile to investigate some of the possibilities.

Figure 2.6   A computer spreadsheet can make keeping track of student information much easier.

class schedules, and so on. You can easily design and modify the database so that you have access to all relevant information pertaining to a particular student. This is particularly useful in emergencies when student information is needed quickly.

In Linda's school she is responsible for student learning and attendance documentation as well as organizing and maintaining locker distributions, equipment usage, and student participation. During a typical day the quantity of information she tracks pertaining to class maintenance, learning assessment, and grading often overwhelms her.

Although teachers traditionally use a simple grade book to keep particular information, one of the advantages of using a **database application** is that you can sort and display information with the stroke of the key. You can also select only the relevant information for presentation. This advantage can be particularly useful when a field such as medicinal needs is part of the student record section. Finally, as more information becomes represented in digital form, it may become possible to send information stored in database and spreadsheet applications electronically to administration offices for grades and record keeping. Possibilities exist for data to be accessible online for parents to keep track of their children's progress. In addition, stu-

dents could also access their records and be more aware of and responsible for their progress.

Displaying Relevant Information

Computers are certainly appropriate for updating, managing, and displaying data for teachers. If, for instance, you need information on what classes Jackie Jones has missed during a particular unit, database software will be able to provide you with instant feedback. This information could be valuable in assessing her overall mastery of the unit objectives. If the information indicated that she missed classes that covered valuable components for successful skill acquisition, you would understand poor performance. Jackie Jones could also access the information any time during the semester. You might require her to be aware of how she is doing in the class. She would have access only to her particular records, and you could address confidentiality in ways that you could not when using a traditional grade book. Every teacher can relate to the situation in which several students stand over the teacher, each asking, "How am I doing in this class?" As you are trying to find Jackie Jones's row of information, you are also trying to make sure that other students are not looking at her personal information. A traditional grade book is organized linearly in pages, rows, and columns. Software databases and spreadsheets can be recalled to display only the information needed at the time. Other fields in the database, such as a locker combination number and Jackie's class schedule, would not be displayed. You would sort out those fields and display only the pertinent information to aid in your assessment.

Keeping Attendance

One of the major time-consuming activities involves taking roll and marking classroom attendance. Databases can be useful for recording attendance. A setup similar to one used by some fitness clubs would have students enter their own identification for attendance each day. Other fields could have them answer the question of the day (for example, "Name an area that you will be focusing on in today's class.") The idea is for students to communicate more than just their presence by responding in ways that can help you assess how ready they are to work.

A concern about having students enter their attendance data is that one student might sign in for a classmate who is not there. Databases track the number of log-ins, so you can compare that number with the number of students physically in class on that day. You can address any discrepancies through rules and disciplinary procedures.

Finally, as computers become smaller, handheld and palm personal computers (PCs) have become popular for having access to databases while teaching (figure 2.7). These devices are particularly useful to physical education teachers who conduct classes in various settings. With the power of the computer at your fingertips, you can enter and assess grading and attendance data in the "field." Handheld and palm PCs, however, have several shortcomings. Because of the small keyboard pad, entering information can be awkward. The attention and fine motor skills needed to enter and access data correctly may outweigh what you gain in convenience and portability. Sunlight can severely affect screen visibility, and battery power may fail unexpectedly. Such circumstances can be frustrating and require excessive time and attention from the teacher. Teachers who use computers primarily for data management of the class would probably more efficiently accomplish the task by designating a particular area for the students to log in on a desktop or laptop computer. As mentioned earlier, teachers can print out certain fields of information to guide them when offering assistance and feedback to their students. Teachers must carefully weigh the cost and benefits of entering data with a handheld or palm PC during the instructional period.

A learning environment that maximizes time on task while minimizing time off task will clearly yield

Figure 2.7 As technology improves, physical education teachers have more options at their fingertips.

positive results for students. Any choice of technology in this matter must ultimately reflect the following question: will this help me maximize my time for engaging students in active learning? Simply put, a technology that saves time on tasks not directly related to the learning can still be considered instructional because the time saved allows more time to be spent on learning. If the teacher can use a system that permits students to sign in before class or during the warm-ups, time and effort can be spent in more useful teaching and learning activities. Likewise, a technology that manages and reports specific information about students could be particularly useful when providing instruction and feedback.

Using Technology for Assessment

One of the most important roles for teachers involves assessing student learning in a way that is meaningful and encourages continued effort by the student. In chapter 12 we explore ways of assessment in physical education in the four domains of learning: cognitive, affective, psychomotor, and health-related fitness. Certain technologies can be

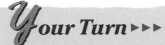

Your Turn ▸▸▸

Make a list of all of the activities associated with a typical physical education class from start to finish. Be specific. Go over each item of your list and determine if the activity is learning or nonlearning in nature (for example, taking roll is a nonlearning activity). Finally, being as creative as possible, consider all the nonlearning activities and determine whether you could shorten or eliminate them by using a specific technology. Spare no expense in making your technology choices. You may even invent and include unreal technologies, such as a retina-scanning machine at the locker-room doors that instantaneously identifies students and records attendance.

particularly useful for teachers to assess student progress creatively (figure 2.8).

Using Video for Assessment Levels

In chapter 9, we expand the concept of learning environment to include the various skill levels of your students. A typical class will feature a spectrum of individuals ranging from the skilled and

Figure 2.8 Videotaping a class can be a creative way to assess student progress and a teacher's classroom design and management.

motivated to the unskilled and unmotivated. To let all of your students participate in tasks in which they can experience success, you need to know what tasks to plan, based on a variety of skill levels. One of the best techniques to help you determine the predominant skill proficiency in your classes involves the use of video recording and playback technology. While you are engaged in conducting class, searching for correct cues, providing feedback, and demonstrating proper techniques, you may find it difficult to step back and assess how the class as a whole is doing with the skills. A simple video session to establish existing group skill levels as well as skill progression can be an extremely useful assessment tool. The saying that the "camera never blinks" is applicable in using video recording technology in class. The teacher should review video sessions shortly after recording them so that she will be able to recall any circumstances or contexts that may have affected the learning. Differences in abilities among students will also be highlighted.

Teachers may want to share a small portion of each video recording with the class to show improvement. One caution about doing this is that certain students may choose to act in a noticeable way to distinguish themselves from the group. Some may purposefully mess up or use exaggerated movements to gain attention. In addition, if some students perform at an obviously lower level than the norm, other class members may ridicule them. If such occurrences seem likely, the teacher should view the video alone. In any case, group videotaping is probably most useful to establish entry-level skills, to recognize areas in which students need to improve, and to identify new concepts to teach. There are better ways to use video recording during practicing of skills.

Video Feedback for Student Practice

Depending on whether teachers are using blocked, variable, or random practice, the ability of students to receive clear feedback and evidence of improvement makes practice more meaningful and enjoyable. Photography, motion pictures, and video have been widely used in physical movement and physical education studies. Videographers and editors are regular members of professional sport franchises. Professional athletes spend almost as much time in the film room as they do on the practice field. Using video in physical education classes may have once seemed too troublesome or expensive, but the size and the prices of recording units con-

Purpose

To acquire a better understanding of what movement skill experiences the class members possess and to provide specific information about the needs of the students

Technique

Video recording and keeping tape archive of various skill and movement progression of the group

Procedure

Step 1. Before introducing a lesson unit, have the class perform certain aspects of the unit that they will be working to master.

Step 2. Set up a video camera in the farthest corner of the room. Establish the widest shot possible that will include all the students and their movements.

Step 3. Set the camera on record and interact with class members completing various movements. Provide feedback and encouragement. The camera and the shot should remain static throughout the activity. You should ignore the camera and keep the students active on tasks so that recording does not distract them.

Step 4. Stop recording after the class and label the tape with identifying information (class, date, time).

Step 5. Review the recording and make notes on which skills and movements were apparently evident. Who possessed which skills? Did a significant number of students make the same errors?

Step 6. Perform video recording at least twice during the lesson unit and compare the progress of the group as they progress through the unit.

Step 7. If a student is not following a particular protocol or is breaking a rule, direct her to the bulletin board for immediate feedback and reflection.

tinue to shrink. A physical education teacher who does not use video is overlooking a tremendous tool for helping students learn.

Unlike the group shot, individual recording of students must involve a focused camera shoot with regard to student movement. The camera operator must have more familiarity with shooting and setting up an ideal situation for capturing an individual's movement. Because the image will be used for feedback, it is vital to achieve the richest representation possible through good use of lighting and competent shooting.

Purpose

To provide an individual student with visual feedback concerning personal acquisition and development of skills

Technique

Videotape recording and tape archiving of various skill and movement progression of an individual

Procedure

Step 1. Require all students to bring in a labeled videocassette VHS tape.

Step 2. Set up the camera in an area or spot where individuals can perform certain skill movements.

Step 3. As the class is engaged in activities, select an individual to come to the designated spot and perform the skill movements.

Step 4. Using the student's individual VHS tape, record the segment in real time (do not stop the student as if you were a movie director). Have the student perform a repetitive activity for roughly five minutes. Record the whole segment. Vary shots from wide to medium to a close-up of the most relevant parts of the body.

Step 5. Have students review tape for homework, jotting down which movements they performed naturally, which they performed with more difficulty, which they attempted unsuccessfully, and what cues they feel they need to achieve success.

Step 6. Perform several individual recording sessions throughout the school year. An average VHS tape will hold two to six hours of video, so you can record subsequent sessions on the same tape.

Through the use of video recording sessions students will be able to receive visual feedback, identify particular strengths and weaknesses, and engage in self-correcting techniques. Clearly, motivation to practice should increase as students become more aware of how the movements they are practicing relate to achievement of a particular skill. The videotape also provides a way for students to share certain class activities with their friends and family. The videotape will also have an audio track of your voice providing verbal cues and feedback to the student. You should not show the individual taped sessions to the whole class. Video can be intimidating because it shows a representation of the student's ability, both the good and the bad. Use particular care with the individual when using video recording in class.

Using Computer-Aided Technologies for Assessment

One of the most efficient ways of offering assessment of physical activity involves the use of computer **heart rate monitors.** These devices, usually in the form of a watch, present heart rate data during a workout and give instant feedback to the user about the duration and intensity of the workout (figure 2.9). When the user appears to fall out of her target rate zone, the monitor produces a visual and audio signal to alert her to increase the

Figure 2.9 Students can now use a computer and printer to instantly display data obtained from heart rate monitors that they wear.

intensity of the workout. In addition, the user can retrieve data after the activity session through a computer-generated graph that shows the heart rate throughout the session. The user can pinpoint particular areas of the workout to demonstrate which parts of the activity were intense and which parts were not. A creative physical education teacher can have students assess activities in terms of their fitness as well as the relative benefits inherent in different activities.

Significant uses for this technology involve teaching concepts as well as designing curriculum for the class. In teaching students how different activities affect their cardiovascular intensity, students can wear the heart rate monitors when playing basketball. Areas of the graph will indicate where the student was less active and where he was performing at or near his target heart rate capacity. By combining a video recording of what the student did with visual representations provided by the heart rate graph, a complete assessment tool could be developed that would directly compare cause (movement) to effect (cardiovascular activity). This method would also reinforce the relationship between the intensity of a workout and the efficiency of burning fat. Finally, teachers who observe students' heart rate data have a tremendous aid to designing appropriate curricula for fitness development. They would be able to explore and validate nontraditional fitness activities that adolescents are more likely to enjoy.

Using Word Programs

Simple word software is valuable in creating and producing task sheets to use for assessment. The ease of copying, pasting, and updating digitally stored information means that teachers can easily develop task sheets, evaluation score sheets, checklists, and so forth. By saving different variations of task sheets, you can produce specifically customized sheets for different fitness or skill levels and update them easily. The biggest advantage to using this technology is that you can create something once, apply variations to it, save those variations, and have custom sheets to reflect student variations.

Another effective use of the word programs is to develop handouts containing visual cues that you can use in the peer review process. You can hand out these sheets to your students, who can refer to them as you are demonstrating a particular skill movement. Thus, students can process the live correct movement with the verbal cues provided by your instruction and the visual representation on the cue sheet. This method will help ensure consistency throughout all phases involved in learning. The concepts that students learn at

the initial stage and repeat at the practice stage are reinforced later during the peer partner feedback stage. Powerful and user-friendly word programs now make it easy to include visuals within the body of the text. Sketches that emphasize the correct body placement or movement can more effectively communicate an acceptable standard or practice than a real-life still photograph of someone successfully completing the movement. This is especially true when novices are attempting to model what they see in the visual.

You can easily create sketches and still photos digitally or scan them from actual sketches into digital format. These graphics can be easily inserted into a document. The advantage of having digital representations becomes clear if you are interested in having students review them on a Web page, view them in a demonstration poster, or refer to them in a test. Having the same visual cue appear in various forms throughout the learning process will provide the student with a source for self- and peer assessment.

Using Technology During Atypical Learning Context

In chapter 13, we provide a basic message about being prepared by planning for the unexpected. We include examples of what happens when inclement weather severely alters the learning environment. Although your students may think that rainy days give them an excuse to blow off the learning for the day, you can have alternative lesson plans and strategies on standby and be ready to deliver them in a way that augments your current lesson plans.

Technology can be a valuable tool during days when you are unable to conduct regular activities. Although the use of technology should be consistent and build on the regularly planned learning objectives, you can use an alternative media-driven learning experience when other rainy-day activities are either not appropriate or have worn out their welcome. The key is to look at rainy days as opportunities to be creative by providing your students with memorable and effective instruction despite the unusual learning setting.

We are all aware of the stereotypical rainy-day learning activities that often amount to little more than standing around and wasting time. Teachers all agree that wasting time has no place in a curriculum. But what do you do when bad weather interrupts a particular learning activity? You can fill that time with entertaining, enjoyable, and relaxing activities that reinforce what your students are learning by providing opportunities for insight and reflection. Using appropriate technology in your class not only results in procedural and declarative knowledge acquisition but also encourages your students to explore additional relevant learning experiences on their own. Rainy days provide opportunities for just those types of experiences.

VCR Technology

Video is a popular technology on rainy days. We can all remember sitting down in a class to watch a movie or television show that had little relevance to what we had been studying. If you show a video for a rainy-day activity, you are responsible for communicating the viewing contexts and learning expectations to your students before showing it. Otherwise, you are leaving it up to your students to determine how they are to interpret and acquire the relevant information. Explaining learning expectations is essential for overcoming one of the major limitations of video, passive viewing. You must work to counteract the tendency in all of us to sit passively in front of a movie on a rainy day. To engage your students, you should use a particular instructional strategy when using video in the classroom for instructional purposes. The teacher must not give up complete control of the learning environment to the video player.

The number one strategy when showing video in a learning context is to avoid showing long uninterrupted programs. The pace of information in video programs is determined primarily by production and editing concerns rather than the goal of providing opportunities to learn. An alternative tactic is to show shorter, more focused video segments of an existing program. One such example is PE TV, a 15-minute program produced by Channel One and designed to be shown in its entirety in class. An appealing possibility is for a teacher to collect related concepts demonstrated in different programs. The teacher could then show a series of such segments to augment a concept he is teaching. Say, for example, that you are teaching the concept of weight transfer and want to show visual examples of the concept in various movement contexts. With proper collection of the various programs, storage, and retrieval, you will have a supplemental activity that can seamlessly advance your curriculum goals and be a teaching tool when inclement weather limits activity. You can introduce concepts, check for retention with your students, and then demonstrate concepts with the video segments. You can refer to these video segments in the future when activities resume.

Requiring students to record and bring in video demonstrations of the concepts from home can introduce and reinforce particular concepts. In keeping with our earlier example of weight distribution, students can choose one of their favorite sports events shown on television. Require them to record and select examples from the event of athletes demonstrating the particular concept. By having students bring in examples, you have an excellent opportunity to assess how well they recognize the concept. In addition, you could copy and save particularly effective examples for your archive of video concepts.

World Wide Web

An alternative solution to weather interruptions is to conduct class at the school's computer lab or library. Students could use computer terminals hooked up to the Internet to research particular issues associated with your learning objectives. They could search the **World Wide Web** for sites that attempt to provide instruction in various physical activities. These sites range from a true instruction site to advertising for books, software, and devices to aid in physical activities. A worthwhile assignment would be for students to visit sites that market devices for easier ways for getting in shape. You may have your students analyze the claims and provide a critical review. Other sites worth using are those that include video segments that students can view from the computer. Again, students could develop reviewing skills by attempting to learn from the educational videos and providing an evaluation of their effectiveness in helping people to learn and improve skills.

Purpose

To develop students' critical analysis skills of physical skill acquisition instruction provided on the World Wide Web

Procedure

Step 1. Students select a particular physical activity and enter it into an online search engine such as Yahoo, Ask Jeeves, MSN Search, or Hotbot.

Step 2. Students should visit educational sites until they find one that teaches a physical activity concept. There are many sites associated with popular activities such as golf, tennis, fencing, swimming, and archery.

Step 3. Students record what they believe to be the site's learning objectives for the chosen activity.

Step 4. Students should attempt to follow the instruction provided at the site and record positive and negative experiences in attempting to achieve the objectives under that instruction. They should also include a summary statement, reporting if this instruction is a valuable resource for the class in the future.

Step 5. The instructor should save the site addresses that students have deemed valuable, creating a resource library of sites that you can include later in your curriculum when you are teaching a particular skill. Before long you will have a library that includes numerous activities and skills that can be used as references and demonstrations.

Motivating Effects of Using Technology

One of the great rewards of using technology in your class is that it can strongly motivate students to learn new concepts, participate in new activities, and achieve new levels of competency. Comparing video segments of a student performing at a low level at the beginning of a lesson unit with segments of the same movement performed later at a higher level can give the student a visual artifact that shows learning and progression. Regularly scheduled video of the student can be stored and reviewed throughout the lesson unit. Imagine the possibilities for students who can visually track successful mastery of a skill.

The use of a heart rate monitor can also provide graphic presentation of progress. You can print out intensity levels during workouts to motivate students to increase or maintain their efforts in the future. Likewise, pedometers can be used to motivate students who are interested in monitoring how far and how fast they have moved during a particular activity.

Motivation for activity varies from student to student. Technology will not provide the answer for everyone, but feedback and assessment that students can use individually stand a better chance of providing additional motivation, especially when compared with performance feedback and assessment that put students in the spotlight. Technologies with storage and playback capability can provide the student with personal information that he can access at any time.

Summary

Any discussion about using technology should begin by asking what you hope to accomplish. Answering this question leads to a process of determining learning goals and objectives before looking at technology issues. Also, it is important to understand both the advantages and limitations associated with the use of technology in the learning environment. We need to explore ways to introduce technology so that it enriches rather than distracts the learners. The GOT-IT model suggests that we address questions at each level to ensure sound implementation of technology. Specific technologies are particularly effective at setting up expectations and rules in the learning environment. Likewise, many computer-enhanced technologies can be valuable in helping students engage in self-assessment and evaluation of physical activities within typical and atypical class settings. Although we could find more examples of how technology can affect the learning environment, one thing is clear: the more open you are to the possibilities of implementing appropriate technologies and techniques into your class, the richer and more meaningful the learning environment can be.

Checking for Understanding ▸▸▸

- What is the most important question you should ask when first trying to determine if you should include instructional technology in your class?

- What are the two main ways that teachers use instructional technologies in the classroom?

- Describe a major hurdle associated with implementing instructional technologies into the classroom.

- According to the GOT-IT model, what are the major questions you should ask yourself about implementing technology into the classroom?

- What are the three major negatives you must be aware of when implementing technology into the classroom?

- What major benefit can you gain by communicating your rules and protocols to your students by visual displays on a bulletin board?

- What major benefit can you gain by communicating your rules and protocols to your students through video and still pictures?

- How can you use video to assess student achievement?

- How can students use video to assess their own achievement?

- What strategy should you use when presenting video during an atypical class setting?

- How can you use the World Wide Web in a meaningful way during an atypical class setting?

For Reflection and Discussion ▸▸▸

- How can you best express your philosophy regarding the use of technology to enhance learning?

- How has technology had an influence on your personal knowledge about physical education?

- How are physical education teachers and physical education portrayed in popular video and television programs?

- Can you think of instances where technology inhibits someone to be physically active?

- Can you think of instances where technology encourages someone to be physically active?

References

Mohnsen, B. 1998. *Using technology in physical education.* Champaign, IL: Human Kinetics.

Suggested Readings

Anderson, M., R. Mikat, and R. Martinez. 2001. Digital video production in physical education and athletics. *Journal of Physical Education, Recreation and Dance* 72(6):19.

Beighle, A., R.P. Pangrazi, and S. Vincent. 2001. Pedometers, physical activity, and accountability. *Journal of Physical Education, Recreation and Dance* 72(9):16.

Kemp, J.E., and D.C. Smellie. 1994. *Planning, producing, and using instructional technologies.* 7th ed. New York: HarperCollins.

Mitchell D. 2001. Digitizing video. *Journal of Physical Education, Recreation and Dance* 72(4):11.

Norton, P., and K.M. Wiburg. 1998. *Teaching with technology.* Orlando: Harcourt Brace.

Ryan S., S. Marzilli, and T. Martindale. 2001. Using digital cameras to assess motor learning. *Journal of Physical Education, Recreation and Dance* 72(8):13.

Chapter *3*

Adolescents and Physical Activity

**A teacher affects eternity;
no one can tell where his influence stops.**

— *Henry Adams*

One day at work, Laurence, who is in his 50s, comes across an article in the newspaper about "new PE." He reads that physical education is now aiming at helping all young people develop skills in a variety of activities that they can enjoy throughout their lives. The article makes him think about his own physical education experiences and his current sedentary lifestyle. "My PE classes were not like that at all. Do you think that has anything to do with my being a couch potato?" he asks his wife over dinner. Laurence is recalling what it was like to always be chosen last for team sports. He remembers how his classmates made fun of him when he failed the pull-up test in front of them. He's wondering whether his granddaughter, Elise, is having a better experience, and he promises his wife that he will ask her about PE this weekend when they see her. "The way they describe this new PE in the article, I think it could be of some value in a child's education," he tells his wife. "I don't even bowl or play golf because I always felt like a loser and a klutz in PE! Maybe if it were taught in the appropriate way, physical education could have the opposite effect."

Learning Objectives

After reading this chapter thoroughly and discussing the issues in class you should be able to

- state NASPE's definition of a physically educated person,
- explain why physical activity, not physical fitness, should be the focus of physical education programs,
- explain the current activity levels of American youth and the adult population,
- list a majority of the determinants for physical activity in youth,
- synthesize the information in chapters 1 and 3 and describe what teachers can do to help students become physically active for the rest of their lives,
- explain how long adolescents need to be active each day and what kinds of activities lead to health enhancement,
- define lifetime health-enhancing activities and list the two main questions that you should ask before you focus on any activity in your curriculum, and
- explain how teachers can discourage physical activity enjoyment and participation.

Key Terms and Phrases

Physically educated person
Physical activity
Physical fitness
Determinants for physical activity
Biological factors
Psychological factors
Sociological factors
Environmental factors
Self-efficacy

In chapter 1 we outlined why the focus of physical education should be to guide students in the process of becoming physically active for the rest of their lives, and we discussed how we can change secondary school physical education to reach that goal. You may remember that a variety of national guidelines for physical education and activity, as well as the National Association for Sport and Physical Education (NASPE) standards, support that goal. In this chapter we will show you how the research related to physical activity participation supports these guidelines and standards. Many prominent researchers, teacher educators, and physical education teachers agree that the purpose of physical education should be to help students become active for the rest of their lives. In this chapter you will learn more about why they arrived at this conclusion.

Purpose of PE: Active for Life

Pate and Hohn (1994) stated in the introduction to their text *Health and Fitness Through Physical Education* that guiding students to be active for life should be the mission of physical education. That goal has become the official mission statement for many physical education programs around the nation, as well as Web resource sites, advocacy organizations, and teacher education programs. George Graham, well-known teacher educator, author, and the "brain" behind PE Central, has coined the phrase "Guiding youngsters in the process of becoming physically active and healthy for a lifetime." The statement explains the main premise of this book. To guide students effectively, a teacher must know the factors that influence activity levels, teach the skills and concepts that will lead to activity, and boost students' confidence in their abilities. Beyond that, she must be a role model and be involved in the community. The teacher must recognize that becoming active for a lifetime is indeed a process. Becoming physically active doesn't happen overnight. To help students become active for a lifetime so that they can care for their bodies, minds, and souls, the teacher must teach lifetime skills that enhance health.

Do we know why people become active or become couch potatoes? Are kids more out of shape than they once were? Can a quality physical education program lead to lifelong physical activity? You may have your own thoughts about what the answers are, but in this chapter you will learn what researchers have found about these and similar topics in the last three decades. The results of the research on determinants of physical activity, for example, have shown that teachers *can* do certain things to help children and youth become physically active, now and in their future. Our national standards and guidelines for physical education, which we discussed in chapter 1, reflect this finding. For instance, the NASPE standards for physical education state that students should be physically educated by the time they graduate from high school. NASPE's definition of a physically educated person puts a great deal of emphasis on the factors that lead a person toward an active lifestyle. A **physically educated person,** according to NASPE (1995, v), is one who

- has the skills necessary to perform a variety of physical activities,
- is physically fit,
- participates regularly in **physical activity,**
- knows the implications and benefits of involvement in physical activity, and
- values physical activity and its contributions to a healthy lifestyle.

Many students who major in PE teacher education would have a difficult time saying that they fit the preceding description. Ask yourself if you are physically educated. If your answer is no, ask yourself why not. In which of the categories do you fall short? Does that have anything to do with your physical education experiences? Should teachers be concerned about making sure that all students become physically educated? Obviously, the members of NASPE, our national organization of physical education professionals, believe they should. Four of the five parts of the NASPE definition of a physically educated person deal with physical activity values, knowledge, skills, and participation. As you will learn in this chapter, the definition of a physically educated person is largely based on the research of determinants for physical activity. Research in this area supports the idea that physical activity (the process), not **physical fitness** (the product), should be the focus in physical education. This finding is exactly what we expressed in chapter 1: the main goal of physical education should be to help students learn the skills and concepts they need to become physically active for the rest of their lives. Improved physical fitness is usually a product of regular participation in physical activity. In other words, fitness will follow eventually if a person is active enough. The argument you will hear is that physical activity habits carry over into adulthood, but fitness levels don't. Ultimately, the physical education teacher should see it as her responsibility to teach students the skills and concepts needed to become a lifelong participant in sport and physical activity rather than just a spectator (figure 3.1). To be able to do that, the teacher must know and understand the determinants for physical activity, and address them as in the examples presented in the GET ACTIVE FOR LIFE factors in table 1.4 (in chapter 1). Physical education teachers have the obligation to use all available resources to do what they can to overcome the barriers to physical activity in children and youth.

Focus on Activity, Not Fitness

A physical educator must understand the difference between physical fitness and physical activity and know how to address each in a physical education curriculum. Think about Laurence from our opening scenario. He was probably active during his childhood—most kids are—but as he grew into an adolescent, physical activity turned him off because of the inappropriate teaching methods used by his teachers. He felt like a klutz in most activities, and the class environment ac-

Purpose

Have students research via the Web people's activity levels during the course of a lifetime and determine why levels change throughout different stages of life.

Resource and Procedure

As you prepare students for the new year, explain why certain activities will be presented for the purpose of sustaining physical activity for a lifetime. For a homework assignment, challenge your students to search the Web and chart the average person's physical activity levels. You may want to provide a general Web site such as CASPER (Concerned Adults and Stu-

dents for Physical Education Reform, **www.helpcasper.org**) or the Centers for Disease Control and Prevention (**www.cdc.gov**) and have them search the site (who knows—they may find other things that interest them and are of value to them as well). Have students reflect on why there is such a difference between activity levels in younger adolescents, late teens, and adults. Have them list activities that they could see themselves engaging in regularly at an advanced age. Post the list of activities and constantly refer back to them during the unit. This helps to bring home the idea of activity for life.

Figure 3.1 Effective physical education classes should result in adults who become active rather than spectators.

centuated that feeling. The focus was on fitness, but teachers did fitness testing in a way that did not help him understand how he could improve. The method of testing was one in which he felt he was put in the spotlight (figure 3.2). His classmates ridiculed his weaknesses, and the teachers let it happen. His attitude toward physical education and physical activity became negative. As he grew older he lacked the skills and knowledge he needed to become involved in physical activity settings.

Why Not Fitness?

If we wanted to make sure that children became fit in our physical education classes, we could not focus on much else. We agree with Corbin (2002) when he states that fitness is important, but that physical education should not focus on getting children fit. Although the fitness of America's youth is an intermittent concern of politicians and the media, physical educators must resist the temptation of aiming to please these groups by "teaching to the fitness test."

The fitness focus in the media and among politicians may be due to the annual release of fitness scores in most states and nationally. We can easily become lost in the numbers, but we need to use caution when analyzing fitness test results and not fall into the trap of judging the success of physical education based on these tests. Remember that numerous factors influence the fitness levels of children, including heredity, age, and maturation, all of which are out of the teacher's control (Bouchard 1993; Corbin and Pangrazi 1992). In fact, studies have found that in youth the relationship between activity level and fitness is weak (Morrow and Freedson 1994; Pate, Dowda, and Ross 1990), so there is not much point in trying to answer the public's concern about fitness

Figure 3.2 Teachers need to make certain their students don't feel like they are being set up to be ridiculed for their inadequacies.

levels by making this the focus of physical education. Besides, Corbin and Pangrazi (1992) found that young children nowadays are *not* less fit overall than in earlier decades, as we have been led to believe from reports in the media and by some professionals who examined normative rather than criterion-referenced data.

We must also remember that fitness tests are often administered by teachers who have little or no training in the test procedures, see little value in the testing and thus are sloppy with the administration of the tests (affecting reliability and validity of the tests), and use inappropriate practices that cause children to give up to escape embarrassment. Many of the regularly used fitness tests have doubtful validity. In addition, errors can occur in the reporting of results, and students sometimes cheat on the tests. Does this mean we should not test the fitness of our children and youth? No, but we should use fitness testing to help our students develop goal-setting and problem-solving skills that they can use to check and improve their fitness when they want to later in life. We need to educate the public about why we do fitness tests and why our focus in physical education should be activity, not fitness.

Taking the focus off fitness does not mean that we should not address it. When we do address fitness in physical education, however, we should be teaching the *process* of lifetime fitness and not worry about the *product* of physical fitness activities (Pangrazi 1994). The product can only happen when the process is in place. You can improve your health-related fitness safely only by being physically active. The bottom line is that fitness levels don't automatically carry into adulthood, but physical activity levels do have that potential (Sallis and McKenzie 1991). This is especially true if the activities that children and youth learn and participate in include those that they are likely to participate in throughout their lives (American Academy of Pediatrics Committees on Sports Medicine and School Health 1987; American College of Sports Medicine 1988; Sallis and McKenzie 1991; U.S. Department of Health and Human Services, Public Health Service 1991). Later in this chapter we will look at this concept of lifetime activities.

Although our leading physical activity and fitness experts seem to agree that we should focus on activity levels rather than fitness in physical education, some express concern about certain areas of health-related physical fitness, especially increasing obesity levels of children and adolescents. Children in America are fatter than they were in previous decades (U.S. Department of Health and Human Services 2000; Flegal, Dietz, Srinivasan, and Berenson 1988). This circumstance is a major cause of concern for parents, health practitioners, politicians, and, of course, physical education teachers. The main reason for this concern is the fact that obesity is related to the two main categories of killers in the United States—heart disease and cancer (Centers for Disease Control and Prevention 2002).

Physical activity is a major factor in combating obesity, and lack of it is one of the reasons we have this problem today (Centers for Disease Control and Prevention 2002). We believe that by focusing physical education classes on helping students become physically active for the rest of their lives, our profession can be part of the solution to the problem of increased obesity levels in our society. We discuss childhood and adolescent obesity and overweight further in chapter 4.

Purpose

Use e-mail technology to obtain present activity levels and types of activities your students are currently engaging in away from school.

Resource and Procedure

A good year-opener activity is to have students reflect on their current activity levels. Prompt them with specific questions (for example, "In the past week, how many times have you participated in a physical activity of moderate intensity?"). Have them describe the types of activities they predominantly take part in and enjoy. You also can provide them with a longer time frame, such as "over the past summer." Be creative! You may also want to provide them with a list of activities that are considered moderate and vigorous to help them understand the difference. Have them e-mail their responses to you. If students do not have e-mail, show them how to sign up for a Web-based e-mail system such as Yahoo, Earthlink, MSN, or Hotmail. These particular services are free and can be activated on any computer that has Web access. When you teach using technology, it can be valuable for students to have e-mail accounts. Once they have sent you their e-mail assignment, save student addresses into groups, possibly by periods. All e-mail systems are equipped with this grouping feature and have instructions on using it.

The New Focus: Physical Activity

We clearly have a problem of inactivity in our society. Most people are not physically active on a regular basis (U.S. Department of Health and Human Services 1996, 1997, 2000). Researchers have extensively studied the causes for this and usually refer to them as determinants for physical activity. We summarized the determinants in chapter 1 as the GET ACTIVE FOR LIFE factors, and later in this chapter we will, as promised, explore them further.

By focusing our physical education programs on helping youth develop the skills and concepts they need to become physically active for the rest of their lives, we increase their chances of living healthy, active lives. As mentioned earlier, activity is more likely to carry over into adulthood than is fitness (figure 3.3). A child or adolescent who enjoys being physically active, has confidence in

Figure 3.3 The habits and strategies that lead to consistent physical activity begin when we are children and continue, hopefully, into old age.

her abilities, is competent in many movement forms and proficient in a few (NASPE 1995), and has the problem-solving and self-management skills to overcome real and perceived barriers to being active is more likely to be active now and in the future (Sallis et al. 1992).

Why Should Adolescents Be Physically Active?

The benefits of regular physical activity are many, ranging from improved self-esteem and sense of well-being to decreased risk of heart disease and certain forms of cancer. The benefits in the end are the same for teenagers as they are for adults, but teens don't tend to think long-term. When you're 15, you think 40 is old, and any benefits of exercise at an older age may not sound important to you. Learning about the short-term and long-term benefits of regular physical activity should be part of the physical education curriculum, but the focus should be on the benefits that matter most to teens. Research has shown that knowing why one should be physically active is not a strong influence on participation in physical activity. Nevertheless, it may have some influence, and teaching children why activity and fitness are important is considered an appropriate practice (Middle and Secondary School Physical Education for Children [MASSPEC] 1995, 1998).

Figure 3.4 summarizes the benefits of regular physical activity. The benefits adolescents may be most interested in are in boldface type. Most teenagers care about how they look, so they may be interested in the fact that regular physical activity helps improve body composition in a healthy way by increasing muscle mass and reducing body fat. They may also be interested to know that exercise reduces anxiety, increases self-esteem, and improves strength and endurance.

As discussed earlier, obesity is a growing problem in America (no pun intended). The percentage of children and adolescents who are overweight has more than doubled in the past 30 years (U.S. Department of Health and Human Services 1997) (figure 3.5). By the early 1990s 11% (4.7 million) of children ages 6 through 17 were reported to be seriously overweight. Sadly, obese children are more likely to become obese adults, so it is crucial to help them avoid or tackle this problem in a healthy way at an early age. Recently the American Heart Association declared obesity a "major risk factor" for heart disease (it used to be a "contributing risk factor"), adding to the list that now includes a sedentary lifestyle, high cholesterol, high blood pressure, and smoking (see chapter 4 for more details about obesity).

Regular Physical Activity:

- reduces the risk of dying prematurely,
- reduces the risk of dying from heart disease;
- **increases self-esteem;**
- reduces the risk of developing diabetes;
- reduces the risk of developing high blood pressure;
- may improve blood pressure and cholesterol levels;
- **improves strength and endurance;**
- reduces the risk of developing colon cancer;
- **reduces feelings of depression and anxiety;**
- **helps control weight;**
- **helps build and maintain healthy bones muscles and joints;**
- helps older adults become stronger and able to move about without falling;
- **promotes psychological well-being;**
- **helps prevent and reduce obesity;** and
- **promotes a healthy body composition.**

Figure 3.4 Benefits of physical activity (U.S. Department of Health and Human Services 1996, 1997). The benefits adolescents may be most interested in are in boldface type.

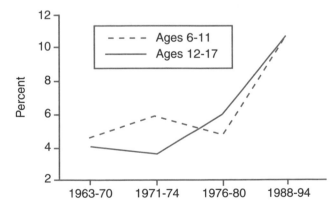

Percentage of Young People Who Are Overweight*

*Overweight defined by the age- and sex-specific 95th percentile of body mass index (1963-70 data). Source: Trojano RP, Flegal KM. *Pediatrics* 1998; 101 (3); 497-504.

Figure 3.5 Percentage of young people who are overweight.

Purpose

Have students become aware of media messages related to activity.

Resource and Procedure

Have students watch some of their favorite television shows and keep a log that shows how often teenagers were depicted engaging in physical activity during each show. To integrate math, have them calculate what percentage of the time the programs showed teenagers being physically active. You could also tape a few shows that illustrate this point and have them ready for an inclement-weather activity. Also ask them to compare male characters' physical activity to female characters' physical activity. At the end of this activity, ask why the television networks would want students to think that teenagers don't exercise.

Your Turn ▶▶▶

- Why do you think that so many people don't see the connection between physical education and the prevention of obesity and certain chronic diseases?
- What was the focus of your middle school physical education program?
- What was the focus of your high school physical education program?
- How do you think your experiences in physical education have influenced your activity level?

Sufficient, regular physical activity can help prevent or combat obesity in most people. Physical education teachers can at this point become important preventive health figures. Every physical education program deals directly with one of the solutions to obesity—physical activity. The programs that guide students in the process of becoming physically active for a lifetime help solve the problems of obesity in America. Unfortunately, however, many physical education programs still do more harm than good, as evidenced by the physical activity participation patterns of American youth.

How Active Are America's Youth?

If we are moving toward a focus on physical activity rather than physical fitness in physical education, we need to know how active children and youth currently are and how we can improve those levels. We know from the research that young children are active (U.S. Department of Health and Human Services 1996), but we also know that activity levels drop as children get older. The most dramatic drop in physical activity levels occurs around age 14, and the decline continues throughout adolescence (U.S. Department of Health and Human Services 1996). Figure 3.6 shows data from the Centers for Disease Control's National Youth Risk Behavior Survey in 1992. The percentage of teens and young adults involved in moderate and vigorous physical activity is shown by age and sex. In early adolescence children are active, but as they get older their participation in both vigorous and moderate activities drops to about half of what it was earlier. Notice that males are more active than females all through the teenage years and even into adulthood if you look at vigorous activities only. When it comes to participation in moderate activities, males level off around age 17 and females increase slightly around age 19. In this area women catch up with men by age 20.

Figure 3.7 shows similar results from the 1995 Youth Risk Behavior Survey but highlights the high school years, when the most dramatic drop in activity levels occurs for both boys and girls. The sad part is that this inactivity in the teenage years has a lasting effect on both sexes. By the time they reach young adulthood less than 50% of males and less than 40% of females are physically active on a regular basis. The numbers become a little worse as people settle into adulthood, with more than 60% of adults not achieving the recommended amount of physical activity for health and 25% of adults completely inactive (U.S. Department of Health and Human Services 1996).

Note that the largest drop in physical activity during adolescence occurs around the time when most students are no longer required to take physical education. Daily participation in physical education by high school students dropped throughout the 1990s (figure 3.8). Most high schools in the United States do not require more than two years of physical education, and daily physical education in the 7th through 10th grades is no longer a sure thing. If that isn't enough bad news, we should also look at how active students are in their physical education classes.

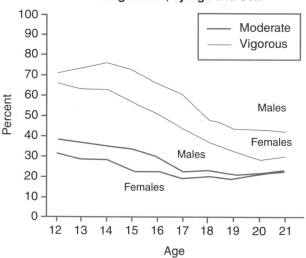

Physical Activity Levels of Adolescents and Young Adults, by Age and Sex

Source: CDC 1992 National Health Interview Survey/Youth Risk Behavior Survey

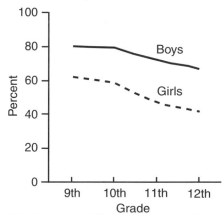

Regular Participation in Vigorous Physical Activity* by High School Students, 1995

*On 3 or more of the 7 days preceding the survey, at least 20 minutes of participation in activities that made the students breathe hard and sweat.

Figure 3.6 Physical activity levels of adolescents and young adults by age and sex.

Figure 3.7 Regular participation in vigorous physical activity by high school students.

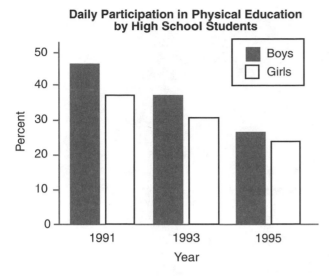

Daily Participation in Physical Education by High School Students

Source: CDC National Youth Risk Behavior Survey.

Figure 3.8 Daily participation in physical education by high school students.

How Active Are Students in Physical Education Classes?

The number of students reporting to be physically active for at least 20 minutes during an average physical education class is too low. With most classes in middle and high school lasting at least 50 minutes, it would be helpful if students enrolled in physical education would get the moderate to vigorous activity they need on the days that they have physical education. This is not an impossible task because the activity time does not have to be continuous and bouts of activity can be as short as 8 to 10 minutes. But in 1995 only 70% of students said they were physically active for at least 20 minutes (on the average) in physical education, a drop from 81% in 1991 (U.S. Department of Health and Human Services 1997). In chapter 7 you will learn teaching techniques that will help you increase learning time in physical education and decrease time wasted.

Although keeping students active in physical education class is a worthy goal and a by-product of good teaching (see chapters 7 and 8), it should not be the ultimate focus. Students can be active for most of the class period but fail to learn the skills and concepts they need to be active on their own. A good secondary physical education program will focus on what students need to learn to become active for the rest of their lives. A good teacher will be able to do this and still keep students active for a large portion of the class. If those are your goals, it is important that you understand what causes adolescents to become physically active.

Your Turn ▶▶▶
- Why do you think activity levels drop during the early teenage years?
- Why do you think girls are less active than boys?

What Makes Adolescents Physically Active?

Adolescents probably have slightly different reasons for being physically active than adults do, and researchers have tried for years to find exactly what those reasons are. Although over 300 studies have looked at what influences people to be physically active, we have no single clear answer to the question, "What makes people active?" Numerous factors are involved, and we usually refer to them as **determinants for physical activity.**

Although we don't know exactly what happens during the teenage years to reduce physical activity levels, forever for most people, we should be aware of some important indicators. When asked in a national survey why they like physical activity, adolescents answered that they like it "because it's fun; they do it with friends; and it helps them learn skills, stay in shape, and look better" (U.S. Department of Health and Human Services 1997, 1). These are important statements for physical educators to consider when they plan their curriculum and lessons (figure 3.9). Researchers have identified these and other factors as important influences on physical activity levels in adolescents (table 3.1).

In chapter 1 we introduced them to you as the GET ACTIVE FOR LIFE factors. We will now explain some of those factors in more detail, but here we have categorized them into four main groups: **biological factors, psychological factors, sociological factors,** and **environmental factors.** They no longer spell out GET ACTIVE FOR LIFE, so for easy memorization of these determinants for physical activity in youth, use table 1.4 in chapter 1.

Biological Factors

One of the major determining factors when it comes to teens and their physical activity level is gender. Boys are far more physically active than girls all through adolescence, as they are throughout the rest of their lives (Sallis 1993; Corbin 2002).

Figure 3.9 Young students enjoy physical activities such as dancing that are fun, social, and help them look better.

Researchers are not sure if they should categorize this as a biological factor, because after puberty boys increase muscle mass while girls increase fat mass, or attribute it to social and cultural factors, because adolescent boys receive more opportunities and encouragement to be active than do girls (Sallis et al. 1992). This issue can be argued, but many physical education professionals think it has more to do with social and cultural factors than it does with biology. They claim that historically women have not been encouraged to be physically active and the gap between activity levels of teenage boys and girls seems also to be affected by ethnic and cultural influences (Corbin 2002; Pate et al. 1995). Either way, teachers can help by encouraging girls to be active and including activities in the curriculum that appeal to a wide variety of interests for both genders.

The other factor in this category is age. People tend to become more inactive as they grow older. For this reason it is important to teach students skills and concepts in physical education that will help them stay active for the rest of their lives. We will discuss this in more detail later in this chapter.

Psychological Factors

One of the most important determinants for physical activity is **self-efficacy,** which is a psychological concept that deals with a person's confidence in his ability to do something, in this case use motor, problem-solving, social, and self-management skills in a sport or activity. Several studies have found self-efficacy to be a strong influence in adolescents' level of participation in physical activities (Corbin 2002; Sallis et al. 1992). This is good news for physical educators because they are the ones who, for the most part, rule in this area. The potential is there to reach all students during physical education, and teachers should make sure they develop programs in which students can improve their self-efficacy in a variety of activities (NASPE 1995).

The next factors require that you understand the difference between *knowing why* and *knowing how.* Adolescents' knowledge of the health benefits of physical activity (knowing why) may have a limited influence on their activity levels, but their knowledge of how to be active is an important factor (Pate et al. 1995; Sallis et al. 1992; U.S. Department

Table 3.1   Factors That Influence Activity Levels in Youth

Biological and developmental factors

Gender

Age

Psychological factors

Perceived barriers to physical activity, such as time

Perceived benefits of physical activity

Self-efficacy about physical activity (confidence in one's abilities)

Knowledge of how to be physically active

Attitude toward physical activity and PE, and subjective norms (perceptions of what others think about activity)

Enjoyment

Goal setting

Intrinsic motivation

Social and cultural factors

Socioeconomic status

Peer influences

Parental and sibling influences

Economic status

Cultural influences

Gender

Environmental factors

Weather

Unsafe neighborhoods, lack of bike trails and sidewalks

Lack of access to facilities, equipment, and recreational programs

Television viewing and videogame playing

Compiled from Pate et al. (1995), Sallis et al. (1992), and U.S. Department of Health and Human Services (1997).

of Health and Human Services 1997). Studies of health behaviors have found, for example, that although people know why they should be active, stop smoking, wear seat belts, and eat healthy foods, they don't. But research has also shown that adolescents who know how to be physically active are more likely to participate in physical activities (Sallis et al. 1992). Physical education teachers can play a major role in this area by teaching students how they can be active in their com-

munities and by making sure that they are competent and feel confident in a variety of activities that are available or possible where the students live.

Most of us perceive several barriers to physical activity. Time is probably the most common one. When it comes to finding time and overcoming other barriers to physical activity, teachers can help their students by teaching strategies for how to get around some of these barriers. Knowledge about how to be active should include information on how to overcome these barriers. Students should learn what activities are available in the area in and out of school, including facilities that are available for the students to use on their own. This should include information about problem-solving and self-management skills that can help students manage their time so that they have some left over for physical activity. Teachers should offer suggestions for all levels of skill, for a variety of interests, and for all time frames—for each season, on weekends, and before, during, and after school. Studies have shown that adolescents are more likely to be active when facilities are available, when the weather is good, and on weekends when they have more time (Sallis et al. 1992). Many students will not be aware of the opportunities available to them in their community, especially if they come from a family that is not physically active.

Finding time for physical activity can be a challenge for all of us, but you can get your students involved in the creative problem-solving process to find time in a busy schedule. For example, if students watch television at all during the day (very likely), they can figure out ways to perform physical activity such as jumping rope, doing crunches, running stairs, or doing squats or push-ups during this otherwise sedentary activity. Dancing while watching music videos is another way to sneak activity into a "busy" day. We will discuss other barriers to physical activity in the section on environmental factors.

As teenagers' physical activity levels drop, so do their positive attitudes toward physical activity (Sallis and McKenzie 1991; Godin and Shepard 1986). Why does this happen? If you watch children playing, you can't help but notice the joy they express when moving. Is there something we do to kids in school as they grow older to cause their positive attitudes and level of physical activity to fall off? Chances are the answer is yes (other chapters in this book cover in detail what we can do to maintain or improve positive attitudes toward physical activity and desire to stay active). But do adolescents' attitudes toward physical activity influence their activity levels? Researchers have found a moderate influence when we look at attitudes alone (Sallis et al. 1992). But attitudes could be more indicative of behaviors if we look at two other factors at the same time: perceived behavioral control and subjective norm (Fishbein and Ajzen 1975).

Perceived behavioral control is a person's feelings about her control over the behavior (for ex-

ample, "I will get my homework and chores done quickly, then I will go for a bike ride"). Subjective norm is a person's beliefs about what other people (who matter to that person) think about the behavior (for example, "All my friends think it's cool to in-line skate"). Subjective norm in the teenage years is mainly about what peers think. What parents and other family members think matters also, especially in early adolescence, but peers become more important as the teenager grows older. Together, attitudes, perceived behavioral control, and subjective norm have been shown to be good predictors of behavior (Fishbein and Ajzen 1975).

Enjoyment is another psychological factor that strongly influences people's activity levels (Pate et al. 1995). It seems logical that people would prioritize the things in their lives that they enjoy. If physical activity seems like a drag, chances are it will not become part of a person's schedule. Physical education teachers can do much in this area. The most important thing to remember is first that enjoyment and fun do not mean rolling out the ball and letting students do whatever they please. To enjoy a physical activity, one must have some competence and confidence. As a teacher you should understand the concept that enjoyment comes from confidence and competence, which in turn come from well-designed lessons (more in chapters 7, 8, and 11).

Another aspect of enjoyment is choice. The Diamond Conceptual Framework addresses choice in the pursuit of proficiency in activities at the high school level (see chapter 1). But many other ways of providing choices in physical education throughout secondary school are available. Teachers can offer choices in each lesson in different ways, such as allowing students to choose a specific task, equipment, location of skill practice, or level of difficulty. When you give students a choice, they recognize that their feelings matter and that when possible you will let them have a say in what is going on in your class (more in chapters 7, 8, and 11).

The perceived benefits of physical activity that matter to adolescents center around the issue of enjoyment. Teens like having fun, learning skills, and improving their appearance and fitness levels (U.S. Department of Health and Human Services 1997). The disease-preventing benefits do not seem to matter much to adolescents. This doesn't mean that you don't teach those benefits, just that you focus on the factors that matter more.

A related factor that also allows for student input is goal setting. When students learn self-regulatory skills in physical education, such as goal setting, self-monitoring of progress, and self-reinforcement, they are more likely to continue participating in physical activity once they have started (Pate et al. 1995). Teachers can help students learn the process of goal setting by emphasizing the acronym COST: goals should be Challenging, Obtainable, Specific, and a Timeline should be involved. They should also teach their students how to monitor their progress by simple self-assessment techniques such as keeping an exercise or activity journal. Students can write in their journals about their physical activities, how they felt after exercising, how they feel about their bodies, and so forth. Students can also learn strategies for self-reinforcement. For example, a student who loves to watch television or play video games can make a deal with himself that for every hour of participation in a physical activity, he can watch television or play video games for one hour. We discuss these issues further in chapters 7 and 8.

Purpose

Have students see the benefits of physical activity.

Resource and Procedure

Borrow or buy a few heart rate monitors and have students wear the monitors for an entire day. Have them keep track of the various activities they are engaged in: both purposeful exercise *and* day-to-day activities like walking home, sweeping the porch, and ironing clothes. Have them see which activities provide the best workout. It is also a good opportunity to pick a time in the past (for example, early 1900s) and brainstorm the amount of work that people needed to do without the aid of machines. Have students determine how many active moments were built into the day then versus now. This assignment could be coordinated with a history teacher.

Sociological Factors

Several factors that influence adolescents' participation in physical activity fit in the sociocultural category. One of these is socioeconomic status; another is level of education. These usually go hand-in-hand, as people with higher levels of education usually make more money. Researchers have found that people with more education are more physically active on their time off than are people with less education (Pate et al. 1995). For adolescents the parents' level of education and socioeconomic status would be the relevant factor. This area is difficult, if not impossible, for a physical educator to deal with directly, but teachers should be aware of which students may be most at risk for a sedentary life. Teachers can help by focusing on strategies to overcome real and perceived barriers (see earlier discussion).

We also see a difference in people's activity levels when we consider race and ethnicity. Research has shown, however, that the difference is mostly because of differences in socioeconomic status and level of education (Pate et al. 1995). Teachers can help by being aware of cultural factors that influence activity and by encouraging and teaching *all* students strategies for becoming more physically active.

Earlier we discussed the difference in physical activity levels for boys and girls. One could argue that this discrepancy is as much a sociocultural factor as it is a biological factor. Either way, you should be aware of how society influences activity levels of boys and girls in different cultures. Teachers should make an extra effort to motivate girls by catering to their interests. Expanding girls' perceived possibilities becomes an important task if we want girls to catch up with boys in this area (Corbin 2002).

When it comes to participation in physical activity, adolescents are influenced by their parents, siblings, and peers. This point relates to several we have discussed earlier. This is another area where teachers have to think outside of the box to be of help. The use of peer modeling, including celebrity peers, can help (figure 3.10). For example, show your students that popular teen singers and musicians must exercise to be able to perform during concerts. Teachers can also involve the students' families in the curriculum by organizing activity days and giving physical activity homework for the whole family.

Environmental Factors

Most environmental factors that influence people's activity levels are related to factors in the psychological and social categories. Lack of access to facilities and equipment, for example, is related to socioeconomic status. People living in poor

Figure 3.10 The influence of celebrities can help encourage youth to choose a healthy lifestyle.

neighborhoods usually do not have the same access to safe parks, sports clubs, and country clubs. Unsafe neighborhoods and lack of bike trails and sidewalks are real barriers to involvement in physical activity. Although teachers can do little to change this directly, they can help by working with community leaders to create safe alternatives for all their students, not just the athletically gifted. Every community needs programs that cater to all its children and focus on involvement in physical activity (U.S. Department of Health and Human Services 1997).

The last factor we will discuss relates to how students use their leisure time. Excessive television viewing and video game playing seem to influence adolescents' activity levels. The logic is plain. The more time you spend in front of the television set, the less time you have to be physically active. Several of the factors discussed earlier relate to this issue. The upshot is that teachers can help students find strategies to increase their physical activity in an enjoyable way that helps them achieve benefits that they think are important.

What's Most Important?

With so many factors to remember, it is probably wise to make a list of priorities. If the main goal of your physical education program is to help students become active for life, you should consider the factors that influence activity level and concentrate in the areas where you'll have the most influence. Physical educators can probably have the greatest influence on enjoyment and self-efficacy. You can do this everyday in your physical education classes by teaching students skills and concepts in an enjoyable way that makes them all feel successful (more on this in chapters 7 and 8). You may also help by teaching them how to be active, by helping them develop problem-solving and self-management skills related to physical activity, by being a positive role model, and by encouraging all students to be active, because they all influence each other. Keep the GET ACTIVE FOR LIFE list from chapter 1 handy in your room or office to remind yourself how important you are in this national effort to increase people's activity levels. In addition, make sure you educate others about how you are helping to solve a national health problem. Your charge has come from the U.S. Department of Health and Human Services (1997), as well as many other health-related organizations and researchers (see chapter 1). Let people know that you are part of the solution to the problem by teaching lessons that help students become active for the rest of their lives.

Your Turn ▶ ▶ ▶

- Do you think the fact that girls are less active than boys is due to biological or sociological reasons? Does it matter? Why or why not?

- Considering all the determinants of physical activity, which have been the main factors in your life so far?

How Active Is Active Enough?

You now know that enjoyment is a major point to consider if you want people to stay active. Most people do not enjoy activities that are extremely strenuous, and they drop out of exercise programs that involve vigorous activity sooner than they discontinue activities of moderate intensity (Pate et al. 1995). Research shows that regular participation in moderate physical activity is adequate for good health and that getting off the couch is well worth the effort (figure 3.11). Adolescents must learn this important message because many adults have the misconception that exercise must be painful to be useful. If people learn that the route to getting in shape need not involve pain but can instead include enjoyment, more adults and teens might be physically active.

The current CDC guidelines for physical activity suggests that adolescents should be active every day for 30 to 60 minutes. The intensity level recommended for health benefits is moderate, which translates to about 3 to 6 METs (metabolic equivalents) or 4 to 7 kcal/min (kilocalories per minute). The activity time can be divided into shorter bouts of as little as 8 to 10 minutes. Biking or walking to school, mowing the lawn, vacuuming the house, playing a quick pickup basketball game after school, walking the dog, cleaning the bathroom, and skateboarding to a friend's house all count. If the activity is more intense, 15 to 20 minutes per day may be sufficient for health benefits. Note, however, that higher intensity enhances health only to a point. If the intensity level

is too high, the risk of injuries and other health problems increases. As mentioned earlier, people are less likely to stick with intense exercise routines, so that's another reason that we should encourage moderate and somewhat vigorous activities, not the extremely intense kinds. Figure 3.12 shows examples of activities young people can be involved in to enjoy good health without having to join a team or work out until their muscles become sore, and figure 3.13 shows examples of moderate activities that can provide health benefits to people of all ages.

Lifetime Physical Activities

We mentioned in the beginning of the chapter that we believe that a physical education program in the secondary schools should focus on lifetime activities. So what are lifetime activities? This question creates lively discussion among physical education professionals. We believe that the category of lifetime activities can be broad as long as we keep some form of ranking in mind. For example, we can define a lifetime activity as any activity that a participant can modify so that participation is likely throughout most of his or her life. So which activities qualify? We could name

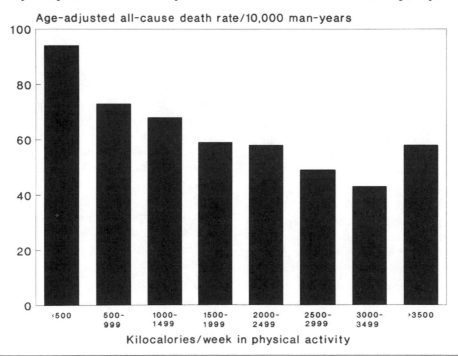

Figure 3.11 Age-adjusted, all-cause death rates per 10,000 man-years of follow-up are plotted across physical activity categories for 16,936 Harvard alumni followed for up to 16 years.

Reprinted, by permission, from R.S. Paffenbarger et al., 1986, "Physical activity, all-cause mortality, and longevity of college alumni," *New England Journal of Medicine* 315:605-613.

How much physical activity do young people need?

Everyone can benefit from a moderate amount of physical activity on most, if not all, days of the week. Young people should select activities they enjoy that fit into their daily lives. Examples of moderate activity include

- walking 2 miles in 30 minutes or running 1 1/2 miles in 15 minutes,
- bicycling 5 miles in 30 minutes or 4 miles in 15 minutes,
- dancing fast for 30 minutes or jumping rope for 15 minutes, and
- playing basketball for 15 to 20 minutes or volleyball for 45 minutes.

Increasing the frequency, time, or intensity of physical activity can bring even more health benefits, up to a point. Too much physical activity can lead to injuries and other health problems.

Figure 3.12 Examples of activities young people can participate in without having to join a team.

From *Guidelines for School and Community Programs to Promote Lifelong Physical Activity: At-A-Glance,* CDC, 1997.\No permission needed.\

scores of them. But if we focus on the word *likely,* we can probably identify some activities that are better possibilities for lifelong participation than others. For example, a busy parent will find it more difficult to get a group of people together to play football, basketball, softball, or baseball than to get one friend to play tennis or to go in-line skating alone or with the kids. The difficulty of assembling a group is one reason that most adults do not participate in team sports. According to a recent study, however, the most common sports in physical education in the United States are football, basketball, soccer, and baseball or softball (Simons-Morton, Eitel, and Small 1999). Wouldn't it be better to focus on helping students develop skills in activities that they are more likely to participate in throughout their lives? This proposal does not mean that you exclude team sports, but it would be more cost efficient to focus on individual and dual activities and include strategies for lifelong participation when you teach team sports. For example, students should learn about

available community leagues and how to modify team sports to play with a smaller group than normally required. They should also learn how to overcome perceived barriers to physical activity. For example, they should learn how to stay active when they have a job and a family. By learning how to modify sports and activities, they can teach their children and play with them.

Some physical education professionals argue that the activities should not only be lifelong but also health enhancing (Ross 1994). If we add this qualifier, we could again stir up some discussion. We choose to take a holistic approach to the term *health enhancing.* We believe that activities should promote at least one area of health-related physical fitness (cardiovascular endurance, muscular strength and endurance, flexibility, and body composition), but we also think that social, mental, and emotional well-being are important factors. Playing chess, however, despite its mental benefits, should not be a priority in physical education because it provides no health-related physical fitness benefit. Many activities may score low on the health-related fitness benefit scale but still be worthwhile to include. Golf, for example, is an activity that promotes health-related physical fitness to a larger or smaller degree depending on whether the participant walks or rides in a golf cart while playing. Using a golf cart would remove any cardiovascular benefits from the activity. But walking 18 holes on a regular basis (golfers tend to become hooked on the game and as they grow older they find more time to become regulars on the course) is recommended by many fitness experts as a way to stay in cardiovascular shape into retirement (U.S. Department of Health and Human Services 1996) (figure 3.14). Golfers who ride the cart may receive some health-related benefits, such as muscular endurance and flexibility from hitting the ball 90 or 100 times (for most of us) in a round.

So how do you decide which activities to include in your program to help promote physical activity into adulthood? Ask yourself these questions before you decide to spend considerable time on an activity:

- Are my students likely to continue this activity into adulthood? Is this an activity that participants can do alone or with one other person? If it is a team sport, can they modify the activity so that they can do it alone or with one other person? (Basketball, for example, can be a qualifying activity if you emphasize how it can be played 1-on-1 or 2-on-2.) Are recreational leagues available

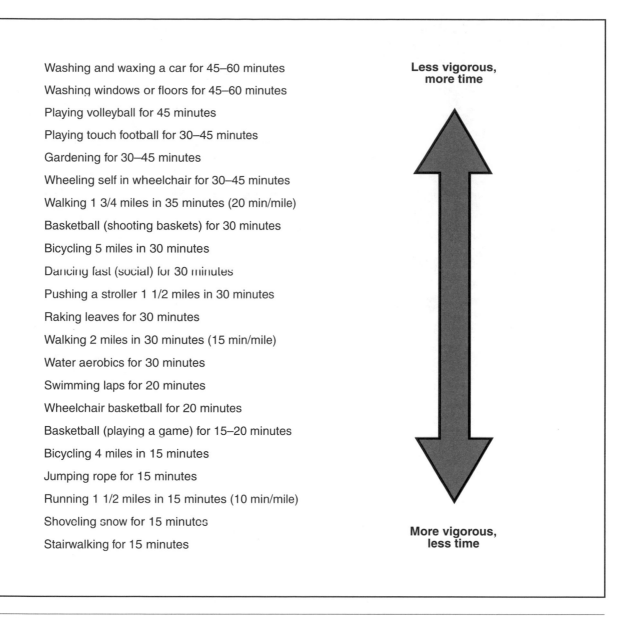

Washing and waxing a car for 45–60 minutes

Washing windows or floors for 45–60 minutes

Playing volleyball for 45 minutes

Playing touch football for 30–45 minutes

Gardening for 30–45 minutes

Wheeling self in wheelchair for 30–45 minutes

Walking 1 3/4 miles in 35 minutes (20 min/mile)

Basketball (shooting baskets) for 30 minutes

Bicycling 5 miles in 30 minutes

Dancing fast (social) for 30 minutes

Pushing a stroller 1 1/2 miles in 30 minutes

Raking leaves for 30 minutes

Walking 2 miles in 30 minutes (15 min/mile)

Water aerobics for 30 minutes

Swimming laps for 20 minutes

Wheelchair basketball for 20 minutes

Basketball (playing a game) for 15–20 minutes

Bicycling 4 miles in 15 minutes

Jumping rope for 15 minutes

Running 1 1/2 miles in 15 minutes (10 min/mile)

Shoveling snow for 15 minutes

Stairwalking for 15 minutes

Less vigorous, more time

More vigorous, less time

Figure 3.13 Examples of moderate activities that can provide health benefits.

in most communities for all ages in this team sport?

♦ Will this activity help my students develop at least one category of health-related fitness (cardiovascular, body composition, muscular strength and endurance, or flexibility)?

You should, in our opinion, be able to say yes to these two main questions before you devote serious time to an activity or sport in PE. The ultimate question is whether teaching the skills and concepts involved in an activity will help students become active for the rest of their lives.

Your Turn ▶▶▶

♦ How would you rate bowling according to the preceding questions?

♦ How would you rate football according to the preceding questions?

♦ How would you rate rock climbing according to the preceding questions?

♦ How would you rate table tennis according to the preceding questions?

Figure 3.14   Golf can provide a cardiovascular workout when golfers walk rather than ride carts during their round.

Discouraging Youth From Becoming Physically Active

Unfortunately, some physical educators use practices that discourage children and youth from becoming physically active, including public humiliation like the experiences that Laurence remembered in our opening scenario. Organizations and institutions such as the CDC, NASPE, Council on Physical Education for Children (COPEC), CASPER, PE Central, and others have stated that teacher-controlled practices such as using exercise as punishment, having captains publicly pick teams, using elimination games, and conducting physical fitness testing in which students are in the spotlight are counterproductive to the mission of helping students become physically active for the rest of their lives.

Although an abundance of research is not available in this area, what we have supports the concerns of these organizations. Children and youth do not feel good about their abilities in physical education when their shortcomings are constantly highlighted. If you think about it, that reaction makes sense. A person who is not as skilled or fit

as the rest of the students in a class will not have high self-efficacy for a skill or an activity if she is always chosen last for teams. Nor would a person who is always eliminated from an activity, such as knockout in basketball or a tag game, feel confident in his ability to do those activities. Can teachers avoid the negative effects that some physical education practices have on the least skilled and least fit students? Of course they can, but only if they stop using those practices. Now that you know how important confidence in one's abilities is in determining whether a young person will be active later on, you should understand the harm that these kinds of practices cause. After reading the rest of this book you will know *how* to avoid using them.

Appropriate Practices for Middle School Physical Education and *Appropriate Practices for High School Physical Education* are two NASPE documents that describe these and other inappropriate practices in physical education. For each inappropriate practice described, they offer suitable alternatives (see chapter 1). Another organization, CASPER, devotes a Web site (**www.helpcasper.org**) to educating people on the practices that help students become active, and those that should be avoided because they are counterproductive. Unfortunately, inappropriate teaching practices, such as those condemned by COPEC, NASPE, and CASPER, are still flourishing in many schools (Ladd 2000). If we know which practices are counterproductive to the goal of helping youth become physically active for the rest of their lives, we must all help stop those we can control. This means that even if everyone else at your school is using inappropriate practices, you should take a stand and use appropriate versions.

Summary

A major health concern in America is that too many people are leading a sedentary lifestyle. If we want to encourage people to become physically active for the rest of their lives, we must target students in the secondary schools. We see a sharp decline in physical activity levels among adolescents, and this inactivity seems to carry over into adulthood. We divide the many determinants for physical activity into four categories: biological, psychological, sociological, and environmental. We know that physical educators can do certain things in each category to help students become active for the rest of their lives. The most important of these may be to foster enjoyment and self-efficacy in health-enhancing lifetime activities, to teach students self-management and problem-solving skills, and to show students *how* to be physically active. Thirty minutes of moderate physical activity per day can provide substantial health benefits, although children and adolescents should be encouraged to be physically active for at least an hour per day. This activity can be intermittent, and bouts as short as 8 to 10 minutes seem to be beneficial. Teachers must help students find ways to work moderate physical activities into their schedules. They must avoid the use of inappropriate teaching practices that might discourage students from becoming physically active.

When Laurence's granddaughter, Elise, came to visit the following weekend, he asked her about her physical education classes. "I love PE," she said. "We're learning so many fun activities!" Elise was in eighth grade at one of the newer schools in town. "So far this year, I've learned how to swing dance, in-line skate, kayak, rock climb, and play lacrosse. I'm not very good at lacrosse, but I'm great at dancing, rock climbing, and in-line skating. We're doing kayaking again in three months, so I think I'll get better at that, too." Laurence felt relieved, but he was curious to find out if Elise's teachers used any of the humiliating practices he had experienced in PE. He asked her how they did fitness testing and found that the emphasis was on goal setting and self-improvement. Elise's teachers didn't post the scores and never had students perform the tests in the spotlight. "My teachers even give fun homework assignments," said Elise. "Last week we had to take our parents either to the ice-skating rink or to the park for a bike ride. Mom and Dad were a little annoyed at first, but then I explained how important it was that they help me become a physically active person, and they seemed to get it, and we went ice skating. It was a lot of fun!" Laurence laughed at the thought of his son on ice skates, but he told Elise how pleased he was to hear all this. He explained to her what he had been thinking about when he read the newspaper article the previous week. Elise wasn't shocked to hear about what her grandfather had gone through. Several of her friends who went to another middle school in town hated PE. She had more than once realized that she was lucky to have teachers who seemed to care about their students and had a purpose for physical education.

Checking for Understanding ▸▸▸

- What is NASPE's definition of a physically educated person?
- Why should physical activity, not physical fitness, be the focus of physical education programs?
- What are the current activity levels of American youth and adults?
- Can you list most of the determinants for physical activity in youth?
- How long should adolescents be active each day?
- What kinds of activities lead to health enhancement?
- What are the two main questions you should ask before you focus on an activity in your curriculum?
- What are five examples of lifetime health-enhancing activities?
- How do some teachers discourage participation and dampen enjoyment of physical activity?

For Reflection and Discussion ▸▸▸

♦ When you become a physical education teacher, what will you do to help your students become physically active for the rest of their lives?

♦ Why do you think many physical education teachers choose to focus on traditional sports such as football, basketball, volleyball, baseball, and softball?

♦ How will you make your physical activity choices for your curriculum?

♦ How will you deal with colleagues who may disagree with your philosophy of physical education, including your choices of activities?

♦ How would you explain your choice of physical activities (in your curriculum) to your students?

♦ Are you willing to commit to not using inappropriate practices in your physical education classes?

References

American Academy of Pediatrics Committees on Sports Medicine and School Health. 1987. Physical fitness and the schools. *Pediatrics* 80:449–450.

American College of Sports Medicine. 1988. Physical fitness in children and youth. *Medicine and Science in Sports and Exercise* 20:422–423.

Bouchard, C. 1993. Heredity and health-related fitness. President's Council on Physical Fitness and Sports. *Physical Activity and Research Digest* 1(4):1–8.

Centers for Disease Control and Prevention. 2002. Physical activity and good nutrition: Essential elements to prevent chronic diseases and obesity, At A Glance 2002. [Online.] Available: **www.cdc.gov/nccdphp/dnpa/dnpaaag.htm** [May 29, 2002].

Corbin, C. 2002. Physical activity for everyone: What every physical educator should know about promoting lifelong physical activity. *Journal of Teaching Physical Education* 21:128–144.

Corbin, C., and R. Pangrazi. 1992. Are American children physically fit? *Research Quarterly for Exercise and Sport* 63:96–106.

Fishbein, M., and I. Ajzen. 1975. *Belief, attitude, intention and behavior.* Reading, MA: Addison-Wesley.

Flegal, K., W. Dietz, S. Srinivasan, and G. Berenson. 1998. Overweight and obesity in the United States: Prevalence and trends. *International Journal of Obesity* 22:39–47.

Godin, G., and R. Shepard. 1986. Psychosocial factors influencing intentions to exercise of young students from grades 7–9. *Research Quarterly for Exercise and Sport* 57:41–52.

Ladd, A. 2000. Developmentally inappropriate practices used in K–12 physical education. Master's thesis, California State University, Chico.

MASSPEC. 1995. *Appropriate Practices for Middle School Physical Education.* National Association for Sport and Physical Education.

MASSPEC. 1998. *Appropriate Practices for High School Physical Education.* National Association for Sport and Physical Education.

Morrow, J., and P. Freedson. 1994. Relationship between habitual physical activity and aerobic fitness in adolescents. *Pediatric Exercise Science* 6:315–329.

NASPE. 1995. *Moving into the future: National standards for physical education.* St. Louis: Mosby.

Pangrazi, R. 1994. Teaching fitness in physical education. In *Health and fitness through physical education,* ed. R. Pate and R. Hohn, 75–80. Champaign, IL: Human Kinetics.

Pate, R., and R. Hohn. 1994. *Health and fitness through physical education.* Champaign, IL: Human Kinetics.

Pate, R., M. Dowda, and J. Ross. 1990. Associations between physical activity and physical fitness in American children. *American Journal of Diseases in Children* 144:1123–1129.

Pate, R.R., M. Pratt, S.N. Blair, W.L. Haskell, C.A. Macera, C. Bouchard, D. Buchner, W. Ettinger, G.W. Heath, A.C. King, et al. 1995. Physical activity and public health. A recommendation from the Centers for Disease Control and Prevention and the American College of Sports Medicine. *Journal of the American Medical Association* 272:402–407.

Ross, J.G. 1994. The status of fitness programming in our nation's schools. In *Health and fitness through physical education,* ed. R. Pate and R. Hohn, 21–30. Champaign, IL: Human Kinetics.

Sallis, J. 1993. Epidemiology of physical activity and fitness in children and adolescents. *Critical Review of Food Science and Nutrition* 33(4/5):403–408.

Sallis, J., and T. McKenzie. 1991. Physical education's role in public health. *Research Quarterly for Exercise and Sport* 62:124–137.

Sallis, J., B. Simons-Morton, E. Stone, C. Corbin, L. Epstein, N. Faucette, R. Iannotti, J. Killen, R. Klesges, C. Petray, T. Rowland, and W. Taylor. 1992. Determinants of physical activity and interventions in youth. *Medicine and Science in Sports and Exercise* 24(6):S248–S257.

Simons-Morton, B., B. Eitel, and M. Small. 1999. School physical education: Secondary analysis of the school health policies program study. *Journal of Health Education* 30:S21–S27.

U.S. Department of Health and Human Services, Public Health Service. 1991. *Healthy people 2000: National health promotion and disease prevention objectives.* DHHS pub. no. (PHS) 91-50213. Washington, DC: U.S. Government Printing Office.

U.S. Department of Health and Human Services. 1996. *Physical activity and health: A report of the surgeon general.* Atlanta: U.S. Department of Health and Human Services, Centers for Disease Control and Prevention, National Center for Chronic Disease Prevention and Health Promotion.

U.S. Department of Health and Human Services. 1997. *Guidelines for schools and community programs to promote lifelong physical activity: At-a-glance.* Centers for Disease Control and Prevention.

U.S. Department of Health and Human Services. 2000. *Healthy people 2010: National health promotion and disease objectives.* Washington, DC. U.S. Government Printing Office.

Suggested Readings

Blair, S.N., and M.D. Meredith. 1994. The exercise-health relationship: Does it apply to children and youth? In *Health and fitness through physical education,* ed. R. Pate and R. Hohn. Champaign, IL: Human Kinetics.

Sallis, J., and K. Patrick. 1994. Physical activity guidelines for adolescents: Consensus statement. *Pediatric Exercise Science* 6:302–314.

Part II

The *Adolescent*

Chapter 4

Adolescent Growth and Development

> If we don't change, we don't grow.
> If we don't grow, we aren't really living.
>
> — *Gail Sheehy*

Dominique had just finished putting her ninth grade physical education class into small groups to work on skills and task cards for badminton. She took a moment to observe students as they collected equipment and began skill practice. For some reason, students' shapes and sizes stood out for her today. She thought, *Wow, most of these 30 students are approximately 14 years old. They may be about the same age, but*

they look amazingly different. Some are tall, some short, some thin, some medium, and others large. Some of the girls physically look like young women of about 18, while other girls' bodies remain childlike. Same with the boys: Some boys look similar to what they looked like in seventh grade, whereas others seem to be sporting light beards, mustaches, and crackling voices. Dominique wondered whether these noticeable physical differences affected students' participation in her physical education classes. Although she worked hard to account for individual differences, she couldn't help but wonder about the effect of physical growth and development on students' motor, cognitive, and affective abilities.

Learning Objectives

After reading this chapter, you should be able to

- identify indicators of growth and development,
- define the terms *growth* and *maturation,*
- note national differences in height, weight, and body-mass statistics between adolescent boys and girls,
- discuss a greater awareness about puberty,
- express general concepts of adolescent cognitive development,
- describe general concepts of adolescent affective development,
- consider the impact of eating disorders on adolescent growth and development,
- explain the effect of select street drugs on adolescent growth and development,
- show an awareness about child abuse and its effects on adolescent growth and development, and
- identify resources that will help students collect accurate information about topics discussed in this chapter.

Key Terms and Phrases

Adolescence
Puberty
Growth
Maturation
Body composition
Body mass index
Somatotype
Endomorphy
Mesomorphy
Ectomorphy
Menarche
Anorexia nervosa
Bulimia
Binge eating
Licit drugs
Illicit drugs
Anabolic steroids
Child maltreatment

ake a moment to look around and do some people watching. When you take time to observe people you can't help but notice that everyone is different. People vary by size, shape, weight, body type, and physical features. They also express personality in different ways through such things as behavior, dress, and hairstyle. Engaging in people watching while sitting at a cafe, in traffic, or at the airport is similar in a way to observing students in our physical education classes. In physical education, students may be dressed similarly with shorts, T-shirts, sweats, and athletic shoes, but they still emerge as individuals, each of them unique.

On the surface, most of us understand that students differ from one another. With this realization, we know that we must plan lessons that account for individual differences and promote student success as much as possible. But how well do we understand the nature of individual differences? Perhaps Dominique was on to something important when she asked, "What effect does physical growth and development have on stu-

dents' motor, cognitive, and affective abilities?" In this chapter we will examine critical elements of human growth and maturation to help us understand the nature of human differences and determine strategies to get to know our students better. Understanding the growth and development process of students will help us as we work to tolerate, accept, appreciate, value, and respect student differences in our classes.

Understanding individual differences is necessary when teaching. Understanding adolescence is a challenge. Often described as moody, irritable, sarcastic, critical, unmotivated, lazy, rebellious, defiant, and as know-it-alls, adolescents go through a period of time that was difficult for most of us. Adolescence is clearly the bridge between childhood and adulthood. Erik Erikson (1963) described adolescence as the "conflict between identity acquisition and identity diffusion." Identity acquisition and identity diffusion are addressed when adolescents work to answer two questions: "Who am I?" and "What am I going to do?" (Erikson 1963 as reported by Holmes 1995) (figure 4.1).

Figure 4.1 Adolescents often look to popular magazines when trying to answer the difficult questions, "Who am I?" and "What am I going to do?"

Dominique ponders several issues: "Why are some boys and girls taller than their peers? Why do some students look more physically and sexually mature than others? It boggles my mind to see these differences; after all, most of my students are the same age." To address Dominique's comments and thoughtful questions, we must first define the terms *growth* and *maturation*.

We define **adolescence** as the second stage of life, ages 10 to 22, when young people experience significant biological, psychological, and social changes necessary to prepare for adulthood (Holmes 1995). We divide adolescence into two parts, early and late adolescence, with ages ranging from 10 to 14 and 15 to 22, respectively. The beginning of adolescence is marked by the onset of puberty.

"**Puberty** is the point in human development when sexual maturity begins" (Caissy 1994, 2). The beginning of puberty sets the process of sexual development in motion. Sex organs mature, ancillary sex traits appear, and individuals experience growth in height and weight. Hormones secrete unevenly throughout the body, causing behavior to become unpredictable and emotions to flare. Throughout adolescence, youths struggle with their identities. They relate less to their parents and family and more to their friends. They become greatly concerned with appearance. Adolescents want to act more like adults, yet they really are not quite sure how to do so (Caissy 1994). All these adolescent experiences, events, and behaviors are normal. Youth, especially during the early years of adolescence, are trying to make sense of and understand their feelings related to the growth they are experiencing. It is just as important that we, as physical educators, understand the challenges associated with adolescent growth and maturation.

According to Malina (1986) and Malina and Bouchard (1991), growth and maturation are critical biological activities that generally occur in the first 20 years of life. Growth and maturation are related, yet different, processes. **Growth** means to change in size, which is directly related to biological activities such as an increase in cell number (hyperplasia), an increase in cell size (hypertrophy), and an increase in intercellular materials (accretion) (Malina 1986, 4). **Maturation,** on the other hand, is biological progress toward a mature, or adult, state. Progress varies from one individual to another. In fact, growth and maturation vary among individuals. Each student has his or her own biological clock. Thus, each student grows and matures at an individual rate. As Malina (1986) so wisely pointed out, growth and maturation are not neatly tied to the days, months, and years of the calendar. Instead, they are directly tied to the genetic code and biological clock ticking inside each of us. Dominique found this to be true when she looked around her class of predominately 14-year-olds and found that they varied greatly.

Primary Indicators of Growth and Maturation During Adolescence

Previously, we mentioned that the age range for adolescence is 10 to 22. Note, however, that adolescence generally occurs between the ages of 10 to 19 for girls and young women and between the ages of 10 to 22 for boys and young men (Malina 1986; Pangrazi and Darst 1997). Adolescence is often described by many rapid changes occurring to the body, mind, and emotions. Let's begin with the examination of indicators that mark change in physical growth and maturation.

Growth

Height and weight are the most commonly used measures of growth. Many adolescents will experience a growth spurt of 2 1/2 to 3 years during which they will attain about 20% of their adult height. Girls may experience this growth spurt around their 10th or 11th birthdays, and boys' growth spurts may occur during the ages of 12 and 13 (Payne and Isaacs 1995). Girls are often slightly taller than boys during the early years of adolescence. We often see evidence of this during their time at middle school.

Height

By the time males and females have reached the ages of 18 and 16 respectively, they have grown to approximately 98% of their adult height. Final growth often occurs by the age of 18 for young women and by around age 20 or 21 for young men (Payne and Isaacs 1995). To determine whether individuals are growing at a rate similar to others in their age group, one can compare individual data to norm-referenced charts produced by the National Center for Health Statistics (NCHS) (Kuczrnarski, Ogden, Grummer-Strawn et al. 2000).

T'nT Find norm-referenced charts for adolescent growth on the World Wide Web at **www.cdc.gov/nchs/data/ad/ad314.pdf**.

Figures 4.2 and 4.3 are the NCHS percentile charts for the height (stature) of boys and girls (December 2000). Comparing student heights from your classes to these norm-referenced charts will give you an idea of common growth patterns and where your students fall within them. This assessment may also alert you to growth abnormalities, about which you should consult the school nurse for advice and assistance.

Dominique witnessed growth in height among her students every day. She remembers a student named Joshua, whom she met when he was a freshman. At 14, he was shorter than most of the girls in his physical education class. In his sophomore year, many of his buddies grew several inches, leaving Joshua behind in height. He was beginning to think that he would be shorter than most of his male friends and many of his female friends for the rest of his life. He was bummed. When Joshua returned from summer vacation to begin his junior year, Dominique had to take a second look. He had grown a lot. By the end of his junior year Joshua was taller than most of his friends, both male and female. Dominique thought to herself, *It just goes to show you that youths answer to their own biological clock.*

Weight

As their bodies change and they grow taller, adolescents also put on weight. According to Payne and Isaacs (1995) it is not uncommon for girls to gain about 35 pounds during their adolescent years while boys typically add 45 pounds. The growth velocity charts for variable body weight from the NCHS (figures 4.4 and 4.5) illustrate the change in body weight that occurs during adolescence.

Simple measures of weight do not determine how much of the body tissue is lean mass or fat. An individual may weigh more than a normative chart suggests yet be below the recommended percentage for body fat. This individual has more lean body mass than fat. Because of this limitation of the chart, we often hesitate to assume that individuals who weigh more than what the chart suggests for their height and weight are fat. That may not be true. Therefore, the concern is not about being overweight. It is about being overfat, which increases one's risk for a number of diseases, including heart disease and type 2 diabetes.

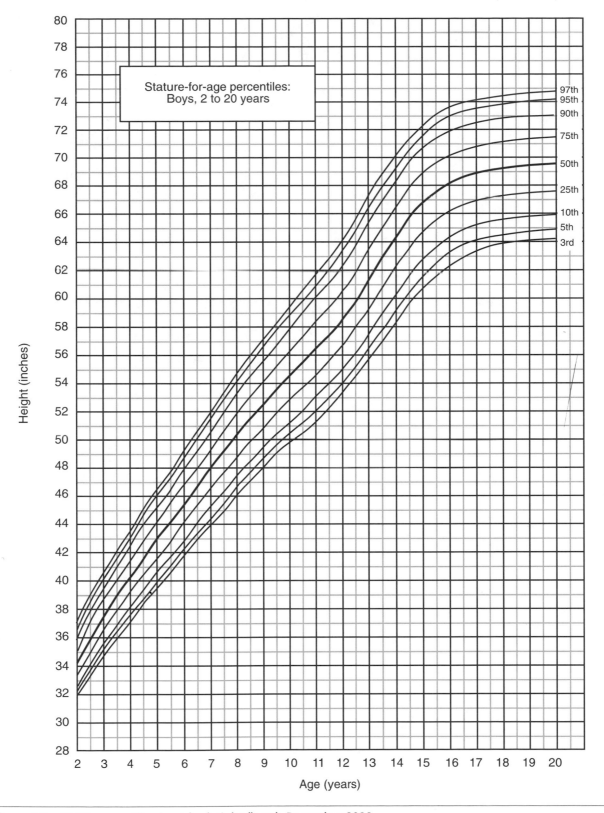

Figure 4.2 NCHS percentile chart for height (boys), December 2000.

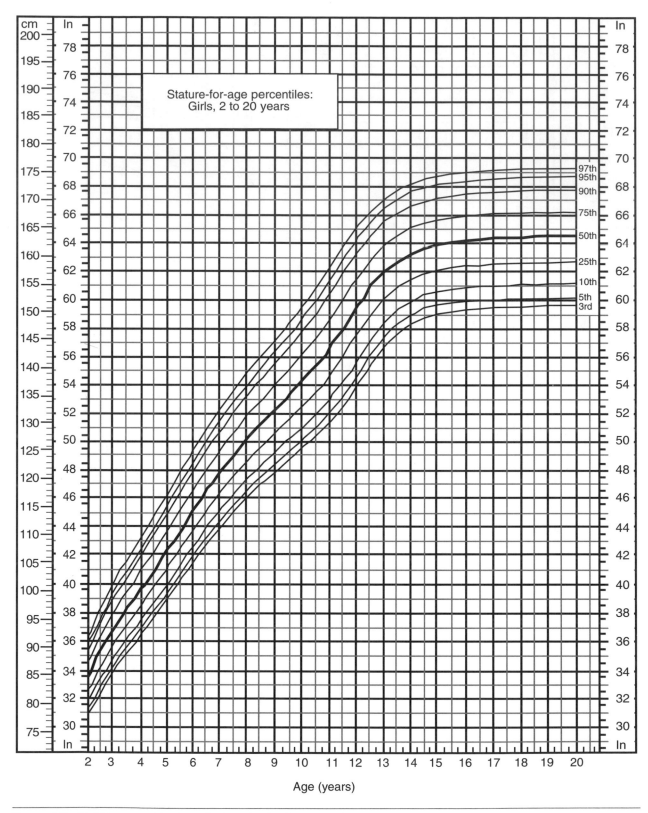

Figure 4.3 NCHS percentile chart for height (girls), December 2000.

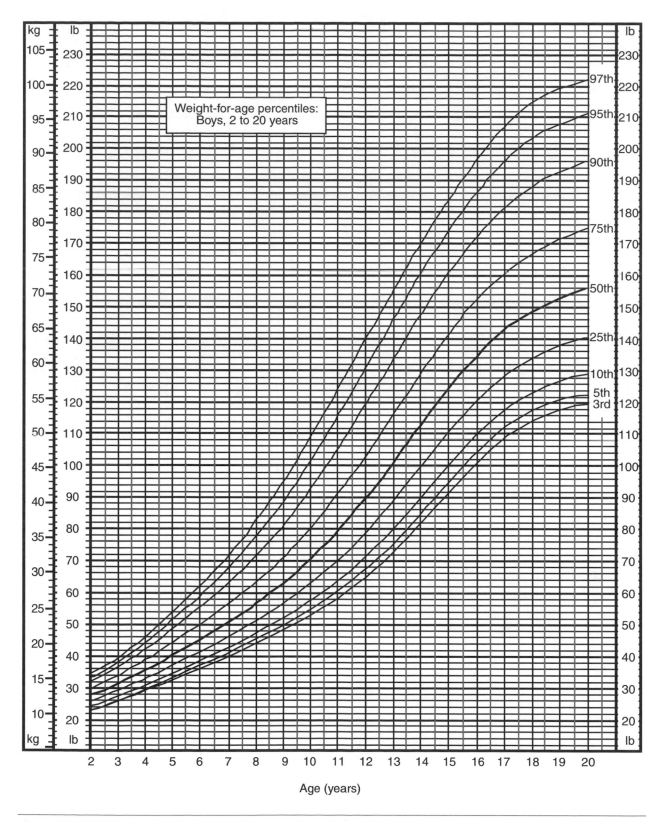

Figure 4.4 NCHS growth velocity chart for variable body weight (boys).

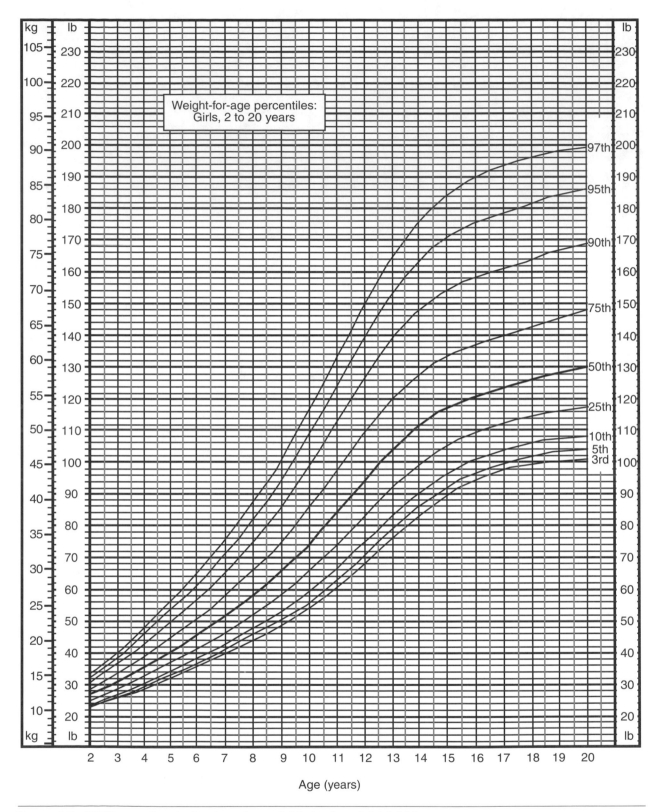

Figure 4.5 NCHS growth-velocity chart for variable body weight (girls).

Body Composition

The study of **body composition** enables us to examine closely the amount of fat-free mass and fat mass in an individual's body. Fat-free mass, or "lean body mass," includes all of the body's nonfat tissue such as bones, muscles, organs, and connective tissue (Wilmore and Costill 1994; American Alliance for Health, Physical Education, Recreation and Dance [AAHPERD] 1999). Fat mass pertains to all body fat. Several techniques exist to measure total body fat or fat-free mass (figure 4.6). Many of these techniques require special equipment, procedures, and training. Hydrostatic, or underwater weighing, technique is one of the most accurate measures of body composition. The measure of skinfold thickness using calipers is the technique most often used with fitness testing in schools. This technique involves measuring skinfold thickness at several sites on the body. Individuals trained in the use of skinfold calipers can provide reasonably accurate estimates of total body fat (Wilmore and Costill 1994). The reality is that many physical educators who use skinfold calipers do not have adequate training. They may have received training during a college course, from a workshop, or by reading the teacher's manual in a fitness testing kit. If you have this kind of training, exercise caution when using skinfold data. Errors can occur.

Body mass index (BMI), another method for determining body composition, is a mathematical formula used to compute body fat (AAHPERD 1999). Physical educators use the method to help students determine an approximate percentage of body fat. This simple tool must be used responsibly because it has limitations. Calculating BMI is easy: BMI = weight (kg) divided by height squared (m²). The sum is rounded to the nearest whole number. Charts are available to convert the BMI computation to pounds and inches (see table 4.1). Note that students with the same BMI can have different lean body mass and fitness levels.

Unfortunately, many body-composition techniques are designed for adults. With this in mind, some research literature reports that fatness is often overestimated by 4% when techniques for measuring body fatness in adults are used with children. Although measures of body composition yield important information, there are limitations (Malina 1986; Malina and Bouchard 1991; AAHPERD 1999). Some of those limitations relate to students' self-perception and self-concept. We will address these limitations later in this chapter. Because limitations exist in the measurement of body composition, we as teachers must use techniques for measuring body composition thoughtfully and carefully.

Body Type

While observing our students, we tend to notice that they come in different shapes. Body shape

Figure 4.6 There are many ways to measure body composition, including many that are much more reliable than this lobster's approach. As a teacher, be aware of the errors common to skinfold measurements.

Purpose

Use technology to provide fat analysis measurements that don't require uncomfortable and potentially embarrassing skinfold measurements.

Resource and Procedure

Body fat analyzers such as those made by Futrex™ use near-infrared light beams that allow the fat to absorb the light and the lean mass to reflect the light back. It allows a quick testing situation that does not require a person to disrobe. Students could track their fitness progression by measuring themselves without being in the spotlight. If you are interested in using such a technology, always try it out first before purchasing it. Make sure such machines are accurate. It's better to not have a test at all than to have one riddled with inconsistencies. Go online and see what companies have to offer in the way of "smart" measuring technologies.

Table 4.1 Body Mass Index Table

Height (inches)	NORMAL						OVERWEIGHT					OBESE										EXTREME OBESITY															
BMI	19	20	21	22	23	24	25	26	27	28	29	30	31	32	33	34	35	36	37	38	39	40	41	42	43	44	45	46	47	48	49	50	51	52	53	54
												Body Weight (pounds)																								
58	91	96	100	105	110	115	119	124	129	134	138	143	148	153	158	162	167	172	177	181	186	191	196	201	205	210	215	220	224	229	234	239	244	248	253	258
59	94	99	104	109	114	119	124	128	133	138	143	148	153	158	163	168	173	178	183	188	193	198	203	208	212	217	222	227	232	237	242	247	252	257	262	267
60	97	102	107	112	118	123	128	133	138	143	148	153	158	163	168	174	179	184	189	194	199	204	209	215	220	225	230	235	240	245	250	255	261	266	271	276
61	100	106	111	116	122	127	132	137	143	148	153	158	164	169	174	180	185	190	195	201	206	211	217	222	227	232	238	243	248	254	259	264	269	275	280	285
62	104	109	115	120	126	131	136	142	147	153	158	164	169	175	180	186	191	196	202	207	213	218	224	229	235	240	246	251	256	262	267	273	278	284	289	295
63	107	113	118	124	130	135	141	146	152	158	163	169	175	180	186	191	197	203	208	214	220	225	231	237	242	248	254	259	265	270	278	282	287	293	299	304
64	110	116	122	128	134	140	145	151	157	163	169	174	180	186	192	197	204	209	215	221	227	232	238	244	250	256	262	267	273	279	285	291	296	302	308	314
65	114	120	126	132	138	144	150	156	162	168	174	180	186	192	198	204	210	216	222	228	234	240	246	252	258	264	270	276	282	288	294	300	306	312	318	324
66	118	124	130	136	142	148	155	161	167	173	179	186	192	198	204	210	216	223	229	235	241	247	253	260	266	272	278	284	291	297	303	309	315	322	328	334
67	121	127	134	140	146	153	159	166	172	178	185	191	198	204	211	217	223	230	236	242	249	255	261	268	274	280	287	293	299	306	312	319	325	331	338	344
68	125	131	138	144	151	158	164	171	177	184	190	197	203	210	216	223	230	236	243	249	256	262	269	276	282	289	295	302	308	315	322	328	335	341	348	354
69	128	135	142	149	155	162	169	176	182	189	196	203	209	216	223	230	236	243	250	257	263	270	277	284	291	297	304	311	318	324	331	338	345	351	358	365
70	132	139	146	153	160	167	174	181	188	195	202	209	216	222	229	236	243	250	257	264	271	278	285	292	299	306	313	320	327	334	341	348	355	362	369	376
71	136	143	150	157	165	172	179	186	193	200	208	215	222	229	236	243	250	257	265	272	279	286	293	301	308	315	322	329	338	343	351	358	365	372	379	386
72	140	147	154	162	169	177	184	191	199	206	213	221	228	235	242	250	258	265	272	279	287	294	302	309	316	324	331	338	346	353	361	368	375	383	390	397
73	144	151	159	166	174	182	189	197	204	212	219	227	235	242	250	257	265	272	280	288	295	302	310	318	325	333	340	348	355	363	371	378	386	393	401	408
74	148	155	163	171	179	186	194	202	210	218	225	233	241	249	256	264	272	280	287	295	303	311	319	326	334	342	350	358	365	373	381	389	396	404	412	420
75	152	160	168	176	184	192	200	208	216	224	232	240	248	256	264	272	279	287	295	303	311	319	327	335	343	351	359	367	375	383	391	399	407	415	423	431
76	156	164	172	180	189	197	205	213	221	230	238	246	254	263	271	279	287	295	304	312	320	328	336	344	353	361	369	377	385	394	402	410	418	426	435	443

Source: Adapted from Clinical Guidelines on the Identification, Evaluation, and Treatment of Overweight and Obesity in Adults: The Evidence Report. Available: **www.nhlbi.nih.gov/ guidelines/obesity/bmi_tbl.pdf**

may be referred to as body physique. Three categories generally describe body physique, or **somatotype:** endomorphy, mesomorphy, and ectomorphy (Sheldon 1940; Heath and Carter 1967; Payne and Isaacs 1995; Pangrazi and Darst 1997). A student who falls into the **endomorphy** category often looks soft and round with an excessively protruding abdomen. We typically think of an endomorphic person as obese. **Mesomorphy** refers to those students who appear to be muscular, and students who fall within the category of **ectomorphy** are thought of as very thin, or skinny. Somatotype influences a student's ability to perform motor tasks. Students who are endomorphs will probably perform poorly on most aerobic and anaerobic motor tasks. Their weight places them at a disadvantage for many physical activities (Pangrazi and Darst 1997). Mesomorph students may display good strength. The illustrations presented in figure 4.7 will help you visualize each body type.

You will have students of all shapes and sizes in your classes (figure 4.8). When teaching students about body types and body composition, remember that this is a sensitive issue for most individuals. Adolescents who are particularly sensitive about their bodies and how people perceive them may feel embarrassment about examination of body composition. Present an attitude of acceptance for all body shapes and sizes (AAHPERD 1999). Expect your students to demonstrate ac-

ceptance of differences among students. Respect the privacy of students' results. Don't post body-composition results in the gymnasium. Remember that substantial error may occur when computing body composition. Use the information responsibly by helping students understand the meaning of the numbers and the health benefits associated with an acceptable range of body fat. Help students accept who they are and help them set goals for achieving improved fitness levels. You will learn about goal setting in chapter 7.

Awkwardness and Motor Skill Development

What effect does growth and maturation have on motor-skill development? Some research literature strongly suggests that some students experience a period of clumsiness and awkwardness when they are in a phase of rapid growth. Keeping this in mind, physical educators may observe some students who demonstrate efficient motor performance and then suddenly become uncoordinated for a time. When this occurs, teachers would do well to reassure students that the clumsy stage is temporary and related to physical changes associated with puberty and growth.

Because adolescents experience rapid growth spurts, many of them feel self-conscious about their bodies and general appearance (figure 4.9).

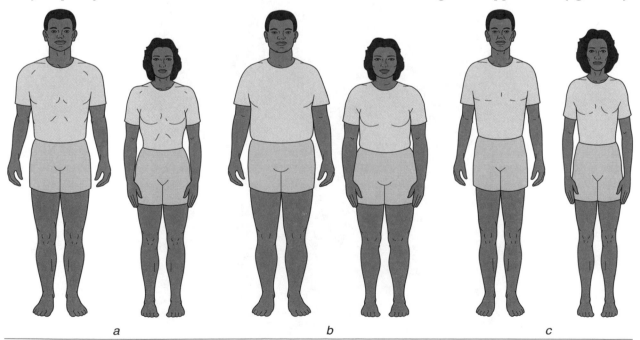

a   b   c

Figure 4.7 Knowing these three categories of body type can help teachers understand the physical differences among students in their classes. *(a)* Mesomorphs; *(b)* endomorphs; and *(c)* ectomorphs.

Reprinted, by permission, from National Strength Conditioning Association, 2000. The Biomechanics of Resistance Exercise. In *Essentials of Strength Training,* edited by T.R. Baechle and R.W. Earle (Champaign, IL: Human Kinetics), 173.

Figure 4.8 Your students will range greatly in size and body type, creating challenges for physical education teachers to make class time valuable for all students.

Figure 4.9 Adolescents are serious and inquisitive about trying to make sense of their place in the world.

Some students may wonder, "How tall will I be?" "Will I remain this height forever?" "How much weight will I continue to gain?" or "Is it OK to gain this much weight?" In looking around the school, you will see students who have recently undergone growth spurts. They may appear taller and heavier than their peers. Early in adolescence, girls will generally appear taller and heavier than boys. Later, boys will catch up and become taller and heavier than most girls. Rapid growth spurts in height and weight may affect adolescents' motor coordination, making some students clumsy and awkward.

> **D**ominique recalls this happening recently to Suzanne, captain of the volleyball team. Suzanne is athletic, meaning she is coordinated. Several months ago, Dominique remembers noticing that Suzanne appeared bigger all the way around. Not fat, just bigger. Suddenly her clothes seemed a little too short and tighter. In physical education class Dominique also noticed that Suzanne seemed clumsy. She would walk into things or seem to trip over lines on the gym floor. Dominique thought it was strange that a student so gifted would have periods of clumsiness. She assumed it was because Suzanne was just not paying attention to things around her. It was not until Dominique read more about adolescent development that she realized Suzanne's awkwardness was related to growth spurts.

The research literature has examined the issue of adolescent awkwardness. Payne and Isaacs (1995) point out several studies with findings supporting adolescent awkwardness. For instance, Tanner (1990, as reported by Payne and Isaacs 1995) reported that balancing abilities were disrupted for six months when adolescents entered a growth spurt phase. Beunen and Malina (1988) found that up to 33% of the males in their study exhibited a decline in motor performance during growth spurts. Clumsiness doesn't happen to everyone, but it does happen. The effect it has on motor performance appears to be temporary.

Maturation

Remember, maturation is one's progress toward adult stature. Height and weight are inadequate measures of maturation because individual results vary so much. A set of "predictable physiological parameters" (Payne and Isaacs 1995, 141)—skel-etal age, dental maturity, and sexual maturity—can describe individual maturation. As a physical educator, you may not have reason to use these physiological parameters with your students, but you should be aware of them.

Skeletal Age

Maturation is measured most often by comparing chronological age to skeletal age. Skeletal age is the result of predictable changes in bone structure during growth. When we are young our bones are made up of soft cartilaginous tissue. As the body matures, bones ossify and harden. The rate of ossification provides us with an accurate indication of maturation (Pangrazi and Darst 1997; Payne and Isaacs 1995; Wuest and Lombardo 1994). During the middle school years ossification is not complete. Usually, the body completes the ossification process at the end of high school.

Dental Maturity

Teeth are also an important predictor of physical maturity. Evidently, indicators of maturation occur with the study of deciduous (temporary) and permanent teeth (Payne and Isaacs 1995). Radiographs are used to determine dental maturity. Using radiographs provides a way to track human development over time.

Sexual Maturity

The onset of puberty (sexual development) occurs during adolescence, and for most youth it happens between the ages of 10 and 14. In some instances girls as young as 8 years old report menarche. Both girls and boys can be late bloomers by entering puberty after age 14. So again, it is important for us to be aware of individual differences among our students.

Puberty is at the mercy of the central nervous system and the endocrine gland, with the hypothalamus commanding the helm. At puberty the endocrine gland becomes more active and releases hormones into the child's system. Released hormones trigger growth spurts (as discussed earlier) and begin the process of sexual development. Obese children and tall children tend to enter puberty before short and thin children. Nutrition also plays a central part in the onset of puberty. Poor nutrition on the part of the pregnant mother or in the child's early years may delay the onset of puberty. Physical and emotional stress may also delay puberty (Caissy 1994). We describe sexual development in two stages.

Puberty in girls

According to Caissy (1994) girls will complete puberty over a three- to four-year period. Between the ages of 10 to 12 many girls begin to experience stage one of sexual development and growth. Breast buds and the widening of the pelvis are typically the first sign of sexual development, followed by the appearance of pubic hair. Next, breasts become larger and begin to grow rapidly. It is not uncommon for one breast to grow more rapidly than the other, giving the appearance of uneven size. Girls who express concern about this should be reassured that the uneven growth rate of breasts is temporary. Hair will also begin to grow in the underarm area. During stage one of sexual development, girls will also experience significant gains in height and weight (Caissy 1994; Feldman and Elliott 1990; Payne and Isaacs 1995).

Menarche, or the first menstrual period, marks the ending of stage one in sexual development and the beginning of stage two. Girls experience menarche at different ages. Girls getting their period at the ages of 8 and 9 are very early developers, those at 10 and 11 are early, those at 12 and 13 are average, and those at 14 to 15 are late developers. Any of these ages fall within the realm of normal developmental stages (Caissy 1994; Holmes 1995). During the first two years of menstruating, girls may experience irregular bleeding from slim to heavy and varied length in period from 4 to 7 days or longer. The menstruation cycle usually occurs every 25 to 31 days. When girls begin complaining of cramping or other discomfort associated with menstruating, one can assume that ovulation has begun. During menstruation girls continue to grow in height and increase weight, but the process slows. Stage two is also a time when the body becomes more rounded.

Many teachers often wonder why girls choose not to participate in physical education during their periods. Reasons for nonparticipation vary. For some girls, their culture may strongly demand that they remain inactive during the time of menstruation. Other girls may feel strong cramps and experience heavy blood flow. One or both of these may make them feel poorly. Some girls may believe the myth that girls should refrain from doing anything physical while menstruating. A few girls may simply use their period as an excuse to avoid physical education. Regardless of their reasons, girls should be encouraged to remain physically active during menstruation. Many anecdotal reports suggest that regular physical activity has a positive influence on menstruation. Many girls have reported feeling "less physical distress associated with the cycle and increased regularity when moderate physical activity is part of their lifestyle" (President's Council on Physical Fitness and Sports 1997).

Purpose

Provide female students with a resource for fitness activities during menstruation.

Resource and Procedure

Some female students use their menstrual periods as an excuse to miss class. You may want to find a source that you can print out and assign to a student who is looking for an excuse to avoid exercise. Provide her with an article of the results of a study or an advice column encouraging women to not interrupt their workout schedule because of menstruation. Try to find articles that include the things to consider when exercising during menstruation. Go online and connect to a database of periodicals. You can access electronic copies of fitness and young women's magazines that have articles about the topic. Once in the database of a particular magazine, enter "exercise" and "menstruation" and you may find an article or two that is just right for your students. Print out the most valuable articles and keep it as a class resource. The first time a student asks to be let out of class, allow her to do it but supply her with your reading materials. Ask her to write a short essay during class that is a reflection and reaction to the readings.

The term for menstrual cramps is *dysmenorrhea* (Brooks-Gunn, Gargiulo, and Warren 1986). Most women and girls experience menstrual cramps at some point in their lives. Note, however, that the majority (75% to 80%) of them rate their cramps as mild, not severe (Brooks-Gunn, Gargiulo, and Warren 1986). Some of your students will experience severe cramps, and you may want to dismiss them from participation. Most of your students will experience mild cramping. As mentioned earlier, anecdotal evidence shows that girls notice less cramping when they exercise, but scientific evidence on the matter remains ambiguous (Shangold and Mirkin 1994). If you aspire to earn a master's or doctoral degree, or conduct research as you teach, you may want to investigate this topic further and contribute to an inadequate database. In the meantime, treat your female students with respect and examine the issue of "I can't play because I have my period" on an individual basis.

Dominique has many stories about girls and their periods during physical education class. Girls in class often seem reluctant to participate because they don't think they should. They don't know that exercise may help them feel better. Dominique remembers a student who didn't want to participate because she was afraid she would soil her gym uniform and everyone would see it. Dominique believes teachers should work hard to educate girls and young women about the benefits of exercise during menstruation. But, she recalls, "You always will have a student who tests your patience." Taneeka was one of those students. It seems that Taneeka was having her period during every physical education class. After the second week of continuous flow, Dominique called Taneeka's mom. Taneeka, her mom, and Dominique met. Taneeka confessed that she was using her period to be excused from participating in physical education. She never again used her period to justify nonparticipation.

Puberty in boys

Boys tend to enter puberty two years after girls. Most often they begin sexual development around the ages of 12 to 14. On average, boys complete the process in four years. As with girls, boys experience growth in height and weight as they enter puberty. Stage one for boys includes the appearance of pubic hair along with enlargement of the genitals and broadening of the shoulders. With growth the body begins to look more muscular and defined. As boys enter stage two of development, they continue to experience growth in their reproductive organs along with growth of hair on the face, upper lip, legs, and abdomen. Ejaculation, or spermarche, marks the onset of puberty for boys. Little is known about the meaning spermarche has for males. Researchers speculate that the occurrence of ejaculation is as significant for boys as menarche is for girls (Feldman and Elliot 1990). Boys may experience a spontaneous erection or nocturnal ejaculations commonly known as "wet dreams." Boys who are uninformed about pubertal changes may experience confusion and or embarrassment from these events (Holmes 1995). As physical educators we need to be aware of these changes and understand individual differences. By 16 to 17 years of age, both males and females have generally completed sexual development (Caissy 1994).

Additional Indicators of Growth and Maturation

Growth and maturation include changes beyond those that occur in height, weight, body composition, dental maturity, and sexual maturity. Other systems in the body undergo change as well, including the endocrine, voice, circulatory, respiratory, central nervous, and digestive system. Cognitive and affective development also produce changes in adolescents.

Endocrine System

The increased activity of the endocrine gland produces increased levels of sebum, an oily substance, to the skin. Skin becomes oilier. Many adolescents, particularly early adolescents, experience acne. Hair also becomes oilier and may require more washing. Adolescents also tend to produce more sweat. With sweat comes increased body odor, particularly from underarms and feet (Caissy 1994).

Students may not be aware of their heightened body odor, particularly after physical exertion. Many physical educators will discuss body odor and the need for good personal hygiene with students, especially middle school students. Teachers should encourage students to clean up after physical education classes and give them time to shower. Many teachers reduce the time they allow for students to change before class so that they can add a few minutes for changing and showering after class. Because students are more concerned with appearance and what their peers think, they need extra time for grooming to enjoy the physical education experience. They should also listen closely to your advice on personal grooming. In chapter 7 we will explore how you can organize your time wisely in physical education classes so that you can spare a few more minutes for grooming after class while still having sufficient time for learning.

Voice changes also occur for boys and girls during adolescence. The pitch for both sexes becomes lower, and their voices sound more adultlike. The change is particularly noticeable in boys (Caissy 1994).

The circulatory, respiratory, central nervous, and digestive systems experience significant change as well. The heart grows in both size and weight. The lungs and their capacity grow. The central nervous system continues to grow and mature into late adolescence. The digestive system continues to grow and mature during this time as well (Wuest and Lombardo 1994).

Cognitive Development

Many adolescents believe they know it all. They may perceive themselves as infallible and indestructible. In other words, a period of egocentric behavior can mark adolescence. This know-it-all perception is a guise for cognitive development. Adolescents are able to think more abstractly than their younger cohorts. As a result they are able to solve abstract concepts like algebraic equations. Adolescents also begin to consider possibilities and move to a more idealistic perspective. Finally, adolescents display greater ability to solve problems and think logically. In doing so, they can identify problems and systematically test for solutions (Allen and Santrock 1993). We will explore cognitive development further in chapter 5, "How Adolescents Learn."

Affective Development

Affective development refers to the personal and social development of adolescents. We often stereotype adolescence as a time of moodiness, extreme behaviors, laziness, anger, and a know-it-all attitude. Well, stereotypes usually contain some element of truth. With hormones raging, many adolescents experience mood and emotional swings. An adolescent may be jubilant one hour and miserable the next (Caissy 1994). In fact, one may observe a student go from giggling to laughing to extreme pouting during the same class period. For many, adolescence may be a time of extreme mood swings.

Emotions

Anger is another emotion that younger adolescents commonly express. Feelings of frustration often trigger anger. Anxiety about social situations is another emotion we observe. Anxiety often occurs when students are concerned about their physical appearance. Middle school and high school students, both boys and girls, spend a lot of time dressing. They need to make sure their hair, clothes, footwear, and general physical appearance are acceptable or "cool" to their peers. Many adolescents worry greatly about what other people think about them (Caissy 1994; Holmes 1995). Adolescents may display these three emotions and others in extreme forms. In other words, students may say that they "absolutely love something" or they "hate it." They may even state that events leave them thrilled or devastated for a lifetime. Besides observing this kind of behavior in class or in the halls, reflect back to when you were an adolescent and recall some of the extreme mood swings that you may have experienced.

Your Turn ►►►

♦ Describe some of the mood swings that you remember you or your friends having as adolescents.

♦ Can you remember any "totally devastating" issue that was going to ruin your life but that later seemed almost unimportant?

Self-Concept

In physical education, we are working to provide students with quality movement experiences that will help maintain and enhance positive student self-concept and self-esteem. Self-concept refers to how an individual assesses her own abilities (also called self-efficacy), behavior, and personality (Mercier and Hutchinson 1998). Self-esteem, on the other hand, is how one describes herself based on how she believes others perceive her (Mercier and Hutchinson 1998; Gallahue 1996).

Researchers have identified six components that are essential in developing positive self-concept and self-esteem (Borba 1989; Hellison 1995; Gallahue 1996; and Mercier and Hutchinson 1998). These components are security, selfhood, belongingness, purpose, competence, and virtue.

Security

When students feel secure and safe in their environments, they will be more open to learning the lesson at hand. Teachers develop a sense of security among students when they establish clear class rules and consequences, when they maintain consistent and fair behavior around those class rules, and when they structure classes with positive routines and appropriate learning activities that maximize student learning time.

Selfhood

Selfhood is another word for individual uniqueness. Adolescents are interested in developing and discovering their individualism. Physical education is a wonderful place for students to learn about their physical, personal, and social abilities and limitations. Developing selfhood leads to a better understanding and acceptance of oneself.

Belongingness

Adolescents, like most of us, thrive when we feel a part of something. Belongingness means that individuals feel accepted by others (Mercier and Hutchinson 1998, 163). Feelings of appreciation and respect foster belongingness. At times, adolescents might find themselves engaged in an internal tug-of-war as they struggle to determine their selfhood while striving for belongingness.

Purpose

Purpose defines the reason for being alive. When students have a sense of purpose, they become empowered and are more able to set goals and achieve them. Purpose helps to foster a positive sense of self-worth.

Competence

Competence refers to one's ability to master skills. Again, physical education class is an ideal setting for students to engage in skill practice and develop competence in motor skills as well as self-management and problem-solving skills. Competence is directly related to one's self-confidence or self-efficacy (Gallahue 1996). As students increase their competency, they enhance their self-concepts and self-esteem. The Diamond Conceptual Framework for physical education, as described in chapter 1, puts confidence and competence at the forefront in the pursuit of lifelong participation in physical activity.

Virtue

Virtue is often overlooked or receives a wink and nod as if to say, "Yeah, sure." Virtue is the recognition that one is operating within the boundaries of an established moral code. We hope that students will learn and practice a moral code that is consistent across cultures. A moral code would include such behaviors as fairness, honesty, mutual respect, and ability to resolve conflicts peacefully.

Dominique recalls seeing the effect of these six components on the self-concept and self-esteem of a junior named Mark. Most people thought of Mark as a quiet, nerdy kid who kept to himself and didn't appear to have many friends. During class activities, Dominique noted that he would always put himself down before attempting practice or game play. He would say, "Oh, man, I won't be able to serve over the net" or, "I can't do that." When Mark made a mistake, he would also put himself down by saying, "Mark, you are so stupid. You can't do anything." Dominique wanted to find a way to improve Mark's self-concept and self-esteem. She decided the outdoor adventure unit would be an excellent place to try. In the outdoor adventure unit, Dominique created a safe environment where her students could try and succeed, or try and fail, or simply try. She worked hard to cultivate a class in which students trusted, encouraged, and supported each other. Only after a few weeks of group initiatives and problem-solving activities did members of the class really begin to trust each other. With the support of classmates, Mark finally felt like he belonged somewhere. He felt that classmates appreciated his efforts, particularly after the "treacherous traverse" activity during which he brainstormed an idea that safely delivered his team over an imaginary ravine. From that moment on, Mark seemed to take more risks in class, both socially and physically. He started hanging out with classmates outside class. He smiled more, and his classmates witnessed his witty humor as he became more outgoing. Dominique reflected on his growth: "Wow, in a safe and consistent environment (security) where Mark had support and encouragement (belongingness), he realized some of his abilities and limitations (selfhood). Classmates who took him seriously shared his successes and failures (purpose). As his sense of self-worth improved, Mark was willing to take more risks (competence), thus discovering more about himself and his abilities. Finally, Mark ventured out of his shell and took more risks socially and behaved toward others in a supportive and inclusive way (virtue)." Dominique then wondered how she could create a similar environment in all her classes.

Personal Identity

Searching for identity occupies most adolescents' time. Moving from childhood to adulthood means declaring independence from the adults significant in one's life. We have all experienced the process of rebelling from our parents and guardians to some degree. Now, as teachers, you will witness firsthand adolescents making the break from their parents and from you as a supervising adult. Because students will at times reject you and criticize you, it is best not to take it personally. Their judgmental behavior, although potentially hurtful, represents an important developmental step, and it will not last forever (Caissy 1994; Holmes 1995).

As adolescents strive to make sense of who they are and rebel from their parents or guardians and other adults, they also search for role models. You may find that some students really think you are cool and that your class, your office, and the team you coach are the places to be. Serving as a close mentor to students can be a rewarding experience. Many beginning physical educators feel it is cool to act as a friend to students. Our recommendation here is that beginning physical educators clearly define their professional boundaries. As a role model, you are better off remaining in the role of accessible, friendly teacher-coach and adult confidant than as a friend and perceived peer.

Speaking of peers, friendships with peers become increasingly important as adolescents advance through their developmental years. Peers become significantly more influential to individuals' behaviors. Students with strong, positive self-concept and self-esteem will choose positive and healthy peer relationships.

Other Considerations

We can use national norms to define and predict physiological growth and maturation. But as we know, physiology is only one piece of the complex human development puzzle. Our students face challenges in the environment each day. We work with students who are affected by their home life, peers, violence, abuse, and addiction. In this section, we will examine influences that affect the body, such as nutrition, eating disorders, drug abuse, and child abuse. In chapter 9 we will discuss peer influences and the nature of verbal and physical harassment.

Nutrition

According to the National Center for Chronic Disease Prevention and Health Promotion (2001) 14% of youth are overweight. This figure represents an increase of 3% since 1994. The percentage of overweight youth is expected to continue to rise. This is not surprising when we look at the U.S. obesity trends for adults (see figure 4.10). Currently, the National Health and Nutrition Examination Survey (NHANES) 1999 reported that approximately 61% of U.S. adults are overweight or obese. "Among U.S. adults aged 20 to 74 years, the prevalence of overweight people (defined as BMI 25.0–29.9) has increased to 35% of the population in 1999 (based on NHANES II and NHANES 1999 data). In the same population, obesity (defined as BMI greater than or equal to 30.0) has nearly doubled from approximately 15% in 1980 to an estimated 27% in 1999" (National Center for Chronic Disease Prevention and Health Promotion 2001). Because the number of overweight and obese moms and dads has increased greatly, we can only speculate that the trend will continue among our youth.

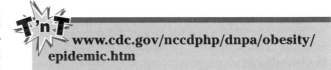

www.cdc.gov/nccdphp/dnpa/obesity/epidemic.htm

We are a people who like to eat fast food, which is typically high in fat and empty calories. We often see students snacking on candy and chips and then washing it down with soda or other high-sugar drinks. Today, many school lunch programs contract out their meals to fast-food restaurant chains. Some school programs provide students choices of healthy meals or trendy foods high in fat and calories.

You must also be aware that many physical education programs place soda and candy machines inside their locker rooms to help balance inadequate physical education and athletic budgets. Several physical educators have told us that name-brand soft-drink companies have approached them with appealing offers. For instance, one teacher reported that a cola company offered to place a football scoreboard in the school football stadium in return for showing their logo on it and placing their soda machines in the locker rooms.

The challenge of managing an inadequate budget for physical education and athletic programs creates an ethical dilemma for physical educators. Some physical educators are beginning to realize that having soda and candy machines in the locker room sends a contradictory health message to youth. As a result, they have begun to replace them with water and juice machines (figure 4.11). One day you may face a similar decision. How will you respond?

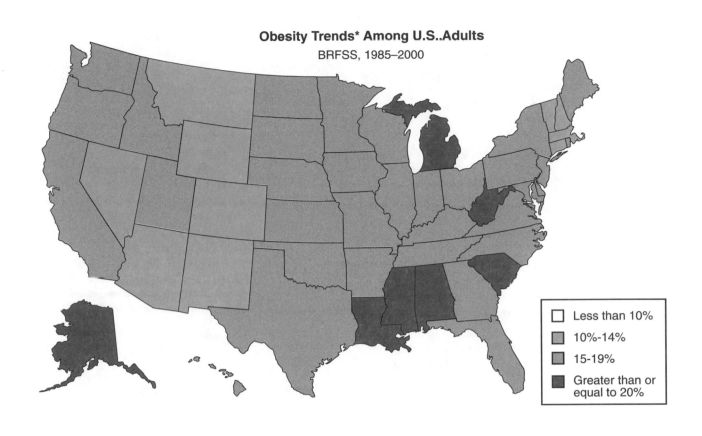

Obesity Trends* Among U.S..Adults

BRFSS, 1985–2000

	Less than 10%
	10%-14%
	15-19%
	Greater than or equal to 20%

Obesity Trends* Among U.S..Adults; BRFSS, 2000
(*BMI greater than or equal to 30, or about 30 lbs overweight for 5'4" person)

10%-14%	Arizona, Colorado, Connecticut, Massachusetts, Montana, Nevada, New Hampshire, New Mexico, Vermont, Wyoming
15-19%	Arkansas, California, Delaware, Florida, Georgia, Hawaii, Idaho, Illinois, Indiana, Iowa, Kansas, Kentucky, Maine, Maryland, Minnesota, Missouri, Nebraska, New Jersey, New York, North Carolina, North Dakota, Oklahoma, Ohio, Oregon, Pennsylvania, Rhode Island, South Dakota, Tennessee, Texas, Utah, Virginia, Washington, Wisconsin
Greater than or equal to 20%	Alabama, Alaska, Louisiana, Michigan, Mississippi, South Carolina, West Virginia

Source: Mokdad AH, et al. JAMA 1999;282:16.

Figure 4.10 U.S. obesity trends for adults, 2000.

Reprinted, by permission, from A.H. Mokdad, 2001, "U.S. obesity trends 1985-2000," *Journal of American Medical Association* 286:10.

Your Turn ▶ ▶ ▶

♦ A popular soft-drink company approaches you with a tempting offer. They will supply you with two soft-drink machines, one for the boys' locker room and one for the girls' locker room. Your department will keep a percentage of the profits for the physical education program. And, if you sell a certain number of soft drinks in the first month, the company will reward your department with a new scoreboard in the gymnasium. Your principal is strongly encouraging you to take the deal. Will you take it? Why or why not?

♦ What's going on in your local schools? Survey the local middle and high schools in your area to determine what kinds of lunch and snack programs they offer. What is the nutritional value of the foods offered to students? Ask students what their favorite on-campus lunch, snack, and drink are. After you have gathered the information, what sense can you make of it? Are the schools in your area supporting healthy nutrition, or are they serving fast food and fat food?

Figure 4.11 Setting up a juice machine at your school rather than a soda or candy machine avoids sending a contradictory message to students.

Foods high in fat and sugar make poor nutritional choices. Students often choose their favorite culinary delights and leave behind foods that would be better for them. Daily, we witness poor eating habits among youth. Because today decides tomorrow, we can assume that youth who have poor eating habits will mature into adults with poor eating habits. Heavy to obese children will mature into heavy and obese adults, raising the risk of heart disease and other chronic illnesses. We can encourage and educate our youth to eat better foods through the content we teach in physical education. Teachers must also be aware of problems other than foods high in fat and sugar. Some students encounter eating disorders that seriously affect their health.

Purpose

Use technology to make students think about the relationship of food choices and physical activity.

Resource and Procedure

Find an interactive online site that allows students to record the food they ate for the past day. The site will calculate the amount of calories consumed. You can then provide them with the recommended daily allowance for achieving their personal fitness goals. Try the Interactive Healthy Eating Index at **http://147.208.9.133/**

Eating Disorders

Eating disorders center on issues with weight and food. Both women and men, girls and boys, experience eating disorders. Typically, we tend to think that only women and girls are susceptible to eating disorders, and they are, in fact, more at risk. Eating disorders affect 5 to 10% of teenage girls and women (Eating Disorders Awareness and Prevention, Inc. 1999), or 5 to 10 million girls and women nationwide. Researchers are noting a downward trend in age, with girls as young as three years old suffering from eating disorders. Boys are not immune to the problem. Research studies have found that the percentage of boys suffering from eating disorders has increased as well. Approximately 1 million boys and men suffer from eating disorders (Eating Disorders Awareness and Prevention, Inc. 1999). We must deal seriously with eating disorders, which include anorexia nervosa, bulimia, and compulsive overeating. All are complex emotional problems that may have life-threatening consequences.

Anorexia nervosa is an eating disorder that involves "the pursuit of thinness through starvation" (Allen and Santrock 1993, 476). Sufferers of anorexia nervosa have distorted body images and an intense and irrational fear of becoming fat. They believe they are fat even when they are dangerously thin. They will do everything in their power to continue to lose weight by starvation and exercise. The disorder typically afflicts adolescent females, but adolescent males can have it too. Most adolescents with this disorder come from white, middle- to upper-class, well-educated families. Experts have suggested many factors as the cause of anorexia nervosa, but the cause is truly unknown at this time. Anorexic youth need immediate counseling and care. If anorexia nervosa remains untreated it can lead to death.

Bulimia, another eating disorder, is defined by individuals who engage in a binge-purge eating pattern. It is characterized by self-perpetuating and self-defeating cycles of binge eating and purging. Binging means eating a large volume of food in one sitting. For example, someone may eat a half gallon of ice cream, a large bag of potato chips or cookies, or an entire large box of cereal. The person may consume the food rapidly. As the person eats, she appears to be in a zone. Eating looks automatic and helpless. Bulimics may eat to a point of discomfort. Feeling physical discomfort numbs the person to other pressing feelings like anger, loneliness, and depression. After stuffing herself with food, the bulimic becomes concerned with weight gain and thus engages in acts of purging. Purging is an action to expel food after eating by vomiting, taking laxatives or diuretics, or engaging in long exercise bouts. This eating disorder is more common among adolescent girls than it is boys, but boys may be afflicted by the disorder.

Compulsive overeating, or **binge eating,** includes periods of continuous eating or gorging. Typically, a compulsive overeater will not purge. The binge eater will overeat occasionally or frequently. The purpose for overeating is similar to the motive behind bulimia in that it is a way to suppress or stuff emotions. Binge eaters may eat alone or socially.

As a teacher, you should keep an eye open for symptoms of eating disorders. Should you suspect that a student is suffering from an eating disorder, consult the school nurse or a qualified counselor before addressing the issue with a student. Keep the following warning signs in mind:

Dominique gets chills when she remembers the difficult time her lacrosse team captain had with anorexia nervosa. It was Dominique's third year of teaching and coaching, and Tiffany was an awesome athlete and student scholar. She played center on the girls' lacrosse team. Preseason began in February. Tiffany came out strong and fit for practice. She quickly earned the center varsity position. Practices came and went as the team readied for their first game. A month into practice, Dominique noted that Tiffany had lost a lot of weight. Dominique asked if she was OK. Tiffany said yes. Another week passed, and Tiffany looked as if she had lost even more weight. Concerned, Dominique sat down for a talk with Tiffany. Tiffany confided that she was anorexic and was having a difficult spring with her disorder. Tiffany also stated that her parents and two brothers were aware of her situation and that the whole family was pursuing counseling in hopes of helping her recover. Dominique followed up with the parents and asked how she could help. As the season progressed, Tiffany lost more weight. She would still practice with the team and attend games, but her physical condition deteriorated so much that she was unable to exert herself for long periods. By the end of the season, Tiffany couldn't run even one lap around the field because she was too thin and weak. Dominique found it difficult to deal with the situation, although she remained supportive of Tiffany and took advice from Tiffany, her parents, and the school nurse. Fortunately, Tiffany recovered in her senior year and finished school quite healthy. She stayed in touch with Dominique throughout her time in college, where she did well academically and continued to play lacrosse.

- Excessive weight gain
- Excessive weight loss
- Preoccupation with food
- Withdrawn behavior
- Preoccupation with weight or body image
- Development of abnormal eating habits such as severe dieting, secretive bingeing, ritualized mealtimes, or withdrawn behavior at mealtime
- Overuse of laxatives, diet pills, or diuretics
- Self-induced vomiting, which you may hear in the bathroom or notice as an extremely sweet smell on the student's breath
- Compulsive or excessive exercising

If you would like to learn more, Lemberg and Cohn (1999) offer more information about eating disorders.

T'nT The National Eating Disorders Association Web site at **www.nationaleatingdisorders.org** offers facts and curriculum ideas about eating disorders.

Drug Abuse

Drug use and abuse affect the growth and development of our youth. Many youth do not heed the warnings that drug use may permanently damage their bodies both physically and mentally. This unfortunate circumstance should not surprise us too much because adolescents often have a sense of immortality and feel that they will not sustain lasting consequences from drug use. What they often fail to realize is that they are extremely vulnerable to drug abuse. Their state of physical and psychological development makes them more highly susceptible to the consequences of drug use (Office of National Drug

T'nT Office of the National Drug Control Policy. **www.whitehousedrugpolicy.gov/publications/drugfact/pulsechk/fall2001/index.html**

Control Policy 2002). One episode of drug use may cause a lifetime of physical, emotional, or psychological problems.

Drug use and abuse among teens rose dramatically in the 1990s (figure 4.12). According to the *Monitoring the Future (MTF)* survey (National Clearinghouse for Alcohol and Drug Information [NCADI] 2001), drug use among 10th graders in the 1990s doubled from 11.6% to 23.2%. Use among 12th graders increased by 50% during this period, moving from 16.4% to 24.6%. More surprising was the drop in age of reported drug use, with the incidence of usage among 8th graders doubling from 5.7 to 14.6%. The *MTF* survey found that drug use among youth had leveled off overall from 1997 to 2000. Findings revealed, however, that the usage of some drugs had increased. As a physical educator, you will encounter drug use and abuse both during and after school. Be clear about the policy of your school district regarding drug use. Also, know what your responsibilities as a teacher are in reporting and helping students with drugs.

Figure 4.12 Drug use among teens rose in the 1990s. It remains an issue that physical educators need to familiarize themselves with.

Dominique has had several close encounters of the drug kind. First, was the incident with Dennis. Dominique was late for a boys' basketball game one winter night. As she walked to the gym across the parking lot, she noticed three students just beyond the security light in the shadows. She thought nothing of it until Dennis raised a can and yelled, "Hi, Ms. D." Dominique yelled "Hi" back, but caught the label of the can in the security light. It was a can of beer. She was aware of her responsibility as a teacher and knew that she had to report the students. Inside the gym, she found the athletic director. The athletic director grabbed a police officer and both followed Dominique to the parking lot, where they found the three students just finishing their cans of beer. The students were suspended from school and brought up on misdemeanor charges.

Drugs fall into two categories: **licit drugs,** which are legal, and **illicit drugs,** which are illegal. The licit and illicit drugs that youth obtain are commonly called street drugs. Many Web sites and other resources are available to help teachers educate themselves and their students about the effects of using these drugs.

Licit Drugs

Alcohol and tobacco are two licit drugs easily available to youth. The *Monitoring the Future* survey (NCADI 2001) reports a significant decline in cigarette use from 1997 to 2000. Levels peaked about 1996. Despite recent declines, the *MTF* survey found that 63% of 12th graders have tried cigarettes. About one-third of seniors surveyed are smokers. Of the 8th graders surveyed, 41% had tried cigarettes and 15% were smokers. These statistics are troublesome when we consider the deleterious effects of tobacco products (NCADI 2001).

It appears that smokeless tobacco use such as chew and snuff has declined in recent years too. Smokeless tobacco use remains concentrated with males (NCADI 2001).

Alcohol remains highly popular among teens. According to the *MTF* survey, 80% of students questioned had tried alcohol before the end of their senior year in high school. Approximately half of the students surveyed had tried alcohol by the time they entered the 8th grade. In addition, 62% of seniors and 25% of 8th graders reported having been drunk at least once in their lives.

Illicit Drugs

There are numerous illicit drugs. This section will briefly review several common among youth today. Drugs reviewed include marijuana, inhalants, methamphetamine, club drugs, and steroids. Discussions will focus around answers to three questions: What is the drug? What is the trend among adolescents? What are the health risks associated with the drug? We cannot examine in detail these selected illicit drugs or look at the many other street drugs that affect and threaten our youth. We therefore encourage readers to seek other sources, including those listed in this chapter, to deepen their understanding of drug use and abuse among adolescents. Keep in mind that all drug use and abuse affects the growth and development of adolescents who use them.

What is marijuana? Marijuana is a mixture of green or gray dried, shredded leaves of the cannabis sativa, a hemp plant (National Institute on Drug Abuse [NIDA] 2001b). The main active ingredient in marijuana is delta-9-tetrahydrocannabinol, or THC. THC binds to protein receptors on specific nerve cells. The result is a high that includes problems with memory and learning, distorted perception, difficulty with problem solving, loss of coordination, increased heart rate, anxiety, and panic attacks. Among the slang terms for marijuana are herb, boom, gangster, chronic, weed, pot, grass, reefer, ganja, Mary Jane, blunt, roach, and nail.

Marijuana has remained the most widely used drug among adolescents for the past 25 years (NCADI 2002). Users consume it orally, in food, or by smoking it. The most common use of marijuana in this country is smoking. Users roll it in paper (joint), place it in a pipe or bong, or place in a hollowed-out cigar called a blunt (figure 4.13).

What is the trend among adolescents? According to the *MTF* survey, marijuana use has been steady, but a small decline in use has occurred since 1996. It remains the most widely used drug by teens. In the year 2000 16% of 8th graders surveyed had used marijuana, 32% of 10th graders had used it, and 37% of 12th graders had used it. Marijuana is easily available to youth. Many teenagers may have friends who are users and know where to obtain the drug. The 2000 *MTF* results revealed that 47% of all 8th graders surveyed said that marijuana was highly accessible to them. As students graduate to higher grade levels, accessibility becomes greater. Seventy-eight percent of 10th graders and 89% of seniors surveyed stated that marijuana was easy to get.

Figure 4.13 Marijuana comes in many forms.

What are the health risks associated with marijuana? THC, the active ingredient of marijuana, suppresses nerve fibers in the information-processing system of the hippocampus. Therefore, marijuana affects learning, memory, the integration of sensory experiences, and motivation. Recently, it has been determined that learned behaviors that are facilitated through the hippocampus also deteriorate. Long-term use of marijuana creates changes to the brain similar to the changes caused by long-term use of other drugs. "Tips for Teens: The Truth About Marijuana," a fact sheet published by the National Clearinghouse for Alcohol and Drug Information (NCADI 2002), warns teenagers about the harmful effects of marijuana. A marijuana user will experience effects in many areas:

- ◆ Brain. Marijuana damages nerve cells responsible for learning, memory, sensory integration, emotions, motivation, and learned behaviors.
- ◆ Self-control. Marijuana affects sense of time and motor control.
- ◆ Lungs. One joint contains four times as much cancer-causing tar as a filtered cigarette (NCADI 2002). A person who smokes marijuana regularly will have the same respiratory problems as a tobacco smoker.
- ◆ Immune system. The user will be less able to fight colds and infections.
- ◆ Heart. The heart rate of a marijuana user has been shown to increase by 29 beats while sitting quietly (NIDA 2001b). Using marijuana and engaging in vigorous physical activity may overload the cardiovascular system.
- ◆ Social behavior. According to the National Institute on Drug Abuse (NIDA 2001b), longitudinal studies conducted on marijuana use among young people in high school and middle school indicate that they have lower achievement scores than nonusers, more deviant behavior and aggression, greater rebelliousness, poorer parental relations, and more associations with friends using drugs.

T'nT NIDA (2001b) *Infofax: Marijuana*: **http://165.112.78.61/Infofax/ marijuana.html**.

Many people believe that marijuana use is not addictive. Addiction is a compulsive, obsessive craving for the drug. Many users fall into this category because they crave and relentlessly seek marijuana. According to NIDA (2001b) approximately 120,000 people enter treatment for addiction to marijuana each year (figure 4.14).

What are the symptoms of marijuana use?

1. Change in school grades (lower)
2. Change in behavior—more aggressive, rebellious, withdrawn
3. Acting silly for no apparent reason
4. Uninterested in friends, family, school, regular activities
5. Difficulty remembering things
6. Difficulty learning or problem solving
7. Red bloodshot eyes
8. Limited or no expression
9. Dizziness
10. Trouble with walking or other motor coordination

Figure 4.14 Symptoms of marijuana use. If a student has one or more of these symptoms, he or she may be using marijuana.

National Institute on Drug Abuse (2001b).

One of Dominique's colleagues turned in a stoned student just the other day. Evidently, Charlie, an English teacher, was standing outside his classroom while students passed to first period. Charlie's classroom is across the hall from the boys' restroom. Just before the bell rang, Charlie got whiff of a smell that he immediately recognized as marijuana. The odor was seeping out from the boys' restroom door. After the bell rang and students cleared the hallway, Charlie decided to wait in the hallway for a few more minutes. When no one exited the boys' restroom, Charlie entered. In the back stall, Charlie found a student named Tim toting on a blunt. Apparently, the junior had arrived at school stoned. As the student followed Charlie to the office, he was giggling and staggering. The boy was suspended and charged with public intoxication and possession.

What are inhalants? Inhalants are any gases or fumes, typically from household or commercial products, that people intentionally abuse through sniffing or "huffing." The intent behind abusing these products is to achieve a mind-altering, or psychoactive, effect. Inhaled gases and fumes are highly toxic to the body and may cause irreversible physical and psychological harm. Because so many household and commercial products may be inhaled, it is difficult to list or categorize them. One classification system described by NIDA (2000) lists four general categories for inhalants:

1. Volatile solvents are liquids that vaporize at room temperature. The following are examples: glues (airplane, rubber cement, household), felt-tip markers, white-out or correction fluid, nail polish remover, gasoline, household degreasers, paint thinners, paint removers, furniture stains, and dry-cleaning fluids.

2. Aerosols are pressurized spray cans that contain propellants and solvents. You will find a number of these around the house such as hair spray, deodorant sprays, vegetable oil sprays, oven cleaner, furniture polish, air fresheners, spray starch, and other fabric protectors.

3. Gases are used in household and commercial products. Gases also include medical anesthetics. Some of the medical anesthetic gases used as inhalants include nitrous oxide (laughing gas), ether, chloroform, and halothane. Nitrous oxide, the substance most commonly abused, is easily accessible in products such as whipped cream sprays and automobile products that boost octane levels or clean carburetors.

4. Nitrates, according to NIDA (2000), are a separate class of inhalants that are primarily used to relax muscles and dilate blood vessels. Thus, they are often used as a sexual enhancer. Examples include cyclohexyl nitrite (room odorizers), amyl nitrite, and butyl nitrite. Amyl nitrite is used in medicine to assist some patients with heart pain. Butyl nitrite is an illegal substance. Street names for amyl nitrite and butyl nitrite include poppers and snappers.

Street slang for inhalants include air blast, bagging, bang, bolt, buzz bomb, climax, discorama, glading, gluey, hardware, head cleaner, high ball, hippie crack, kick, locker room, medusa moon gas, Oz, pearls, poor man's pot, quicksilver, rush, rush snappers, Satan's secret, shoot the breeze, snappers, snotballs, thrust, toilet water, toncho, whippets, and whiteout (ONDCP 2002b).

What is the trend among adolescents? Inhalants seem to be used more by younger students, with boys using them more than girls (NIDA 2000).

According to the American drug and alcohol survey, inhalant use peaks with the 8th grade and then begins to decline. For the year 2001 *MTF* reported the number of 8th, 10th, and 12th graders who used inhalants in the previous 12 months as 9.4%, 7.3%, and 5.9%, respectively.

What are the health risks associated with inhalants? Most inhalants affect the central nervous system, damaging nerve fibers. Extensive damage to these nerve fibers may cause chronic symptoms similar to those caused by neurological diseases such as multiple sclerosis. Prolonged abuse of inhalants will damage parts of the brain responsible for cognition, movement, vision, and hearing.

Use of inhalants can induce irregular and rapid heart rates and rhythms. The primary cause of this condition is lack of oxygen in the brain, which in turn causes the heart rate to increase in an attempt to pump more oxygen. Death may result from a single session of sniffing or huffing. This syndrome is known as sudden sniffing death. Death may also occur by asphyxiation from repeated inhalations, by suffocation when the user places a plastic bag over the head to inhale toxins, by choking on vomit after inhalant use, and through fatal injuries that occur while intoxicated.

Be aware that experimentation with and use of inhalants are prevalent. See figure 4.15 for a list of symptoms of inhalant use. Although use declined slightly from 1996 to 2000, the number of adolescents who have tried inhalants remains high.

What are the symptoms of inhalant use?

1. Slurred speech
2. Lack of motor coordination
3. A drunk appearance
4. No affect or emotion, dull look
5. Behavior that is not with it
6. Nausea or loss of appetite
7. Chemical odors on breath, body, or clothing
8. Stains on face, hands, or clothing

Figure 4.15 Symptoms of inhalant use. If you notice one or more of these symptoms in a student, you should suspect inhalant use.

Data from National Institute on Drug Abuse (2000).

What is methamphetamine? Methamphetamine (meth), called speed in the 1970s, is a highly addictive stimulant that affects the central nervous system. It can be snorted, injected, smoked, or taken orally. The use of meth fell off in the 1970s, but picked up again in the 1980s with the development of crystal meth, or "ice." A user could obtain the crystallized form of meth in chunks, heat it, and inhale the fumes. Methamphetamine is made in makeshift laboratories around the country. Anhydrous ammonia, a highly volatile chemical used as an agricultural fertilizer, is one of the materials to make methamphetamine. Other materials for making the drug are easily bought or acquired (figure 4.16). The production of methamphetamine is called cooking. Cooking is an extremely dangerous activity for the cook, workers, surrounding community, and law enforcement officers who find the lab. Easy access to methamphetamine coupled with its highly addictive qualities has created an increase in its use across the nation (ONDCP 2002). Street names for meth include biker's coffee, chalk, chicken feed, crank, crystal, crystal meth, glass, go-fast, ice, meth, methlies quick, poor man's cocaine, shabu, speed, stove top, trash, and yellow bam.

What is the trend among adolescents? In certain regions of the country concern is growing that methamphetamine use is on the rise. In northern California, for instance, the National Drug Intelligence Center (2001) (**www.usdoj.gov/ndic/pubs/653/meth.htm**) states that methamphetamine use and trafficking is the most significant drug threat. According to the Office of National Drug Control Policy (2002) (**www.whitehousedrugpolicy.gov**), 7.9% of high school seniors had tried methamphetamine at least once in their lifetime. Use among 8th and 10th graders was 4.2% and 6.9% respectively. Approximately one-quarter of seniors surveyed responded that methamphetamine was easy to obtain.

What are the health risks associated with methamphetamine? Chronic methamphetamine use can lead to anxiety, panic attacks, confusion, insomnia, and violent behavior. People who are addicted to this drug suffer withdrawal and experience depression, anxiety, fatigue, paranoia, and aggression. Users also may suffer extreme cravings for methamphetamine. Users may demonstrate psychotic behaviors such as hallucinations, mood disturbances, delusions, and paranoia, "possibly resulting in homicidal or suicidal thoughts" (NIDA 2001c). Damage to the brain after methamphetamine use is detectable fairly soon after drug use.

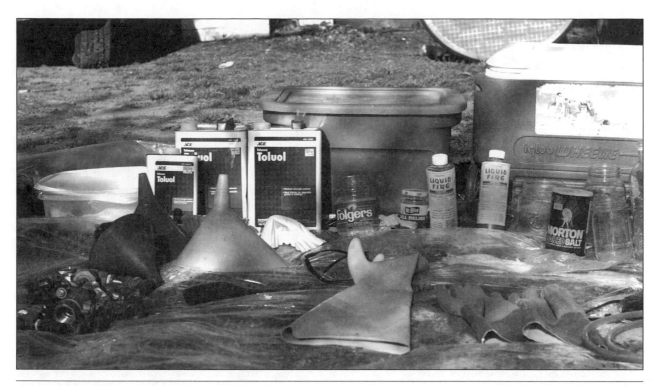

Figure 4.16 Methamphetamine is a popular drug among teens today. The materials needed to acquire and produce the drug are easily found.

What are club drugs? Club drugs are a category of drugs that are popular among youth at dance clubs and all-night dances called raves. The most publicized club drugs are MDMA (methylenedioxymethamphetamine), or ecstasy, rohypnol (flunitrazepam), GHB (gamma-hydroxybutyrate), and ketamine (ketamine hydrochloride).

Ecstasy is a stimulant that produces psychedelic effects. The drug is popular at parties because it enables users to remain physically active for longer periods. Rohypnol and GHB are depressants. Recently, these drugs have received media attention because people use them to sedate and intoxicate unsuspecting victims and then sexually assault them. They have been labeled "date rape" drugs because they render the victim helpless and impair memory of events that take place while the victim is under the influence of the drugs. Both drugs are colorless and odorless.

Ketamine, a tranquilizer used in veterinary medicine, is similar to PCP and LSD in that it produces hallucinatory effects. Although hallucinations may last only about an hour, a user may suffer impaired judgment, coordination, and senses for 24 hours. The drug comes in both liquid and powder form. Users may inject the liquid form or mix it into drinks. They can mix the powder ketamine into drinks, smoke it, or snort it. Table 4.2 provides a list of street terms commonly used to refer to different drugs.

What is the trend among adolescents? According to the *MTF* survey, 8.2%, 5.4%, and 3.1% of 12th, 10th, and 8th graders respectively used ecstasy in the past 12 months. The largest number of users are young people between the ages of 18 and 25. The number peaked at 1.4 million in the year 2000.

The *MTF* survey revealed that in 2000, 1.0%, 1.3%, and 1.5% of 8th, 10th, and 12th graders respectively had used rohypnol over the previous 12 months. The survey found similar percentages for the use of GHB, with usage rates of 1.2%, 1.1%, and 1.9% for 8th, 10th, and 12th graders respectively. Rates for the use of ketamine over the past year in the 8th, 10th, and 12th grade were reported as 1.6%, 2.1%, and 2.5% respectively.

What are the health risks of using club drugs? As a stimulant, ecstasy can cause lasting psychological and physical damage. Physically, a user may experience rapid heart rate, an increase in blood pressure, nausea, and faintness. The drug may also cause muscle tissue to break down and cause kidney and cardiovascular systems to fail. Psychologically, a user may become confused,

Table 4.2 Street Terms for Club Drugs

GHB	MDMA	Rohypnol	Ketamine
Soap	XTC	R-2	Jet
Scoop	Go	Mexican valium	Super acid
Max	Disco biscuit	Rophies	Special K
Liquid ecstasy	Crystal	Rope	Honey oil
Grievous bodily harm	X	Roofies	Green
Goop	Adam	Roaches	K
Georgia home boy	Ecstasy	Forget-me drug	Cat valium

Office of National Drug Control Policy (2002b).

depressed, anxious, and paranoid. Ecstasy stays in the body for a long time, and one may experience consequences weeks after use.

Rohypnol, a depressant, may cause muscle relaxation in low doses. Higher doses of rohypnol may cause loss of motor control and consciousness as well as create partial memory loss. Combining this drug with alcohol may be a mistake that results in death. Rohypnol begins to work 15 to 20 minutes after consumption, and its effects may last six hours.

GHB, another depressant, creates feelings of drowsiness, nausea, unconsciousness, seizures and severe respiratory depression, and coma. Ketamine produces hallucinogenic effects similar to those produced by PCP and LSD.

Anabolic Steroids

Anabolic steroids, synthetic substances related to hormones, receive a lot of press these days. They promote growth and development and enhance athletic performance. Scientists discovered anabolic steroids in the 1930s as they looked for effective ways to treat hypogonandism. Today, the primary medical use of anabolic steroids is to "treat delayed puberty, some types of impotence, and wasting of the body caused by the HIV infection and other diseases" (NIDA 2001a, 1).

Back in the 1930s scientists also discovered that anabolic steroids increased the growth of skeletal muscle in lab rats. When the world of sports got wind of this information, weightlifters and body builders began using them to increase muscle mass and athletic performance. Relatively quickly,

anabolic steroids made their way into other sporting arenas. Today, the use of anabolic steroids is widespread, and we are beginning to see an increase in the use of anabolic steroids by adolescents.

What is the trend among adolescents? Anabolic steroid use is more prevalent among adolescent males than it is females. According to the *Monitoring the Future* 2001 survey, 2.2% of 8th grade boys, 3.6% of 10th grade boys, and 2.5% of 12th grade boys had taken anabolic steroids at least once in their lives (NCADI 2001). Use among 8th, 10th, and 12th grade girls was 1.0%, 0.8%, and 0.9%, respectively. Results from this survey revealed a significant rise in steroid use among adolescents since the first survey was conducted in 1991. It is important to note that steroid use among young women is increasing.

Adolescents report various reasons for taking anabolic steroids. Some adolescents are interested in making their bodies appear more fit and attractive. Some boys and girls seeking bodily improvement may have distorted body images. For instance, boys may think they look small and weak. Many of us remember the saying "He looks like a 95-pound weakling." Girls, too, may have distorted body images and believe that they look fat and flabby when they may in fact be lean and fit (NIDA 2001a).

Boys seeking to look more fit often want to add weight and muscle mass. That is a reasonable goal considering the social messages boys receive from our culture at a young age. The image of male attractiveness centers on big, bulky, and muscular.

Magazines geared toward men often promote becoming more muscular as an effective strategy for gaining women's attention. In addition, little boys often play with action figures that possess more muscle mass than realistically possible. One study pointed out that the degree of muscularity in selected action figures anthropometrically sized to the average male build would be more than most body builders could achieve (Pope, Olivardia, Gruber, and Borowiecki 1999).

Other reports found that boys and girls who have been physically or sexually abused may turn to anabolic steroid abuse. Increased body mass may be one way to protect oneself. NIDA conducted interviews with male weightlifters and found that 25 percent of those who abused anabolic steroids recall events of childhood physical or sexual abuse. In a study of women weightlifters, many who had been raped reported steroid abuse. The women reasoned that increasing body mass would help deter men from raping them in the future because the women would appear intimidating or unattractive (NIDA 2001a, 1).

Anabolic steroids come in all forms. Some can be taken by injection. Others come in pill form to be swallowed, and some are creams or gels to be rubbed into the skin. Whatever the means of ingesting steroids into the body, abusers often use an amount 10 times or more greater than what a doctor would prescribe to a patient (NIDA 2001a).

The health risks associated with taking anabolic steroids are far greater than the benefits of increased muscle mass, strength, and endurance. On the surface of the body, anabolic steroid abuse may cause acne, cysts, oily hair, oily skin, fluid retention, and muscular cramps (NIDA 2001a; Fahey and Fritz 1991, 51). Other effects can occur in the hormonal system, musculoskeletal system, cardiorespiratory system, liver function, and behavior.

Hormonal system

Because steroid abuse is about taking synthetic hormones, it is little wonder that use of these drugs would affect the normal functioning of the hormonal system. Use of anabolic steroids may even disrupt the normal production of hormones in the body. The damaging effects may be both reversible and irreversible. In boys and men some reversible side effects include reduced sperm count, shrinking of the testicles, and infertility. Irreversible effects may include breast development and hair loss from the scalp. In girls and women, anabolic steroid use may decrease body fat and breast size, increase muscle mass and body hair, deepen the voice, and create an enlarged clitoris. With continued abuse these effects may be irreversible.

Musculoskeletal system

Adolescence is a time of important physical growth and development. Increased levels of synthetic hormones may alert the body to stop growing. When epiphyseal growth plates prematurely close, bone growth ends. Therefore, youth may stunt their growth with use of steroids. Tendons and muscles will be more prone to injury.

Cardiorespiratory system

Research shows that anabolic steroids lead to cardiovascular disease. Steroid users make themselves prone to heart attacks, strokes, increased cholesterol and triglyceride levels, atherosclerosis, and high blood pressure. Anabolic steroids can lead to an enlargement of the heart and heart wall. When this happens, the heart requires more oxygen to function properly (Fahey and Fritz 1991, 91).

Liver

According to NIDA (2001a) anabolic steroid use can cause tumors filled with blood to form in the liver. When this occurs, enlarged tumors may burst and cause internal bleeding. Anabolic steroid use may also lead to liver cancer.

Abnormal behavior

Changes in a person's daily behavior can occur with the use of anabolic steroids. Some users become depressed. Many demonstrate more aggressive, even violent, behaviors. Case studies have reported events in which participants experience delusions, schizophrenia, and homicidal rage.

Drugs affect our students regardless of ethnicity, gender, or socioeconomic status. Our role as physical educators is to inform adolescents about street drugs and the many adverse effects they may have on their bodies. Adolescents are at high risk for these damaging effects because their minds, bodies, and behaviors are still developing. Many Web sites, books, and articles provide valuable information and links to other sources that may help you educate your students and athletes about the use of licit and illicit drugs. When educating students, remember that the adolescent mind is an analytical mind. Offer accurate information about the benefits and health risks of using drugs. Point out clearly that the risks far outweigh the benefits and help them reach a healthy decision.

Child Abuse and Neglect

Hundreds of thousands of children (youth under the age of 18) are neglected and abused each year. **Child maltreatment** transcends ethnicity, culture, gender, and socioeconomic status. In 1999, 54% of all victims were between 0 and 3. African Americans had the highest maltreatment rates followed by American Indians–Alaska Natives, Hispanics, Whites, and Asian–Pacific Islanders (U.S. Department of Human Services, Administration of Child, Youth, and Families 2001).

T'nT

www.acf.dhhs.gov/programs/cb/ publications/cm99/cm99.pdf

Abuse and neglect, or maltreatment, is defined as an act or failure to act "on the part of the parent or caretaker which results in death, serious physical or emotional harm, sexual abuse or exploitation of a child." Each state has specific definitions, policies, and laws regarding child abuse and neglect. As a physical educator, you should be aware of the policies affecting your school and district.

Maltreatment is of several types: physical abuse, neglect, sexual abuse, and emotional abuse. Although state definitions may vary, the following definitions from the U.S. Department of Health and Human Services are a useful starting point.

- Physical abuse—physical injury caused by punching, beating, kicking, biting, burning, shaking, or other harmful intent.

- Child neglect—failure to provide for a child's basic needs. Neglect may be physical, emotional, medical, or educational.

- Sexual abuse—includes fondling a child's genitals, intercourse, incest, rape, sodomy, exhibitionism, and commercial exploitation such as prostitution. This may be the most underreported form of abuse.

- Emotional abuse—emotional injury caused by verbal abuse, bizarre forms of punishments, neglect, and any act or omission on the part of the caregiver that causes severe changes to behavioral, cognitive, emotional, and mental status.

Most perpetrators of child abuse (87.3%) are a parent of the child. Sixty-one percent of the perpetrators are female and tend to be responsible for physical abuse and neglect. More male parents are responsible for sexual abuse.

Abuse or neglect at any age is horrific and may have lasting physical, cognitive, and emotional effects on the child. Adolescents are not immune from abuse and neglect. Some states report that abuse of adolescents ranges from 15 to 40% of all cases reported. Because they are older and more independent, abused adolescents may be more difficult to identify than abused younger children. Should you suspect that a child is being abused you should report it to your principal, who will report it to Child Protective Services (CPS), or you may report it to Child Protective Services yourself. After receiving a report of potential abuse, CPS will conduct an investigation to determine if abuse is taking place.

Child abuse is real and can have a serious effect on an adolescent's development. We must be cognizant of the possibility that one day we may meet a student who is or has been abused. The trauma from this experience will influence the abused student's participation in school and in your physical education class. Be sure to get to know each of your students so that you are better prepared to help them in time of need.

Summary

Adolescent growth and development is affected by physiological and psychological maturation as well as the environment. Eating disorders, drug use and abuse, and child maltreatment transcend ethnicity, gender, and socioeconomic status. As a physical educator, you must at times look past the student in a uniform to understand how environmental issues are affecting his or her life. At that moment, you must decide if you can help, if you are in over your head, or if resources available at school can help the student.

Checking for Understanding ▶▶▶

- Define the terms *growth* and *maturation*.
- What is puberty? How does it occur in boys and girls?
- Explain general concepts of adolescent cognitive development.
- Describe general concepts of adolescent affective development.

For Reflection and Discussion ▶▶▶

- What experience did Dominique have with a student-athlete's eating disorder? How would you handle a student with an eating disorder?
- How will you deal with students and street drugs in your classes or athletic teams?
- If you suspect that a student is being physically and emotionally abused, how will you deal with the situation? Explain the steps you would take to help.

References

AAHPERD. 1999. *Physical education for lifelong fitness.* Champaign, IL: Human Kinetics.

Allen, L., and J.W. Santrock. 1993. *Psychology: The contexts of behavior.* Madison, WI: WCB Brown and Benchmark.

Beunen, G., and R.M. Malina. 1988. Growth and physical performance relative to the timing of the adolescent spurt. In *Exercise and Sport Sciences Reviews,* ed. K.B. Pandolf. New York: Macmillan.

Borba, M. 1989. *Self-esteem builders resources.* Torrance, CA: Jalmar Press.

Brooks-Gunn, J., J. Gargiulo, and M.P. Warren. 1986. The menstrual cycle and athletic performance. In *The menstrual cycle and physical activity,* eds. J.L. Puhl and C.H. Brown. Champaign, IL: Human Kinetics.

Caissy, G.A. 1994. *Early adolescence: Understanding the 10–15 year old.* New York: Plenum Press.

Eating Disorders Awareness and Prevention. 1999. *Eating disorders in the U.S.A.: Statistics in context.* [Online.] Available: **www.edap.org/edinfo/index.html** [June, 2001].

Erikson, E. 1963. *Childhood and society.* New York: Norton.

Fahey, T., and B. Fritz. 1991. *Steroid alternative handbook: Understanding anabolic steroids and drug-free scientific natural alternatives.* Walnut Creek, CA: Sport Science.

Feldman, S.S., and G.R. Elliott. 1990. *At the threshold: The developing adolescent.* Cambridge, MA: Harvard University Press.

Gallahue, D.L. 1996. *Developmental physical education for today's children.* 3rd ed. Madison, WI: Brown and Benchmark.

Heath, B.H., and J.E.L. Carter. 1967. A modified somatotype method. *American Journal of Physical Anthropology* 27:57–74.

Hellison, D. 1995. *Teaching responsibility through physical activity.* Champaign, IL: Human Kinetics.

Holmes, G.R. 1995. *Helping teenagers into adulthood: A guide for the next generation.* Westport, CT: Praeger.

Kuczrnarski, R.J., C.L. Ogden, L.M. Grummer-Strawn, et al. 2000. *CDC growth charts: United States. Advance data from vital and health statistics of the Centers for Disease Control and Prevention.* No. 314. Hyattsville, MD: National Center for Health Statistics. **www.cdc.gov/nchs/data/ad/ad314.pdf**

Malina, R.M. 1986. Physical growth and maturation. In *Physical activity and well-being,* ed. Vern Seefeldt. Reston, VA: AAHPERD.

Malina, R.M., and C. Bouchard. 1991. *Growth, maturation and physical activity.* Champaign, IL: Human Kinetics.

Mercier, R., and G. Hutchinson. 1998. Social psychology. In *Concepts of physical education: What every student needs to know,* ed. B. Mohnsen. Reston, VA: NASPE.

National Center for Chronic Disease Prevention and Health Promotion. 2001. *Obesity and overweight: A public health epidemic.* Atlanta, GA. **www.cdc.gov/nccdphp.dnpa/obesity/epidemic.htm**

National Clearinghouse for Alcohol and Drug Information (NCADI). 2001. *Monitoring the future. 2001 data from in-school surveys of 8th, 10th, and 12th grade students.* Rockville, MD: Center for Substance Abuse and Prevention. **www.health.org/newsroom/mtf/2001/menu.htm**

National Clearinghouse for Alcohol and Drug Information (NCADI). 2002. *Neighborhood characteristics and youth marijuana use.* Rockville, MD: Center for Substance Abuse Prevention. **www.health.org/govstudy/shortreports/marijuana/**

National Drug Intelligence Center. 2001. 319 Johnstown, PA 15901-1622 **www.usdoj.gov/ndic/pubs/653/meth.htm**

National Institute on Drug Abuse (NIDA). 2000. *Inhalant abuse.* Bethesda, MD: National Institutes for Health. **http://165.112.78.61/ResearchReports/Inhalants/Inhalants.html**

National Institute on Drug Abuse (NIDA). 2001a. *Anabolic steroid abuse.* Bethesda, MD: National Institutes for Health. **http://165.112.78.61/Steroid/AnabolicSteroids4.html**

National Institute on Drug Abuse (NIDA). 2001b. *Infofax: Marijuana.* Bethesda, MD: National Institutes for Health. **http://165.112.78.61/Infofax/marijuana.html**

National Institute on Drug Abuse (NIDA). 2001c. *Research reports: Methamphetamine abuse and addiction.* Bethesda, MD: National Institutes for Health. **http://165.112.78.61/ResearchReports/methamph/methamph.html**

Office of National Drug Control Policy (ONDCP). 2002a. *Pulsecheck: Trends in drug abuse November 2001.* Executive Office of the President. Washington, DC: U.S. Government Printing Office. **www.whitehousedrugpolicy.gov/ publications/drugfact/pulsechk/fall2001/index.html**

Office of National Drug Control Policy (ONDCP). 2002b. *Drug facts: Club drugs.* Executive Office of the President. Washington, DC: U.S. Government Printing Office. **www.whitehousedrugpolicy.gov/drugfact/club/ index.html**

Pangrazi, R.P., and P.W. Darst. 1997. *Dynamic physical education for secondary school students.* 3rd ed. Boston: Allyn & Bacon.

Payne, V.G., and L.D. Isaacs. 1995. *Human motor development: A lifespan approach.* Mountain View, CA: Mayfield.

Pope, H.G., R. Olivardia, A. Gruber, and J. Borowiecki. 1999. Evolving ideals of male body image as seen through action toys. *International Journal of Eating Disorders* 26:65–72.

President's Council on Physical Fitness and Sports. 1997. *Physical activity and sport in the lives of girls.* Center of Research on Girls and Women in Sport, University of Minnesota.

Shangold, M., and G. Mirkin. 1994. *Women and exercise: Physiology and sports medicine.* Philadelphia: F.A. Davis.

Sheldon, W.H. 1940. *The varieties of human physique.* New York: Harper and Row.

Tanner, J.M. 1990. *Fetus into man.* Cambridge, MA: Harvard University Press.

U.S. Department of Human Services, Administration of Child, Youth and Families. 2001. *Child maltreatment 1999.* Washington, DC: U.S. Government Printing Office. **www.acf.dhhs.gov/programs/cb/publications/cm99/ cm99.pdf**

Wilmore, J.H., and D.L. Costill. 1994. *Physiology of sport and exercise.* Champaign, IL: Human Kinetics.

Wuest, D., and B. Lombardo. 1994. *Curriculum and instruction: The secondary school physical education experience.* St. Louis: Mosby.

Suggested Readings

Andrich, D., and I. Styles. 1994. Psychometric evidence of intellectual growth spurts in early adolescence. *Journal of Early Adolescence* 14(3):328.

Elkind, D. 1988. *The hurried child: Growing up too fast too soon.* Reading, MA: Addison-Wesley.

Herman-Giddens, M.E., and E.J. Slora. 1997. Secondary sexual characteristics and menses in young girls seen in office practice: A study from the pediatric research in office settings network. *Pediatrics* 99(4):505–513.

Humphrey, J.H. 1988. *Children and stress.* New York: AMS Press.

Joseph, J.M. 1994. *The resilient child: Preparing today's youth for tomorrow's world.* New York: Plenum Press.

Kohl III, H.W., and K.E. Hobbs. 1998. Development of physical activity behaviors among children and adolescents. *Pediatrics* 101(3):549–555.

Larson, G.A., and L.D. Zaichkowsky. 1995. Physical, motor, and fitness development in children and adolescents. *Journal of Education* 177(2):55.

Lemberg, R., and L. Cohn, eds. 1999. *Eating disorders: A reference sourcebook.* Phoenix, AZ: Oryx Press.

McCreary, D.R., and D.K. Sasse. 2000. An exploration of the drive for muscularity in adolescent boys and girls. *Journal of American College Health* 48(6):297–303.

Puhl, J.L., and C.H. Brown, eds. 1986. *The menstrual cycle and physical activity.* Champaign, IL: Human Kinetics.

Roche, A.F. 1992. *Growth, maturation and body composition: The Fels longitudinal study 1929–1991.* Cambridge, UK: Cambridge University Press.

Troiano, R.P., and K.M. Flegal. 1998. Overweight children and adolescents: Description, epidemiology, and demographics. *Pediatrics* 101(3):497.

Wagner, W.G. 1996. Optimal development in adolescence: What is it and how can it be encouraged. *Counseling Psychologist* 24(3):360–400.

Chapter **5**

How Adolescents Learn

> The teacher does not bid you enter the house
> of her wisdom, but rather leads you
> to the threshold of your own mind.
>
> — *Kahlil Gibran*

Ajeet and Devon are veteran physical education teachers at a high school. One day while rearranging the equipment room after school, they got into a discussion about how their students learn. Devon remembered an eye-opening experience that caused him to view a student in a different light. He remembered working with sophomores in a track and field unit. One student, Sandy, was somewhat awkward when she moved. Devon could see that Sandy was not comfortable with her body or confident in her ability to move. Teaching an average-size class of 32, Devon made an extra effort to work with this young woman. During class he offered her lots of feedback and encouraged her to try harder when practicing various track skills. Her motivation, along with her skill, seemed to remain unchanged. The unit came and went. Devon met her again in his health class, held in a classroom with 25 students total. Devon made sure he included interactive learning activities along with lecture content, much as he did in his physical education classes. To his delight, Sandy was in his class. Impressions from the physical education class led Devon to believe that Sandy would be quiet, shy, and somewhat unmotivated in this class. Much to his surprise, Sandy was assertive, knowledgeable, and seemed to enjoy lectures and problem-solving activities. She was a quick thinker and easily comprehended health content and complex ideas. Devon was amazed! He recognized then that students might not behave in the same way in physical education classes as they do in other classes. He became more determined to examine how students learn and find ways to involve and improve the learning of students like Sandy in his classes.

Learning Objectives

After reading this chapter you will be able to

- define learning,
- better understand how students learn,
- describe several findings of brain research,
- describe eight multiple intelligences,
- understand metacognition as a learning process,
- explain the three stages of motor learning,
- provide an overview of learning disabilities, and
- determine ways to create effective learning environments in physical education.

Key Terms and Phrases

Learning
Brain research
Intelligence quotient (IQ)
Multiple intelligences
Metacognition

Many of us have had experiences with students like Sandy. Some physical education teachers assume that students like Sandy are unmotivated and disinterested in physical activity. In other words, they just don't try. Some concerned teachers work harder to find ways to motivate students like Sandy to learn. Others try for a while and eventually give up, casting Sandy into a student category like wallflower, nondresser, poor student, or simply lazy. We contend that students' participation or nonparticipation in physical education class may have a great deal to do with the ways that students prefer to learn. As teachers we must understand better how students learn so that we can create enriched learning environments where they find success.

What Is Learning?

When we think of **learning** in physical education, we typically think of students improving their motor skills and game play. Usually these improvements are marked by changes in growth, physical maturation, and skill acquisition (Rink 1998, 16) (see chapter 4, "Adolescent Growth and Development"). Note that learning in physical education is not limited to motor-skill acquisition and improved motor performance. Learning includes a holistic or constructivist approach in which students work to improve a variety of skills and concepts (as defined in chapter 1), personal fitness, social abilities, and self-esteem. These aspects of student learning are clearly illustrated by the seven outcomes for becoming a physically educated person stated in the physical education national standards (National Association for Sport and Physical Education [NASPE] 1995) (see table 1.1).

The word *learn* means to gain knowledge, skill, comprehension, or mastery through study or experience. As teachers, we are committed to creating a learning environment that will motivate and challenge students. Before we talk about how students learn, let's dispel three myths about students and learning (Berryman 1991).

Myths About Learning

Myth: Students predictably transfer learning from one situation to another.

Research literature tells us that students do not predictably transfer knowledge from classroom settings to new situations (for example, from physical education class to health class or from physical education class to home situations). To help students transfer learning from the classroom to other situations, teachers must help them find meaning in what they learn and ways to apply that meaning to situations outside physical education. As students apply fitness concepts to their lives, they may participate in fitness activities more often.

Myth: Students are passive receivers of knowledge and wisdom.

Some believe that students are simply empty barges waiting for teachers to load them with the knowledge, wisdom, and skills they will need to sail away and be successful in life. This idea is simply not true. This myth comes from the traditional perspective that the purpose of education is to impart knowledge and culture upon young people. This particular myth encourages a direct style of teaching (see chapter 8) in which the teacher is in charge and students have little responsibility for their own learning. According to Berryman (1991, 2) teachers who control all aspects of learning limit students' opportunities to develop important learning skills such as goal setting, strategic planning, monitoring, evaluating, and revising. Students who receive this kind of instruction may lack confidence in their ability to learn and make sense of physical education content. Students may adopt a "waiting it out" (Berryman 1991, 2) attitude in this kind of class. They may choose not to dress for class, to hide behind bleachers, or to go through the motions of game play. Passive learning encourages students to go through the motions. They pretend to learn but rarely make sense of or internalize content, and they certainly do not transfer learning to situations outside class.

Another important point associated with this myth is thinking that students enter your classroom as blank slates (tabula rasa) waiting to be inscribed with appropriate and necessary skills and knowledge. The reality is that students enter your classroom with their own designer luggage, filled with experiences, beliefs, and perceptions. If we do not help students examine the contents of their luggage, if it remains untouched, students may hang on to inaccurate facts, unhealthy beliefs, and possibly poor physical activity behaviors when they confront situations outside school.

Myth: Learning is directly related to strengthening "the bonds between stimuli and correct responses."

This myth is based on cause and effect, which was an instructional strategy that emerged from behavioral theories of learning. A cause-and-effect approach to learning isolates content from context and requires students to learn many disconnected skills and concepts. For example, if we were to teach students the tennis serve on an unmarked surface and without a net, they would be learning the skill out of context. They would not know that the game requires them to place the ball over the net and into the service box diagonally across from the server. Teaching the tennis serve on a tennis court and providing other information about the serve, such as its purpose, places the skill in context. Students who can place a skill in context will understand it better and know how to use it in game play. The tennis serve will take on meaning that they can apply to other situations.

These mistaken assumptions about students and learning limit the educational potential of each lesson taught. Now that we have dispelled these myths, let's move on to how students learn.

Learning and Learning Styles

Over the years, learning theorists have developed many models for learning. By consulting education and adolescent development texts you may review a number of these models. For the purpose of this chapter we refer to a modified version of Bloom's taxonomy, and we then discuss brain research, multiple intelligences, and metacognition.

Bloom's (1956) taxonomy refers to a classifying system for learning. Bloom and his colleagues divided learning into three domains or categories: cognitive, affective, and psychomotor. Each domain consists of levels of behavior placed in a hierarchy. The cognitive domain focuses on the acquisition and application of knowledge. The affective domain emphasizes the development of attitude and values. The psychomotor domain includes the physical and neuromuscular skills of the body (Harrison, Blakemore, Buck, and Pellett 1996, 95). Corbin (1976, 2002) introduced another domain called health-related fitness (see chapters 3 and 12 for more information on health-related fitness). We will use each of the four learning domains (figure 5.1) to examine how students learn.

Cognitive Domain

Six levels of behavior make up the cognitive domain (figure 5.2). These levels are considered hierarchical. In other words, a student must com-

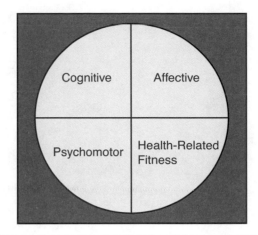

Figure 5.1 Learning can be categorized into four domains.

plete the first level, knowledge, before moving to the second level, comprehension. Each time a student learns something new, she will work through the cognitive levels. As a physical educator your role is to provide students with opportunities to practice at different levels based on individual needs.

Affective Domain

Developing attitudes and values refers to our emotional side. The affective domain has five levels of behavior that describe emotional growth: receiving, responding, valuing, organizing, and characterizing (figure 5.3).

Psychomotor Domain

The psychomotor domain is the learning of physical and neuromotor skills. This domain is particularly important because it provides a way to describe steps that many students take to learn motor skills and concepts. Physical educators have developed their own motor-learning models or modified Bloom's over the years.

Fitts and Posner (1967) developed a sound motor-learning model that we will explain in a later section. George Graham and colleagues (1998) have outlined the generic levels of skills proficiency in which the process of learning motor skills is divided into four categories: precontrol, control, utilization, and proficiency. Refer to chapters 8 and 12 for further details.

Although taxonomies enable us to identify and classify hierarchical levels of learning behavior, we should remember that each student is unique and will engage at the level that best suits his abilities

1. Knowledge:	Observes and recalls information
	Knows facts and terms
	Knows dates, places, and events
	Knows rules and categories
	Question cues: list, define, describe, identify, show, label, name
2. Comprehension:	Understands information
	Grasps meaning
	Interprets facts
	Compares and contrasts information
	Translates information into a different context
	Predicts results and/or consequences
	Question cues: summarize, interpret, compare, predict, estimate, discuss, contrast
3. Application:	Uses information in a variety of situations
	Applies methods, concepts, and principles to new situations
	Solves problems with information learned
	Question cues: apply, demonstrate, complete, illustrate, adapt, examine, solve
4. Analysis:	Breaks down whole into parts
	Sees patterns
	Sees organization of parts to a whole
	Discovers meanings and relationships
	Question cues: analyze, explain, compare, infer, order
5. Synthesis:	Uses information learned to create new ideas
	Generalizes from given facts
	Relates knowledge to several areas
	Relates information in new ways
	Question cues: integrate, plan, create, design, formulate, invent, modify
6. Evaluation:	Compares and discriminates between ideas and information
	Assesses value
	Recognizes subjectivity
	Question cues: assess, evaluate, examine, decide, rank, discriminate, conclude

Figure 5.2 Six levels of behavior make up the cognitive domain.

Adapted from Bloom, B.S. (Ed.). 1956. *Taxonomy of educational objectives, handbook I: Cognitive domain*. New York: McKay.

1. Receiving:
Pays attention
Willing to listen
Willing to attend to a task
Behavior examples: listens to others; remembers names

2. Responding:
Actively participates
Attends and reacts to a particular situation
Complies
Follows directions
Finds satisfaction or enjoyment in responding
Behavior examples: participates in activity, presents to group, asks questions, follows rules to the game

3. Valuing:
Places worth on a particular object, phenomenon, or behavior
Expresses a strong opinion or belief
Expresses preferences
Demonstrates a commitment to values
Behavior examples: demonstrates belief in class rules, sensitive toward individual differences, plans improvement, and follows through

4. Organizing:
Organizes values into priorities
Resolves conflicts between values
Understands relationships among values
Places values into an hierarchy
Behavior examples: recognizes how one's behavior affects the class, accepts responsibility for one's behavior, demonstrates how to get along with others

5. Characterizing:
Internalizes values
Demonstrates consistent behavior
Integrates beliefs, values, ideals, and behavior
Behavior examples: self reliant, able to work independently, able to work cooperatively in group settings, uses ethical practice consistently, resolves conflict peacefully, values others and their opinions

Figure 5.3 The affective domain consists of five levels of behavior.

Adapted from Bloom, B.S. (Ed.). 1956. Taxonomy of educational objectives, handbook II: Affective domain. New York: McKay.

and needs. To gain a broader understanding of how students learn, we turn now to a brief discussion about brain research, multiple intelligences, and metacognition.

Learning and Brain Research

We know that learning is not merely the result of cause and effect. A physical educator can stand before a class of 35 and explain and demonstrate the basketball set shot, but it is unlikely that all students in the class will learn to perform the shot. A physical educator can provide a task sheet that explains the behavioral characteristics of fair play, but it is unlikely that everyone in class will learn and demonstrate fair play. Common sense tells us that learning cannot take place in isolation and that students must find meaning in what they are learning. Learning must take place in appropriate contexts.

Over the past few decades, researchers have been learning more about how the brain works.

Educators have reviewed these findings with great interest. Many want to know if they can apply the findings from **brain research** directly to instructional strategies and curriculum development processes used in public education (figure 5.4). The answer to date remains uncertain. Many brain research findings provide insight about how people learn, but none have been studied significantly in the classroom or gymnasium. As we await the results from studies that apply the findings of brain research to education and physical education, we can review with earnest some findings from brain research to understand better how people learn.

Brain research tells us that the brain will make physiological changes as a result of hands-on experience (figure 5.5). The environment that embraces each individual can strongly influence the development of the person's brain and the learning process. Therefore, we discard our thinking that IQ, or "brains," is predetermined at birth and replace it with the idea that "brains" will continue to develop and evolve throughout a person's life (figure 5.6). Diamond and Hopson (1998) have found and established the concept "neural plasticity," which means that the brain has incredible ability to change its structure and function constantly as a direct response to external experiences. In addition, it seems that the brain has some inherent abilities important to individual learning.

1. The brain needs to make sense of information. Interactive teaching strategies in which students have responsibility to be involved in their learning help them organize and make sense of information.

2. The brain has many abilities, all of which seem to develop in an integrated fashion. It makes sense that teachers who use multiple instructional strategies will assist the integrated development of the brain.

3. The brain is naturally curious. Students are inherently interested in the world around them, and they seek to make connections between what they are learning and what they know. Our job as physical educators is to help students with that process.

4. The brain is naturally social. Teaching strategies that encourage students to work together as well as separately enhance the overall learning process and meet the brain's need to interact (Wolfe and Brandt 1998).

5. IQ is not fixed at birth, a principle we will discuss further in the next section.

6. Some abilities of the brain can develop more easily during certain times of life. These periods are windows of opportunity. For example, a child can more easily learn a second language at a young age than he can later on. An adult may learn a second language only through years of struggle and hard work, whereas a child may seem to pick it up effortlessly.

7. Daniel Goleman points out in his book *Emotional Intelligence* (1997) that "learning is strongly

Figure 5.4 Teachers are anxious to use brain research to help them understand how to reach students in the classroom.

Figure 5.5 When people participate in physical activity, not just their bodies but their brains undergo important physiological changes.

influenced by emotion." It appears that the stronger one's emotion toward a meaningful experience, the stronger the memory of that experience. In other words, if a student is excited about learning to play soccer, setting personal goals for improving her soccer skills, or demonstrating fair play while involved in a game, she will have a strong memory of those experiences.

Multiple Intelligences

The brain is highly complex. We should review findings from brain research carefully and apply to our teaching those concepts and insights when and where appropriate. One of the most important points to come out of brain research is the reminder that students are individuals who differ from one another in many ways, including the ways in which they learn. Individuals are unique, which means they may learn in ways similar to or different from others. Acknowledging a spectrum of learning styles implies that we expand our definition of intelligence. Let's begin.

Figure 5.6 Infants begin trying to make sense of their surroundings once they enter the world, starting the process of brain development that will continue throughout childhood and adolescence.

In 1904 French school officials were trying to reduce overcrowding that plagued the country's schools. The French Ministry of Education commissioned Alfred Binet, a psychologist, to develop a way to determine which children were unable to learn in school. The strategy was to take children who were unable to learn by traditional classroom teaching and place them in special schools and classrooms. Binet and a student developed an intelligence test consisting of 30 questions. Binet also developed the concept of mental age (MA), which is an indication of a person's mental development compared with the development of others. He tested this theory by developing averages for intelligence on 50 children ages 3 to 11 whom he tested. Binet concluded that average MA scores corresponded directly to chronological age (CA), which is age from birth to adolescence. Therefore, "a bright child would have an MA above the CA and a dull child would have an MA below the CA" (Goleman 1997).

By 1912 William Stern devised the **intelligence quotient (IQ),** which consists of a person's mental age divided by his or her chronological age and multiplied by 100. Individuals whose MA was the same as their CA would have an IQ of 100. People whose mental age was higher than their chronological age would score higher than 100 and be considered above average. Mental age scores that were lower than chronological age would score lower than 100, indicating a lower than average intelligence. Over the decades, researchers at Stanford University revised the Binet tests many times. We now know them as the Stanford-Binet tests, or simply IQ tests.

A Stanford psychologist named Lewis Terman conducted many of the IQ test revisions. One revision was used in mass during World War I when over 2 million American soldiers were tested and their intelligences analyzed (Goleman 1997, 38). Terman also conducted the IQ test with thousands of children and adults of different ages, selected at random from different regions in the United States. Administering these tests to large numbers of people, Terman and other researchers were able to create a normal distribution for intelligence. According to Goleman and Gardner (Goleman 1997, 38) revising the IQ test and testing thousands led to a popular trend, "the IQ way of thinking." In other words, we believed that people were born with a certain amount of intelligence. This belief had serious implications for teaching in that we treat students in one of two ways: students either

can or cannot learn (Checkley 1997). This narrow view of academic intelligence and knowledge leaves out the importance of emotion on our ability to think and learn, not to mention the fact that we can improve our intelligence with opportunity and practice. Gardner (1983) realized the limitations of IQ and developed a model of what we now know as multiple intelligences.

Gardner first described **multiple intelligences** in *Frames of Mind* (1983). In doing so, he encouraged us to move away from the narrow view of intelligence that described people as either smart or not smart. Gardner recognized the limitations of the traditional model and realized that many people were smart in some aspects of their lives and not so smart in others (figure 5.7). Through Gardner's work we realize the brilliance of a variety of people like Martina Navratilova (tennis), Michael Jordan (basketball), Cheryl Swoopes (basketball), Mark McGwire (baseball), Katarina Witt (ice skating), Mozart (music), Beethoven (music), Cassatt (painting), Picasso (painting), Martin Luther King (political action and social leadership), Einstein (science), Mother Theresa (social leadership), Ida B. Wells (journalism and political action), and so on. Through his work we realize that those in the preceding list did not all have the same kind of intelligence. Their intelligence varied, yet each was brilliant.

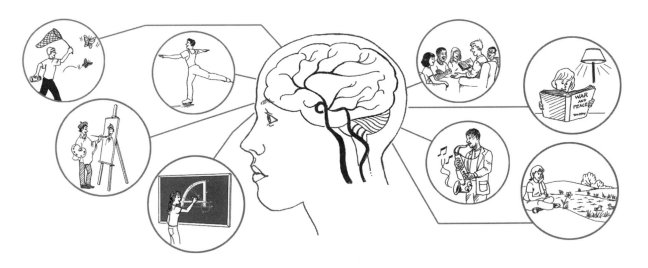

Figure 5.7   The concept of multiple intelligences tells us that different people have skills in different areas instead of the antiquated idea of people being either smart or not smart.

Gardner identified eight kinds of intelligences (Boggeman, Hoerr, and Wallach 1996; Checkley 1997). Each form of intelligence is grounded on Gardner's (1983, xxii) criteria for defining intelligence. Intelligence must

1. be isolated by brain damage,
2. be highlighted by exceptional individuals,
3. contain an identifiable core set of operations,
4. have a definite set of outcome performances,
5. have developed over time,
6. show support from experimental and psychological tasks,
7. have support from psychometric findings, and
8. be susceptible to encoding from a symbol system.

Gardner identified the following eight intelligences (Checkley 1997):

1. Linguistic—sensitivity to the meaning and order of words.
2. Logical-mathematical—the ability to handle chains of reasoning and to recognize patterns and order.
3. Musical—sensitivity to pitch, melody, rhythm, and tone.
4. Body-kinesthetic—the ability to use the body skillfully and handle objects adroitly.
5. Spatial—the ability to perceive the world accurately and to re-create or transform aspects of that world.
6. Interpersonal—the ability to understand people and relationships.
7. Intrapersonal—the ability to access to one's emotional life as a means to understand oneself and others.
8. Naturalist—the ability to make distinctions in the natural world and use that ability in a productive manner (for example, to be able to recognize and classify things in the natural world like animals, birds, rocks, or cultural artifacts like art or cars) (Guignon 1998).

Each intelligence is well defined. The naturalist intelligence is Gardner's most recent one. He developed this category after taking many questions about where he would place someone who excelled in biology and ecosystems. Investigating this topic further, Gardner decided that another intelligence existed. The finding of the eighth intelligence informs us that the list may yet be incomplete. As researchers learn more about the brain and cognitive development, other intelligences may appear on the list.

Multiple intelligences describe how people learn. Someone who excels in the body-kinesthetic style learns well by moving. When we think about our physical education classes, we can easily identify the students who move skillfully and handle objects adroitly. Just as readily we notice the students who do not move well at all. Those who do not move well or who show limited confidence in moving may excel in another intelligence. Let's think back to the introduction to this chapter. Devon was concerned about Sandy's ability to learn in a track and field unit. When Devon met Sandy in the classroom for health, he found her to be a different person. She excelled in language and interpersonal skills. Devon learned without realizing it that Sandy probably did not learn best in the body-kinesthetic area but stood out in linguistic and interpersonal intelligences. This revelation about Sandy does not mean that we ask her to write about track and field and not engage in movement activities. But we have found that Sandy learns best in a particular way and that we should find ways to use some of her strengths to help her find meaning in activities. We want her to gain confidence while practicing her weakness, which in this scenario was performing track skills.

Devon began to brainstorm ideas that would help Sandy find meaning in the track and field unit. One thought he had was to have Sandy read about male and female track Olympians and find out how track and field helped them on and off the track. Devon thought that by helping Sandy connect with these athletes through language, she could use her interpersonal skills to relate their experiences to her own. From there, Devon thought he might use Sandy's interpersonal skills in class by placing her in a leadership role to help other students in class with track and field. He would de-emphasize the importance of perfect performance and focus on skill development and cognitive understanding. He would encourage Sandy to use her language and interpersonal skills to help others.

Gardner has received criticism (Goleman 1997) for his lack of attention to the effect of emotion on thinking and learning. Gardner acknowledges this limitation (Goleman 1997) and comments that it may have something to do with his training in cognitive and behavioral science, which in the past was devoid of the study of emotion. Gardner also explained to Goleman that he attempted to address the importance of emotion in the intrapersonal intelligence. According to Goleman (1997) emotions are important to the thinking and learning process. Emotional intelligence includes self-control, zeal, persistence, and ability to motivate oneself. We will talk further about this in the next section, metacognition.

Learning and Metacognition

Now we have a good idea about how students learn. We may even have a better idea about how we ourselves learn. How can we use information about multiple intelligences to enhance the learning process for our students? One way would be to teach students about **metacognition,** which is the ability to be aware of and monitor one's own learning process. That's right; metacognition occurs when students consciously take responsibility for their own learning. We can teach students how to self-monitor their own learning.

First, let's consider the characteristics of a well-developed thought process (Jacobson 1998). Using metacognition with self-monitoring learning strategies includes

1. a relevant knowledge base,
2. careful observation and classification of ideas,
3. reflection and elaboration of those ideas,
4. self-assessment,
5. appropriate application (knowing why, when, and where to apply learning), and
6. feedback from an appropriate source.

As students engage in these important critical thinking skills in your class, they will come to understand the importance of metacognition in their learning. Students will find that the metacognitive process can be developed through the use of relevant hands-on learning activities in which they plan, make decisions, and assess results. All of this improves academic performance. Teaching for metacognition is important if we want to help our students become physically active for the rest of their lives. In chapters 7, 8, 11, and 12 we will give you examples of ways that you can encourage metacognition through the learning activities and assessments you provide for your students.

Learning and Motor Skills

Learning styles, brain research, multiple intelligences, and metacognition lend insight into the ways students gather, organize, and make meaning of skills and concepts. Now, we will turn our focus to findings in motor-learning research to deepen our understanding about how students learn and improve motor skills. This information coupled with what we have learned about cognitive development will inform us about how to create rich learning environments in physical education.

Purpose

Use technology to be aware of what other professionals do to facilitate students' motor learning.

Resource and Procedure

Select a couple of Web resources that have been set up to facilitate communication among physical educators on a variety of topics. Many of the topics centering on facilitating motor skill learning can be found at PE Central (**http://pe.central.vt.edu**) and **www.pelinks4u.org** Web sites. Various listservs (a stream of posted messages cataloged by topic) are available to physical educators; these serve as sounding boards, question-and-answer sessions, sources for refreshing your spirit, and sources of encouragement. When posting a question or a response, remember to be courteous, patient, and brief. Also, listserv members appreciate that you post relevant information to a particular forum. No one likes to scroll through a series of unrelated and off-topic postings.

Understanding how students learn will help us do our jobs better. We will be more adept at helping students learn and improve motor-skill performance and learn and apply movement concepts. We said earlier that students improve motor-skill performance through growth, physical maturation, and learning. It is a matter of physiology to note that as students grow taller and stronger, they will naturally improve at some skills, particularly those that require force and effort like jumping and kicking. The ability to improve the form of a motor skill is not dependent on physical growth and maturation (Rink 1998). Maturation does provide, however, a capability for learning (Nichols 1994, 80). Once an individual has achieved a certain neuromuscular maturity, opportunity and practice play an increasingly significant role in learning and improving motor skills.

Individuals progress through three stages of motor learning to become competent and proficient at motor skills (Fitts and Posner 1967).

Stage 1: Verbal-Cognitive Stage

During this stage the learner is trying diligently to understand and perform the skill correctly. The stage includes both mental and physical rehearsal of the skill. A teacher may witness a student declaring under his breath the steps to an overhand throw in softball: "Side to target, elbow back, step with opposition." Students at this stage will show deep levels of concentration while performing. The skill will not appear fluid, and performance will vary. Sometimes students will experience success by demonstrating correct form. At other times they will not be able to execute the skill correctly. In addition, a student in the cognitive stage may know that he did some aspect of the skill incorrectly, but not know which part he did poorly or how to correct his error (Rink 1998; Magill 1989).

Stage 2: Motor Stage

Notable improvement occurs as students progress from the cognitive stage to the motor stage. In this stage, students consistently demonstrate the fundamental mechanics of each skill learned (figure 5.8). Errors occur less frequently than they did in the cognitive stage, and when errors occur they are on a lesser scale. In the motor stage, learners are working to refine their skills. They have developed some ability to detect and correct errors as they occur. The ability to provide feedback to self enables the learner to make changes to practice

Figure 5.8 Delaying motor development can prove costly in the future, just as not performing regular maintenance on a car can be.

and performance. In addition, the learner begins to apply newly learned skills to a variety of situations that may occur in actual motor-skill performance and game play. For example, in golf a student may perform the chip shot with some consistency and accuracy. She is able to detect and correct gross errors in performance. She begins to experiment with varying lies such as the downhill lie in which the feet stand higher than the golf ball (Rink 1998; Magill 1989).

Stage 3: Autonomous Stage

At this stage, motor-skill performance flows. It appears effortless. The students are able to detect all kinds of errors and correct them. Students are able to perform the skill in a variety of physical settings. For instance, a young woman who has learned to dribble and dodge opponents with a soccer ball is now able to do so with stationary and dynamic defense. In dynamic situations she is able to assess her defender, maintain control of the ball, and execute a successful dodge past her defender. She makes it look easy; thus the skill appears automatic (Rink 1998; Magill 1989).

Sometimes people assume that a person who excels in one sport like basketball will automatically excel in another sport like team handball. Making this assumption can be foolish. A person in the autonomous stage in a sport or activity like field hockey may be at the verbal-cognitive stage in another sport or activity like in-line skating. To illustrate this point, complete the task in figure 5.9.

In the left-hand column list 10 to 20 physical activities or sports. In the columns to the right of this list, check whether you perform these activities/sports at the verbal-cognitive, motor, or autonomous stages.

Physical activity	Verbal-cognitive	Motor	Autonomous
ex: field hockey			✓
ex: unicycle	✓		
ex: swimming		✓	

Figure 5.9   Determine your stages of motor skill for your favorite activities.

Understanding how students learn cognitively, affectively, and motorically is essential to thoughtful lesson planning and effective teaching (see chapters 7, 8, and 11). In every class, however, some individuals will have learning disabilities. Examining the characteristics of learning disabilities will enable you to continue your development as an effective physical educator (see chapter 6).

Learning and Students With Disabilities

People with learning disabilities may be one of the largest and most misunderstood groups of learners (Craft 1990, 177). Over the course of your teaching career, you will have the opportunity to work with many children and adolescents with learning disabilities. Learning disabilities come in many forms. No single profile offers a clear representation of a student with a learning disability. Craft (2000) provides an overview of what a student with a learning disability may look like. Imagine your middle school or high school physical education class. A student with a learning disability may be that 15-year-old boy who seems intellectually bright but does poorly in his schoolwork. He may have difficulty reading, distinguishing left from right, or organizing things. He may appear clumsy when performing gross and fine motor tasks. He may be the one who cannot skip, gallop, walk on a balance beam, or change directions quickly in games.

Students with learning disabilities are often difficult to detect. They appear normal in their physical, social, and mental development, but for some reason they fail to reach their academic achievement potential in school (Gallahue 1996). Craft (1990, 177) explains four factors commonly used to describe learning disabilities that may help you detect students with learning disabilities in your classes.

1. Academic performance does not match intellectual potential.

2. There are learning problems that are not caused by mental retardation, emotional disturbance, or environmental disadvantage.

3. Development of cognitive, affective, and motor skills is uneven.

4. Clear signs of central nervous system dysfunction may or may not be present.

Learning disabilities are highly complex and unique to the individual. The causes of learning disabilities are largely unknown and are a key area of investigation for researchers. We do suspect, though, that neurological, genetic, and environmental factors may be the causes of learning disabilities.

A student with a learning disability has difficulty receiving and processing information. Information processing includes four stages, initiated by an external stimulus: sensory input, decision making, output or behavior, and feedback for the assessment and planning of future information processing (Craft 1990). Craft explains that students with learning disabilities may experience a breakdown in one or more stages of the information-processing cycle. For example, one student in your class may have difficulty watching demonstrations or listening to instructions. This student has trouble attending to external stimuli and thus may have difficulty with sensory input. Another student may pay attention in class but have difficulty performing motor tasks. This student may know what to do and how but be unable to translate that information from sensory input through the decision-making and output stages. She thus appears uncoordinated and clumsy. Students with learning disabilities will exhibit many combinations of difficulty with information-processing stages. Your responsibility is to help identify those difficulties and provide students with opportunities to work through them. Many characteristics of learning disabilities illustrate a breakdown in one or more stages of information processing.

Students with learning disabilities are unique, just like every student in your class. Effective instructional strategies are those that are multisensory. Consult chapter 6 for more information regarding students with disabilities.

Creating Effective Learning Environments in Physical Education

A wise professor once told us, "Now that you have a lot of information about this subject, so what? How do you make sense of it and how will you apply it to your teaching?" At first, we thought she was being sarcastic when she asked, "So what?" We soon realized that her short question was profound. We ask the question again here. Now that you have a better understanding of how students in physical education classes learn, so what?

Making sense of how students learn so that you can establish effective learning environments and improve your teaching in physical education is the next step. Although we will discuss effective learning environments in detail in chapters 7 and 9, we want to leave you with a few important points here.

    Students will achieve at higher levels when they have a more continuous learning environment.

The lesson here is that less is more. That's right—less is more. Imagine that you are starting your first day on a new job. When you arrive at the locker room, your supervisor gives you a lock and locker and tells you that you must report to your spot in the gymnasium within 7 minutes of the ringing of the bell. Once on your spot, the supervisor tells you that you have 30 minutes or less, three to four times each week, to learn and complete the tasks of your job. You are told to keep quiet and stand in long lines while waiting to perform. In addition, you learn that your job and your supervisor will change every three weeks. You may do well in your new job, be labeled "talented," and earn good ratings. Others will do OK, and still others will be labeled "dumb." They may lose interest in the job, or even lose the job. After nine months at this job, you move on to the next level and start the process again. You have no control over any of these rules or procedures. How do you feel? How will you perform? What will be the quality of your work? Of course, many students in traditional physical education classes may feel this way. Darling-Hammond (1998) strongly encourages us to challenge the educational system or the physical education system that we inherit as teachers. One way to do that is to provide our youngsters with units of content that allow for learning to take place. As we discussed in chapter 1, units should be four weeks long or longer in middle school and at least eight weeks long in high school. Units of that length allow students to learn the skills and concepts they need to become physically active for the rest of their lives.

Motor learning should encourage thinking.

Our students should learn to think as well as move in physical education. We should make every effort to make learning purposeful and meaningful for our students and steer away from conditioned responses that require no thinking (Nichols 1994). This process should include how the body moves and how to vary movements depending on conditions. One way to help students achieve higher levels of cognition is to have them engage in the movement processes of perceiving, refining, vary-

ing, applying, and creating (Nichols 1994). In the process of perceiving, we introduce the student to a concept or motor skill. Here the student will develop an understanding of how to perform the skill and identify several cues that will help him perform the skill. Once the student perceives the task, he focuses on refining the skill. He gives attention to mastering the fundamental mechanics of each skill or concept involved. For instance, in a softball unit when students are learning to catch the ball, they would pay particular attention to lining up the body with the ball when fielding a grounder. Next, they would give attention to varying the conditions in which they performed the skill. You can see that this type of practice would help a student move from the motor stage to the autonomous stage. Applying skills and concepts to appropriate situations would follow. Students would learn to analyze complex and changing environments and apply the appropriate skill or concept. Once students have established the foundation of perceiving, refining, varying, and applying, they can work on creating their own movements to match complex and changing situations. As teachers we will create tasks that enable students to practice perceiving, refining, varying, applying, and creating. The teaching styles presented in chapter 8 will give you ideas about how to do this.

Students should learn reflective strategies.

Metacognition is awareness and monitoring of one's own learning. Helping students explore and examine how they learn will enhance their ability to learn physical education content. Reflection will help students identify errors and provide corrective feedback to themselves and others. Metacognition strategies should include having students plan, monitor, and regulate their own behavior, give feedback to themselves and others, and assess improvement in motor-skill performance and knowledge. Using the teaching styles you will learn about in chapter 8 will be key to helping your students become competent at metacognition.

The learning environment should be positive and emotionally supportive.

Students learn best in an environment where it is safe to take risks and explore learning potential. The learning environment should be social. Students should have many opportunities to work collaboratively and cooperatively with other students. When students work together we note a scaffolding effect. In other words, students witness other perceptions, interpretations, performances, and answers to content. As a result they examine lesson content in depth and from differing perspectives. For challenged and gifted students alike, a social environment will stretch cognitive, social, personal, and motor abilities (Wolfe and Brandt 1998). Positive and emotionally supportive environments provide an enjoyable atmosphere that promotes exploration and the fun of learning. Chapter 9 will explore this concept further.

Teachers should use multiple instructional strategies.

Teachers should strive to use all the senses of their students, although not necessarily all at once (Wolfe and Brandt 1998). By using a variety of instructional strategies, teachers can capitalize on the preferred learning modalities of each student, such as visual, auditory, tactile, and kinesthetic, as well as each student's preferred intelligence. Chapters 2 and 8 should help you understand more about how to use multiple instructional strategies.

As students work to connect to content, teachers should connect to students.

We understand the importance of helping students find meaning in what they are learning. We also know that students must find ways to apply what they learn to what they know to internalize learning and transfer it from one situation to another. In addition, research findings show that students do better when they build positive personal relationships with their teachers. Students who are simply a number in a squad may not achieve their academic potential in physical education. Smaller class sizes and blocked time will help teachers get to know their students better. Most of the responsibility of getting to know students rests on the shoulder of the teacher. Building a relationship takes time. When teachers see between 150 and 200 students per day, it may be the middle of the school year before they form a relationship with half to two-thirds of their students. Teachers should make a strong effort to overcome any barriers that might prevent them from getting to know their students and how they learn best.

Summary

Based on findings from cognitive research and motor learning, we know that students are unique and learn in different ways. Students do not predictably transfer knowledge from one situation to another. They are not empty barges waiting for physical educators to load them with the knowledge, wisdom, and skills they will need to sail away and be successful in life. Student learning is not just a cause-and-effect response; it is deeply related to the meaning students create for their learning. When we understand these three points, we increase students' potential to learn in our classes. Brain research tells us that a person's IQ is not fixed at birth and that the brain continues to develop, particularly when we provide individuals with hands-on practical experiences. The model of multiple intelligences informs us that students may have different kinds of intelligence. We know about at least eight forms. Students in our classes may have strength in some of these intelligences but not in others. By offering students activities that incorporate multiple intelligences, we may help students connect with and make sense of the content they are learning. Metacognition is a process by which students monitor their learning. Providing activities that help students learn how to set personal goals and self-assess their learning progress makes them reflective learners, critical thinkers, and problem solvers. Brain-based research, multiple intelligences, and metacognition represent findings in cognitive theory. Turning our attention to motor learning, we understand that students pass through three stages as they practice and acquire motor skill competency: verbal-cognitive, motor, and autonomous. We must remember that all students are unique and that some will come to us with learning disabilities. Learning disabilities may include characteristics such as inattention, distractibility, perceptual deficits, disorganization, and impulsivity. All this information reinforces the need for us to use a variety of instructional strategies in physical education to maximize student learning.

Checking for Understanding ►►►

- What are the three domains of Bloom's taxonomy? Why are they important to learning in physical education?

- What are the eight multiple intelligences? Of the eight multiple intelligences, which one best represents the way you learn and why?

- What is metacognition and why is it important in physical education?

- What are the three stages of motor learning? Why is it possible for a middle school or high school student to be in any motor-learning stage?

- What are learning disabilities?

- What are the six attributes of effective learning environments?

For Reflection and Discussion ►►►

- List several scenarios about why Sandy did not excel in Devon's track and field unit.

- Apply the components of the cognitive domain to student learning in physical education.

- Apply the components of the affective domain to student learning in physical education.

- Plan a physical education unit or lesson and prepare several instructional strategies that will engage students in several multiple intelligences.

- How do we include students with learning disabilities in our classes?

References

Berryman, S.E. 1991. Designing effective learning environments: Cognitive apprenticeship models. *Brief from the Institute on Education and the Economy.* New York: Teacher College, Columbia University.

Bloom, B.S., ed. 1956. *Taxonomy of educational objectives, Handbook I: Cognitive domain.* New York: McKay.

Boggeman, S., T. Hoerr, and C. Wallach. 1996. *Succeeding with multiple intelligences: Teaching through the personal intelligences.* New City School. St. Louis, MO.

Checkley, K. 1997. The first seven . . . and the eight: A conversation with Howard Gardner. *Educational Leadership* 55(1):8–13.

Corbin, C.B. 1976. *Becoming physically educated in the elementary school.* 2nd ed. Philadelphia: Lea & Febiger.

Corbin, C.B. 2002. Physical activity for everyone: What every physical educator should know about promoting lifelong physical activity. *Journal of Teaching in Physical Education* 21(2):128–144.

Craft, D. 1990. Learning disabilities. In *Adapted physical education and sport,* edited by J.P. Winnick. Champaign, IL: Human Kinetics.

Craft, D. 2000. Learning disabilities and attention deficits. In *Adapted physical education and sport,* 3rd ed. Edited by J.P. Winnick. Champaign, IL: Human Kinetics.

Darling-Hammond, L. 1998. *Using standards to support student success.* Restructuring brief: A publication of the California Professional Development Consortia. No. 15., 1–8.

Diamond, M., and J. Hopson, eds. 1998. *Magic trees of the mind: How to nurture your child's intelligence, creativity, and healthy emotions from birth through adolescence.* New York: Plume/Penguin.

Fitts, P.M., and M.I. Posner. 1967. *Human performance.* Belmont, CA: Brooks/Cole.

Gallahue, D.L. 1996. *Developmental physical education for today's children.* 3rd ed. Madison, WI: WCB Brown and Benchmark.

Gardner, H. 1983. *Frames of mind: The theory of multiple intelligences.* New York: Basic Books.

Goleman, D. 1997. *Emotional intelligence: Why it can matter more than IQ.* New York: Bantam.

Graham, G., S.A. Holt/Hale, and M. Parker. 1998. *Children moving: A reflective approach to teaching physical education.* 4th ed. Mountain View, CA: Mayfield.

Guignon, A. 1998. *Multiple intelligence: A theory for everyone.* Wallingford, CT: Education World. **www.education-world.com/a_curr/curr054.shtml**.

Harrison, J.M., C.L. Blakemore, M.M. Buck, and T.L. Pellett. 1996. *Instructional strategies for secondary school physical education.* Dubuque, IA: Brown and Benchmark.

Jacobson, R. 1998. Teachers improving learning using metacognition with self monitoring learning strategies. *Education.* 118 (4):579–90.

Magill, R.A. 1989. *Motor learning: Concepts and applications.* 3rd ed. Dubuque, IA: Wm. C. Brown.

National Association for Sport and Physical Education (NASPE). 1995. *Moving into the future: National standards for physical education.* Reston, VA: National Association for Sport and Physical Education.

Nichols, B. 1994. *Moving and learning. The elementary school physical education experience.* St. Louis: Mosby.

Rink, J.E. 1998. Motor learning. In *Concepts of physical education: What every student needs to know,* ed. Bonnie Mohnsen. Reston, VA: National Association for Sport and Physical Education.

Wolfe, P., and R. Brandt. 1998. What do we know from brain research? *Educational Leadership* 56(3):8–13.

Suggested Readings

Allen, L., and J.W. Santrock. 1993. *Psychology: The contexts of behavior.* Madison, WI: WCB Brown and Benchmark.

Bogan, M.B. 1998. Metacognition in environmental education: A study of the relationship between the manifest and received curriculum. *College Student Journal* 32(1):93–111.

Bruer, J.T. 1998. Brain science, brain fiction. *Educational Leadership* 56(3):14–18.

Cicourel, A.V. 1974. *Cognitive sociology: Language and meaning in social interaction.* New York: Free Press.

D'Arcangelo, M. 1998. The brains behind the brain. *Educational Leadership* 56(3):20–25.

Dickinson, D. 1998. Learning through many kinds of intelligence. *New Horizons for Learning: Electronic Journal* [Online]. Available: **www.newhorizons.org/art_/rnthrumi.html**.

Fosnot, C.T., ed. 1996. *Constructivism: Theory, perspectives and practice.* New York: Teachers College Press.

Furth, H.G., and H. Wachs. 1972. *Thinking goes to school: Piaget's theory into practice.* New York: Oxford University Press.

Gardner, H. 1991. *The unschooled mind: How children think and how schools should teach.* New York: Basic Books.

Gardner, H. 1991. *To open minds: Chinese clues to the dilemma of contemporary education.* New York: Basic Books.

Gardner, H. 1993. *Multiple intelligences: The theory in practice.* New York: Basic Books.

Jones, B.F., A.S. Palincsar, D.S. Ogle, and E.G. Carr. 1987. *Strategic teaching and learning: Cognitive instruction in the content areas.* Alexandria, VA: Association for Supervision and Curriculum Development.

Lederman, N.G., and M.L. Neiss. 1998. What's in style. *School Science and Mathematics* 98(2):57–59.

Lowery, L. 1998. How new science curriculums reflect brain research. *Educational Leadership* 56(3):26–30.

Marshall, H.H., ed. 1992. *Redefining student learning: Roots of educational change.* Norwood, NJ: Ablex.

Mettetal, G., C. Jordan, and S.M. Harper.1998. Attitudes towards a multiple intelligence curriculum. *Journal of Education Research* 91(2):115–122.

Mohnsen, B.S. 1997. *Teaching middle school physical education: A blueprint for developing an exemplary program.* Champaign, IL: Human Kinetics.

Payne, V.G., and L.D. Isaacs. 1995. *Human motor development: A lifespan approach.* 3rd ed. Mountain View, CA: Mayfield.

Resnick, L.B., and L.E. Klopfer. 1989. *Toward the thinking curriculum: Current cognitive research. 1989 Yearbook of the Association for Supervision and Curriculum Development.* Alexandria, VA: Association for Supervision and Curriculum Development.

Silver, H., and R. Strong. 1997. Integrating learning styles and multiple intelligences. *Educational Leadership* 55(1):22–27.

Slywester, R., and J-Y Cho. 1992. What brain research says about paying attention. *Educational Leadership* 50(4):71–76.

Swanson, P.N. 1998. Teaching effective strategies to students with learning and reading disabilities. *Intervention in School and Clinic* 33(4):209–18.

Sweet, S. 1998. A lesson learned about multiple intelligences. *Educational Leadership* 56(3):50–51.

Thomas, A.M. 1991. *Beyond education: A new perspective on society's management of learning.* San Francisco: Jossey-Bass.

Tishman, S., D.N. Perkins, and E. Jay. 1995. *The thinking classroom: Learning and teaching in a culture of thinking.* Boston, MA: Allyn & Bacon.

Tomlinson, C.A., and M.L. Kalbfleishch. 1998. Teach me, teach my brain: A call for differentiated classrooms. *Educational Leadership* 56(3):52–55.

Winnick, J.P., ed. 1990. *Adapted physical education and sport.* Champaign, IL: Human Kinetics.

6

Including Students With Disabilities

A child miseducated is a child lost.

— *John F. Kennedy*

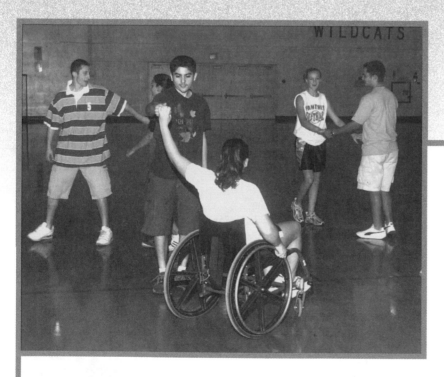

Joan Montgomery is a new teacher at Central High School. She just graduated from college with a teaching credential, so this is her first teaching job. Joan's schedule includes two sections of freshmen, two sections of sophomores, and one section of juniors and seniors. Today is the first day of school, and she will be meeting her junior and senior weight-training and fitness class during first period. The juniors and seniors are sitting in the bleachers waiting for class to begin when Joan enters the gym. She introduces herself, conducts several instant activities that help students become acquainted with one another, passes out her weight-training syllabus, explains class rules briefly, and begins the tedious process of assigning lockers and locks. Joan looks up from the table where she's sitting to greet the next student and finds him at eye level. She didn't see this student during class. Greg gives Ms. Montgomery a big smile, offers his hand, and says, "Hi, I'm Greg McFarlene, and I've just been reassigned to this class." Joan greets Greg back, shakes his hand, takes his schedule, and notices that this friendly student is in a wheelchair.

Greg asked to have a locker on the bottom row at the beginning of an aisle. He explained that a locker there would give him more room for wheeling around. Greg also asked if he could bring a key lock because combination locks were difficult for him to maneuver. In addition, he said that he would be on time for class but could use a head start of a few minutes at the end to change in time for the bell. Joan, impressed with this young man's maturity, agreed and realized that she would not have thought of those details on her own.

During her second period prep, Joan reflected on first period. She was excited to have a full class of 32 students. Wednesday the class would dress out and begin weight training and fitness training. She wondered how Greg would do. She also wondered how she would help accommodate Greg's needs in class. Suddenly, Joan began looking for her notes and resources about working with people with disabilities. She also wondered whether Greg had an established IEP. She would have to ask in the office as well as ask Greg about that. Joan wanted to make sure that Greg and other students with disabilities felt included in her classes. She knew that she would have to work hard to make sure that all students felt included.

Learning Objectives

After reading this chapter you will be able to

- demonstrate general knowledge of disability laws,
- express awareness for students with disabilities,
- examine strategies for modifying physical education instruction in order to meet student needs,
- define IEP,
- explain the process for developing and implementing a student IEP,
- reflect on your own open mindedness toward people with disabilities, and
- describe the steps you will need to take to achieve inclusion in your classroom.

Key Terms and Phrases

P.L. 94-142
IDEA
Section 504
Individualized Education Program (IEP)
Transition plans
Cognitive delays
Intellectual impairment
Down's syndrome
Fetal alcohol syndrome
Fragile X syndrome
Learning disabilities
Attention-deficit disorder/hyperactivity
Asthma
Diabetes
Cerebral palsy
Epilepsy
Spina bifida
Arthritis

As mentioned in chapter 3, adolescent growth and development is based on observations of youth without disabilities. Although we can predict general growth and maturation patterns in youth without disabilities, these patterns vary from one individual to the next. Growth and development information can aid our understanding of all students, including students with disabilities.

Remember that motor-skill acquisition is a highly complex process that depends on the "integrity of the motor system and complex interaction between maturation and experience" (McClenaghan 1990). Delayed motor-skill acquisition in adolescents with disabilities is often the result of some impairment to the motor system coupled with limited opportunities for motor-skill practice.

Children with learning disabilities, mental retardation, developmental delays, sensory impairments, central nervous impairments, musculoskeletal impairments, and chronic diseases may have delayed motor development (McClenaghan 1990; Auxter, Pyfer, and Huettig 1997). As physical educators we have a responsibility to provide students with disabilities an inclusive and nonrestrictive environment for learning. To do so, we must identify student needs, develop learning objectives, and provide appropriate learning activities for students. This process is typically written down and formalized into an individualized education program, or IEP.

To help students effectively, physical educators need to understand not only human growth and development and motor development but also general characteristics associated with various disabilities. Because many disabilities and impairments affect our students, and because each student is unique in ability and need, your ability to seek appropriate resources and help will be critical to your success in providing meaningful physical education experiences to students with disabilities.

Purpose

Use technology to provide assistance and obtain ideas for teaching students of various ages and with various needs.

Resource and Procedure

Select a couple of Web resources that are set up to provide support for physical educators facing special needs. Investigate documents, adapted lesson plans, funding opportunities, and support sources. Web sites mentioned earlier in the book could be good starting points, but information on individualized education programs can be located at **www.washington.edu/doit.**

Disability Law

The number of children and youth with disabling conditions is increasing each year. According to the year 2000 annual report submitted to Congress by the Department of Education, Office of Special Education and Rehabilitative Services (OSERS 2000), 5.5 million children ages 6 through 21 received educational services in the United States, including Puerto Rico. Of the 5.5 million, 2.5 million were ages 12 through 17. These data were based on a count conducted in 1998 with an update completed in 1999. The OSERS annual report categorizes children by disability as well as by ethnicity and disability. Figure 6.1 is an overview of the numbers of children and youth (ages 6–18) served, by disability. For more detailed information about numbers and ethnicities served, visit their Web site at **www.ed.gov/offices/OSERS/OSEP/Products/OSEP2000AnlRpt**.

The number of students with disabilities continues to grow at a rate greater than the rate of growth in population or student enrollment. State reports indicate that improved methods for diag-

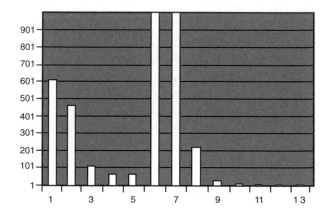

Index:
1. Mental Retardation = 610,000
2. Emotional Disturbance = 463,000
3. Multiple Disabilities = 107,000
4. Hearing Impairments = 70,000
5. Orthopedic Impairments = 69,000
6. Learning Disabled = 2.8 million
7. Speech/Language Impairment = 1.1 million
8. Other Health Impairments = 220,000
9. Visual Impairments = 26,000
10. Autism = 5,300
11. Deaf/Blindness = 1,600
12. Traumatic Brain Injury =1,200
13. Developmental Delay = 1,100

Figure 6.1 Number of children and youth (ages 6–18) served, by disability.

noses and identification are the primary reasons for increased numbers (OSERS 2000). Improved diagnostics and increased educational services are the direct results of disability laws.

Purpose

Use the Web as a resource to help you adapt fitness activities for students with particular illnesses and conditions.

Resource and Procedure

Check out the Web MD site at **www.webmd.com** and access the interactive search engine that allows you to search the entire site for information on specific conditions. You will then have access to numerous reference materials that help you in choosing safe alternative variations of activities. You will also know what signs to look for when a student may be unable to complete a particular activity.

The year 2000 marked the 25th anniversary of the passage of **Public Law (P.L.) 94-142**, the Education for All Handicapped Children Act. Before the act became law, educational services were minimum to nonexistent for children and youth with special needs. Many children who were deaf, blind, or had emotional and behavioral problems received no services. Children with mental retardation and other severe developmental disabilities did not receive services; instead, they were institutionalized. Today, data illustrate that most of these children live at home and receive special services and education through public schools (OSERS 2000). In 1997–1998 75% of the 5.5 million youths from 6 through 21 years of age with disabilities were educated in public schools with their able-bodied peers.

When P.L. 94-142 was passed, Congress was concerned that many students with special needs would not be identified. This concern spurred the passage of the 1975 amendment that focused on "child find," or identifying students with disabilities. This amendment helped to improve processes and evaluation techniques for identifying children and youth with special needs.

In the 1980s implementation of P.L. 94-142 was emphasized. Each year educators improved educational programs and services for students with disabilities. Three important transitions occurred in this decade. First, parents were strongly encouraged to play a central role in making education decisions for their children. Second, legislation (P.L. 99-457) addressed preschool and toddler education and programs. Third, secondary school programs were required to focus on transition skills and **transition plans** that would lead to independent living after graduation (Auxter, Pyfer, and Huettig 1997).

For 15 years P.L. 94-142 referred to children as handicapped. The 1990s brought a change in terminology reflecting a change in the nation's attitude. In the 1990 Individuals with Disabilities Education Act (**IDEA**, P.L. 101-476), Congress changed all references to "handicapped children" to "children with disabilities" (OSERS 2000). The intent was to inform the public that disability is a natural part of the human experience and that individuals with disabilities deserve all the rights and privileges afforded other citizens in this country. In addition, the 1990 IDEA continued to improve services and programs for children with disabilities.

The 1996 IDEA strengthened services to at-risk children. Amendments to IDEA passed in 1997 provided several important changes to the existing law (Winnick 2000). First, it included provisions for free appropriate education to all children with disabilities aged 3 through 21. Second, it provided an extension to the provision for developmental delay for children aged 3 through 9. Third, the amendment emphasized educational results and required that children with disabilities receive progress reports similar to those provided to students without disabilities. Fourth, changes were made to the IEP process (Winnick 2000).

Given all the amendments to IDEA over the years, the original tenets have remained intact since 1975:

1. To ensure that all children with disabilities have an opportunity to receive free appropriate public education that emphasizes special education and related services designed to meet their needs

2. To ensure that the rights of children with disabilities and their parents or guardians are protected

3. To assist states and communities in providing for the education of all children with disabilities

4. To assess and ensure the effectiveness of efforts to educate children with disabilities

Students who do not qualify for services under IDEA may be eligible for services under **Section 504** of the Rehabilitation Act (1973) (Auxter, Pyfer, and Huettig 1997). Students who qualify under Section 504 may include those with the following conditions:

- Drug or alcohol dependency
- Attention deficit disorder or attention deficit hyperactivity disorder
- Communicable diseases including human immunodeficiency virus (HIV)
- Learning disabilities without severe discrepancy between ability and achievement
- Social maladjustment
- Other health compromises such as insulin-dependent diabetes, asthma, severe allergies, arthritis, epilepsy, and temporary disabilities (modified from Auxter, Pyfer, and Huettig 1997)

Over the past 25 years amendments and legislation have continued to expand the educational services and programs provided to all children and youth with disabilities.

IEP Process

P.L. 94-142 and the amendments and legislation that followed have had a direct effect on physical education programs. Physical education was specifically included in the writing of P.L. 94-142 back in 1975. The primary purpose of physical education programs for students with disabilities is to help improve students' quality of life. Educators can accomplish this by focusing on the development of physical and motor fitness, fundamental motor skills, and movement concepts and specialized skills like those found in aquatics, dance, and individual and group games and sports (Auxter, Pyfer, and Huettig 1997) (figure 6.2). Delivering appropriate, high-quality physical education to students with disabilities will require physical educators to follow curriculum, use student-centered instructional strategies, modify activities to meet students needs, and determine and implement student individualized education programs (IEPs).

The **Individualized Education Program (IEP)** is required for all who have been identified as students with special needs and disabilities (Houston-Wilson and Lieberman 1999). All teachers, including physical educators who provide services to students with disabilities, must be involved in the IEP process. If you have not had access to the

Figure 6.2   A goal of physical education programs for the past quarter century has been to integrate disabled students into the general student population and teach them the same fundamental skills and movement concepts.

IEP process, or if you have simply been overlooked, consult your principal or special education director about the matter. Ask to be involved in the IEP process for students in your physical education classes (Houston-Wilson and Lieberman 1999).

All IEPs include physical education. The extent to which a student can participate in regular physical education classes depends on the student's abilities. Some students with disabilities are able to participate in regular physical education classes without modifications. Others will require teachers to make modifications. We refer to modifications of regular physical education as adapted physical education. The IEP will reflect modifications that students with disabilities need for physical education.

The IEP process follows deliberate steps. First, the student is identified as possibly needing special education, adapted physical education, and related services. Next, the student is evaluated using reliable instruments that will help determine education performance. An evaluative statement about a student's present level of physical education performance is also necessary. Physical education performance may include descriptions of

- motor output, including evidence of sensory input system dysfunction, inappropriate reflex behavior, sensory integration deficit, and motor-planning deficit;
- locomotor, nonlocomotor, and manipulative competency;
- physical fitness level;
- ability to participate in a variety of dance, games, and sport activities;
- ability to engage in leisure and recreation activities; and
- ability to use community-based resources to fulfill movement and participation needs (Auxter, Pyfer, and Huettig 1997, 62–63).

After evaluations take place, a qualified team reviews the findings and decides if the student is eligible for special education and related services. If the student is eligible, the IEP team has 30 days to meet and write an IEP. Specific individuals make up an IEP team. A team member may fill more than one team position if he or she is qualified to do so. Members include the student when appropriate, parents or guardians, a special education teacher, an evaluation interpreter, individuals with knowledge or expertise about the child, regular teachers including physical educators, a school-system representative, and transition services agency representatives. The team writes out the steps and immediately implements them. The IEP team continues to meet periodically to assess student progress on the IEP. Goals are measured and evaluated annually, and the IEP is reassessed and revised.

IEP content is specific and includes the following sections (OSERS 2000; Auxter, Pyfer, and Huettig 1997):

1. Current performance: This is an assessment of student's education performance.

2. Annual goals: Goals that a student can reasonably achieve in one school year. Goals may address academic, social, and behavioral needs. All goals must be measurable so that progress may be determined.

3. Short-term instructional objectives: Goals are broad measurable statements. Objectives are more specific and measurable statements. Short-term instructional objectives should be stepping-stones toward achieving annual goals.

4. Special education and related services: The IEP should list all the special education and related services that will be provided to the student. An example of a related service would be assistance provided by an adapted physical education specialist or occupational specialist to a physical educator who cannot fulfill progress on specific motor skills and movement concepts. Another example would be professional development and training provided as a means of helping the student.

5. Participation with nondisabled students: The IEP includes a statement that describes the extent of the student's participation with nondisabled students.

6. Participation in state and districtwide tests: The IEP must state clearly modifications that will be made to the administration of required achievement tests.

7. Dates and places: An IEP must clearly state when services begin and end, how often they will be provided, where they will be provided, and how long services will last.

8. Transition (ITP) service needs: When a student becomes 14, the IEP must address a student's transition service needs with a statement about the courses and services the student needs to reach his or her postschool goals.

9. Needed transition services: When a student becomes 16, an IEP must include a statement about what transition services the student needs to prepare to leave school.

10. Age of majority: One year before a student reaches legal age, the IEP must include a statement that the student has been informed of any rights that will transfer to him or her on attaining legal age.

11. Measuring progress: The IEP must clearly spell out assessment techniques used to evaluate progress on goals and objectives. In addition, the IEP must state how parents will be informed of that progress.

See figure 6.3 for an example of an IEP. Note that the law doesn't specify the format of an IEP. Therefore, you may find that IEPs vary in format from school to school.

TRINITY COUNTY SPECIAL EDUCATION LOCAL PLAN AREA
INDIVIDUALIZED EDUCATION PROGRAM

IEP Date: _____   Page _____ of _____

ANNUAL GOALS AND BENCHMARKS/SHORT-TERM OBJECTIVES

22. Student: _Amanda Smith_

Informed of Progress: ☒ Quarterly ☐ Trimester ☐ Semester ☐ Other: _____

How? ☐ Annotated Goals/Obj. ☐ Summary Progress Report ☐ Other: _____

Area of Need: _____ ☐ Enables student to be involved/progress in general curriculum and/or
☐ Addresses other educational needs resulting from the disability

---

23. Annual Measurable Goal # _____   **By June 1st**

Amanda will serve a volleyball over the net from 30 feet successfully 4/5 times.

Baseline:
Amanda can currently hit a beachball for a serve with proper mechanics and minimal assistance.   **(Nat. Standard #1)**

Person(s) Responsible: ☐ Teacher ☒ Specialist ☐ Student ☐ Parent ☐ Other: _____

Reviewed: ___/___/___
☐ Met ☐ Not Met
Comment:

---

24. Benchmark/Short-Term Objective: By _5/1_

Amanda will serve a volleyball over the net from 15 feet on 4/5 trials.

Reviewed: ___/___/___
☐ Met ☐ Not Met

Benchmark/Short-Term Objective: By _5/11_

Amanda will serve a volleyball over the net from 20 feet on 4/5 trials.

Reviewed: ___/___/___
☐ Met ☐ Not Met

Benchmark/Short-Term Objective: By _5/19_

Amanda will serve a volleyball over the net from 25 feet on 4/5 trials.

Reviewed: ___/___/___
☐ Met ☐ Not Met

Area of Need: _____ ☐ Enables student to be involved/progress in general curriculum and/or
☐ Addresses other educational needs resulting from the disability

---

Annual Measurable Goal # _____   **By June 1st**

By June 1st Amanda will demonstrate positive social behavior by complimenting or giving high fives to three other classmates during PE on 3 consecutive days.   **(Nat Standard #5)**

Baseline:

Person(s) Responsible: ☐ Teacher ☒ Specialist ☐ Student ☐ Parent ☐ Other: _____

Reviewed: ___/___/___
☐ Met ☐ Not Met
Comment:

Benchmark/Short-Term Objective: By _5/3_
Amanda will demonstrate positive social behavior by refraining from any negative comments to classmates on 3 consecutive days.

Reviewed: ___/___/___
☐ Met ☐ Not Met

Benchmark/Short-Term Objective: By _5/11_
Amanda will demonstrate positive social behavior by giving one positive comment or high five to a classmate on 3 consecutive days.

Reviewed: ___/___/___
☐ Met ☐ Not Met

Benchmark/Short-Term Objective: By _5/19_
Amanda will demonstrate positive social behavior by giving 2 positive comments or high fives to a classmate on 3 consecutive days.

Reviewed: ___/___/___
☐ Met ☐ Not Met

Parent Initial _____

Figure 6.3 Example of an IEP form.
Adapted, by permission, from Trinity County Special Education.

T n T For further information on IEPs examine *A Guide to the Individualized Education Program* (OSERS 2000) at **www.ed.gov/offices/OSERS/OSEP/Products/IEP_Guide**.

Your Turn ▶▶▶

◆ Examine what you have just learned about the Individuals with Disabilities Education Act and discuss its effect on physical education classes.

◆ All adolescents might benefit from an individualized education program (IEP). Why should students with disabilities have special consideration under the law?

Overview of Disabilities

Children and youth are protected by IDEA and Section 504 of the Rehabilitation Act, which states that public schools must provide an education in an inclusive and unrestrictive environment.

We will cover the broad categories of impairments in this chapter, but examining these impairments in depth is beyond the scope of this book. We encourage you to seek further information from credible Web pages, texts, and other information sources.

Cognitive Delays and Intellectual Impairments

We understand today that **cognitive delays** and **intellectual impairments** are dynamic processes that respond well to appropriate stimuli. In the past, people diagnosed with cognitive delays and intellectual impairments were considered incurable, and they were institutionalized (Auxter, Pyfer, and Huettig 1997). Society once considered mental retardation genetic and unresponsive to environmental conditions. People with forms of mental retardation were taken from their homes and loved ones and placed in institutions where they were looked after for the duration of their lives. After decades of research, we now know that improvements to cognitive abilities depend on the readiness of the individual and appropriate stimulus from the environment. Because of these findings

and years of educational program development, individuals with cognitive and intellectual impairments today have more opportunities to learn, work, recreate, and contribute to the community (Auxter, Pyfer, and Huettig 1997; Krebs 2000).

As a nation, we tend to group many people into the category of having cognitive delays and intellectual impairments. Because individuals in this group are so diverse in their cognitive abilities, no single set of characteristics defines them. Some general characteristics, however, may guide your search for the best strategies to include these individuals in your classes.

We have established that cognitive abilities and intellect vary greatly among individuals with developmental delays. It stands to reason, then, that some people may also appear clumsy and awkward, have difficulty with balance, and lack the ability to perform motor tasks efficiently. According to Auxter, Pyfer, and Huettig (1997), a review of literature reveals that a number of perceptual and cognitive characteristics may inhibit the learning of motor skills. Individuals with cognitive delays may have had less practice with motor skills, and they may have slower movement times. Individuals may have language difficulties that inhibit their ability to communicate. Some individuals with cognitive delays and intellectual impairments may have difficulty with postural reflexes; thus they may have trouble grasping things or holding up their heads. Cognitive impairments also contribute to less developed cardiorespiratory systems, which in turn play a part in poor fitness levels. In addition, those with cognitive impairments may be slower or less able to interact spontaneously with dynamic movement environments. But because cognitive abilities continue to grow and develop with chronological age and in effective environments, physical educators can create programs that meet individual needs and contribute to fitness and cognitive development.

The three most common causes of cognitive delays and intellectual impairments are (1) Down's syndrome, (2) fetal alcohol syndrome (FAS), and (3) fragile X syndrome.

Down's Syndrome

Down's syndrome is the most common chromosomal disorder that leads to cognitive delays and intellectual impairments (figure 6.4). Down's syndrome most often results from an extra #21 chromosome, giving the individual 47 chromosomes instead of the normal 46. Approximately 5,000 children are born with Down's syndrome each year

Figure 6.4 Effective physical education programs are believed to improve the physical and psychomotor abilities of people with Down's syndrome.

(Krebs 2000). Many children with Down's syndrome have IQ scores between 25 and 50. Researchers and educators believe that effective physical education programs greatly improve the physical and psychomotor abilities of people with Down's syndrome.

Fetal Alcohol Syndrome

Fetal alcohol syndrome (FAS) is caused by a mother's abuse of alcohol during pregnancy. Alcohol impairs the brain development of the fetus, resulting in cognitive delays and intellectual impairments. FAS is the leading cause of cognitive delays and intellectual impairments in live births. The severity of impairments relates directly to the level of alcohol abuse (heavy to mild) by the mother. FAS typically results in poor motor coordination, hypotonia, and attention deficit/hyperactivity disorders (Auxter, Pyfer, and Huettig 1997).

Fragile X Syndrome

Fragile X syndrome (FXS) is considered the most common inherited cause of cognitive delays and impairments (1 in 1,250 males and 1 in 2,250 females). FXS is caused by an abnormal X chromo-

some that looks fragile at its ends. FXS appears more often in males because they only have one X chromosome (XY). Because females have two X chromosomes (XX) a healthy X can cover for an abnormal one. Children with FXS may be hyperactive, experience attention deficits, and demonstrate aggressive outbursts. In addition, children with FXS may experience poor balance, poor coordination, and tactile defensiveness (Auxter, Pyfer, and Huettig 1997).

Down's syndrome, fetal alcohol syndrome, and fragile X syndrome are three common causes of cognitive delays and intellectual impairments in children. As a physical educator you will encounter these and others. To meet the needs of these students, you must work to create an inclusive environment. Remember that all children and youth with cognitive delays and intellectual impairments can grow and improve cognitive and motor function. You have the responsibility to create an unrestrictive and inclusive environment for these students. To accomplish this, consider doing the following:

- Assess student needs and performance abilities.
- Use effective methods for individualized instruction.

- Engage students in activities in which they will be successful.
- Facilitate interaction with other students and group activity.
- Be patient, reinforcing, and consistent in your behavior and expectations.
- Work to help the student make the transition to lifelong activity and community events.

Learning Disabilities

According to OSERS (2000) more than 2.8 million students between the ages of 6 and 12 are served under IDEA. Children and adolescents with learning disabilities form the largest group of learners with special needs in this country. The cause of learning disabilities is relatively unknown (Craft 2000). During your teaching career you will have the opportunity to work with many students with learning disabilities. Learning disabilities come in many forms. No single profile describes a student with a learning disability. That 12-year-old boy who seems bright but does poorly in classes may have a learning disability. Reading, organizing things, or distinguishing left from right may be difficult for him. He may perform motor tasks awkwardly and be unable to skip, walk on a balance beam, or change directions quickly in games.

The Education for All Handicapped Children Act (1975), P.L. 94-142, defines learning disability as

a disorder in one or more of the basic psychological processes involved in understanding or in using language, spoken or written, which may manifest itself in an imperfect ability to listen, think, speak, read, write, spell or do mathematical computations. The term includes such conditions as perceptual handicaps, brain injury, minimal brain dysfunction, dyslexia, and developmental aphasia. The term does not include children who have learning problems which are primarily the result of visual, hearing, or motor handicaps, of mental retardation, of emotional disturbance, or of environmental, cultural or economic disadvantage (section 121a.5(b)(9)).

Students with learning disabilities appear normal in physical, social, and mental development, but for some reason they fail to reach their academic achievement potential in school (Gallahue 1996). You may therefore be able to identify them. Craft (1990, 177) explains four factors that may help you identify students with learning disabilities in your classes.

1. Intellectual potential and academic performance do not match.
2. There are learning problems that are not caused by mental retardation, emotional disturbance, or environmental disadvantage.
3. Cognitive, affective, or motor development may be uneven.
4. Clear signs of central nervous system dysfunction may or may not be present.

Learning disabilities are highly complex and unique to the individual. The causes of learning disabilities are largely unknown; researchers continue to investigate the topic. We suspect, however, that neurological, genetic, and environmental factors play a role. For instance, neurological factors may imply some degree of brain damage that may have been caused by such circumstances as infection, trauma to the brain, anoxia, and fetal alcohol or drug syndrome (Craft 2000).

Incidence of genetic factors may be higher among youth whose parents and grandparents had characteristics of learning disabilities. Environmental factors may include such things as stimulus deprivation, limited opportunity for motor experiences, and lack of or minimum opportunity to develop academic readiness. The cause of learning disabilities may not always lie with the environment outside of school. Poor instructional practices, poor curricular choices, and inappropriate learning environments may be part of the cause of learning disabilities (Craft 1990, 179).

A student with a learning disability has difficulty receiving and processing information. Information processing includes four stages, initiated by an external stimulus: sensory input, decision making, output or behavior, and feedback for the assessment and planning of future information processing. Craft (1990) explains that students with learning disabilities may experience a breakdown in one or more stages of the information-processing cycle. For example, a student in your class may have difficulty watching demonstrations or listening to instructions. This student has trouble attending to external stimuli and thus may have difficulty with sensory input. Another student may pay attention in class but have difficulty performing motor tasks. This student may know what to do and how to do it but be unable to translate that information from sensory input through the decision-making and output stages. She thus appears uncoordinated and clumsy. Students with learning disabilities will exhibit many combinations of difficulty with information-processing stages. Your responsibility is to identify those difficulties and help students work through them. Many characteristics of learning disabilities illustrate a breakdown in information processing. Several characteristics—inattention, distractibility, perceptual deficits, disorganization, and impulsivity—may indicate that a student has a learning disability (Craft 1990, 179–182).

Students who have difficulty paying attention to tasks and controlling impulsive behavior may have **attention-deficit/hyperactivity disorder** (ADHD). You may have several students with attention-deficit/hyperactivity disorder. Students are often diagnosed with ADHD at an early age (four to six years old). Students with ADHD will have difficulty paying attention to instructions, tasks, assignments, and social interactions. You may find that they rush through their work carelessly, making many mistakes. They also may have difficulty organizing schoolwork or even their personal things. Students with ADHD may speak out of turn and behave in ways that are perceived as disruptive. According to Auxter, Pyfer, and Huettig (1997) 10 to 20% of the school-age population experience some form of ADHD. There are three identified disorders. Many of you may have heard of ADHD, which means attention deficit disorder with hyperactivity. ADHD is categorized by a short attention span, poor listening skills, impulsiveness, restlessness, and easy distractibility. Attention deficit disorder without hyperactivity (ADD-WO) is a condition in which students lose their thought patterns, show delays in delivering their responses, and experience delays in recalling names and descriptions of things. The third form of ADD is attention deficit disorder–residual (ADD-R), which identifies the adolescent who has not outgrown ADD. According to Auxter, Pyfer, and Huettig (1997) 30 to 60% of ADHD children do not outgrow their attention-deficit/hyperactivity disorders.

Like every other student, students with learning disabilities are unique. The most effective instructional strategies are multisensory, as explained in the next section and in chapter 8. In the meantime, you should be sure to determine the motor-functioning level of the student with a learning disability and then determine goals and activities that can improve motor deficiencies. You should establish daily routines and structured activities to assist students with learning disabilities.

Your Turn ▶▶▶

- ◆ Discuss how you will accommodate individuals with ADHD in your classes.
- ◆ What recreational activities are available in your community for people with cognitive delays? How can an individual become involved in these activities?

Chronic Illnesses

We believe that students with chronic illnesses benefit from physical activity and exercise. Increased fitness levels will benefit not only physical health but also emotional, psychological, and social well-being. You should identify youth with chronic illness in your classes and, when necessary, modify their physical education program to ensure participation and opportunities to experience success through physical activity. Many types of chronic illnesses affect our children and youth. The scope of this chapter and text will not permit us to provide information about many of them, but to broaden your awareness of youth with chronic illness, we have selected those that we have most often encountered in schools.

Asthma

Asthma is a chronic lung disease that is categorized by obstruction to the airways and airway inflammation (figure 6.5). People who live with asthma experience asthma "attacks." When this occurs three changes take place in the lungs. First, an excessive amount of mucus is produced. Mucus is thick and sticky and tends to clog the bronchial tubes. Second, the bronchial tubes swell, constricting the airways. Third, the muscles around the airways tighten. A student who experiences an asthma attack may feel tightness in the chest, shortness of breath, wheezing, dizziness, and dry cough. The student may have trouble talking. Students with asthma should have medication registered with the office or school nurse. When an attack occurs the student should stop exercising and take the medication.

Many things can cause a student to have an asthma attack. Some attacks occur because of exposure to allergens such as cat hair, dust, pollen, grasses, or molds. Changes in temperature may trigger an attack. Sometimes exercise may bring one about.

Figure 6.5 Asthmatic students sometimes use inhalers to improve their breathing.

Asthma attacks need to be addressed immediately. An attack that is not treated and stopped can become life threatening. Evidence of a severe attack will be a tensing of the neck muscles, inability to talk, and grayish or blue fingernails. Skin around the ribs and chest may appear as if it is sucked in as well. A severe attack requires immediate emergency medical attention (American Lung Association 2002).

Most people with diagnosed asthma will be under a doctor's care that will include medications and inhalers. Many people with asthma can ward off an asthma attack by using their medications and inhalers as prescribed, which often includes taking it just before exercise. Be sure to review an asthmatic student's medical history and know what medications he is taking. Never allow students to share medications because doing so may result in severe or fatal consequences. Each student with asthma should have an individualized physical education program. Many students who have asthma are capable of performing all activities conducted in class. Intensity of performance may vary depending on their ability to breathe that day.

Diabetes Mellitus

Diabetes mellitus is a general term that refers to an array of metabolic disorders caused by deficient insulin source. Students with diabetes mellitus strive to balance blood sugar through diet, exercise, and insulin or other medications to prevent hypoglycemia (low blood sugar) or hyperglycemia (high blood sugar). Unfortunately, diabetes mellitus is on the rise in this country, particularly among school-age children. There are four types of diabetes mellitus:

Type 1—insulin-dependent diabetes, which is controlled by insulin, diet, and exercise.

Type 2—non-insulin-dependent diabetes, which may be controlled by diet, exercise, or oral medication. In some cases insulin is used to help control type 2 diabetes.

Type 3—gestational diabetes, which often occurs for a short period during pregnancy.

Type 4—secondary diabetes that results from other conditions and syndromes such as cystic fibrosis, organ transplants, renal dialysis, and drug use.

Many of the students you meet with diabetes have type 1 or type 2 diabetes. You should be aware of the proper medical treatment of a person with diabetes of either type.

Both type 1 and type 2 diabetics check their blood sugar using a glucometer, a small computer that reads blood glucose level (figure 6.6). The many kinds of glucometers on the market all work in similar ways. Students place a special chemical stick inside a glucometer. Next, they prick their fingers and apply a small amount of blood to the stick. Within 5 to 45 seconds the computer displays a blood glucose level. A blood glucose level between 80 and 120 is considered acceptable. Blood glucose over 120 is considered high, and blood glucose under 80 is considered low.

Students who experience hyperglycemia may show signs of

- tiredness,
- sluggishness,
- crankiness,
- increased thirst, or
- frequent urination.

Symptoms of high blood glucose must be treated. If left unattended, high blood glucose can lead to

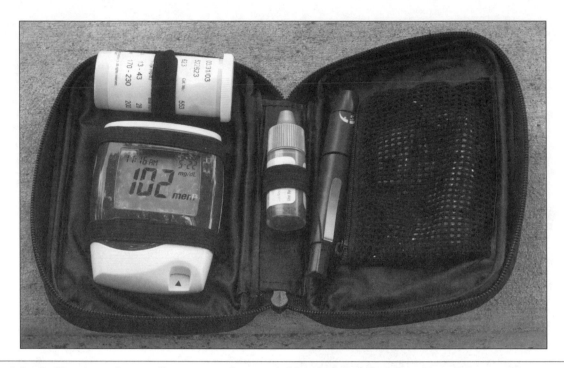

Figure 6.6   A glucometer is a small computer that reads blood glucose levels.

ketoacidosis, a serious medical condition. Symptoms of ketoacidosis include dehydration, drowsiness, nausea, sugar in the urine, ketones in the urine, and a fruity-smelling breath. A student with high blood sugar should not participate in moderate or vigorous physical activity until his blood sugar level falls within an acceptable range. Consult your school nurse about this situation.

Low blood sugar can also have severe consequences. Students who have low blood sugar lack energy and feel agitated, lightheaded, and confused. Their palms may become sweaty; they may feel shaky all over; and they may look pale. When students have low blood sugar, they need to take some form of sugar quickly, such as juice, raisins, fruit, or candies such as Lifesavers or Starbursts. Within minutes you should see an improvement in appearance, and the student should feel better. When the student feels better, it may be wise to offer her a more substantial carbohydrate like crackers or graham crackers. After 15 to 20 minutes the student may be able to resume activity. In most cases, it may be better for the student not to resume activity after an incidence of low blood sugar. If a student becomes unconscious, seek medical attention immediately.

People with type 1 diabetes must take insulin daily. Many type 1 diabetics take insulin injections several times a day to balance their blood sugar levels. More people with diabetes are now taking

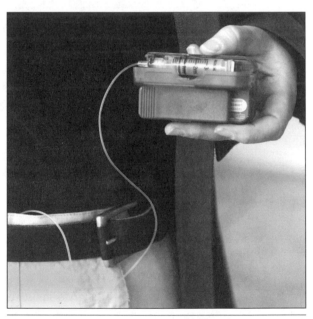

Figure 6.7   An insulin pump, which attaches to the belt or waistband, is becoming a popular way for diabetics to regulate their blood sugar level.

insulin through an insulin pump (figure 6.7). The insulin pump, about the size of a pager, attaches to the belt or the waistband of clothing. Tubing stretches from the pump to the student's abdomen area, where it is inserted under the skin. The pump pumps a constant insulin dose. Students wearing the pump can suspend or reduce their insulin basal rate when necessary. If your students wear a pump or take injections, ask them and the school nurse about how insulin works and how you can be prepared to assist in the event of low or high blood sugar.

Exercise is important to the student with diabetes because it helps in balancing blood sugar. Controlled blood sugar levels can deter or slow the onset of complications that most people with diabetes face in their future. Physical education class can be an important ingredient in a diabetic's care. You should assess the student's abilities. Many students will have a good idea about how exercise affects their blood sugar levels. You should consult the school nurse as well. Together, you, the student, the parents (when necessary), and the school nurse can determine a participation level that will most benefit the student. Many people with diabetes enjoy physical activity. Many students with diabetes participate fully in physical activity and school athletic programs.

As a physical educator, you will encounter students with a variety of chronic illnesses and diseases. You may work with students who have HIV, cancer, cystic fibrosis, Tourette's syndrome, and more. Whatever the illness or disease, be sure to learn more about it and work with the student, parents, school nurse, and other professionals to assess and design a physical education program that will most benefit the student.

Physical Disabilities

Many physical disabilities afflict people. In this section, we will review some of those that teachers with whom we work most often describe. They include cerebral palsy, epilepsy, spina bifida, and arthritis.

Cerebral Palsy

Cerebral palsy (CP) is a condition that impairs voluntary movements. It begins with a lesion to the brain that may occur before, during, or after birth. In addition, central nervous system abnormalities such as enlarged ventricles to the brain and decreased brain hemisphere size cause impaired motor function (Auxter, Pyfer, and Huettig 1997). CP occurs in 1 or 2 live births per 1,000. Poor postural adjustments contribute to the difficulty of performing simple gross motor movements such as kicking, running, jumping, throwing, and striking (figure 6.8).

Joan thinks about a student with type 1 diabetes that she had in class this year. Kurt, a sophomore, was in her sixth-period class, scheduled right after lunch. Kurt was sociable and athletic. Joan had no idea that he had diabetes until the third day of class when he looked a bit pale after warming up. When Joan inquired, Kurt said he thought that he might have low blood sugar. He asked Joan if he could go check. Joan said yes and sent Kurt with one of his friends to the locker room to check his blood sugar level on the glucometer and drink a box of juice that he had in his locker. Kurt and his buddy reappeared about 15 minutes later. Kurt said his blood sugar level was 64 and that the juice made him feel better. Kurt experienced low blood sugar in several class periods in a row. Concerned for Kurt, Joan went to the Internet and school nurse to learn more about diet, exercise, and insulin. Joan learned that the three must be in balance to fend off high and low blood sugars. When she quizzed Kurt, Joan learned that he wasn't eating much at lunch and that physical education class occurred when his insulin was peaking. Joan worked with Kurt and the school nurse to determine that Kurt needed to eat more carbohydrates with lunch to make it through physical education class. Kurt seemed pleased with the result because he disliked having to stop his activity when he had low blood sugar.

Dealing with Kurt was different from dealing with Melissa and her type 1 diabetes. Melissa, who also took insulin injections, seemed to always be having high or low blood sugar. One day during field hockey class Melissa showed Joan her glucometer reading of 480. Joan immediately had her stop all activity and drink lots of water. She asked another student to accompany Melissa to the school nurse, where she could focus on immediately reducing her blood sugar level. Throughout the year, Melissa had very high or very low blood sugar. On two occasions her blood sugar was so high that she had to be hospitalized for several days. Working with the school nurse and other professionals in school didn't seem to help. Melissa seemed disinclined to take care of herself. As a result she was skinny, didn't look healthy, and had pale skin. She appeared tired much of the time and became sick a lot. Joan was struck by how two students with the same disease could handle it in such different ways.

Figure 6.8 Students with cerebral palsy present a challenge for the physical educator because they have impaired motor function.

The extent to which neuromotor dysfunction damaged the brain is difficult to establish and varies greatly from one infant to the next (Porretta 2000). Severe brain damage may be easily assessed shortly after birth. Milder damage may not show clearly until the child become three or four years old. Children with cerebral palsy will have varying degrees of motor impairment. Many children with CP experience muscular spasticity, which is characterized by muscular contractures that restrict muscle movement. Hypertonicity will give the child an appearance of stiffness. Muscle movements will be stiff and jerky.

Sensory and perceptual delays may lessen with training. Therefore, students with CP can improve and maximize their movement abilities through well-planned physical education and other movement programs. We should encourage high school students with CP to improve their physical fitness and body mechanics and to continue practicing motor skills and relaxation techniques. The high school student with CP must also begin thinking and working toward a transition from school-based activities to community-based activities.

Epilepsy

Epilepsy is present in about 2% of the population. Many people experience their first epileptic episode during childhood. Epilepsy is a condition that results from abnormal electrical activity of the brain (Auxter, Pyfer, and Huettig 1997). Students with epilepsy may experience brief episodes of altered consciousness, motor activity, sensory phenomena, or inappropriate behavior caused by abnormal excessive discharge of cerebral neurons (Berkow 1992).

Many students with epilepsy and other seizure disorders control their seizures with medications. Students who demonstrate good control of their condition should be able to participate fully in physical education classes. Students with epilepsy should avoid activities that may involve direct blows to the head, such as heading a soccer ball, as well as height activities like climbing ropes. Teachers should carefully supervise swimming and prohibit underwater swimming (Auxter, Pyfer, and Huettig 1997).

Spina Bifida

Spina bifida occurs in about 1 child out of every 1,000 live births, and 80% of these children are born with the most severe form of spina bifida, myelomeningocele (Kelly 2000). Spina bifida is the result of a defective closure of the vertebral column. Spina bifida may create varying degrees of neurological impairment. Symptoms range from mild muscle imbalance to paralysis that usually affects the bladder and rectum. Sometimes children and youth will have a shunt inserted to drain cerebrospinal fluid that the body is unable to reabsorb. The shunt helps protect the child from brain damage.

Children with spina bifida may need modifications made to their physical education programs. You should work with others in your school to conduct a needs assessment and provide a program that meets the individual's needs.

Arthritis

Arthritis is an inflammation of the joints. Arthritis is a progressive disease that with time results in fatigue and muscular stiffness. Rheumatoid arthritis affects more than 3 million people in this country. To date, it is the number one crippling disease. Some children also have arthritis. Juvenile arthritis, or Still's disease, usually afflicts children before the age of seven. More than 250,000 children in this country have juvenile arthritis.

Treatment for arthritis includes healthy diet, stress reduction, exercise, and medication. Physical exercise works well in reducing pain and improving motor function. Because arthritis is inflammation of the joints, stretching and improving range of motion is important. Physical educators should provide programs of "static stretching, isometric muscle contraction, and reduced weight-bearing aerobic exercise" (Auxter, Pyfer, and Huettig 1997).

Cerebral palsy, epilepsy, spina bifida, and arthritis are four physically disabling conditions on a list of many. You may encounter students with these physical disabilities or others. When you do, be sure to review their medical histories and work with qualified professionals along with the student and parents or guardians to develop an IEP that meets students needs and provides the best opportunities for success.

Hearing and Visual Impairments

We rely on hearing to assist our communication and interaction with others. When people suffer hearing loss, they will lose some of their ability to communicate (figure 6.9). Children who experience permanent hearing loss will have difficulty with language comprehension, social interactions, and motor development (Auxter, Pyfer, and Huettig 1997). Individuals are categorized as either hard of hearing or deaf. The degree to which a person is deaf or hard of hearing will depend on the amount of decibel loss they have incurred as well as their ability to carry on a conversation.

Because communication is one area of difficulty for students with hearing impairments, physical educators must find ways to interact effectively with students. Instructional strategies that use visual and kinesthetic techniques are helpful. Learning sign language may assist you with communication. Many students with hearing impairments will be able to participate fully in physical education class. Modifications may simply entail using effective communication techniques.

Visual Impairments

Persons with visual impairments are classified as blind or partially sighted. About 1% of the population is visually impaired. The percentage of school-age children and youth who have visual dysfunctions but are neither blind nor partially sighted may be as high as 20 to 30% (Auxter, Pyfer, and Huettig 1997). Vision loss greatly affects child and youth development as well as academic, emotional, psychological, and social growth. Visual impairments often limit physical activity and active exploration of the environment. Thus, motor development in the visually impaired adolescent may be delayed. Depending on the individual, emotional, psychological, and social well-being may be adversely affected as well.

Again, we as physical educators must assess the needs of our visually impaired students and provide beneficial learning opportunities for them (figure 6.10).

When communicating with a deaf person, remember to

- maintain eye contact throughout the conversation,
- use paper and pencil to augment conversation,
- signal that you understand only when you really do (do not pretend to understand),
- use polite ways to gain a deaf person's attention,
- learn to use a teletypewriter (TTY) to transmit typewritten words over the telephone lines to another TTY,
- discourage interruptions to the conversation,
- correct a deaf person's English only if asked, and
- appreciate that many people's hearing is not improved through the use of hearing aids (Graybill & Cokley, 1993).

Figure 6.9 Tips for communicating with deaf students.

Reprinted, by permission, from J.P. Winnick, 2000, *Adapted physical education and sport,* 3rd ed. (Champaign, IL: Human Kinetics), 173.

Figure 6.10 Teachers need to find methods of providing beneficial learning opportunities to visually impaired students.

But we must also learn to be more creative because our main avenue of presentation, the demonstration, has limited effectiveness in instruction. To assist visually impaired students with learning, we need to provide other sensory stimuli, such as verbal and tactile instructions. Because student vision may be impaired, we must take extra steps to provide a safe environment so that students have sufficient trust to try activities and so that no one is injured.

Steps to Inclusion

Creating an environment that includes all students, including students with disabilities, requires that physical educators teach with an open mind and sensitivity toward others. You must be willing to walk into the gym, locker room, and field and observe the facilities and curriculum from a different point of view. You must realize that your program may present barriers that make it difficult for some students to participate to their potential. When evaluating your program for inclusiveness begin with the physical structures, such as facilities and equipment (figure 6.12).

Figure 6.12 Your locker room should be designed for all students to have easy access.

Facilities and Equipment

School sports complexes typically include locker rooms, gymnasium, pool, weight room, outdoor hardtop area, tennis courts, and field space. Many of these facilities are decades old. Original building plans did not consider people with disabilities; construction plans had the physically able in mind. Many schools have upgraded their facilities to make them user friendly to students with special needs. But many others have not because costs are prohibitive or, frankly, because no one has thought about it. Many physical education facilities remain inaccessible to people with disabilities. Are the physical education facilities at your school or at schools that you observe accessible to students with disabilities? Consider answers to the following questions (Auxter, Pyfer, and Huettig 1997):

1. Can a student who uses a wheelchair, leg braces, crutches, or has difficulty with locomotion get into the locker room and maneuver with ease around lockers, showers, and toilets?

2. Can a student who uses a wheelchair, leg braces, crutches, or has difficulty with locomotion enter the gymnasium, pool, and weight room with ease and move about teaching areas freely?

3. Can a student who uses a wheelchair, leg braces, crutches, or has difficulty with locomotion move easily (without barriers) from the locker room to indoor facilities to outdoor facilities? If not, what accommodations can be made?

4. Can a student who uses a wheelchair, leg braces, crutches, or has difficulty with loco-

motion move easily onto field space? If not, what accommodation can be made?

5. What adaptations can be made to equipment to provide students with disabilities opportunities for success?

6. Are quality audio sources available to assist visually impaired students?

7. Are all teaching stations safe for students with and without disabilities?

8. Can everyone, including students with disabilities, evacuate safely in an emergency?

Purpose

Use video to record your facilities and assess potential problems of student accessibility.

Resource and Procedure

Videotape your facilities and vocally record any potential accessibility problems you see. When viewing the tape, try to come up with potential problems through the "eyes" of your students. Have other educators view the tape and share their ideas. Make a list of possible improvements. Prioritize your list based on things you can do and things that may require outside help. The video becomes a good rationale for making the changes.

Physical Education Program

Auxter, Pyfer, and Huettig (1997) provide a wonderful section describing ways to establish the least restrictive environment for students with disabilities. Physical educators should examine several areas of their program and make decisions that will benefit all students, including students with disabilities. These areas include curriculum, support personnel, equipment, program participation, management of behavior, teaching style, and grading. We will describe these briefly here, but we encourage readers to consult this text for more in-depth information about adapted physical education.

Curriculum

Physical educators should work together to create a program that includes everyone and is grounded in the NASPE standards. As you review the NASPE standards (see chapter 1) you will note that the standards guide physical educators in the process of helping students become physically educated. The language used is inclusive of students with special needs and students with disabilities. Inclusion means that every student has access to the same curriculum. Using the NASPE standards may not be enough. Physical educators should also use state, region, and district standards and curriculum framework to guide program development.

Support Personnel

When creating inclusion, a physical educator is working to establish the least restrictive environment possible for learners. To accomplish this, the physical educator may need help from others. Support personnel for students with disabilities can be extremely helpful. Some students with disabilities may not need any assistance in class; others may. Several kinds of support personnel can assist students with disabilities who need help:

- Class buddy—students in class who help students in need
- Teacher assistant—student helper who volunteers to assist the teacher during a free period
- Teacher aide—paraprofessional assigned to assist a specific student throughout the day
- Adult volunteer—adult who volunteers to help a teacher with classes and specific assignments

All support personnel should receive appropriate training so that they can assist students with disabilities. At the secondary level you may want to meet with the volunteer or aide and the student with the disability to discuss the physical education IEP and strategies for implementing it during class. Discuss thoroughly the role of the helper. You must educate support personnel and train them to be involved in class (Murata and Hodge 1997).

Joan remembers working with Shandra, a student with severe cerebral palsy, in her fourth-period class. She was a sophomore who had mild cognitive delays. She was also animated, outgoing, and loved to participate. She had an adult aide who accompanied her to each class. When she met the aide Joan was excited because she thought the aide would be able to help Shandra in class. Joan was disappointed when the aide took a chair at the side of the gym and read a newspaper. Joan decided that from that day forward the aide would be more involved, but she knew she would have to train him first.

Equipment

In most physical education classes that you observe, all students use the same equipment. Teachers should consider providing alternative equipment based on student needs. For instance, in a class on volleyball you will see students striking regulation volleyballs with varied degrees of success. Students who are beginners may find more success if they have an opportunity to strike balls that are lighter and stay up in the air longer, like a beach ball or a volley foam. As physical educators, we should often modify equipment to meet student needs, particularly for students with disabilities.

Program Participation

When the IEP committee meets to determine student learning goals, objectives, and an action plan, they will also determine the type of participation. To provide the least restrictive environment possible, the committee must seriously consider the student's level of participation. Auxter, Pyfer, and Huettig (1997) list nine possibilities:

1. Full, independent participation in regular physical education

2. Full, independent participation in regular physical education with younger students

3. Full, independent participation in some units, with support in others, in regular physical education

4. Full, independent participation in some phases of the daily lesson, with support in other phases, in regular physical education

5. Participation with support in some units, with separate physical education for other units

6. Participation with support in some phases of the daily lesson, with separate physical education for other phases

7. Separate, but equal, adapted physical education in the school building with typically developing peers

8. Separate, but equal, adapted physical education in the school building with peers with disabilities

9. Adapted physical education at home, a hospital, or an institutional setting

Behavior Management

Students with disabilities are often excluded from regular physical education classes because of poor behavior. A behavior management plan may be part of a student's IEP. You should consider a behavior management plan for each of your students. Use positive reinforcement with your management plan to encourage desired behavior. At times, consequences for episodes of undesirable behavior will be necessary, such as a verbal warning, time-out from activity, removal from an activity, detention during or after school, or other disciplinary action determined by you and the school principal in consultation with the parents.

Teaching Styles

Effective teaching is based on finding appropriate teaching styles that will meet student needs. The same holds true when working with students with disabilities. You need to assess student needs and determine teaching styles that will work effectively with those students. Some teaching styles that you might consider will be command, practice, self-check, reciprocal, and guided discovery (see chapter 8).

Grading

Grading should focus on assessing student learning. When it is time to grade, return to the IEP and review the short-term objectives. These objectives use measurable terms that should be part of the grading process. You should expect students with disabilities, like all students, to achieve in all aspects of the grading process. In some instances you will have to make modifications. Overall, focus on student learning and help students set measurable and achievable learning objectives. Remember too that grading or assessment is an excellent form of feedback for students, so be sure to include it in the process.

Summary

As teachers we have a responsibility to understand the diversity that exists among our students and to embrace each individual for his or her uniqueness. This goal requires that we provide quality physical education for students who are different from ourselves, who are not gifted movers, and who are with disabilities. Some disabilities are noticeable, and some are not. Work hard to know your students and their needs. When working with students who qualify under disability law, including Section 504, seek to be a member of student IEP teams. Your involvement will benefit the student in several ways. First, you will help set appropriate goals for the student. Second, you will have an opportunity to help other educators understand the importance of developmentally appropriate physical education. Remember that inclusion is a cornerstone of equitable education.

Checking for Understanding ▸▸▸

- Define Public Law (P.L.) 94-142. Why is this law important?
- What is the Individuals with Disabilities Education Act? How did it affect physical education?
- Explain the IEP process. As a physical educator how will you become involved in the IEP process?
- How many children (ages 6 through 12) with learning disabilities are served by IDEA each year?
- What is an ITP? Why is it important for students with disabilities to have one? How will you involve yourself as a physical educator in the ITP process?
- Define learning disability.
- How will you help a student with a physical disability?

For Reflection and Discussion ▸▸▸

- Visit a local middle or high school and find out how they implement the IEP process. Talk with physical educators about their involvement in this process. Describe the steps you would take to establish inclusion in your classroom.
- Collect accurate information about learning or physical disabilities that are unfamiliar to you. Develop strategies for sharing this information with colleagues and for including students with this disability in your class.

References

American Lung Association. 2002. Facts about asthma: Attacks. [Online.] Available: **www.lungusa.org/asthma/astasthmatk.html** [May 29, 2002].

Auxter, D., J. Pyfer, and C. Huettig. 1997. *Principles and methods of adapted physical education and recreation.* 8th ed. Madison, WI: Brown and Benchmark.

Berkow, R. (1992) as printed in Auxter, Pyfer, Huettig, 1997, p. 378.

Craft, D. 1990. Learning disabilities. In *Adapted Physical Education and Sport,* edited by J.P. Winnick. Champaign, IL: Human Kinetics.

Craft, D. 2000. Learning disabilities and attention deficits. In *Adapted physical education and sport.* 3rd ed. Edited by J.P. Winnick. Champaign, IL: Human Kinetics.

Gallahue, D.L. 1996. *Developmental physical education for today's children.* 3rd ed. Madison, WI: Brown and Benchmark.

Houston-Wilson, C., and L.J. Lieberman. 1999. The individualized education program in physical education: A guide for regular physical educators. *Journal of Physical Education, Recreation and Dance* 76(3):60–64.

Kelly, L. 2000. In *Adapted physical education and sport.* 3rd ed. Edited by J.P. Winnick. Champaign, IL: Human Kinetics.

Krebs, P. 2000. In *Adapted physical education and sport.* 3rd ed. Edited by J.P. Winnick. Champaign, IL: Human Kinetics.

McClenaghan, B.A. 1990. In *Adapted physical education and sport.* 3rd ed. Edited by J.P. Winnick. Champaign, IL: Human Kinetics.

Murata, N.M., and S.R. Hodge. 1997. Training support personnel for inclusive physical education. *Journal of Physical Education, Recreation and Dance* 68(9):21–25.

Office of Special Education and Rehabilitative Services (OSERS). 2000a. *22nd annual report to Congress, executive summary.* [Online.] Available: **www.ed.gov/offices/OSERS/OSEP/Products/OSEP2000AnlRpt/ExecSumm.html** [May 29, 2002].

Office of Special Education and Rehabilitative Services (OSERS). 2000b. *A guide to the individualized education program.* [Online.] Available: **www.ed.gov/offices/OSERS/OSEP/Products/IEP_Guide/** [May 29, 2002].

Porretta, D.L. 2000. In *Adapted physical education and sport.* 3rd ed. Edited by J.P. Winnick. Champaign, IL: Human Kinetics.

Winnick, J.P., ed. 2000. *Adapted physical education and sport.* 3rd ed. Champaign, IL: Human Kinetics.

Suggested Readings

Craft, D., and L. Lieberman. 2000. In *Adapted physical education and sport*. 3rd ed. Edited by J.P. Winnick. Champaign, IL: Human Kinetics.

Doyle, M.B. 2000. Transition plans for students with disabilities. *Educational Leadership* 58:46–48.

French, R., H. Henderson, L. Kinnison, and C. Sherrill. 1998. Revisiting Section 504, physical education, and sport. *Journal of Physical Education, Recreation and Dance* 69(7):57–63.

Goldman, V.E. 1993. Teaching dance in secondary school for children with moderate learning difficulties. *British Journal of Physical Education* 24(3):7–9.

Kinchin, G.D., and M. O'Sullivan. 1999. Making physical education meaningful for high school students. *Journal of Physical Education, Recreation and Dance* 70(5):40–54.

Maeda, J.K., N.M. Murata, and S.R. Hodge. 1997/98. Physical educators' perceptions of inclusion, A Hawaii school district perspective. *Clinical Kinesiology* 51(4):80–85.

Mosston, M., and S. Ashworth. 1994. *Teaching physical education*. 4th ed. New York: Macmillan.

National Information Center for Children and Youth With Disabilities. 2002. Office of Special Education Programs, Washington, DC 20013. **www.nichcy.org**

National Institute of Arthritis and Musculoskeletal and Skin Diseases. 2002. National Institutes of Health, Bethesda, Maryland 20892. **www.nih.gov/niams/healthinfo/juvarthr.htm**

National Institute of Mental Health. Learning Disabilities. [Online.] 2002. NIMH Public Inquiries, 6001 Executive Boulevard, Rm. 8184, MSC 9663, Bethesda, MD 20892-9663. Available: **www.nimh.nih.gov/publicat/learndis.htm**

Piletic, C.K. 1998. Transition: Are we doing it? *Journal of Physical Education, Recreation and Dance* 69(9):46–50.

Reams, D. 1997. Using teacher assistants in physical education classes: Serving students with disabilities. *Palestra* 13(2):16–25.

Rizzo T.L., and B. Lavay. 2000. Inclusion: Why the confusion? *Journal of Physical Education, Recreation and Dance* 71(4):32–36.

Skelton, J. 1993. Totally blind in a secondary school: What programme can be offered? *British Journal of Physical Education* 24(3):13.

Suggested Web Sites

American Diabetes Association. 1701 North Beauregard Street, Alexandria, VA 22311. **http://diabetes.diabetesjournals.org/**

American Epilepsy Society. 342 North Main Street, West Hartford, CT 06117-2507. **www.aesnet.org**

American Lung Association. Asthma: General Information Index. **www.lungusa.org/asthma/**

Internet Special Education Resources. 2002. Special Education, Learning Disabilities Resources. **www.iser.com/index.shtml**

Rowley, L. 1998. *Family Village Project. Resources for people interested in spina bifida and related disorders.* **www.familyvillage.wisc.edu/spinabifida.html**

Part III

The Teacher

Chapter 7

Effective and Reflective Teaching

> I hear and I forget. I see and I remember.
> I do and I understand.
>
> — *Chinese Proverb*

After finishing his first year of teaching at Pablo Valley High School, Damon is looking back on the year with mixed emotions. He is still excited about his job and wants to make a difference for the students, but he's worried about their learning. He assessed his students throughout the school year, and it just seems that they should have learned more. He's not sure what he's doing wrong, but he knows he's doing many things right. His students seem to respect him because, with few exceptions, they follow instructions and stay on task. Damon plans his lessons to ensure that all students can experience success. His students seem to enjoy his classes, but he's not sure about the amount of time they spend being active and learning the skills and concepts. He knows he tends to talk too much. He also suspects that he needs to improve his management and organizational skills. His students seem to spend a lot of class time waiting for things to happen, although they do so without causing much trouble. As he reflects back on his first year, Damon remembers reading about these issues in college. He wonders where he put the old textbook from his secondary methods class.

Learning Objectives

After reading this chapter thoroughly and discussing the issues in class, you should be able to

- explain what is meant by being "caring but demanding,"
- explain the difference between rules and protocols,
- devise a set of rules and protocols for your future class,
- list at least five ways to use your time wisely to save valuable learning-activity minutes,
- explain the KISS principle of instruction,
- explain the concepts of inclusion, success, and flow,
- explain the difference between repetitive and mixed practice and the best time to use each type,
- list three characteristics of good performance cues and know how many cues you should use at one time,
- list three characteristics of effective feedback,
- explain how to motivate students in physical education, and
- explain what considering the COST of your goals means.

Key Terms and Phrases

Caring but demanding
Use time wisely
KISS
Inclusion
Flow
Repetitive practice
Mixed practice
Cues
Feedback
Motivation
Goal setting
COST of goals

What does it take to become an excellent teacher? The answer to this question will vary depending on whom you ask, but one observation is hard to ignore: excellent teachers keep learning throughout their careers. When you take a lifelong approach to teaching and learning, you realize that you are on a journey. The excellent teacher is not an end product, something you become one day or a destination at which you arrive. Excellent teachers, of any subject area, never stop learning how to become great at what they do. This habit is exactly what makes them excellent. They constantly reflect on the activities they choose for their students and the effectiveness of their teaching. Reflection usually leads to trying new things, and with each new discovery, teachers figure out what works best. In this way they constantly improve their teaching. If you take advantage of the opportunities to reflect on and develop your teaching philosophy, communication, and teaching skills throughout your career, you too will be on the path to becoming an excellent teacher. It is your choice to make.

In this chapter we will introduce you to some of the skills and techniques effective teachers use to create the best possible learning environment for their students. Remembering your years as a student in physical education and other classes, did you ever wonder why some teachers had full control over their classes, whereas others always seemed to struggle with students who were off task? Or how some teachers managed to get 30 to 35 minutes of learning activities into a 50-minute class, whereas others had difficulty squeezing in 15 minutes of active learning time? Effective teachers seem to have several things in common. They are caring but demanding; they use their time wisely; they maximize learning opportunities for all their students; and they use a number of teaching tricks and tools to help them in these areas.

Caring but Demanding

Most of us remember one or more favorite teachers from elementary or secondary school. Chances are your favorite teacher was a caring person. We all like to feel special and that others care about us. Some teachers are better than others at expressing warmth and concern. It is difficult, if not impossible, to feign caring. Older students, especially, will know if it's the real thing.

Although caring is an important characteristic of a well-liked teacher, it alone is not enough to make an effective teacher. Effective teachers are **caring but demanding**. Teaching is like parenting. Children need to know that their parents love and care for them, but unless they have guidelines to go by they may take advantage of the caring parent to get what they want. Caring and demanding parents or teachers set the guidelines, teach the children or students to follow the guidelines, and hold them accountable for their choices. As a result, the children or students respect their parents or teachers, and they are less likely to want to disappoint them. Teaching an adult to become a caring person is difficult, but we can give you some suggestions for how to *communicate* that you care about your students. On the other hand, we *can* teach you how to become a demanding teacher. The following sections include practical suggestions about how to communicate that you care and how to become a demanding teacher.

How to Communicate That You Care

We hope you've chosen this profession because you care about children and youth, and that you will continue to care throughout your teaching career. You can't be taught to care, but you can learn how to express caring. There are certain signs that students notice concerning genuine caring. Calling students by their names, for example, shows that you have made an effort and that you care about them as individuals. They are not just numbers on your roll sheet. Learning 150 or more new names each year is not easy, but with some effort it is possible. Making an effort to notice things that are unique about a student, and acknowledging this in a positive way, will also help communicate that you care. You may, for example, learn that a certain student is in the drama group and once in a while ask him about his theatrical endeavors. You may have another student who has younger siblings she cares for after school. An occasional question about how she's doing with all her chores and school will show that you care about her as a person. Being available for students during a certain hour of the day (before or after school, or during lunch) for help with skills, concepts, or physical education homework also shows that you care about them and their learning. Communicating specifically *how* what you teach them will affect *their* lives is another important way to show you care.

In recent years teachers have been told to be careful about touching students because of sexual harassment issues. Many teachers ignore the warnings and communicate to their students that they care by hugging them or patting them on the back. This is a delicate issue, but consider that your hug or pat on the back may be all the physical contact some students receive from a caring adult all day. However, you have to be extremely careful. There are a number of teachers who have been wrongly accused of sexual harassment when all they meant to do was express care, concern, or compassion to a student (see chapter 15).

Respected First, Then Liked

You may have heard the old advice to new teachers: "Don't smile until Christmas." Although we consider that recommendation a little extreme, there is a grain (ever so small) of truth in it. To become a caring but demanding teacher, you must make sure immediately that your students respect you. You can accomplish this in a nonthreatening, friendly way, but accomplishing it is crucial. Most beginning teachers want their students to like them, but many underestimate the importance of establishing who is in charge from the beginning. Don't worry; you can have both! Students will like you if you come across as a caring person, but by gaining their respect first you will ensure that they also view you as a demanding teacher.

Demanding does not translate into *mean,* but it does imply that you let students know who is responsible for their safety and learning—you! By establishing respect up front, you will find that the school year will go smoothly with few problems. One of the best ways to get off to a good start is to establish clear rules and protocols immediately.

Rules and Protocols

Effective teachers spend time in the beginning of every school year establishing rules and protocols for students to follow. Rules usually cover safety and respect issues, and protocols deal with behaviors that make the learning environment more effective (see chapter 9).

Rules

In middle and high school, students are old enough to help you create the rules for the class. Explain to them first that your main concerns are to ensure their safety and help them all to learn as much as possible (figure 7.1). With your leadership,

Purpose

Use a still camera to take pictures of your students correctly, following rules and protocols.

Resource and Procedure

After reviewing the rules and protocols for the class, have students demonstrate their understanding by showing you proper procedures for different situations. Take photos of the students following proper procedures. Display the photos in relevant spots as reference material for your students. The power lies in using your current students for this exercise because it proves that they know and have demonstrated proper adherence to rules and protocols.

Figure 7.1 A teacher should establish clear rules at the beginning of the school year.

together you and the students should be be able to create a set of rules that seem fair to them and will be easy to remember. Students can also help establish the consequences for violating a rule (more on this in chapter 9).

Generally, rules should be clear, stated in a positive way, and few in number. You should discuss and define rules so that students know exactly what each one means. For example, "Wear proper attire for physical activity" may need examples and explanation to be clear to all students. For instance, you should tell them why they cannot wear flip-flops during the dance unit. A rule such as "Use respectful language" may also need some definitions. What does respectful mean? A word that is acceptable and commonly used in one culture may not be appropriate in your class. The

Sample rules for physical education

- ♦ Allow others the opportunity to learn.
- ♦ Respect each other's differences.
- ♦ Handle the equipment with care.
- ♦ Listen when someone is talking to the whole class.
- ♦ Wear attire appropriate for physical activity.
- ♦ Always be safe!

Figure 7.2   This sample list of rules adheres to the guidelines of being clear, positive, and not overwhelming.

rules should encompass all issues important to you in creating an environment that is safe and allows all students the opportunity to learn. In figure 7.2 you will find some sample rules for secondary school physical education.

Protocols

Teachers usually create protocols to help the class time run as efficiently as possible. Some of these protocols relate to entering and exiting the gym, stopping and starting, talking and listening, getting and putting away equipment, and so on. Students don't automatically know what to do in these situations in your class. They may have picked up habits in other teachers' classes that you do not want them to continue in yours, so you have to let them know how you want the class to run. Just as you did with rules, you can have students help you create protocols for your class. This encourages ownership, and later you will be able to remind students that the rules and protocols are their own. Effective teachers establish protocols

early in the school year and consistently enforce them until they become routine. This issue may be difficult for new teachers, because if the teacher slacks off, the students will too. So it is crucial to be consistent, especially in the first few months.

Protocols are necessary for even the most obvious issues. How will your students know when you want them to stop and listen to you? You might use music as the signal. When the music is on, students are active; when you turn it off, they gather around you and listen for new instructions. How do they know what to do with their homework sheets? You might teach them to put their homework sheets in the crate on the floor as they enter the gym. After they've had a chance to practice and get it right a few times, they may do it consistently. How will you take roll? What will your students do when they have to use the rest room during class? What happens if they forget their PE clothes? Another common protocol-related issue in physical education occurs when students play with equipment while the teacher is talking. You may choose to have the students delay getting the equipment until you finish presenting your instructions, or you might teach the protocol that equipment stays on the floor between the students' feet while you are talking.

Many issues fall under the protocol umbrella, and establishing clear ways to deal with those issues will save a lot of time. If you don't do this in the beginning of the school year, you will find yourself answering the same questions and giving students the same instructions repeatedly. If they know what you expect them to do in each situation and they have a chance to practice and become familiar with the protocols, you will have more time for the academic learning activities. Figure 7.3 shows sample protocols for a physical education class.

Sample protocols for physical education

- ♦ Put your homework in the crate as you enter the learning area.
- ♦ When entering the learning area, read and follow the instructions on the board.
- ♦ Go signals: "Go" (said), one whistle blow, or music on.
- ♦ Stop signals: two whistle blows or music off.
- ♦ Stop-and-gather signal: Three whistle blows. Gather around the teacher for instructions.
- ♦ Put equipment on the floor between your feet when the teacher is giving instructions to the class.

Figure 7.3   Protocols such as these can help a teacher establish clear guidelines to deal with a variety of potential problems.

Hold Students Accountable

A caring but demanding teacher establishes the protocols and rules early in the teacher-student relationship and consistently enforces them. If rules and protocols are to increase student safety and improve the learning environment, you must hold students accountable. If they do not seem to understand a protocol, such as your "stop and gather" signal, practice until they have no problem remembering. If they sense that you will be consistent and firm, they will learn the protocols more quickly. Obviously, if students do not follow the rules and protocols, they must experience some consequences after a practice period. The form of the consequences will depend on the type of discipline system you decide to use (see chapter 9). You will probably need a few weeks at the beginning of every school year to get your system to work smoothly, but most teachers find the time well spent.

Be Aware

A commonsense aspect of effective teaching that we must mention is monitoring your students. Graham (2001) calls it "withitness." Students quickly find out if a teacher is "with it" or not (figure 7.4). Some teachers just seem to have eyes at the back of their heads. Students know if you are able to pay attention to *everything*. They may try to get away with inappropriate behavior if they sense that you are not aware of what they are doing. A good technique to practice "withitness" is to have your back to the wall, or if you are outside, to position yourself at the outer edge of the learning area. That way you can always see what is going on. With practice you can develop the habit of constantly scanning the whole learning area to see if all your students are on task. An occasional comment to those at the other side of the room or field will help convince your students that you always know what's going on, even if you are physically at a distance. Being aware will help keep your students on task, and as a result they will learn more in your classes.

Figure 7.4 These students recognize that their teacher has "withitness."

Your Turn ▶▶▶

◆ Did you ever have a teacher who seemed to know everything that was going on in class? If so, how did the students act in that class compared with classes in which the teacher was not so aware?

◆ How can you start developing your "with-itness" immediately?

◆ What is the advantage of not having too many rules and protocols?

◆ How will you go about establishing your rules and protocols?

◆ How will you deal with the possibility that not all students will like you if you are demanding?

◆ How did you know which teachers really cared about you as a student?

Use Your Time Wisely

Teachers spend time on rules and protocols at the beginning of a school year and then maintain them in each class period so that their classes run smoothly and provide students more opportunities to learn. To learn any skill or concept takes practice. If students have more time to practice, they will learn more. Quantity and quality of practice are the two main determinants of success in learning skills and concepts (Schmidt 1991). We will discuss quality later in the chapter. This section will focus on how to find more time for practice in your lessons. As the heading suggests, to free up more time for practice, the teacher must **use time wisely.**

A number of studies have looked at how teachers and students spend their time in physical education classes. One consistent finding is that too much time in physical education is spent on managerial tasks (i.e., lining up, taking roll, collecting homework, handing out and collecting equipment), transitions (i.e., students moving from one place to another, dividing students into groups or teams, or changing learning activities), instructions (teacher talking to students about what they are supposed to do), and demonstrations (teacher using herself or students to demonstrate a skill or activity). The more time the teacher spends on management, transitions, instructions, and demonstrations, the less time students have to prac-

tice skills and be otherwise involved in learning activities. If students must also wait in line for their turn to do the task, it is easy to see how a 50-minute lesson can include only 17 minutes of active learning (table 7.1), or even less if we count the minutes each student is actually involved with the task.

How can you, as a teacher, avoid spending too much time on management, transitions, instructions, and demonstrations? And how can you avoid having students wait in line for a turn at the task? The answers are simple to state but take a good deal of practice to master. The key is to focus on one question: How can I provide my students with the greatest amount of time for practice? The following paragraphs provide some practical suggestions for using your time more wisely.

Purpose

Use video to assess the amount of class time spent on various activities.

Resource and Procedure

During a typical class meeting, set up a video for the widest possible shot of you and the students. Conduct your class as usual. Afterward, view the tape with a stopwatch. Label and time each activity that takes place during the class. How long did you spend in getting the class ready to learn? How long did you spend in demonstration mode? How long did you answer questions and provide feedback? Finally, how long were the students active? With the camera far away from the action, you might consider using a remote wireless microphone to ensure a good recording of your communications. Also, it is better to set up the camera beforehand and have it recording so that students will be less likely to notice the camera. This task could also be beneficial to you when you assess the effectiveness of your learning cues and feedback.

Taking Roll

Once students know and observe the rules and protocols, they should know what to do as soon as they enter your classroom (this could be the gym, a field, tennis courts, or wherever you teach). Effective teachers do not waste time on roll call

Table 7.1 Ineffective Versus Effective Time Management

The examples demonstrate ineffective and effective time management for a 50-minute class in physical education. Notice that the time allowed for dress in the two examples is the same. The difference is in the time spent on management, transitions, instructions, and demonstrations.

Ineffective time management example	Effective time management example
Dress: 5 minutes	Dress: 5 minutes
Roll: 5 minutes	Instant activity: 4 minutes
Instruction (episode one): 5 minutes	Roll: taken during instant activity or warm-up
Demonstration: 3 minutes	Instruction and demo (episode one): 1 minute
Transition: 2 minutes	Transition: 20 seconds
Learning activity: 10 minutes	Learning activity: 10 minutes
Instruction (episode two): 4 minutes	Instruction and demo (episode two): 1 minute
Transition: 2 minutes	Transition: 20 seconds
Learning activity: 7 minutes	Learning activity: 10 minutes
Dress: 7 minutes	Instruction and demo (episode three): 1 minute
	Transition: 20 seconds
	Learning activity: 10 minutes
	Dress: 7 minutes
Total activity time (assuming no waiting in line for turns): 17 minutes (34% of class time)	Total activity time (assuming no waiting in line for turns): 34 minutes (68% of class time), twice as much as in the ineffective example

(figure 7.5). You can take roll in a variety of ways while students are involved in an activity. Here are a few examples:

♦ You start every lesson with a 5- to 10-minute instant activity specific to the lesson content. The activity should not require much explanation, and you can write instructions on a whiteboard or a task sheet. While students are warming up for your lesson this way, you quietly take roll while roaming the area.

♦ You number all your equipment, and as students enter your classroom and pick up their numbers, you quickly mark the unclaimed equipment on your roll sheet.

♦ As students enter the classroom, they mark themselves present on your attendance sheet or directly into your computer. Because you know your students' names, you can quickly identify any mistakes while your students begin their first learning activity.

A teacher can take roll in many ways without wasting valuable learning time. PE Central (**www.pecentral.com**) has numerous suggestions from teachers of all levels. Try a few to find which work best for you.

Figure 7.5 An effective teacher can have her class involved in activity while taking roll.

KISS Long Instructions Good-Bye!

Another way to save valuable minutes is to talk less. Keeping instructions short may be difficult, especially in the beginning of your teaching career. Many new teachers think that the more they explain a task, the better their students will understand it. In reality, if you talk for much more than a minute or two, you lose the students' inter-est and may overwhelm them. In addition, they will probably forget most of what you said because their short-term memory is limited to about 30 seconds and seven items of information (Schmidt 1991). So by talking much more than 30 seconds at one time, you will be wasting your time. A use-ful idea to consider is "less is more." If you can be short and clear, students will be more likely to remember what you said. To help them remem-ber to be brief and concise, people often use the acronym **KISS:** keep it short and simple. Break up your instruction into one- or two-minute episodes instead of trying to explain everything at one time. You will find this method more effective and more conserving of time. In addition, your students will appreciate it! Most importantly, plan carefully what you are going to say ahead of time and practice saying it. When you rehearse, you will be less likely to ramble on.

Don't Overwhelm Them With Demos

Just as you want to keep your instructions short and simple, you should keep your demonstrations to about one minute at a time for the same rea-sons. If you throw too much information at your students at once, you will overwhelm them (fig-ure 7.6). Break it up. Do several shorter demon-strations throughout the lesson and focus on no more than three points each time. A good demon-stration emphasizes the most important cues (which we will discuss later) and should be short, simple, and specific.

Damon found his old secondary methods textbook in one of the boxes of his college stuff in his parents' garage. He was glad he hadn't sold back the books from his major classes. He climbed up on the roof of his parents' house, which had been his favorite think-ing spot during his teenage years. He loved the view of the city from there. As he read the chapter on ef-fective teaching, he remembered practicing many of the techniques in his college classes. He had always had a problem with talking too much, and he just knew his long-windedness was the main reason that his stu-dents did not get enough learning-activity time. But it never *seemed* to him during class that his explana-tions and demonstrations were that long. Time flew when he was on center stage. The students loved to hear him tell his stories as he explained a skill. He was funny, and they loved that about him. But when his friend Michele, a history teacher, had come to help him figure out his time management problem, he was shocked to find that he spent 15 minutes talking to the class in one period. Michele had timed his instruc-tions, demos, transitions, and learning-activity time for three periods, and his talk time ranged from 11 to 15 minutes per class. He knew that was too much, that his verbosity was his main problem. His performance in the other management categories had been accept-able, but how could he fix his tendency to talk too much? He took a deep breath and kept reading. Maybe he would find some helpful hints in the old text-book.

Figure 7.6 Teachers will get a more enthusiastic response and better results when they don't overwhelm students with demonstrations.

Check for Understanding

Once you have finished your short, simple instructions and demonstrations, how will you know that the students understand? Effective teachers use a simple teaching technique called checking for understanding (Graham 2001). You simply ask them to show or tell you the essence of the instruction or demonstration. For example, you may give your students the following instructions: "Get in groups of three or four, pick up a task sheet that will tell you which station to start at, and come to me when you have completed the task." Your checking-for-understanding questions may sound something like this: "How many students should be in each group?" "How will you know which station to start at?" and "What should you do when you have completed the task?" Students who missed the information when you told them the first time have another opportunity to understand what you expect by listening to the answers that come from the whole group (in unison). Likewise, after a demonstration, you may use checking for understanding to see if the students understood the main idea. For example, after telling them that they should use a bow-and-arrow-like position of the arms in the middle of the tennis serve, you could ask them, "Show me the position your arms should be in at the midpoint of the tennis serve."

Checking for understanding is an effective way to get students to pay attention to your instruc-

tions and demonstrations. This method lets them know that you are holding them accountable for the information you give them.

"Rest When You Get Here!"

When students are going from one activity to another, you can speed things up by giving them a time limit. For example, you might say, "Everyone jog to the jump-rope station before I count to 10." Students get the idea that they should hustle and that you expect them all to be there before you say "10." Communicating to students, from day one, that you want to have as much time as possible for the learning activities may help them understand why they should hustle. At our school, Professor Hutchinson has coined the phrase "Rest when you get here." She uses this friendly hustle reminder when she wants her students to speed up their transition from the learning activity to the gathering point where she is ready to give further instructions. This technique seems to work well in both university and secondary school settings.

Avoid Lines

Being able to do what we suggest in this chapter takes thorough planning. In the beginning of your teaching career, you may find that you have to plan management, transitions, instructions, and demonstrations in detail to save valuable minutes for learning activities. But even if you are an extremely effective manager, you will be unable to increase activity time significantly if you have students wait in line for their turn at a task.

Is waiting in line for a turn unavoidable? We think not. Even if you do not have enough equipment for all the students to be involved, you can devise ways to avoid waiting. Many successful teachers use stations when they don't have enough equipment for all students. Here's an example: You have a class of 30 students and are planning a golf lesson toward the middle of your golf unit. You only have six of each club: drivers, putters, 9 irons, 8 irons, and 7 irons. Instead of working on just one skill and having students wait in lines to get their turn to practice, you could set up five stations that each cover a shot: drive, putt, pitch, chip, and full iron swing. In the beginning of the unit, you may have to reduce the number of skills stations, focus on two skills a day, and include other stations where students learn rules and etiquette or work on the fitness areas important for golf.

Time spent waiting in line is time wasted! No learning occurs if students are not actively involved (physically or cognitively) with a task. Chapter 8, which covers a variety of teaching styles in physical education, will give you ideas about how to get around obstacles such as lack of equipment. Students become bored while waiting for turns, and besides not learning anything, they may cause discipline problems. Again, the key to being effective is to use every minute productively. Always remember why you are teaching: to help the students become physically active for the rest of their lives. Several of our national standards and guidelines, which should be the cornerstone for everything we do in physical education according to the Diamond Conceptual Framework in chapter 1, address the issue of ensuring that students have enough practice time to learn important skills and concepts. We teach an important subject matter. Besides making sure that students enjoy our classes, we have a duty to use the time in a way that they can learn what they need to become physically educated people. Figure 7.7 summarizes tips on how to use your time wisely in physical education.

As we said earlier, using your time wisely is easier said than done. Learning how to apply the preceding suggestions will obviously take time. But establishing clear rules, practicing protocols, speeding up transitions, avoiding lines, and keeping your talking time and demonstrations short will help you become a teacher with 68% or more active learning time, instead of 34% (see table 7.1). Effective time management is one part of the puzzle of effective teaching (figure 7.8). Another important piece concerns making sure that students are actually learning something while they are involved in a learning activity. This piece depends on ensuring their success in learning activities and organizing the practice time.

- ♦ Take roll during the instant activity or warm-up.
- ♦ For the warm-up, use instant activities that do not require much instruction.
- ♦ Plan your instructions and demonstrations; make them short and concise. Talk no more than one or two minutes at any one time.
- ♦ Give instructions, review, and assess during quiet exercises such as stretching or abdominal crunches.
- ♦ Use stations or different teaching styles (chapter 8) if you don't have enough equipment for every student. Do not waste valuable practice time by having students wait in lines.
- ♦ Teach your students the protocols for transitions (getting from one place to another, getting and putting back equipment, selecting partners, and so on).

Figure 7.7   Tips on how to use time wisely in physical education.

Figure 7.8 Teachers should strive to give students as much active learning time as possible.

Damon knew what to do. He had to plan his lessons in more detail and practice his instructions and demos. Maybe he could ask Michele to come back and time him again in two or three weeks when he had improved. His goal was to do no more than two minutes of talking or demonstrating at one time and no more than eight minutes total for each class. He would be cutting his current talk time in half, which would be a big improvement if he could do it. The hardest part was going to be resisting the urge to explain everything to death. He could still be funny; he just needed to break things up.

His goal was ambitious, and he'd given himself only three weeks to achieve it. It was a challenge, for sure, but meeting it would make him a better teacher, and his competitive spirit always pushed him to become better. He climbed down from the roof, thinking how lucky he was to be in a profession that he cared so much about. By improving his teaching skills, he knew that he would positively influence his students' ability to learn things that would benefit them for the rest of their lives. His job was important; there was no question in his mind about that. He had become a physical education teacher because of the challenge of helping students become active for the rest of their lives. Continuing to improve his teaching skills was part of rising to that challenge. Damon was proud of his accomplishments so far.

Your Turn ▶▶▶

- Have you ever been in a class (K–college) in which you became frustrated with the amount of lecturing and lack of time spent on discussion and practice?

- How do you feel about the opening quotation in this chapter? Does it ring true?

- Why do you suppose some teachers talk so much?

- Why do you think some physical educators have their students wait in lines for turns, although this practice is rare in other subjects?

- How can teachers avoid making excuses and focus on allowing students enough practice time in physical education?

Maximize Learning Opportunities for All Students

By the time students take a physical education class at the secondary level, they will have had a variety of movement experiences. Some students will have had excellent elementary school physical education, and others will have learned little other than how to wait patiently for their turn. Some will have been involved in extracurricular sports and physical activities from early childhood, whereas others will have no experience with organized physical activities. In some states, such as California, where it is common for elementary classroom teachers to be responsible for physical education requirements, many children will have the idea that physical education is recess or organized play. Nationwide, secondary school teachers have students coming to their classes from programs run by elementary specialists that have no purpose to physical education other than to keep children busy, happy, and well behaved. In such instances, children have had no chance to learn the basic movement concepts and skills that are so important in developing competency in sports and physical activity (Graham, Holt/Hale, and Parker 1998).

There are ways to deal with the fact that your students come to your class with varied backgrounds in movement skills and knowledge. Ultimately, it is your responsibility to teach *all* your students, regardless of their ability, background, and experience. Understanding the concept of inclusion is essential to maximizing learning opportunities for all students. We explain the concept briefly in this chapter, but chapter 8 covers in more detail a variety of teaching styles in physical education and how to use the inclusion concept in each one.

Maximizing learning also involves knowing how students learn best. Besides providing plenty of practice opportunities, as discussed earlier in this chapter, you must work to ensure quality practice time. To achieve this goal, you should organize the practice in a way that helps students really learn (retain) the concept or skill, give performance cues, and provide effective feedback. The last issue we will discuss in this chapter is creating motivation for practice, which in a way summarizes many of the important concepts in this chapter.

Include All Students

The **inclusion** concept is the underlying philosophy for teachers who try to make sure that students at all levels of ability can experience success in physical education (see chapter 6 for details about including students with disabilities). Inclusive teaching implies that the teacher provides tasks with variations of varying difficulty so that each student can find one that is right for him. The key here is that each student should experience some success with the task. The success level should be around 80%. If it is higher than that, the student is likely to become bored with the task. If it is lower, the student may become frustrated. Frustration and boredom lead to off-task behavior. When students are successful with a learning activity at a level of about 80%, they are more likely to stay on task and get the practice they need to improve. This concept is often referred to as "teaching in the **flow**" (Csikszentmihalyi 1990).

How can you ensure that students experience 80% success with a task? Graham (2001) suggests planning several variations that differ in difficulty for each main learning activity. The teacher can either let the students choose their variation of the task, called teaching by invitation (Graham 2001), or help them choose the right one, called intratask variation. Chapter 8 covers these methods of teaching in detail. Because the idea is to have all students experience a high, but not too high, level of success, the method you select will depend on your students' ability to choose what works best for them.

Organize Practice Effectively

Many teachers are not aware of the research that shows the importance of practice organization. This is not a textbook on motor learning, but we feel it will be helpful to discuss some concepts typically covered in motor-learning classes to help bridge the gap between theory and practice.

You can organize practice time in many ways. Depending on the learning stage of your students, some can be more effective for retaining the skills or concepts than others (Schmidt 1991). We will briefly explain two main ways to organize practice. For ease of remembering them, we call them repetitive practice and mixed practice. We will also examine when each kind is most effective. For every new skill they attempt, students go through three stages of learning (refer to chapter 5 for more detail). In the first stage, the verbal-cognitive stage, students tend to talk themselves through the movement. If you remember learning how to dance, you know exactly what we're talking about. When you first learned the steps for swing, you probably talked yourself through it as you moved: "slow, slow, quick-quick." For the cha-cha it was "one-two, cha-cha-cha." These verbal reminders help significantly in the first stage of learning, when a lot of thinking is going on. In this first stage, the improvement is rapid if teaching is effective.

In stage two, usually referred to as the motor stage (also called practice phase in some books), students no longer have to think as much about what they are doing. Here they can start thinking about strategy and stylistic aspects of the skill or activity. In the motor stage, improvement comes more slowly, and students may feel that they reach several plateaus as they advance through the stage. The final stage is the autonomous stage. Most students do not attain this stage in a physical education class except in the most basic skills. Reaching this stage takes a lot of practice, and once in this stage the student may not even notice any improvement because it occurs so slowly. Using the three stages of learning or the generic levels of skill proficiency (explained in chapter 8) to classify students will help you decide which type of practice to use. Keeping in mind the concept of inclusive teaching, you can expand your possibilities to help students experience success by using several variations for practice organization: repetitive for the novices and mixed for the students who are progressing through the first learning stage or beyond.

Repetitive Practice

Repetitive practice lets the student practice a task a number of times consecutively before going on to another task. Motor-learning books refer to this as blocked or constant practice. Blocked practice is a method that involves practicing several skills using many repetitions in several blocks, or sets. Constant practice involves performing one task during the entire lesson. These are both repetitive, so an example of repetitive practice would be hitting golf balls at a driving range or on a field. Hitting 20 shots with the driver, pitching 20 times with the 9 iron, and putting 20 times on the putting green would be classified as blocked practice. This kind of practice is effective only early in the learning process, in the verbal-cognitive stage. Beginners need time to establish a motor pattern, and repetitive practice helps them achieve that. Research has shown, however, that this kind of practice is not effective for someone who is no longer a complete beginner (Schmidt 1991). Let's again use golf as an example. Experienced golfers who go to the driving range and hit a bucket of balls using repetitive practice are often successful in that session, but they cannot understand why their next round of golf is mediocre. Repetitive practice gives a false sense of skill and is unlike the criterion activity or sport, in this instance golf. Golfers who are not complete beginners rarely swing the same club twice in a row, unless it's the putter, and even then they never play the putt from the same place using the same stroke. We observe, however, that repetitive practice is a widely used form of skill practice (i.e., drills) in physical education regardless of the students' level of skill. The advice to take from the motor-learning experts is to abandon repetitive practice as soon as your students have established a motor pattern (for example, the basics of a golf swing) and move on to mixed practice (Schmidt 1991).

Mixed Practice

Mixing up the skills or the way of practicing the skills is beneficial for students who have grasped the basics of a skill. In **mixed practice**, students practice one skill in several ways, such as throwing different distances, or mix several skills and practice them in a random way. This form of practice allows students to get beyond the false sense of competency they experience with repetitive practice. We will use basketball as the example this time. Some of the skills involved in basketball include dribbling, shooting, catching, and passing. Students beyond the verbal-cognitive stage of learning should participate in mixed practice. You can do this by having students practice dribbling in a variety of ways in the same task (the motor-learning texts refer to this as variable practice). Another way to mix things up would be to practice at least three basketball skills in a random order in the same task (called random practice in the motor-learning books). The students could, for example, play modified games in which they use at least three skills. In a two-on-two or three-on-three basketball game, the students would use all four skills—dribbling, shooting, passing, and catching—in a random order.

Mixed practice would be appropriate for students who are in the motor or autonomous stages of learning. Modified games are a motivating and effective way to learn, and if the teacher plays the correct role, they will not be roll-out-the-ball lessons. Students beyond the beginner category but not yet comfortable with their skills in a competitive situation will benefit from working at stations where they practice dribbling, shooting, catching, and passing in a random order, never repeating one skill more than two or three times in a row. The point is to try to make the practice as close to the real thing as possible. In addition, you want to make the students *think* each time they perform a skill. If they think about a skill each time they perform it and try to be consistent with the way they go about producing the movement (thinking about the movement and carrying it out), they will be more likely to retain the skill, and the movements will become automatic more rapidly (Schmidt 1991).

We believe these are the most important issues for physical educators to consider in planning practice time in their classes. If you understand the benefits and limitations of repetitive and mixed practice, and for which learning stage each is appropriate, you will be able to modify them and accommodate your students, regardless of their learning stage for a skill.

Tricks and Tools

Excellent teachers make sure all their students are involved in learning activities that maximize their potential for improvement. To do that, you need to know how to use variations and different types of practice, but you also need to know some other tricks and tools of the teaching trade. Giving good performance cues, offering appropriate feedback,

and constantly looking for ways to motivate your students are keys to effective teaching.

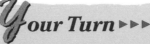

Your Turn ▶▶▶

- Why do you suppose many teachers and coaches use the repetitive form of practice when the motor-learning experts have told us that this is not the most effective way to teach people who are beyond complete beginners?

- What is an example of how to organize a swimming lesson using repetitive practice?

- What is an example of how to organize a swimming lesson using mixed practice?

- What is an example of how to organize a volleyball lesson using repetitive practice?

- What is an example of how to organize a volleyball lesson using mixed practice?

Give Good Performance Cues

You may have a wonderful setup for your lesson to help all your students be successful at practicing the skills, but if they do not know how to perform the skill, your efforts may be of little use. As mentioned earlier, to learn a skill, students should think about it each time they try it. You want them to think about it the correct way every time. This is where students need your help. Giving performance **cues** has been shown to be effective in learning motor skills and concepts. You should give these cues during the instruction or demonstration, but only one or two at a time. You should prepare a short list of cues for each new skill in your lesson plan (more details in chapter 11) and have them ready to use with students as you see that they are ready for another one.

Great cues are short and simple (KISS). The best ones are easy to remember because they are different, funny, or help the student see a clearer picture of the movement in her mind. Figure 7.9 lists some good examples of cues for specific skills. Remember that it is more difficult to simplify things and provide meaningful cues than to rattle on with all kinds of information. Your job as a teacher is to be helpful, not to overwhelm your students with your knowledge. So use your imagination or borrow good cues from other people. A useful cue for kicking the soccer ball is "Use the shoelaces." A memorable cue for basketball shooting that you

Skill	Sample cues	
Step aerobics: V-step	First, third, home, as in baseball (feet go out-out-in-in)	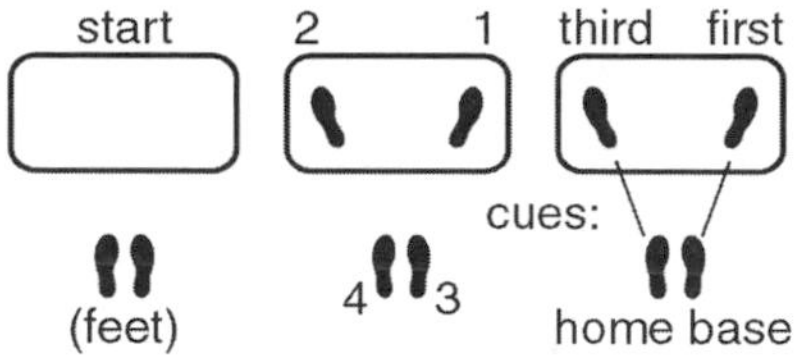
In-line skating: ready position	Knees over toes, nose over knees, rear over heels	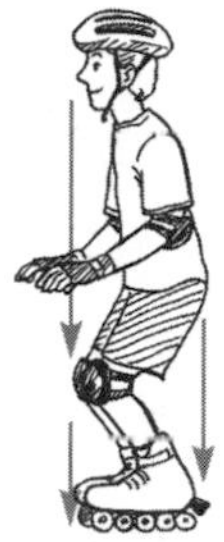
In-line skating: heel brake stop	• Scissor legs • Brake skate in front • "Dirty toilet seat" squat • Lift toe of brake skate	

Figure 7.9 Examples of cues for specific skills.

may have heard is to "Reach for the cookies on the top shelf." Obviously, some cues are more appropriate for certain ages, so you may have to use your imagination to make them age appropriate. Your students may be wonderful resources in this area. You can also visit PE Central (**www.pecentral.com**) to find great cues submitted by teachers around the world for a variety of activities. You might also buy a book on cues. Either way, you may find that as you get better at making the cues short, simple, and memorable, your students will understand the movement better and improve more rapidly.

Provide Effective Feedback

After you have given your cues for a skill you should let students know how they are doing with the task. **Feedback** is crucial for learning, but providing enough feedback to all your students is difficult unless you use self-feedback or partner feedback teaching styles (see chapter 8). Feedback comes in two main types. If it comes from within the person, it's called intrinsic feedback. When it comes from sources outside the person, it's called extrin-

sic feedback. Intrinsic feedback, in which students get messages about their performance from within themselves, is important in learning and in developing the ability to listen to the body and to use that information to improve performance. But the teacher usually must provide extrinsic feedback to help a student develop that ability. Motor-learning texts usually cover intrinsic feedback in detail, but in this chapter we will focus on the extrinsic feedback that teachers provide to their students.

Like cues, feedback is most effective when it is kept short and simple (another example of the KISS principle). Feedback can be described in many ways: it can be positive, negative, general, specific, prescriptive, and congruent with the cues provided. Given too frequently, feedback can cause dependency, which is a problem. But in physical education each teacher usually has at least 25 or 30 students, so this is not an issue if the teacher is the source of the feedback. You don't have enough time to offer much feedback in a lesson unless you have your students provide feedback to each other (see chapter 8, partner feedback style). If that is what you do, you should caution your students that giving feedback too soon will hurt the performer's chance to correct his own mistakes.

Positive feedback is more effective than negative feedback and definitely more appreciated! General feedback is OK and can be motivating if it is positive, such as "Good job," but it is not particularly helpful. In addition, overused phrases, even positive ones, lose their motivating ability. Specific feedback goes into the details of the movement (for example, "Way to follow through high on that backhand, Nicole.") Prescriptive feedback tells the performer how to do better on the next trial, for example, "Good direction on that putt, Gage, but next time try to use the pendulum motion to get the speed right." Prescriptive feedback is by definition specific, but specific feedback need not be prescriptive. Both can be effective.

Besides being specific or prescriptive, feedback should ideally go along with the cues that you have given earlier. Feedback that corresponds with the cues you have given is called congruent feedback (Graham 2001). For example, if one of your main cues for the in-line skating heel stop was "Scissor your legs," your feedback should address that issue. You should refrain from giving feedback on a cue you have not yet used.

A teacher will have to exert a lot of effort to give feedback to each student at least twice in a class period. Consider our example of an effective teacher earlier in the chapter (see table 7.1). If you have 34 minutes of skill practice and 30 students in your class, you would have to give feedback to about two students each minute to reach every student twice during your lesson. Doing this may not sound too difficult, but in observing teachers we find that most have trouble in this area. We do feel, however, that giving students feedback is important for learning and is well worth the effort. In chapter 8, you will learn about several teaching styles that will make it easier for you to tackle the issue of using appropriate amounts of feedback. Quality of feedback is an issue no matter who gives it and how often, so remember that it should be positive, prescriptive, specific, and congruent with the cues, and you will be on the right track. Table 7.2 summarizes the tips for maximizing learning, including using appropriate feedback.

Student Motivation

One of the most common questions we get from teachers and students in pedagogy classes concerns **motivation**. They frequently ask, "How do I motivate my students?" Kids in high school, especially, are often characterized as being uninterested in physical activity. Do they have little interest because the teacher is focusing on activities they don't like? Does the teacher fail to provide choices and thus prevent every student from having a realistic opportunity to become proficient in a few physical activities and competent in many? Do students have little interest because of the way classes are run, because they spend too much waiting for the teacher to finish talking or waiting in line for a turn? Many teachers admit that motivating their students is a major concern. Many other teachers across the nation, however, report no problem with student motivation. These teachers are probably doing something right. It can't just be the local water. We have discussed some of the things that effective teachers do to motivate students. Let's briefly review those here. In addition, we will discuss goal setting, giving students challenges, and using music and choices as motivating tools (figure 7.10).

Table 7.2 Tips for Maximizing Learning	
Beginner (verbal-cognitive stage)	**Beyond beginner (motor and autonomous stages)**
◆ Use repetition to help establish motor pattern.	◆ Avoid repetitions; use mixed practice to help with retention.
◆ Use short, simple cues to help with consistency of movement.	◆ Use short, simple cues to help with consistency of movement.
◆ Use frequent feedback that is positive, specific, prescriptive, and congruent with the cues.	◆ Ask questions that help students figure out how to improve before you give them feedback. This encourages them to think and provide themselves feedback (intrinsic feedback).

Figure 7.10 Giving students ample choices is one way to ensure that motivation is high in your classroom.

One of the things Damon had been most excited about when he accepted the job at Pablo Valley High School was their choice program. As a whole, the student population was excited about physical education because they got to choose three activities per year. Choices included basketball, in-line skating, tennis or pickle ball, golf, ballroom dance, lacrosse, Ultimate Frisbee, orienteering, mountaineering, swimming, volleyball, self-defense, and cardio kick boxing. The school cooperated with the two middle schools in town to make sure that students had an opportunity to experience all these sports and activities before they got to Pablo Valley. That way they knew which activities they wanted to pursue and which they wanted to avoid. The system worked so well that Damon couldn't imagine putting together a curriculum any other way. The teachers enjoyed it as well because they were able to teach the sports and activities in which they were most skilled. Damon was relieved that he didn't have to teach tennis. His expertise in ballroom dancing and in-line skating had been the main reason that he got the job. The other teachers were thrilled to have those two activities added to their choices because students had asked for them for several years.

No, motivation was not really an issue at Pablo Valley, but Damon knew he was lucky. In his previous job, student motivation was always a topic of discussion at department meetings. His old school's traditional curriculum of football, softball, basketball, track and field, and soccer had limited appeal among the students. The curriculum didn't appeal to him either, but his colleagues had not been willing to consider adding "new age" activities. When the job came up at Pablo Valley in the next town over, Damon jumped at the chance. Now he worked with like-minded colleagues whose focus was teaching skills and concepts that would help students be active for the rest of their lives. The students seemed to understand that. The choice curriculum, Damon was sure, was key to their motivation.

Motivation and the Learning Environment

A well-run class in which the teacher uses time wisely, establishes protocols, enforces rules, communicates expectations, and is caring but demanding is no doubt more motivating to most students than a class in which the teacher wastes time and is vague about expectations. In addition, a teacher who is enthusiastic about the subject and becomes involved with the lesson will be more motivating than one who seems detached and less concerned with student learning. The teacher can express this kind of motivation by ensuring that students get plenty of quality practice opportunities and receive ample, appropriate feedback during the learning activities. Mixed practice, as mentioned earlier, is not only a more effective way for those beyond the verbal-cognitive stage to learn but also tends to be more fun because it is less repetitive.

Motivation results when students experience success with a task. Maintaining enthusiasm is tough when failure is the only result or when the task is so easy that further practice seems pointless. Inclusive teaching is therefore essential. A positive environment where students feel safe is also important, a topic we will discuss in chapter 9.

Goal Setting and Challenges

Establishing an effective learning environment will not ensure that all students will be motivated in physical education. So what else can you do? Motor-learning experts suggest that if students learn the concept of **goal setting** and then set their own goals, they are more likely to try harder and be more motivated to improve and learn. Studies have shown that setting goals provides better motivation than the teacher's saying, "Try your best" (Schmidt 1991). Students should set both long-term and short-term goals. For example, a student might write this long-term goal in his physical education journal: "In this unit I will learn the forehand, backhand, serve, lob, and volley well enough that I can be a worthy opponent in a tennis match with my mom." A short-term goal for the same student for a lesson focusing on the backhand would be "Today I'm going to learn three good cues for the backhand, and I will hit at least 10 good backhand shots this lesson."

Teachers can help students set both short-term and long-term goals. To help with the goal-setting process, you should recognize several points. If goals are unobtainable, students will be frustrated. If goals are not challenging enough, they will be useless in encouraging improvement. Specificity makes it easier to hold students accountable, and for goals to work you have to give them a time frame. To remember these issues, we have developed the acronym COST. Consider the **COST of goals**: are they Challenging, Obtainable, Specific, and do you have a Time frame?

Short-term goals that the teacher gives the students during class are also called challenges. For example, the teacher might challenge students practicing with partners in the Ultimate Frisbee unit by saying, "How many successful throws and catches can you perform in a row while varying your distance? See how much you can keep improving your record." Challenges can motivate students to stay with a task, and they are only limited by your imagination. You'll find more examples of challenges in table 7.3.

Your Turn ▸▸▸

◆ What is a sample challenge for a swing dance lesson?

◆ What is a sample challenge for a swimming task?

◆ What is a sample challenge for a basketball learning activity?

Let the Music Play

Most people, especially teenagers, like music of some form. Music at 120 beats per minute or higher is motivating, and the right music can make a student who normally hates fitness exercises tolerate them. Music is even more likely to motivate students if they get to choose it, either from your CD or tape library, or from their own collection of tapes or CDs (unfortunately, prescreening is necessary). You may choose to have theme days and let the students choose from within that theme. Theme days could include country and western, rock, contemporary, reggae, rap, jazz, or even classical music. The type you use depends on your desired outcome. Music with a steady beat at 120 beats per minute or higher is motivating for active tasks, whereas slower music can be a wonderful way to end a lesson by promoting relaxation and a reduction in heart and breathing

Table 7.3 Sample Challenges to Students in a Variety of Activities

Activity	Sample challenges to students
In-line skating	Choose a spot or line on the ground. Can you use your heel brake to stop on that point? How close can you get?
Team handball	How many successful passes can you and your partner make in a row?
Walleyball	Can you make a perfect set for your partner? Can you duplicate that perfect set?
Step aerobics	Can you stay with the beat of the music for the whole routine?
Golf	How many putts can you make in a row, varying the distance and angle with each putt?

rates. Beth Kirkpatrick, a former NASPE Middle School Teacher of the Year, used a different classical composer each month during her "Gravionics" (a balancing strength-endurance and flexibility program) portion of the class. She says, "This has proven to be a great resource for educating students on the powerful effects that music can have on emotional and mental fitness, as well as actually causing physical changes with respect to heart rate and respiration" (Kirkpatrick 1993, 8). Building a small tape or CD library is easy if you involve your students. A homework assignment in the beginning of the school year could be for each student to bring in an audiotape or CD with 10 songs or music pieces of their choice. If some of your students don't have access to a stereo, you could have them complete the assignment in pairs or small groups. You could also provide a portable stereo that students could check out or use at school. Before giving the assignment, be sure to establish criteria for acceptable music, which would exclude music with swear words, violence or gang references, and racial slurs. In addition, listen to student-selected music before playing it in class to make sure that nothing inappropriate slips by you.

Purpose

Use digital technologies to build a library of music with various beat counts for the purpose of enhancing students' physical education experiences.

Resource and Procedure

Research the various options for sharing and downloading digital music on the Web. Many sites can be used for creating and maintaining a diverse music library that fits a variety of class activities. Most of these sites offer music files for a small fee. Music files can be stored on your computer and burned on to CDs to be used in class. You can also use a CD burner to record digital music sources without downloading music files. There are numerous sites set up for presenting information about digital music storage capabilities. Try **www.free-mp3-music-player-downloads.com** for a comprehensive overview of digital music transfers over the Internet.

Give Them Choices

Most of us like the feeling of independence and importance we get when we participate in decision making. Giving students choices can be a great way to motivate them. Choices can be about small items, such as choosing the type of ball to use or selecting the distance from a partner while practicing throwing and catching, or they can involve bigger decisions, such as which body part to work on during the muscle toning portion of the class. This idea relates back to the concept of variations. Teaching by invitation (Graham 2001) is a wonderful way to allow students to have a say in your lesson. Providing choices should never become a free-for-all in which the teacher asks students, "What do you want to do today?" Effective teachers plan their lessons thoroughly, including what kinds of choices they allow the students to make.

According to the Diamond Conceptual Framework (remember chapter 1?), the older the students, the more they should be able to choose which activities they get involved in. A 9th or 10th grader who has been exposed to a variety of sports and physical activities in middle school probably knows what she really enjoys and in what activity she would like to become competent or proficient. If you allow her to choose among three or four (or more if possible) activities in each unit, she is likely to be more excited about physical education and more motivated to learn because she made the decision.

Offering choices, small or large, can be key to motivating your students in physical education, especially when you use this method in conjunction with the other effective teaching methods and tools discussed in this chapter.

Reflect Often

This chapter covers a lot of information about teaching effectively. But you should know that excellent teachers make mistakes all the time! What makes them different, and excellent, is not that they are perfect. They are excellent because they reflect on what they did in every lesson, every day, and constantly find ways to improve. Excellent teaching is not a destination; it's a journey. If you choose to take the path of the excellent teacher, you commit every day to trying to use what you have learned about effective teaching.

But there is an equally important part. You also commit to reflecting constantly on your successes and setbacks. If you do this, you will be on the path of excellence. We believe this is the most challenging and rewarding part of our profession. By reflecting, teachers have a new chance to succeed with each new lesson!

Damon's ability to reflect made him successful as a teacher. A school day didn't pass when he wouldn't think through the day's lessons and critically analyze how he could improve. "Always something to work on" was his response to anyone who commented on his drive to excel.

He reached his goal of cutting down on talk time in the three weeks. His friend Michele was impressed at his tenacity and drive to be the best teacher he could possibly be. When the nomination forms from the school district went out that spring, she had no doubt that Damon would be a deserving recipient of the award. In her nomination letter she wrote, among other things, the following: "Damon's ability to constantly reflect on the effectiveness of his teaching methods, and his ability to focus on teaching students skills and concepts that will help them for the rest of their lives, make him a model for teachers of any subject area." She asked Damon for permission to copy some of the pages in his reflection journal to include in the nomination packet. The journal was a complete collection of short daily entries for the last two years. Damon had shared parts of the journal with her before. He knew it helped him to write things down so that he could look back on them later when he needed a reminder of one sort or another. He agreed to let her copy some entries, and both of them waited with anticipation for the school district to make the decision.

Summary

Becoming an effective teacher takes time and involves much reflection. As you think about what you do well and not so well, you should aim for excellence by remembering the principles of effective teaching discussed in this chapter. An effective teacher is caring but demanding. She establishes clear rules and protocols in the beginning of the school year. She uses her time wisely by taking roll while students are involved in learning activities, by giving short and simple instructions and demonstrations, by avoiding lines, and by shortening transition time. She maximizes learning opportunities for all students by using teaching techniques such as variations and practice organization suitable to the students' skill level. She gives good performance cues and appropriate congruent feedback. By using these effective teaching practices and other tools, such as goal setting, challenges, music, and choices, an effective teacher motivates students to stay interested in learning the skills and activities.

By constantly reflecting on your successes and setbacks in teaching, you will be on the path of excellence. Remember that excellent teachers make mistakes all the time, but they are not afraid to reflect on their mistakes and learn from them. They see having a chance to succeed with each new lesson as the most challenging and rewarding part of their profession!

Checking for Understanding ▸▸▸

◆ What is meant by being caring but demanding?

◆ What is the difference between rules and protocols?

◆ What are five different ways to use your time wisely and allow for more learning-activity time in physical education?

◆ What does KISS stand for, and why is it important when it comes to instructions and demonstrations?

◆ Why is success important in learning, and what happens if there is too much or too little of it?

◆ What is the difference between repetitive and mixed practice? When is the best time to use each type?

◆ What are three characteristics of good performance cues? How many cues should you use at a time? How many cues should you plan for each skill practice?

◆ What are three characteristics of effective feedback?

◆ How do you motivate students in physical education?

◆ What does "consider the COST of your goals" mean?

For Reflection and Discussion ▸▸▸

◆ How will you make sure that you become an effective and reflective teacher?

◆ Have you seen a choice program in place in a high school? If so, how was it set up?

◆ Were students in your physical education classes in middle and high school motivated? Why or why not?

◆ What kind of music motivates you?

◆ How will you use music in your physical education classes?

◆ Do you use goal setting in any area of your life? Does it work for you? Do you consider the COST of your goals?

References

Csikszentmihalyi, M. 1990. *Flow*. New York: Harper & Row.

Graham, G. 2001. *Teaching children physical education, becoming a master teacher*. 2nd ed. Champaign, IL: Human Kinetics.

Graham, G., S. Holt/Hale, and M. Parker. 1998. *Children moving: A reflective approach to teaching physical education*. 4th ed. Mountain View, CA: Mayfield.

Kirkpatrick, B. 1993. *The ultra shuffle: Who's keeping score?* Grundy Center, IA: For Your Heart.

Schmidt, R. 1991. *Motor learning and performance: From principles to practice*. Champaign, IL: Human Kinetics.

Suggested Readings

American Alliance for Health, Physical Education, Recreation and Dance. 1999. *Physical education for lifelong fitness: The Physical Best teacher's guide*. Champaign, IL: Human Kinetics.

Harrison, J., C. Blakemore, and M. Buck. 2001. *Instructional strategies for secondary physical education*. 5th ed. Boston: McGraw-Hill.

McCracken, B. 2001. *It's not just gym anymore. Teaching secondary school students how to be active for life*. Champaign, IL: Human Kinetics.

Metzler, M. 2000. *Instructional models for physical education*. Boston: Allyn & Bacon.

Chapter **8**

Teaching Styles in Physical Education

> Learning is not attained by chance,
> it must be sought for with ardor and
> attended to with diligence.
>
> — *Abigail Adams*

ora has been a high school physical education teacher for five years. She has struggled since the beginning of her teaching career with the issue of skill diversity in her classes. In just about every class she teaches, the students' skill level for a particular activity ranges from complete beginner to almost proficient. No matter what kind of task she plans, about a third of the students find it too easy or too difficult. In addition, Lora's classes are large, at least 40 students in each period. She's finding it hard to give the students enough feedback to help them learn more. Last week at the Virginia AHPERD conference, she heard a speaker talk about using different teaching styles to alleviate many difficulties in teaching. The speaker addressed the two major problems Lora struggles with, skill diversity and being unable to give enough feedback. She is eager to try with her classes some of the teaching styles she's just learned about.

Learning Objectives

After reading this chapter thoroughly and discussing the issues in class, you should be able to

- explain what the inclusion concept is,
- list and define the generic levels of skill proficiency,
- explain the two main kinds of variations,
- list the teaching styles presented in this chapter,
- describe the student's and the teacher's role in each of the teaching styles,
- describe one advantage and one disadvantage for each teaching style,
- describe the progression of the teaching styles, and
- explain how to use teaching styles as variations.

Key Terms and Phrases

Generic levels of skill proficiency (GLSP)
Inclusion
Variations
Teaching by invitation
Intratask variation
Direct teaching style
Teacher feedback style
Partner feedback style
Self-feedback style
Convergent discovery style
Divergent discovery style

In the previous two chapters, we established that effective teachers have many things in common. Among other things, they create an environment for learning that maximizes the opportunities for all students to learn. Being able to do that takes knowledge in the areas of effective teaching as well as willingness to reflect and improve. But it involves even more, including learning about and using a variety of teaching styles. The style you use should depend on what you are trying to accomplish with the lesson. In other words, your learning objectives should guide you. Teaching can be compared to carpentry. If you have only a hammer and a saw in your tool belt, you will be able to do only certain kinds of work. But if you have all the tools imaginable, you would decide which ones to use after you know what you will be building. Likewise, if you as a teacher have only two teaching styles in your repertoire, you will have limited options for reaching all your students and providing opportunities for them to learn more. With more teaching styles in your tool belt, you will open doors for yourself and your students.

This chapter will present a spectrum of teaching styles built on the work of Mosston and Ashworth (1994, 2001). This chapter simplifies and renames some of the styles for easier recognition and memorization. We do not include Mosston's complete spectrum of teaching styles, but have chosen instead to focus on those we believe are most useful for secondary physical education teachers. In addition, we have made the inclusion style the premise for all the other teaching styles we describe in this chapter.

Inclusion Concept

Most teachers are in a situation similar to Lora's. Their students' skill proficiency varies greatly within each class and from activity to activity. In chapters 4, 5, and 7 we discussed some of the reasons that students come to our physical education classes with widely varied levels of skill proficiency. To review briefly, some students have been involved in sport and physical activity of all sorts from early childhood, and others have not. Some grow and develop quickly, and others develop slowly. Some have had quality physical education in earlier grades, and others have not. Some have parents who teach them skills, and others do not.

The result of children's varied movement experiences is that middle or junior high school physical education classes will include students with a variety of levels of skill proficiency, no matter what skills you choose to teach. Because these programs vary as well, and because children continue to have different movement experiences after school, you can count on having a variety of levels of skill proficiency in all your physical education classes in high school, too.

To help teachers pinpoint and understand differences in skill proficiency, Graham, Holt/Hale, and Parker, based on work by Stanley (1977), developed a classification system called the **generic levels of skill proficiency** (GLSP). The GLSP (Graham, Holt/Hale, and Parker 1998) includes four levels that span the three stages of learning described in chapters 5 and 7: precontrol (covers the verbal-cognitive stage of learning), control (verbal-cognitive stage and beginning of the motor stage), utilization (motor stage), and proficiency (late motor and autonomous stages). Table 8.1 describes the stages.

Now you may ask yourself this question: If it is true that I will have such varied GLSP in my classes for most skills and activities, how can I still make sure that all my students will learn? One answer is to use an **inclusion** approach to teaching, one that allows all students to experience success, tackle challenges, and improve self-efficacy (figure 8.1).

As you remember from chapter 1, the guiding lights of our profession tell us that we should be concerned with all our students' learning and make sure that we help them become physically educated people. This is no easy task. But teachers all over the world are able to do just that because they care enough to make it a priority. If a teacher makes a conscious effort to provide all students an equal opportunity to learn skills and concepts at a level appropriate for them, we say he is using the inclusion concept in his teaching. This effort should allow all students to experience success yet confront challenging tasks. We also call this teaching in the flow (Csikszentmihalyi 1990). Students are more likely to stay on task when they are about 80% successful with a task. If they experience more than 80% success, they have a tendency to become bored. If they experience less than 80% success, they tend to become frustrated. Boredom and frustration usually lead to off-task behavior, which in turn causes discipline problems. This affects the learning process because it reduces the time students spend on practicing the skills. So how do

Table 8.1 Generic Levels of Skill Proficiency

Level of skill proficiency	Definitions from Graham. Holt/Hale. and Parker (1993)	Examples
Precontrol	"The precontrol level is characterized by lack of ability to consciously control or intentionally replicate movement" (p. 60).	A child who catches a disk (Frisbee) with inconsistent form and seems awkward and only "accidentally" successful would be at the precontrol level for that skill.
Control	The control (advanced beginner) level is characterized by less haphazard movements. The body appears to respond more accurately to the child's intentions. The child's movements often involve intense concentration because the movements are far from automatic. A movement that the child repeats becomes increasingly uniform and efficient (p. 62).	A child who, with intense concentration, can usually throw a disk (Frisbee) successfully in the direction of her target would be at the control level for that skill.
Utilization	The utilization (intermediate) level is characterized by increasingly automatic movements. A child at this level is able to use the movement in different contexts because he doesn't need to think as much about how to execute the movement (p. 62).	A child who, with concentration, is able to use particular disk (Frisbee) throws and catches in a game situation is considered to be at the utilization level for those skills. He would be able to execute the skills consistently and, with concentration, combine them with the other skills he has learned that apply to the game.
Proficiency	The fourth level of proficiency (advanced) is characterized by somewhat automatic movements that begin to seem effortless. At this level, the child gains control of a specific movement and is challenged by the opportunity to employ that skill in changing environments that require sudden and unpredictable movements (pp. 62–63).	A child who is at the proficiency level for a variety of disk (Frisbee) throws and catches would enjoy the challenges of the game of Ultimate (Frisbee). Even when focusing on strategy, she can perform the skills effortlessly.

Adapted, by permission, from G. Graham et al., 1993, *A reflective approach to teaching physical education*, 4th ed. (Mountain View, CA: Mayfield), 61.

Slam Dunkin' Success

Figure 8.1 Inclusion of all students allows each student to experience some level of success, no matter what the activity is.

you make sure that students are about 80% successful? One way would be to provide an appropriate task for each student. Planning several variations of a task that differ in difficulty can accomplish this. You can choose which variation each student will perform, or the student can choose one. We usually refer to this concept of teaching as inclusion teaching. You should incorporate it into all the styles explained in this chapter.

Variations

Graham (2001) describes two methods of incorporating **variations** of the main task into the lesson to make sure that all students are in the flow. Both are inclusion teaching methods, and both involve planning a main task according to the skill proficiency of the majority of the students for the particular skills, as well as several easier and more difficult variations of each learning activity. In the first method, called **teaching by invitation,** the teacher lets students choose a variation of a learning activity that allows them to experience success but still feel challenged. The teacher has already planned these variations, which are well-defined harder or easier versions of the main task. For example, if the main task is dribbling a basketball while running, an easier variation would be walking and dribbling. A more difficult variation would be running and performing a crossover dribble. In chapter 11, we provide examples for other activities.

The second method of incorporating variations into a lesson is called **intratask variation.** Here the teacher gives selected students variations to try after she has observed their level of success with a task. The variations can be the same as those used in teaching by invitation. The difference is in the manner of presentation.

Which of these two methods you choose will probably depend on your students. Are they able to select a task variation that permits them to be successful about 80% of the time? Many students can make a suitable choice, and with them you can use teaching by invitation. Other students may choose tasks that are either too difficult or not challenging enough. For those students, intratask variation is probably the better method. With proper planning and use, both techniques allow students to experience maximal skill practice and learning and minimal off-task behavior.

Selected Teaching Styles

As mentioned in the beginning of this chapter, the teaching styles we present here are slightly modified from Mosston and Ashworth's (1994, 2001) work. The main difference is that we promote the inclusion concept for each of the styles that we present rather than treat inclusion as a separate teaching style, as they did in their work. In addition, we have renamed many other styles to make them easier to remember. The styles are still on a continuum, however, spanning from most teacher controlled (direct teaching style) to least teacher controlled (divergent discovery style).

Direct Teaching Style

In the **direct teaching style,** the teacher plans the tasks and leads the class through a task step by step (figure 8.2). He tells them what to do and where, when, and how to do it. He makes all the decisions in the learning process. The student's role is to follow the teacher's instructions. Teachers commonly use this style in aerobics classes, martial arts classes, and during calisthenics. A common equivalent term is *command style* (Mosston and Ashworth 1994, 2001).

This style can be useful when you want all students to be active at the same time and doing the same task, such as in practicing routines in aerobics, martial arts, cheerleading, or dance. The style is probably more appropriate for fitness than it is for skill development, but it can be a time-efficient way to teach basic techniques such as the tennis

Figure 8.2 In the direct teaching mode, teachers are responsible for decision making in the learning process.

grip or the golf grip. For example, the teacher could have the students in a half circle with their tennis rackets on the ground. After brief instruction and a short demonstration, on the teacher's command the students would pick up the racket using the grip the teacher had just shown them. When used in this way, the direct teaching style is an effective way to change from instruction and demonstration to another style that allows students to practice the skill on their own and receive more feedback.

Because the teacher is busy leading the class in this style, she will find it almost impossible to provide feedback. The teacher may offer general feedback, such as "Good job," but rarely can she provide specific, individual feedback unless she has help. If a teacher aide, team teacher, or student leads the class, the teacher could walk around, observe, and provide feedback.

Little student-teacher interaction occurs with this style, so it does not lend itself well to teaching social skills and concepts, such as cooperation. Goal setting (chapter 7) can be incorporated, but this technique may also be limited because the direct teaching style requires all students to perform a task at the same time and in a similar way.

At first glance, the direct teaching style does not seem to lend itself well to the inclusion approach. But with simple variations that the teacher can quickly communicate while giving the instructions, the style can be semi-inclusive. A step aerobics routine, for example, could include variations such as lifting the knees higher for more intensity, adding or dropping arm movements for more or less complexity, or doing the steps on the floor for less intensity. The teacher could easily incorporate and communicate these variations to students while providing the other continuous teaching cues.

Teacher Feedback Style

In the **teacher feedback style,** the teacher plans the tasks and lets the students perform them independently, in pairs, or in groups while she observes them and provides feedback. After the teacher has explained the tasks, the students are able to make decisions about how to perform those tasks, such as pace, exact location, interval, starting and stopping time, and so forth. In this style it is useful and time efficient to prepare task sheets for the students. Task sheets explain in detail the tasks to be performed and the number of trials for each one. The task sheet should also have a place for the students to check off when they are done with each task (see figure 8.3).

Skill to practice: _**Serving**_   Name:_____

Directions:

1. Get a tennis racket and six tennis balls.
2. Go to an open serving spot and start practicing your serve. You have three choices:
   a. Serve over the net and aim to hit the ball anywhere inside the court on the other side.
   b. Serve over the net and aim to hit the ball inside the service court.
   c. Serve over the net and aim to hit inside the hoop located inside the service court.
3. Serve six times. Then go to the other side, pick up your tennis balls, and start over. Do five sets of six serves and then hand in your completed task sheet.
4. I will come around and give you feedback based on the things I showed you in the demo today. Here are some of the things I'll be looking for:
   a. Do you start in the ready position with forehand grip, ball, and racket together?
   b. Do you swing the racket down and back with a pendulum motion?
   c. Do you "scratch your back" with the racket and release the ball from the hand straight in the air?

Check here when you have completed each set:

Set 1: _____
Set 2: _____
Set 3: _____
Set 4: _____
Set 5: _____

Challenge: How many times in a row can you hit your target area? _____

Figure 8.3   Sample teacher feedback task sheet for tennis.

Making sure that all students have a chance to be successful but challenged is fairly easy in this style, if you use one of the methods described previously—teaching by invitation or intratask variation. The key is for the teacher to set up ahead of time and have a main task with several easier and more difficult variations. The students would then either choose their specific task difficulty (see table 8.1) or have one assigned by the teacher based on his knowledge of their skill proficiency. Because the teacher equally values all choices or assignments, students should feel free to choose the appropriate task or be happy with the task assigned by the teacher.

The teacher feedback style, probably the most common style of teaching, is a good style to use to ensure that students get lots of skill practice (figure 8.4) but it has one major disadvantage. A teacher with more than 10 students in a class will probably be unable to provide enough feedback to each student. In chapter 7, we discussed the need for feedback in learning motor skills. You may recall that the danger of providing too much feedback is an issue we usually don't have to consider because middle and high school physical education classes usually contain at least 25 students. The problem is definitely lack of feedback. However, teachers who are able to use their time efficiently can be successful with this style. A particularly appropriate use for this style is when teaching a skill that is new to all the students.

The teacher feedback style can be used with students working in pairs or small groups. In this situation, the style lends itself well to teaching social skills such as cooperation. Other affective domain attributes such as self-concept and self-efficacy can also be a focus in this style. For example, students can learn how to set realistic short-term and long-term goals for skill or fitness development. The teacher would use goal setting to motivate and encourage students to keep practicing the skills or keep working on their fitness tasks. When students reach their goals, they feel good about their accomplishments. Consequently, their self-concept and self-efficacy for that activity or skill may improve.

Figure 8.4 The teacher feedback style can be used with students working in pairs or small groups.

Your Turn ▶▶▶

◆ We mentioned several examples of activities for which the direct teaching style would be useful. Can you come up with more examples?

◆ What happens to the teacher feedback style if the teacher neglects to provide feedback to students?

◆ Why do you suppose many teachers are hesitant to venture outside the safety zone of these two teaching styles?

Partner Feedback Style

In the **partner feedback style,** the teacher plans the tasks and writes out specific criteria for how to perform the skills involved (figure 8.5). Students work with partners, and each member of a pair has a chance to do the tasks and observe the partner doing the tasks. In the important role of observer, the student monitors the doer's performance, compares it to the criteria the teacher has given the class for the particular skill, and gives the partner specific, congruent feedback (Mosston and Ashworth 1994, 2001).

The task sheet becomes an important object in this style. Without specific descriptions of each task and criteria for how to do each skill correctly, the teacher will probably spend all his time answering questions when trying to use this style. When task sheets are well planned and written with criteria that are clear and easy to follow, students are able to be self-sufficient for the most part. The teacher's role then becomes to observe the partners and ask questions of the observers if problems occur that the pair cannot work out. The teacher should not override the observer's role in this style. He should resist the temptation to give feedback directly to the doer and instead ask questions that can help the *observer* give appropriate feedback to the doer. The teacher should generally be available for any questions the pair might have about the criteria, the task, or their roles.

You would use the teaching by invitation and intratask variation techniques in this style in much the same way you would use them in the teacher feedback style. The main difference would be to make sure that students respect their partners' choices of tasks without making fun or making

Figure 8.5   The partner feedback style allows students to observe a partner performing a task and give feedback according to the teacher-designed task/criteria sheet.

judgments. This issue makes the partner interaction style a great choice for teaching social skills such as cooperation, appreciation of differences, and respect for others.

The major advantage of this style is that students receive substantial feedback. You might consider teaching your students some of the main concepts of giving appropriate feedback, a topic we covered in chapter 7. Another advantage is that because only half the students are performing the task at one time, your need for physical education equipment is halved. The partner feedback style is a good choice for activities that require more equipment than you may have available. Even if there is not enough equipment for each student, all can be actively involved in the learning activity, either by performing the tasks or by observing the partner.

This style also allows students to study and analyze movement, which can take the learning experience to higher cognitive levels.

A disadvantage of this style is the possibility that it may become a "do and wait" style. Students may not perform their job as observers and instead just wait for their turn. This circumstance is more likely to occur if you do not adequately explain the students' roles. A way to make sure that students stay on task as both doer and observer is to hold them accountable for what they learn in both roles (see assessment ideas in chapter 12) and to collect the task sheets for credit at the end of class. You might use the sheets for grading purposes, put them in the students' portfolios, or use them for taking roll. Figure 8.6 presents an example of a partner feedback task sheet.

Teaching style: *Partner feedback*

Observer's name: _____

Doer's name: _____

Skills to practice: *Stride one, A-frame turn, heel brake stop*

Directions: Practice the skills with a partner. Take turns observing and doing the skills. When you observe, help your partner by giving feedback according to the criteria below. Use the table to check off your partner's technique after each set of five trials. When you have finished all three sets for all the skills, hand in your completed task sheet. Make sure your partner hands in one as well.

Skill	Criteria	Write GI (got it) or NP (needs practice)			
		Set 1	Set 2	Set 3	Comments:
Stride one	Start in ready position with knees bent. Press against the inside edge of your *back* skate as you transfer the weight to the front skate. Aim for a short *glide* and increase the pressure to create a *stride* (glide + pressure = stride). Repeat to make a continuous forward movement.				
Heel brake stop	Start in ready position with knees bent. Take scissors stance (one skate well in front, triangle). Weight on nonbrake leg to start. Use "dirty toilet seat" position. Lift the toe on the brake skate or point toe for cuff-activated brake. Gradually increase pressure on the brake. Keep head up and eyes forward.				
A-frame turn	Practice one side first, then the other. Coast in ready stance. Point toes to form an A. With arms at waist level, rotate upper body in turning direction and look toward where you're going. Push against inside edge of outside skate.				

Figure 8.6   Sample partner feedback task sheet with criteria for in-line skating skills.

The first teaching style Lora decided to try was the partner feedback style. The following week was the start of the self-defense unit. She spent some time with her students to make sure they understood the new style. "When we use the partner feedback style," she explained, "I will take on a new role. You will too. I will become more of a guide on the side, and you will take over many of the responsibilities for teaching each other." The students looked at her. Some seemed excited, others had mischievous grins on their faces, and yet others seemed a little worried. "Don't worry," she continued. "I will not leave all the teaching to you. You will just be responsible for giving each other feedback, but I will help you with that. You will know exactly what to look for. The most important thing to remember is that you consider your partner's feelings and give feedback in a way that is helpful, not hurtful. I will come around and check on how you're doing with that too. So my job is to help the observer give good feedback to the doer." They seemed to get it. A few students had questions, and she clarified. The worried looks disappeared.

When they tried the partner feedback style for the first time the following week, things went well. They were working on blocks. Lora had made sure to use teacher feedback for the same skills the day before. As she looked around the gym and saw most of her students on task and using their criteria sheets, she smiled. She had spent a few hours creating two criteria sheets, but she knew they were effective. She also knew that the work she did now would pay off later because she saved the criteria sheets in a file on her computer, ready for revisions and reuse next year.

Self-Feedback Style

The **self-feedback style** is similar to the partner feedback style in every way except that the learners provide their own feedback by comparing their performance to the teacher's specific criteria for each skill (figure 8.7). The teacher plans the tasks and writes out specific criteria for each skill on a task sheet. After setting up the class and starting the students on the tasks, the teacher observes each student's ability to evaluate his or her own performance. As in the partner feedback style the teacher would have to resist the temptation to give students direct feedback. Instead, if necessary she should ask questions to make sure the student is properly using the task sheet with the skill criteria. The task sheet should have a spot for the learner to check off completion of a task as well as a place to evaluate the quality of the performance (figure 8.8). The teacher must assure students that they will not be graded down for marking "need practice." She must relieve them of the belief that simply checking off "got it" will earn them a better grade for the day. The teacher should emphasize goal setting and personal improvement, and grade students on their ability to analyze their own movements correctly.

Self-feedback can be used even if the students are involved in a group or partner task. For example, the task could be to play a modified game of team handball (i.e., 3-on-3). The task sheet would

Figure 8.7 Learners provide their own feedback in the self-feedback mode.

list the criteria for the skills the students would focus on, for instance dribbling, passing, and shooting goals. The teacher could periodically give a signal for the students to take a short break to check off their criteria sheet.

If students are working with a partner or group, criteria on the task sheet could emphasize cooperation and trust issues.

Skill to practice: __*Dribbling (soccer)*__   Name:_____

Directions:

1. Choose a station (1, 2, or 3) and practice dribbling the soccer ball. At station 1, you will dribble straight down the line. At station 2, you will dribble through cones, and at station 3, you will dribble through a group of defenders.
2. You may switch stations at any time if you feel the one you chose is too hard or too easy for you.
3. Evaluate your own performance by using the criteria below. Use the table to check off your technique after each set of five trials.
4. When you have finished all three sets, hand in your completed task sheet.

Dribbling criteria	Write GI (got it) or NP (needs practice).			
	Set 1	Set 2	Set 3	Comments
I keep my knees bent.				
I contact the ball below the "equator."				
I use the inside or outside of my feet to contact the ball.				
I keep the ball 1 to 2 feet from my feet at all times.				
I look up at where I'm going, not at the ball.				

Figure 8.8 Sample self-feedback task sheet with criteria for soccer.

Advantages of the self-feedback style are that the students learn to analyze their own movements, correct their own mistakes, and become more independent learners. Mastering this skill is a major step on the way to becoming a lifelong learner and participant in physical activity. On the other hand, using this style early in the learning process with students will likely be ineffective because students may be unable to evaluate their own performance or give themselves useful feedback. As a result, they may not learn. The inclusion approach is easy to use with the self-feedback style. Both teaching by invitation and intratask variation would work well as inclusion techniques. In figure 8.8, we present an example of a self-feedback task sheet using teaching by invitation variations.

Your Turn ▶▶▶

♦ Did any of your teachers ever use partner feedback or self-feedback? If so, in which subjects did they use these styles? How did you like being a student in these styles?

♦ What do you think would be the most difficult issue for you in using the partner feedback or self-feedback style?

♦ What issues might you need to address with your students if they have never used task sheets in physical education?

Convergent Discovery

In the **convergent discovery style,** the teacher designs a problem with only one possible solution and lets the students try to discover the answer by themselves, in pairs, or in groups while they perform tasks that the teacher has prepared. This is an excellent style to incorporate into game play (modified or full) to help students learn concepts and strategies. For example, in tennis there is an area commonly referred to as no-man's-land. This is the whole middle area on each side where it is difficult to get to and hit the ball because you are too far away from the net to volley and too far from the baseline to reach a lob easily. The idea is that you should try to avoid being in this area to receive a ball. Your students can discover this concept through singles or doubles game play. The question becomes "Can you find/pinpoint the area on your court where you should avoid being when waiting for the ball to be returned to your side?" The technique is called convergent discovery because the question has only one correct answer. For another example, suppose you had your students practicing the beginning of an A-frame turn in in-line skating. You give them the cues necessary to start practicing, but you want them to discover an important element of the skill. You could ask them, "Which way will you turn if you push against the inside edge of your right skate?" They will solve this problem more quickly than they will the tennis problem, but setting it up may be worth the effort because so many students delight in discovering concepts rather than always having them spelled out.

When your students are ready to play full or modified versions of a game, or they have mastered the basics of a skill and are ready for more complicated tasks and concepts, this style can be especially useful. For example, you could ask students to play a modified game of basketball (three-on-three) and find the answer to the following question: "When playing person-to-person defense, what strategy will best help you prevent the other team from scoring?" The answer would be "To always try to stay between the person you're defending and the basket." Students can work on convergent discovery problems alone or with a partner, but you must hold them accountable for their discoveries and learning. This can rapidly become a roll-out-the-ball style if students are not on task and searching for the solution to the problem.

You can easily incorporate the inclusion concept in this style. You can design variations of each task that are easier and more difficult and teach by invitation or use intratask variation. The important point is that students will be able to solve the same convergent discovery problem no matter which task variation they use. Although it may seem that movement skills and movement knowledge are the most natural concepts to discover with this style, it can also be useful with concepts related to social skills, self-efficacy, and self-concept. If students are working in groups or pairs, this style can be effective in helping them discover the importance of cooperative skills or in boosting their self-image by experiencing success with solving the problems.

Divergent Discovery

In the **divergent discovery style**, as in the convergent discovery style, the teacher designs a problem for students to solve individually, in pairs, or in groups. Here, however, the problem has many possible solutions, and the teacher asks the students either to find as many as possible or to produce one solution different from everybody else's solution. After teaching the students the basics of step aerobics, a teacher could ask his students to create a routine with a partner. He may want to give certain specifications, such as length of the routine and some content guidelines (for example, the routine must incorporate at least five of the steps students learned in class), but otherwise he lets the students create their best solution (figure 8.9). A teacher who wants his students to discover as many solutions as possible to a problem in an in-line skating lesson could ask, "How many different ways can you find to stop?" He would then ask the students to do a task that would lead them to the discovery of many different ways to stop.

Like convergent discovery, divergent discovery is an excellent style to use when your students are ready to play full or modified versions of a game or have mastered the basics of a skill and are ready for more complicated tasks and concepts. For example, if students are playing the game of Ultimate Frisbee, you might ask them to create, with a partner, a defensive play that their team will use in the game that day.

Of course, teachers must hold students accountable for their learning in this style. If students are not held accountable, this style, like the convergent discovery style, can easily become a roll-out-the-ball style, even if the teacher's intentions are good (for more ideas on how to hold students accountable see the assessment sections in chapter 12).

The inclusion approach is simple to incorporate in this style as well. You would handle it the same way you did in the convergent discovery style. The divergent discovery style can help students learn concepts related to movement skills and movement knowledge. Like the convergent discovery style, this style can be effective with students working in pairs or groups by helping them develop cooperative skills. Students may also improve their self-concept and self-efficacy by experiencing success with solving the problems. Figure 8.9 shows an example of a divergent discovery task sheet.

Divergent Discovery Task

Names:

With your dance partner:

1. Create a sequence of at least six swing moves, choosing from the ones you have learned in class (see list below if you need a reminder).
2. Write your sequence on this sheet.
3. Practice your sequence until you feel ready to show it to your teacher.
4. After showing your teacher you may choose to show your dance to another pair or the whole class. Let the teacher know about your decision.

- Choose your moves from this list:
  Basic four-hand hold
  Basic two-hand hold
  Lady's underarm turn
  Gentleman's turn
  Cuddle
  Side kicks
  She goes, he goes
  Pencil turn
  Skin-the-cat
  Pretzel
- Write your sequence here:

Figure 8.9   Sample divergent discovery task sheet for swing dance.

Table 8.2 Summary of Teaching Styles

Teaching style	Description	Teacher's role
Direct teaching style	The teacher leads the class through a task and tells them what to do and where, when, and how to do it. Example: leading calisthenics or aerobics routine.	To plan tasks, lead students through them and provide feedback.
Teacher feedback style	The teacher plans the tasks, lets the students perform the task independently, and provides feedback.	To plan tasks and provide feedback.
Partner feedback style	The teacher plans the tasks and specific criteria for how to perform the skills involved. Students partner up to perform the tasks and take turns being doer and observer (Mosston and Ashworth 1994). The doer does the task while the observer provides specific feedback based on the criteria the teacher has given.	To plan tasks and provide specific criteria for how to perform each skill. To observe partners' ability to work together and provide feedback to each other. To be available when students need help.
Self-feedback style	Same as the partner feedback style, except that the learners provide their own feedback by comparing their performance with the teacher's specific criteria for each skill.	Same as the partner feedback style, except that the teacher observes each student's ability to evaluate his own performance. To be available when students need help.
Convergent discovery style	The teacher designs a problem with one answer and lets the students try to discover the answer by themselves, in pairs or in groups, while they perform tasks that the teacher has prepared.	To design the problem and provide tasks that will help the students discover the solution to the problem.
Divergent discovery style	Same as the convergent discovery style, except that the teacher encourages the students to find different solutions or as many solutions as possible to the problem.	To design the problem and provide tasks that will help the students discover different solutions to the problem.

(continued)

Table 8.2 Summary of Teaching Styles *(continued)*

Learner's role	Advantages	Disadvantages
To follow the teacher's "commands."	Can be time efficient. All students are active at the same time with the same task.	Difficult to provide any specific feedback to individuals. Difficult to provide variations of tasks.
To decide exactly how, when, and where to do the task.	Teacher can provide specific feedback to individuals.	Difficult to provide enough feedback to each student.
To take turns being doer and observer. Doer: To do the tasks that the teacher has planned. Observer: To observe the doer and give specific feedback according to the teacher's criteria.	Students can get a lot of feedback. Students learn to analyze movement by observing their partners and comparing with criteria. Effective style to use for social development goals such as cooperation and trust.	Can become "do-and-wait" style if not well explained and if students are not held accountable for what they learn.
To do the tasks that the teacher has planned and to evaluate their own performance of each skill.	Students learn to analyze their own movement, correct their own mistakes, and become independent learners.	If this style is used too early in the learning process, students may not be able to evaluate their own performance and as a result would not receive any useful feedback.
To do the tasks the teacher has prepared while trying to find the solution to the problem.	Excellent style to incorporate into game play (modified or full) to learn concepts and strategies.	If students are not held accountable for their discoveries, this can become a roll-out-the-ball style.
To do the tasks the teacher has prepared while trying to find different solutions to the problem.	Same as the convergent discovery style. In addition, this style can bring out the creativity within students. Excellent style to use for creating aerobics, dance, and martial arts routines. Good style to use with cooperative activities.	Same as the convergent discovery style.

Lora had fun experimenting with the variety of teaching styles she had just learned. After the students understood what she expected of them in the partner feedback style, teaching them the self-feedback style was a breeze. Later, in using the convergent and divergent discovery styles, she found that her students enjoyed problem solving. She put many hours into creating task and criteria sheets during the first few months. But with practice, that became easier, as did playing her role correctly in each of the styles.

The students still varied considerably in skill proficiency in all her classes. Using a variety of teaching styles had not changed that, but it had nearly removed the problems that disparate skill levels had created before. Now, no matter what the task, she was able to ensure that all her students were working at an appropriate level and could experience success. She found that after a while she could even give her students choices in teaching styles. They quickly found their favorites, and so did she. Camilla, an athletic girl who was far above the other students in most skills, finally met a challenge when she used the self-feedback style. Whenever she had a choice, she would pick that style. Two extremely sociable students, Ryan and Joakim, liked the partner feedback style. The biggest challenge for them was to stay focused on the task. Amber and Brandon, her two most creative students who both were part of the school's drama group, loved the divergent discovery style. Lora was amazed at how their creativity was expressed again and again through this style.

Best of all was the respect she gained from her colleagues. They heard from students about what she was doing, came to check it out, and now wanted her to teach them about the various teaching styles.

Your Turn ▸▸▸

♦ Can you find examples of convergent discovery problems for your favorite physical activities?

♦ Can you find examples of divergent discovery problems for your favorite physical activities?

♦ How will you avoid having the discovery styles become roll-out-the-ball lessons when you teach?

Choosing a Teaching Style

Now that you have been introduced to a variety of teaching styles, you may want to know which ones are the most effective. The answer, of course, depends on what you are trying to accomplish. A summary of each style can be found in table 8.2. Effective teachers have a variety of teaching styles in their repertoires, and they use a certain style when it suits the learning objectives for the lesson or as a variation to maximize learning. The better your grasp of the different styles, the more likely it is that you will use them. Remember the carpenter analogy from the beginning of the chapter? If a carpenter had only a hammer and a saw in her tool belt, she would be able to do only limited kinds of work. Likewise, if you as a teacher know how to use only two teaching styles, you will have fewer ways of reaching all your students (remember the different ways that students learn, discussed in chapter 5). So, when you choose a teaching style you should consider two things:

♦ What are your learning objectives for the lesson? (You will learn about learning objectives in chapter 11.)

♦ Can you use one or several teaching styles as variations to maximize learning for all your students?

Which Teaching Style Fits Your Objectives?

When deciding which teaching style to use, you should start by asking yourself which style will best fit your learning objectives for the lesson. Let's use Lora from our opening scenario as an example. If her objective for a lesson was to have all the students participate in a step aerobics routine to get their heart rates into their target zone for 25 minutes and follow the teacher's lead in a routine consisting of steps they have already practiced, the direct teaching style would be appropriate. On the other hand, if her learning objectives were to have the students learn to cradle the lacrosse stick, belay a partner in rock climbing, or perform the crawl stroke in swimming, teacher feedback, partner feedback, or self-feedback (depending on the skill levels of the students) would be more appropriate styles. If her learning objectives were for the students to use all the steps they had learned in their step unit to create their own 64-count routine or to create a new move for swing dance, the divergent discovery style would be appropriate.

Having a variety of styles available makes your job as a teacher more exciting. You can be creative after you have a few more tools in your teaching belt.

Progressions and Variations

The skill levels of your students should influence your choice of teaching style. Use the teaching styles in a logical progression. Start with teacher feedback and then move to partner feedback. As students improve, you can let them try self-feedback. If a student is at the precontrol or control level of proficiency for a skill (review table 8.1 if necessary), you should not allow him to give himself feedback. He would not be able to analyze his movements properly, even with a detailed criteria sheet. Teacher feedback or partner feedback would be better styles to use because these would allow for feedback from an outside source—the teacher or a partner. Beginners can also learn a lot by analyzing another person's movements in the partner feedback style if clear and simple criteria are available.

You can use the discovery styles when the learner is beyond being a complete beginner, or even earlier as a needs assessment (chapter 12). For example, in a dance unit you can ask students on the first day of class to create a one-minute group routine consisting of any moves they choose (a reminder of appropriateness may be necessary). This divergent discovery assignment would allow you to evaluate the students' rhythmic ability and ability to cooperate with classmates. When using the discovery styles make sure that the questions and tasks are appropriate for the students' skill levels.

Direct teaching is suitable for students of all skill levels. Because of the style's limitations, it is most appropriate when you don't need much feedback. Direct teaching is appropriate when the objective is to have everyone active and working on health-related physical fitness, such as in cardio kick boxing.

When you know how to use different teaching styles it is easy to use them as variations to the main task. If, for example, you see that one student is more highly skilled than the others, you can give him a self-feedback criteria sheet to use with the task he is working on. This variation takes more initial preparation because you must create the criteria sheets, but if you save them on your computer, you can easily revise them for use in similar situations. By using different teaching styles in the same lesson with different students, depending on their needs, you can spend more time giving feedback to those with whom you are using teacher feedback. Table 8.3 presents an overview of the styles that are best suited to enhance learning at each level of skill proficiency.

Knowing and using different teaching styles is another piece of the effective teacher puzzle (chapter 7). Properly used, the teaching

Table 8.3 Generic Levels of Skill Proficiency and Appropriate Teaching Styles

Levels of skill proficiency	Most suitable teaching styles
Precontrol	Teacher feedback and divergent discovery
Control	Direct, teacher feedback, partner feedback, convergent discovery, and divergent discovery
Utilization	Direct teaching (for fitness activities such as step aerobics), teacher feedback (beginning of utilization level), partner feedback, self-feedback, convergent discovery, and divergent discovery
Proficiency	Direct teaching (for fitness activities such as step aerobics), partner feedback, self-feedback, convergent discovery, and divergent discovery

styles presented in this chapter will help you maximize the learning opportunities for each of your students. They will welcome the variety, and we believe you will enjoy it as well. Using a variety of teaching styles also enhances your ability to address the main concern of the Diamond Conceptual Framework: helping your students become physically active for the rest of their lives. Your students will experience more success and learn more. In addition, they will eventually be able to teach themselves skills as they come to rely less on a teacher's feedback through the use of partner feedback, self-feedback, and discovery teaching styles. We want our students to become learners for life. If they can learn from you *how* to learn, they may be more likely to pick up a new activity or sport on their own later in their lives.

Purpose

Use a computer word-processing program to create task sheets that reflect lesson objectives.

Resource and Procedure

Open lesson plans created in your word-processing program and develop task sheets from the learning objectives. The task sheet is easy to create using tables. Word-processing programs also allow you to insert other multimedia such as instructional photos or graphics that can be used to demonstrate skills. You can use these task sheets for all of the teaching styles except the direct teaching style. File the task sheets on your computer according to which activity or sport they represent, and you will be able to modify and print them as needed for a variety of lessons. Task sheets that are well organized, detailed, and professional looking communicate a commitment and seriousness to the learner as well as express your high expectations.

Summary

Effective teachers know how to use a variety of teaching styles in their lessons. This chapter presented a modified and simplified version of Mosston and Ashworth's (1994, 2001) spectrum of teaching styles. The styles are direct teaching, teacher feedback, partner feedback, self-feedback, convergent discovery, and divergent discovery. The inclusion concept of teaching is essential to each style. The style you use depends on your learning objectives and your students' skill proficiency. By using the styles in a progression or as

Checking for Understanding ▸▸▸

◆ What is the inclusion concept all about?

◆ Can you describe the four generic levels of skill proficiency?

◆ What are the two main kinds of variations and how should you use them?

◆ What are the teaching styles presented in this chapter?

◆ What is the student's and the teacher's role in each of the teaching styles?

◆ What is one advantage and one disadvantage for each teaching style?

◆ How can a teacher use the teaching styles in a progression?

◆ How can a teacher use the teaching styles as variations?

For Reflection and Discussion ▸▸▸

◆ Which teaching style appeals most to you? Why?

◆ What are the benefits in having the students solve problems through the discovery style?

◆ What are some specific examples of using the convergent and divergent discovery styles to teach social quality issues such as cooperation and trust?

◆ How would you handle the following situation? You were just hired at a school in which the students have never experienced anything but direct teaching and teacher feedback style in physical education. They resist the change when you start introducing other teaching styles.

variations, you can maximize your students' opportunities for learning.

References

Csikszentmihalyi, M. 1990. *Flow.* New York: Harper & Row.

Graham, G. 2001. *Teaching children physical education, becoming a master teacher.* 2nd ed. Champaign, IL: Human Kinetics.

Graham, G., S. Holt/Hale, and M. Parker. 1993. *Children moving: A reflective approach to teaching physical education.* 4th ed. Mountain View, CA: Mayfield.

Mosston, M., and S. Ashworth. 1994. *Teaching physical education.* 4th ed. New York: Macmillan.

Mosston, M., and S. Ashworth. 2001. *Teaching physical education.* 5th ed. San Francisco: Benjamin/Cummings.

Stanley, S. 1977. *Physical education: A movement orientation.* 2nd ed. New York: McGraw-Hill.

Suggested Readings

Harrison, J., C. Blakemore, and M. Buck. 2001. *Instructional strategies for secondary physical education.* 5th ed. Boston: McGraw-Hill.

Metzler, M. 2000. *Instructional models for physical education.* Boston: Allyn & Bacon.

Rink, J. 1998. *Teaching physical education for learning.* 4th ed. Boston: McGraw-Hill.

Chapter 9

Creating a Positive Learning Environment

> Nonviolence is the answer to the crucial political and moral questions of our time: the need for man to overcome oppression and violence without resorting to oppression and violence. Man must evolve for all human conflict a method which rejects revenge, aggression and retaliation. The foundation of such a method is love.
>
> — *Martin Luther King Jr.*

Lee and Yin are good friends and professors at a small-town university. Lee, a physical education teacher educator, enjoys conversation with Yin, an epidemiologist in the health department. One day over lunch, Lee discussed some of his ideas on establishing positive climates in physical education classes. He was surprised and saddened by a story that Yin decided to share.

Yin: "When completing my doctorate, I conducted a small fitness study with fourth graders at a rural mountain school. One day, students were working at several fitness stations around the playground. I was working at the pull-up station with five students, two girls and three boys. It was Sarah's turn to do pull-ups. She jumped to the bar and effortlessly began to do pull-ups. When she did the first one, everyone in her group cheered. When she reached 3, the three boys and the girl in her group opened their eyes wide with amazement. Students in nearby groups began to watch as Sarah pulled numbers 5 and 6. By the time she reached 9 pull-ups, the entire class had stopped to watch. When Sarah pulled herself up for the 11th time, she realized everyone in class was watching her so she stopped. I'm convinced she could have done a lot more. Sarah did the most pull-ups in class that day. When she finished, I congratulated her accomplishment with the class. I used her feat in a positive way to motivate the students to strive toward their personal best. The whole thing backfired on me.

"The following week, the same fourth grade class was scheduled to repeat the fitness stations and record their personal scores. Earlier on the day of the test and unknown to me, four fourth grade boys got together and decided to hurt Sarah. During recess, these four boys took a playground ball, surrounded Sarah, and threw the ball hard at her head. Sarah fell to the ground, hit her head on the pavement, and sustained serious injury. She was rushed to the hospital. The four boys were rushed to the principal's office. When the principal asked the boys why they had hurt Sarah, one boy spoke up and sincerely said that Sarah was going to do the most pull-ups and she's a girl. Immediately, the principal knew that the boys' actions were premeditated and deliberate."

Learning Objectives

After reading this chapter you will be able to

- state youth risk behavior trends from 1991 through 1999,
- recognize the difference between harassment and violence,
- realize the need for teaching students about social responsibility and social skills,
- define positive discipline and plan strategies for using it in your classes,
- identify personal biases and prejudices about students,
- explain the self-fulfilling prophecy model and how it may affect your classes,
- determine the power of inclusive, equitable, and exclusive language on students,
- define STAR,
- create T charts and H charts, and
- state levels of social responsibility.

Key Terms and Phrases

Harassment
Youth Risk Behavior Survey
Discipline
Positive discipline
Negative discipline
Self-fulfilling prophecy
Self-fulfilling prophecy cycle
Inclusive language
Equitable language
Physical environment
STAR
T chart
H chart

Kids harassing kids has been a part of American culture for centuries. Surely you can remember times in your childhood when you mercilessly teased a sibling or peer or when others relentlessly taunted you. Teasing others to an extent is considered normal verbal play among youth and helps them develop positive social skills and strategies for self-protection (Roberts 2000). But excessive, persistent, and intense teasing and taunting are forms of harassment that are damaging to both the victim and the bully.

Physical and Verbal Harassment

Harassment among youth ranges from verbal assaults (teasing, name calling, threatening, or taunting) to relational assaults (exclusion from social interactions, gossip, and destroying relationships) to physical assaults (hitting, kicking, shoving, and weapon use) (Hanish 2000).

Physical Harassment

Violence and harassment among youth have remained steady over the years. To give you an idea of what adolescents are dealing with on a daily basis, let's look at a few statistics reported in the 1999 *Youth Risk Behavior Survey (YRBS)* (Centers for Disease Control 1999). The *YRBS* sampled thousands of students in grades 9 through 12 and summarized the findings, which you can locate at **www.cdc.gov/mmwr/preview/mmwrhtml/ ss4905a1.htm**.

The second leading cause of death among youth today remains homicide (18.6%). More youth today feel unsafe about coming to and staying at school than did youth from decades ago. Approximately 5.2% of youth surveyed missed school at some point during the 1999 school year because they felt that their safety was threatened.

Looking at youth risk behavior trends from 1991 through 1999, we find that some improvement has occurred around the issue of violence. For instance, in 1993 nearly 8% of students surveyed had carried a gun to school. In 1999 that percentage had dropped to 4.9%. In 1993, 11.8% of all students surveyed had carried a weapon to school. The survey showed that 6.9% of all students had done so in 1999. Overall, physical fighting occurs more frequently than weapon toting. Results show that in 1991, 42.5% of sampled students had been in-

volved in a physical fight. In 1995 that number had dropped to 38.7%. Results reported in 1999 show that the number of students involved in physical fights decreased further to 35.7%. Although we note a decrease in the reporting of physical fighting, we are still looking at 35 students out of 100 engaging in some sort of physical fight during the year. Fighting on school property occurs less often. No data are available for 1991, but in 1993, 16.2% of youth surveyed reported involvement in a physical fight on school grounds. The yearly trend has shown a modest decrease, with 14.2% reporting being in a fight on school grounds in 1999.

Survey results show an increase in the number of students threatened or injured at school from 1997 (7.4%) to 1999 (7.7%).

Physical violence creates barriers that inhibit student learning in school. Physical violence, physical injury, and even death are extreme forms of violence that our students encounter. We don't see much research or reporting on the harassment and taunting students receive on a daily basis.

Verbal Harassment

You have most likely heard the saying "Sticks and stones may break my bones, but names will never hurt me." This folk saying probably originated out of concern for individuals who are verbally assaulted by others. We're convinced that the saying was offered as encouragement to the abused with hope that they would toughen up and ignore the verbal attacks. Many of us have probably tried to live by this saying at least once in our lives. But the reality is that words do hurt. Abusive language, no matter how hard we try to ignore it, is powerful.

Abusive language, by itself or laced with nonverbal taunts, may eventually lead to physical violence. An example is Yin's story of the fourth grade girl seriously injured by several male classmates. Let's also remember that abusive language by itself is hurtful and may leave deep emotional scars. According to Stephen L. Wessler (2000/2001) degrading words, slurs, and put-downs make their way into every high school and middle school every day. In his compelling article "Sticks and Stones," Wessler told a true story of one violent incident that began with hateful and hurtful language at school. Four seventh grade boys began taunting another seventh grade boy, whom Wessler called John (pseudonym), with antigay language. They made comments to John every time they passed him in the hallways or in class. John ignored the comments, hoping that the four bullies would eventually lose interest. Well, they didn't. The boys used degrading language more frequently and became bolder in their attacks. They went from making comments under their breath to making bold public displays, such as surrounding John in the bathroom and yelling antigay slurs. Finally, verbal taunting escalated to physical abuse. Wessler reported that the four tormentors, after yelling slurs at John in the boys' room, pulled his head into a urinal. Sometime later, the boys slipped a rope noose around John's head and tightened it. After John had suffered four months of abuse, another student overheard one of the boys say that he was going to bring his father's handgun to school the next day and shoot John. The student reported what he heard, and adults were finally able to intervene. Although the violence toward John stopped, the emotional hurt from the trauma will linger for years.

Hurtful, degrading language and physical violence among youth come in many forms and for many reasons. Sometimes reasons for bias, prejudice, and hatred are based on race (racism), ethnicity (ethnocentrism), socioeconomic class (classism), gender (sexism), Judaism (anti-Semitism), gang rivalry, sexual orientation (homophobia), and disability (ableism). We cannot discuss in depth each of these social justice topics concerning bias and prejudice, but we can increase your awareness of physical and verbal harassment and provide you with strategies for establishing a positive, inclusive learning environment. For more information about social justice topics, you may wish to consult a book written by Adams, Bell, and Griffin titled *Teaching for Diversity and Social Justice: A Source Book.*

Degrading, hurtful, and violent language left unchallenged will contribute to an environment embedded in bias, prejudice, and physical violence (Wessler, 2000/2001, 30.) As physical educators, how can we help create a positive environment for students? How can we help eliminate the fear, anger, and loss of spirit (Wessler 2000/2001) that students feel when they confront abusive language and physical violence at school? The answer lies in the power of positive discipline. Establishing a positive class climate will help reduce the incidence of abusive language and physical violence, like those we saw in the stories of John and Sarah.

What Is Positive Discipline?

Disciplining students often conjures negative images. When we think of a teacher disciplining students, we may see the stereotypical physical educator who never smiles while calling roll and barking orders. Our imaginary colleague resembles a military drill sergeant who yells at young recruits to stand at attention, look straight ahead, and wipe the smiles from their faces. For our fictional friend, the art of discipline involves catching students doing something wrong and then punishing them severely by having them run laps or do push-ups. In this environment, students learn to fear authority rather than respect it. Negative discipline, as just described, does little to create a positive environment in which students feel safe and willing to take risks to learn and practice skills. Negative discipline also does little to encourage students to engage in positive behavior with one another. Using exercise as punishment does not encourage students to want to be physically active for life. The purpose of this chapter is to present an alternative approach to managing student behavior, an approach we call positive discipline.

The word *discipline* means the training necessary to produce or establish a specific pattern of behavior, especially training that produces moral or mental improvement. The difference between positive and negative discipline is clear. **Positive discipline** recognizes the importance of the classroom environment on student behavior. It strives to eliminate bias and prejudice that threaten student safety as well as learning. Positive discipline works to create an inclusive and warm learning place where students want to participate, where they feel safe and secure, and where they feel they belong. Positive discipline emphasizes catching students doing something good or right.

Negative discipline is often grounded in reactive behavior. It gives no formal consideration to the importance of safe and positive learning environments. And, as mentioned above, negative discipline emphasizes catching students doing something wrong (figure 9.1). Think about your own experiences for a moment and be truthful with yourself. When you received praise for doing something right, how did it make you feel? When you were yelled at for doing something wrong, how did you feel? Most people prefer to receive praise rather than be yelled at. Of course, this doesn't mean that we simply look for things to praise our students about and ignore their poor behavior. Positive discipline asks us to model, expect, and reward positive behavior with the idea that positive behavior breeds more positive behavior. The result is a healthy environment in which students get along with one another and engage willingly in the process of learning.

Using positive discipline doesn't mean that students will never behave poorly or inappropriately. It doesn't mean that when students behave inappropriately they suffer no consequences. The art of using positive discipline involves clear rules regarding classroom routines, student behavior, and learning protocols (chapter 7). It also means that penalties result when students break rules. But tactics that instill fear and humiliation or exercise used as punishment are not used in positive discipline.

Purpose

Use the Web as a resource to find success stories of other educators' discipline strategies.

Resource and Procedure

Select a couple of Web resources that are set up to provide support for physical educators facing special needs. Enter key search words "classroom discipline" to access resources. One of the most comprehensive resources on classroom discipline research is the Northwest Regional Educational Laboratory's Web site (**www.nwrel.org**). PE Central has links and listservs that cover discipline issues in physical education.

Steps to Establish Positive Discipline in Your Class

Right now you may be having visions of kids yelling slurs and obscenities to one another and bullies beating up defenseless victims in the corner of the gym. You may be wondering about whether or not you really want to teach. The information we just provided is not meant to scare you. We present it to inform you of the realities of schools. Most likely, your classes will be overcrowded but relatively peaceful. We believe that by being proactive, you can establish a classroom in which students behave, show respect and tolerance for one another and for you, and rarely cause behavior disruptions. We also believe that teachers have a great deal of power and influence over the climate of their class and the school. So how do we make a positive climate, with a focus on the student affective domain (chapter 4)? Let's get started.

When adolescents are immersed in an environment where teachers and others in authority do not monitor peer harassment and fail to guide students toward positive behavior, students will likely fall victim to verbal and physical assaults. Our responsibility as physical educators is to teach our students how to behave positively and accept responsibility for their own actions. The place to begin is with ourselves.

Teacher Expectations: Self-Fulfilling Prophecy

If you expect students to behave poorly, they probably will. If you expect them to be apathetic, they probably will be. If you expect girls to be wallflowers and sit on the sidelines, they probably will. If you expect boys to have physical altercations in your class, they probably will. You know this old saying too: "Be careful what you wish for, it may come true." This concept is known as the **self-fulfilling prophecy.** Your expectations for students will influence student behavior. They may behave as you expect them to behave.

Because the expectations we hold about students strongly affect their behavior in our classes, it makes sense to expect students to respect one another, take responsibility for their actions, work cooperatively with others, and actively engage in the learning process. Therefore, if we expect students to behave positively in class and be respectful of one another, they probably will. To achieve these results, we must work hard to catch students behaving well and interacting positively with their peers. We also must model effective teaching strategies, which include self-responsibility, self-motivation, and respect for and cooperation with others. And we must provide students with opportunities to practice these positive social skills. The first step in establishing positive discipline, then, is thorough examination of our beliefs and stereotypes about students and thoughtful reflection about how these beliefs and stereotypes affect the learning environment and student behavior.

One activity that helps physical educators examine their beliefs and stereotypes is the **self-fulfilling prophecy cycle** worksheet (Hutchinson

Figure 9.1 Teachers don't always recognize that discipline problems in the classroom may occur because of their own lack of supervision or direction.

1995). The self-fulfilling prophecy cycle includes five parts (figure 9.2):

1. Teacher beliefs about students
2. Teacher expectations for students
3. Teacher behavior toward students
4. Expected student behavior
5. Student outcomes

Take time to fill out this worksheet thoughtfully and honestly. To start, you may want to list some positive and negative beliefs that you hold about students in general and then plug that list into the self-fulfilling prophecy cycle worksheet. For example, you might believe that students who do not dress for class dislike all forms of physical activity. Or you might believe that students who play on organized sport teams make excellent student leaders. After writing down your positive and negative beliefs about students, fill in the self-fulfilling prophecy cycle worksheet as follows (Hutchinson 1995):

1. Select positive or negative beliefs about students in physical education and write those statements under the heading "Teacher beliefs about students."

2. Under the heading "Teacher expectations for students," write one sentence for each belief describing behaviors that you expect from students.

3. Under the heading "Teacher behavior toward students," list for each teacher expectation a corresponding behavior that you may elicit.

4. Under the heading "Expected student behavior," state one student behavior that may occur for each teacher behavior listed.

5. Under the heading "Student outcomes," write outcomes you expect to see because of the interactions that may take place between teacher and student in this cycle.

After you have completed the worksheet, reflect on your answers. Ask yourself the following questions:

1. How may my beliefs about students affect my interactions with them?

2. How may my beliefs enhance student learning and positive student interactions?

3. How may my beliefs limit student learning and encourage negative student interactions?

I. Positive and negative beliefs about students: In the space provided, honestly state some of your beliefs about students in physical education.

Positive: I believe . . .

Ex: Boys are naturally physical and competitive.

1. _____
2. _____
3. _____

Negative: I believe . . .

Ex: Girls can't throw a ball.

1. _____
2. _____
3. _____

II. Fill out the self-fulfilling prophecy cycle

A. Teacher seliefs about students

Ex: Girls can't throw a ball overhand

1. _____
2. _____
3. _____

E. Student Outcomes

Ex: Girls don't learn to throw overhand and graduate high school with limited ability in throwing.

1. _____
2. _____
3. _____

B. Teacher Expectations for Students

Ex: Girls in class will not be able to throw a softball.

1. _____
2. _____
3. _____

D. Expected Student Behavior in Class

Ex: Girls don't practice throwing softballs overhand; girls who cannot throw continue to throw like beginners . . .

1. _____
2. _____
3. _____

C. Teacher Behavior Toward Students

Ex: Does not help girls learn to throw overhand.

1. _____
2. _____
3. _____

Figure 9.2   Self-fulfilling prophecy cycle worksheet.

As you can see from filling out the worksheet, teacher beliefs influence how teachers interact with students. If a teacher believes that girls are not interested in playing sports, he or she may expect girls to be spectators or cheerleaders for sporting events. In class, that teacher may not strongly encourage girls to participate in skill development or game play. The teacher may allow girls to participate minimally in class or even just sit and watch. As a result, the girls in class will not try hard, will avoid action during activity, and will appear content sitting on the sidelines. In the end, we see girls who lack motor skills and seem uninterested in physical activity and sport. Without even thinking about how he or she may have contributed to the students' behavior, the teacher recognizes the lack of skill and interest, which confirms his or her belief and thus completes the self-fulfilling prophecy cycle.

Now you have an idea about how your beliefs and expectations affect the class climate. Knowing this, you should commit yourself to using constructive strategies to build a positive learning environment. Included in that commitment will be the use of inclusive language.

Teacher Language

Language is powerful. Wessler (2000/2001) reminds us that words hurt and, if left unchallenged, can lead to physical violence. When teaching, we must address language in two ways. First, we must be cognizant of the language we choose to use with our students. It should always be respectful, even in situations when we become angry. Remember, language conveys beliefs, expectations, and emotions. Second, we must listen to the language our students use and interrupt their language when it is foul, degrading, hurtful, or hateful.

Inclusive Language

Inclusive language is language that shows respect for all persons in your class and embraces individual diversity. It doesn't offend or exclude anyone. It is language that teachers should use at all times. By using inclusive and respectful language, teachers encourage students to use inclusive and respectful language. The best way to describe inclusive language in physical education is to offer examples.

The easiest and simplest example is the phrase "You guys." We hear people, young and old, use that phrase in everyday conversations. We know what you are thinking: "What's the big deal? Everybody says it." That's right. If you disagree with the argument we are about to present, that's OK. The important thing is that you use this example to think more critically about the language you use in class and its effect on students.

When we ask four-year-olds about the expression "you guys," they tell us that we are speaking about boys, not girls. When we ask seven-year-old girls what we mean by the saying, they say it means boys, but girls are sometimes included. By the time boys and girls make it to middle and high school, they believe the word means both boys and girls. Everyone tends to use it to mean both. However, we find it difficult sometimes to discern its meaning in a phrase. For instance, a group of basketball players are standing outside the gym talking with friends and waiting for practice to begin. This social group of boys and girls are having a wonderful time catching up on the day and making plans for the weekend. After a while, the coach opens the gym door and says to them, "C'mon, you guys, let's go." The players say goodbye to their friends and walk into the gym to practice.

Who are the players? Your first impression in reading the scenario may have been that boys on the basketball team were talking with their girlfriends, a reasonable assumption. The truth is that the scenario may have been about either boys or girls on their respective basketball teams. The meaning of "you guys" as an inclusive phrase was not clear. It probably led us to assume that we were talking about boys. The phrase is not clearly inclusive, and therefore we should not use it while teaching. Instead, we should use more inclusive words like *class, players, students,* or *folks* when addressing groups of students.

> ## Your Turn ▶▶▶
>
> ◆ In referring to groups, what phrases do you or people you know use that should perhaps be more specific or more inclusive?
>
> ◆ What's your opinion about the power of language? Discuss your point of view and then take the opposing point of view and advocate it persuasively.

Language, no matter how small its influence may seem, has a powerful effect on student self-esteem and development. Therefore, you should avoid using language that excludes groups of people based on sex, race, ethnicity, religion, class, sexual orientation, or ability. Keeping that in mind, you should be aware of stereotypical language used for groups of people and make sure that you do not use that language in your speech. You may believe that most people are keenly aware of what is and what is not appropriate language. You would be surprised to learn otherwise. We definitely were when one of our student teachers used a racial slur to refer to several Mexican American students. When we confronted him about it, he was embarrassed and admitted ignorance to the term. Teachers must make a strong effort to be aware of social issues. Although we laugh about the term *politically correct,* the underlying concept encourages us to be humane, honest, fair, and respectful of others who are different from ourselves.

Equitable Language

Equitable language is another aspect of inclusion that teachers should strive for. The reason we use equitable language is that we want to provide messages to students that success is possible for them no matter how different they are from their peers. Inequitable language occurs in many forms.

Let's use another basketball example to illustrate. In Andrea's basketball class, she is ready to teach her students one-on-one defense before she takes them to team defense. As she explains the concept to her students, she describes the defense as "man-to-man." This phrase may immediately exclude half of her class. Girls in the class may not take learning the game of basketball seriously because the language implies that it is really for boys (figure 9.3). An equitable term for this coed situation would be "player-to-player."

In physical education, we often teach students sport skills that require an active defender. An inactive defender is typically part of the progression toward active defense and game play. Many physical educators in the past have referred to this inactive defender as "dummy defense." The word *dummy* implies someone cognitively challenged and is therefore another example of a word we shouldn't use. Other examples of inequitable terms and phrases are "motor moron" and "you play like a girl."

Figure 9.3 Inclusive language can help teachers make sure girls as well as boys are involved in the activity, including those traditionally considered "male sports."

𝒴*our Turn* ▶▶▶

◆ Think of other inequitable terms used in physical education or sport. Offer equitable alternatives.

◆ In small groups, role-play the teacher using equitable terms while speaking to the class.

Sometimes teachers may think that using respectful language (and behavior) is necessary only in class, that using disrespectful language in the locker room or while coaching a team is OK. We contend that it is not. Students often admire and emulate their teachers and coaches. They listen carefully to what you say and observe your behavior in and outside of class. Modeling appropriate behaviors with your students at all times is important.

For instance, we've had many young male football players tell us that a coach will call players on the team girls or fags if they are playing poorly or not aggressively. Comments such as these only perpetuate stereotypes and promote hatred among groups of students and players. In each of your roles, take what you say seriously. Your students will.

Student Language

Earlier in the chapter, we described in John's case how degrading language can lead to physical violence (Wessler 2000/2001). One way that teachers can reduce the amount of violence, whether physical or emotional, is to interrupt any degrading and harmful language they hear. You will have the most control over this in your classes by expecting students to speak respectfully.

Interrupting degrading student language in your class or throughout school must be consistent and firm. Most of the time you can interrupt your students with a low-key response like, "That language is offensive, please don't use that again," or "I'm offended by language like that," or "I will not tolerate offensive language in my class." Students may complain at first, but they will come to respect your expectation. Students who have been hurt by abusive language will appreciate the help. All students will find your class safer because it is free of hurtful comments.

Your Turn ▶▶▶

We are reminded of the framework of developmental assets for youth (*Framework* 1997). Eight developmental assets serve as building blocks to adolescent development (Scales and Leffert 1999). Positive discipline provides several opportunities for students to improve their behavior and self-esteem. As you review this modified list of building blocks, determine which pertain to your behavior, student behavior, and the climate of your school community and your classes.

1. Support—a caring school environment.

2. Empowerment—youth feel safe at home and school.

3. Boundaries and expectations—teachers provide clear rules, expectations, and consequences.

4. Constructive use of time—students are engaged in creative lessons and activities.

5. Commitment to learning—youth are motivated to learn, are actively engaged in learning, and have a sense of belonging in their school community.

6. Positive values—youth understand and value caring, equity, integrity, honesty, responsibility, and restraint.

7. Social competencies—youth demonstrate the ability to plan, make healthy decisions, show empathy and friendship, show comfort with cultural differences, resist negative peer pressure, and engage in peaceful conflict resolution.

8. Positive identity—youth are empowered to take charge of their lives and express a sense of purpose in the world along with a positive point of view.

Physical Environment

A positive climate makes way for positive discipline. The next area to address is the **physical environment,** which includes learning space, visuals, and learning materials. Your learning space will be the locker room, classroom, gymnasium, fields, dance room, weight room, pool, ropes course, and so forth. Make sure that all students have access to these rooms. Ask yourselves questions like the following: Can the boys easily access the dance room if it is located adjacent to the girls' locker room? Can girls access the weight room if it is in the center of the boys' locker room? Can students in wheelchairs easily enter the gym or get out to the field? Can visually impaired students find their lockers? Will ESL (English as a second language) students be able to read locker-room and class rules? Making the learning space accessible and friendly will help students feel safe and promote positive attitudes.

Visuals come in many forms, such as bulletin boards, posters, pictures, murals, and more. Make sure that your visuals represent your student population and school community. Visuals shouldn't be limited to athletic teams and events. Athletics should certainly be part of the environment, but not the only part. Be sure to have posters and bulletin boards representing physical education as well as your diverse student population. You may want to include photos of your students cooperating and getting along in various physical education activities on your bulletin boards.

Learning materials may include things like task cards, books, equipment, worksheets, readings, and so forth. Again, make sure that these represent all students in your classes. Pictures and drawings should include boys and girls, people of color, people with disabilities, and more (figure 9.4). Representing student diversity not only makes students feel as if they belong, but also encourages them to try harder and strive for achievement.

Teaching Strategies for Positive Discipline

Now that you have examined your beliefs and expectations, inspected your use of inclusive and equitable language, and considered the appropriateness of your learning environment, it is time to learn teaching strategies for positive discipline.

The first thing physical educators do is meet their class and begin to learn student names and faces. Physical education classes can be large or small. Either way, teachers work hard to get to know their students. Sometimes we assume that students already know each other or will soon simply because they spend a great deal of time together. This assumption is often false. Students often don't know anyone outside their small group of friends. In class, they may be shy or reluctant to venture away from the safety of their friends.

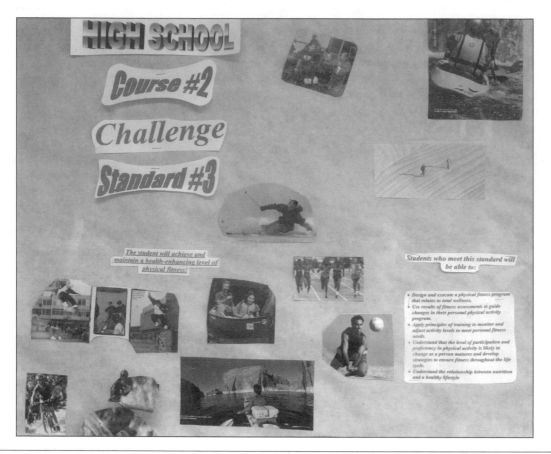

Figure 9.4 Make sure your written materials represent the diversity of your students.

Most young people are more likely to taunt or get in a fight with someone they don't know rather than someone they are acquainted with. Therefore, to develop positive discipline, it is essential for students to get to know one another. The first few days of class should include learning activities in which students learn each other's names and something personal about each other. Most students find this a tall order, so be patient and persistent.

Once students get to know one another a bit, you should establish ground rules for interacting. We cannot assume that students will know how to behave with each other. Creating ground rules or class rules for student behavior makes clear to all students what you expect of them (figure 9.5). Class rules can be determined in several ways. You might simply post the rules and explain them to students. You will get greater commitment from students, however, if you find a way to include them in the process, as we explained in chapter 7. Either way, state the rules positively and try to have seven or fewer rules.

Purpose

Use technology to acquaint students with one another.

Resource and Procedure

Break your students into groups of four or fewer. Take photos of each group of students. Post pictures of your student groups on a class bulletin board or outside your office door. Have your students write their names under the photos and list one thing they like about physical activity. You have now provided a forum for students to share a bit of their personalities with their classmates. This can go a long way in establishing a positive acceptance of everyone on a basic human level. At least everyone will have an opportunity to learn everyone's name and some insight about fellow class members. Digital cameras are useful for taking, storing, and presenting photos in a variety of ways.

Rules for PE

1. Stop, look, and listen on signal
2. Respect others
3. Play fairly and honestly
4. Give 100% during class
5. Help others
6. Participate safely
7. Handle equipment with care

When establishing rules for physical education, phrase them positively and have no more than seven statements. Then post them on the wall so that all students can see them.

Figure 9.5 Sample list of classroom rules.

We will offer two suggestions to get you to think of ways to have students help you determine class rules. One physical educator we know, Bill Silva, has each class he teaches establish a class bill of rights (figure 9.6). In small groups, he has students list rules they believe would be important for the class to run smoothly and for students to get along. He takes the list from each group and compiles it into a large class list. Next, the class brackets together similar rules to reduce the number of rules. Then he has the class vote on the seven most important rules. After the class votes, he places the seven rules on poster paper and has each student sign their class bill of rights. Signed posters hang in the gymnasium for the year. The teacher believes that the routine helps students clearly understand what is appropriate behavior in class.

Another teacher we know asks each of her classes to create a list of rules in a way similar to the process just described. When students finally determine a short list of rules, she gives each student a paper hat or a drawing of a hat. Students take time to decorate their hats with paint, markers, glitter, and stickers. Students then individually sign their own hats. Then, as a group, the class makes a circle around the poster of class rules. The teacher explains the importance of student agreement and the meaning of the folk saying "Throw your hat into the ring." Next, she places a hula hoop over the set of rules. If students believe they can abide by the rules, they throw their hats into the ring. Once all hats are in the ring, the teacher talks about the commitment each person has made. She then posts the rules and the students' hats on the gymnasium walls (figure 9.7).

Bill of Rights

The students of Mr. Silva's eighth grade physical education class have the right to:

1. Learn movement skills and activities
2. Learn movement concepts and sport strategies
3. Enjoy all activities
4. Get a second chance
5. Be treated fairly by the teacher and others
6. Participate in class without getting feelings hurt or have people bother me
7. Play fairly and honestly in all activities
8. Ask questions and be listened to
9. Work cooperatively
10. Participate in a safe environment with safe equipment

These rights were selected by students in Mr. Silva's 4th period eighth grade class during the week of September 1, 2001.

As a student in this class, I will do my personal best to make sure that our class is operated in a manner that adheres to and respects the rights listed above.

Figure 9.6 Example of Bill of Rights. Every student signs a copy.

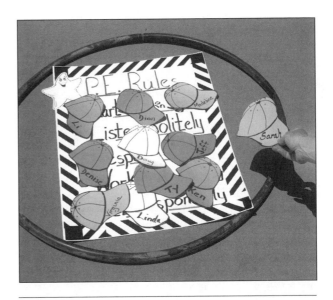

Figure 9.7 "Hats in the ring," showing students' commitment to the rest of the class.

Consequences must result when students break rules. In the previous accounts, the teachers allowed their students to help determine consequences for failing to abide by the rules. Consequences should be clear and straightforward. They should coincide with consequences given by the greater school community and not involve exercise or humiliation. Consequences often include the following protocol:

1. Verbal warning
2. Time-out
3. Detention
4. Detention with call home
5. Detention, trip to principal, call home
6. Behavior contract
7. Removal from class

Teachers find that establishing a positive climate in class and clearly stating class rules reduce disruptive behavior.

Building Class Community and Developing Social Skills

Creating rules doesn't guarantee good behavior. Students also need to learn what positive behavior looks like. Many physical educators aid this process by teaching students social skills and providing activities for classes to bond and unite as groups. Social skill development, then, is essential to positive discipline. The purpose of teaching social skills is to help students learn to cooperate and behave positively with one another. Teachers can also help students understand social concepts such as respect, honesty, integrity, and fairness. Physical educators who teach social skills often find themselves joining other teachers on campus in a common effort. Many principals ask all teachers to help students learn to get along better so that the school community becomes a safer, more positive place. Several teachers with whom we work assist their schools in campuswide social development campaigns. The teachers select one social skill per month to emphasize with students. The teachers report that the strategy works well in improving student behavior.

Our favorite way to introduce social skills to students in physical education is by using acronyms like STAR.

Tara Keegan was an undergraduate student learning to be a physical educator when she created **STAR.** Tara has been teaching physical education at the middle and high school levels for over five years now. Each letter of STAR corresponds to a positive social concept. Hutchinson has further embellished the STAR idea. Each social concept has a working definition that will help students understand its meaning.

- ◆ S = Showing appreciation—the ability to recognize the quality, value, and significance of something. It is an expression of gratitude.
- ◆ T = Trust and trustworthiness—Trust is the ability to place one's confidence in another person. Trustworthiness means that one is worthy of or capable of another person's trust. In other words, a person is reliable.
- ◆ A = Acceptance of others—the ability or willingness to receive or agree upon differences among people. One of the best ways to begin teaching acceptance is to begin with the concept of tolerance. Tolerance means to have respect for or recognition of the opinions and behaviors of others.
- ◆ R = Respect—the ability to show or feel regard for someone else. It is the willingness to show consideration.

What we like about the social skills included in STAR is that they promote positive inclusive behavior among students. The acronym itself is fun because a teacher can do a lot with the word *star*. For instance, some teachers who use the acronym encourage their students to be stars or to reach for the stars. Other teachers use the acronym in their class to promote community with slogans like "Creating a Galaxy of Stars." By using their creative energy, teachers can think of many ways to use this acronym. STAR is not the only social skill acronym that has been created.

Your Turn: Creating Social Skill Acronyms ▶ ▶ ▶

Below is a list of common human virtues or prosocial concepts that you may want your students to learn. Look at the list below and see if you can create a catchy acronym.

Acceptance	Forgiveness	Joy	Respect
Appreciation	Friendliness	Justice	Self-discipline
Compassion	Generosity	Kindness	Service
Consideration	Gentleness	Loyalty	Tolerance
Courtesy	Helpfulness	Moderation	Trust
Cooperation	Honesty	Orderliness	Trustworthiness
Enthusiasm	Honor	Patience	Truthfulness
Encouragement	Humility	Responsibility	Unity

Now that you have introduced your students to the concept of STAR or some other acronym, how will you get them to understand which behaviors correspond with each social concept? In other words, what does showing appreciation look like? How does one demonstrate trust, acceptance, or respect? We cannot assume that students will automatically know how to demonstrate these prosocial concepts. One strategy to help students understand behaviors that are associated with each letter of STAR is to help students brainstorm what the concept would look like and sound like. We do this by describing appropriate behaviors on a **T chart**. The T chart obtains its name from the arrangement of lines used to set up two columns on a piece of paper. One vertical line followed by one horizontal line near the top of the first line resembles the letter *T* (table 9.1).

At the top of the T chart you place the name of the social concept to be reviewed. For example, write "Show appreciation" at the top of the sheet. Next, notice that the T chart is divided into two columns. One column has the word "See" at the top; the other has the word "Hear." Ask students to brainstorm the behaviors they would expect to see or hear from someone showing appreciation. Students may respond that they would see all kinds of nonverbal cues like high fives, pat on backs, thumbs up, raise the roof, and so on. They might hear phrases such as "Good job," "Way to go," and "Thanks for picking up that ball for me."

Create a T chart for each letter of STAR. You may find that what you might see and hear for one social concept would also be applicable to another. That is OK, but try to think of different ones. When you begin to have trouble, review the definition of each social concept. When you have practiced

Table 9.1   T-Chart for Social Skills Show

Showing appreciation

See	Hear
Thumbs up	Thanks
Pat on back	Good job
Raise the roof	I like it

creating T charts, you will be prepared to lead your students through the exercise.

Some teachers elaborate on the T chart by creating an H chart. An **H chart** adds another column to the mix, making the chart resemble the letter *H* (table 9.2). The heading on the third column is "Feel." After students are able to state what they would see or hear for a particular social concept like trust, then they would answer the question "Seeing and hearing those behaviors, how would that make you feel?" Students will respond with positive answers like, "That makes me feel good, safe, or happy." The point of the third category is to encourage students to examine how positive social concepts and behaviors make them feel inside. We want them to feel good about themselves.

Social Responsibility

To build a successful classroom community, you must be willing to care for and respect your students. The safety of the learning environment is also a factor. But even with these things in place, one aspect of community remains missing—students'

Table 9.2   H-Chart for Social Skills

See	Hear	Feel
Thumbs up	Thanks	Appreciated
Pat on back	Good job	Valued
Raise the roof	I like it	Good

willingness to take responsibility for their actions. Hellison's social responsibility model (1995) provides us with guidelines that we can share with students in helping them learn self-control and responsibility (figure 9.8).

The STAR model helps us teach social skills to our students. The social responsibility model provides students with guidelines for appropriate behavior. Our goal as physical educators is to make students aware of these levels of responsibility and provide them with opportunities to develop them. Note that Hellison (1995, 1996) often points out that these guidelines are flexible and adaptable to a number of classrooms and unique contexts.

As a physical educator, you should teach these levels and work to help your students achieve them. Obviously, students will enter your classes at varying levels. Students may be at one level one day and at a higher or lower level the next. Their behavior may change from moment to moment. If students are knowledgeable about their level of behavior, they will be able to focus on ways to improve. Teaching levels of responsibility creates a wonderful vocabulary by which to communicate with your students.

The opening scenario in which the fourth grader suffered serious head injury at the hands of several of her classmates is a true story. Many other incidents of abuse, harassment, and violence in classes have occurred throughout the country. In addition, countless other students don't feel a sense of belonging to their classes or school community. As physical educators, we hold power of influence. We can do much for students' positive development and school experience by using strategies to create positive discipline.

Summary

Besides making your day run more smoothly, positive discipline will assist student development in the cognitive, affective, and psychomotor domains (chapter 5). Cognitive development stems from the opportunity to learn about social responsibility, social skills, and inclusive and equitable language. Affective growth appears as students practice, develop, and advance in the five levels of social responsibility. Psychomotor learning will occur more quickly because students who feel safe in your classroom may be more willing to take risks and practice motor skills.

When you begin to build a positive class community and develop social skills with your students, remember to begin with yourself. Understanding the values and expectations that you bring to the classroom is critical. Once you identify your beliefs and assumptions about your students and understand them more clearly (see figure 9.2), you will be able to work more productively on positive discipline. Make sure your students have a hand in determining positive behaviors for class. Students who help develop the rules for behavior in physical education will be more willing to live by them. Be sure to post the rules and enforce them fairly. Consistency and fairness are essential to maintaining a positive classroom. Finally, don't assume your students will know what positive behaviors look and sound like. Although your students are adolescents (young adults), they may not have had the opportunity to learn and practice prosocial behaviors. Teach them what positive behaviors are. Make sure that your instruction is age appropriate. No one likes to be talked down to or patronized. Positive discipline will create an environment in which students feel safe to interact with others and take risks cognitively, socially, and motorically.

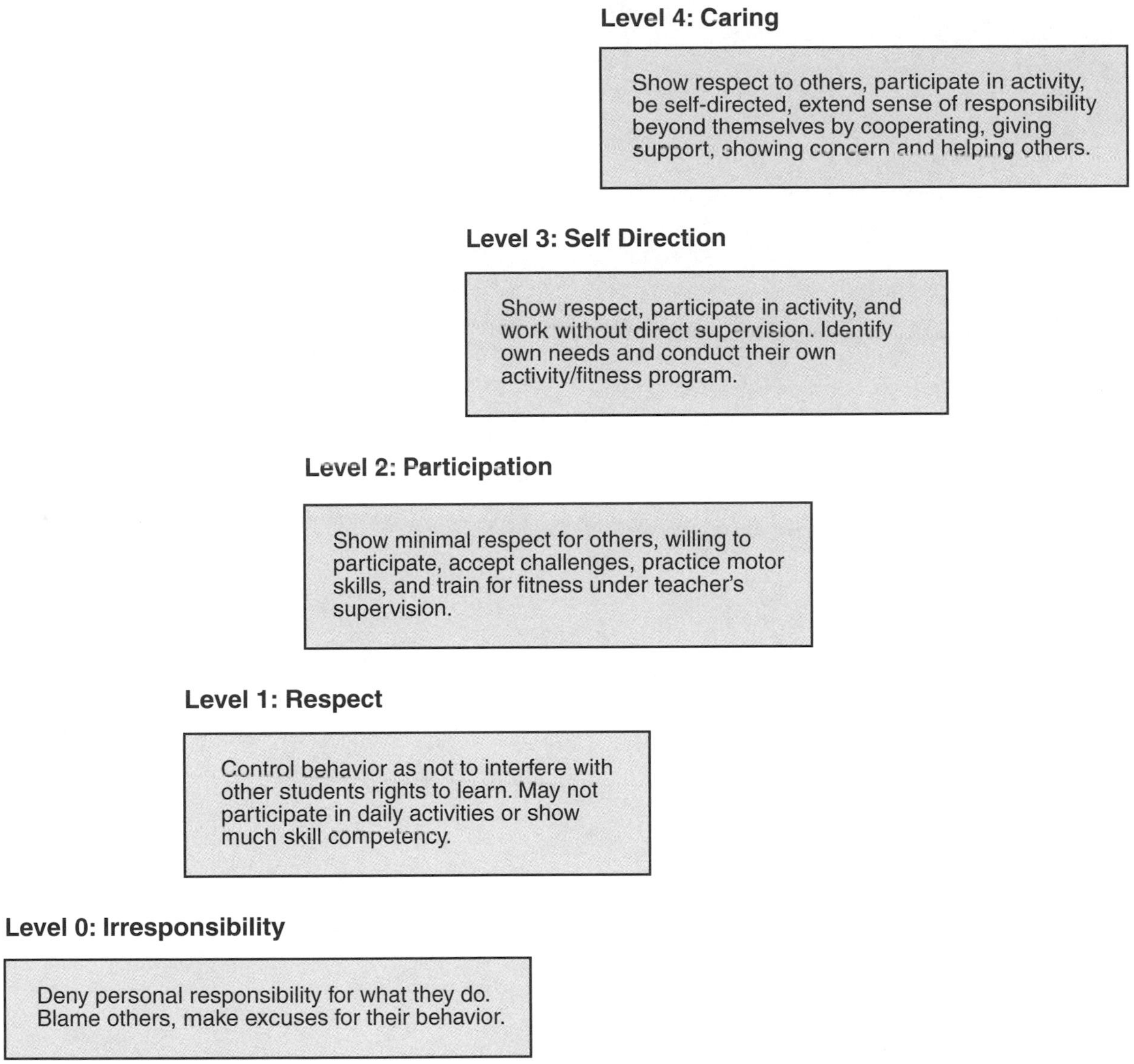

Level 4: Caring

Show respect to others, participate in activity, be self-directed, extend sense of responsibility beyond themselves by cooperating, giving support, showing concern and helping others.

Level 3: Self Direction

Show respect, participate in activity, and work without direct supervision. Identify own needs and conduct their own activity/fitness program.

Level 2: Participation

Show minimal respect for others, willing to participate, accept challenges, practice motor skills, and train for fitness under teacher's supervision.

Level 1: Respect

Control behavior as not to interfere with other students rights to learn. May not participate in daily activities or show much skill competency.

Level 0: Irresponsibility

Deny personal responsibility for what they do. Blame others, make excuses for their behavior.

Figure 9.8   Hellison's social responsibility model.

Checking for Understanding ▶▶▶

- In the opening scenario, what happened to Sarah?

- Define harassment.

- According to the *YRBS* (Centers for Disease Control and Prevention 1999) what percentage of students missed at least one day of school because they felt that their safety was threatened? What sense do you make of this statistic?

- Define discipline.

- What is positive discipline? How does it differ from negative discipline?

- Why should physical educators pay attention to their language as well as student language?

- What does STAR stand for?

- List and define Hellison's (1995) five levels of social responsibility.

For Reflection and Discussion ▶▶▶

- After completing the self-fulfilling prophecy activity, what did you learn about your beliefs about students? How might these beliefs affect your expectations of students and student behavior in your classes?

- Create a plan for establishing a positive learning environment in your classes.

- How would you implement Hellison's five levels of social responsibility into your classes?

References

Adams M., L.A. Bell, and P. Griffin. 1997. *Teaching for diversity and social justice: A source book.* New York: Routledge.

Centers for Disease Control and Prevention. 1999. *Youth risk behavior surveillance survey.* Washington, DC: U.S. Government Printing Office. **www.cdc.gov/mmwr/preview/mmwrhtml/ss4905a1.htm**.

Framework of developmental assets, The. 1997. Minneapolis: Search Institute.

Hanish, L.D. 2000. Children who get victimized at school: What is known? What can be done? *Professional School Counseling* 4(2):113–120.

Hellison, D. 1995. *Teaching responsibility through physical activity.* Champaign, IL: Human Kinetics.

Hellison, D. 1996. Teaching personal and social responsibility in physical education. In *Student learning in physical education: Applying research to enhance instruction,* ed. S.J. Silverman and C.D. Ennis, 269–286. Champaign, IL: Human Kinetics.

Hutchinson, G. 1995. Gender-fair teaching in physical education. *Journal of Physical Education, Recreation and Dance* 66(1):42–47.

Scales, P.C., and N. Leffert. 1999. *Developmental assets: A synthesis of the scientific research on adolescent development.* Minneapolis: Search Institute.

Wessler, S.L. 2000/2001. Sticks and stones. *Educational Leadership* 58(4):28–33.

Suggested Readings

Bosmajian, H. 1996. *The language of sexism.* In *Social diversity and social justice: Selected readings,* ed. M. Adams, P. Brigham, P. Dalpes, and L. Marchesani. Dubuque, IA: Kendall/Hunt.

Burton-Nelson, M. 1994. *The stronger women get, the more men love football.* New York: Avon Books.

Butt, K.L., and M.L. Pahnos. 1995. Why we need a multicultural focus in our schools. *Journal of Physical Education, Recreation and Dance* 66(1):48–53.

Griffin, P., and J. Placek. 1983. *Fair play in the gym: Race and sex equity in physical education.* Amherst, MA: Women's Equity Program and Pat Griffin.

Hellison, D., N. Cutforth, J. Kallusky, T. Martinek, M. Parker, and J. Stiehl. 2000. *Youth development and physical activity: Linking universities and communities.* Champaign, IL: Human Kinetics.

Mercier, R., and G. Hutchinson. 1998. Social psychology. In *Concepts of physical education: What every student needs to know,* edited by B. Mohnsen. Reston, VA: NASPE Publications.

Messner, M. 1992. *Power at play: Sports and the problem of masculinity.* Boston: Beacon Press.

Roberts, W.B. Jr. 2000. The bully as victim. *Professional School Counseling* 4(2):148–56.

Williamson, K.M. 1996. Gender issues. In *Student learning in physical education: Applying research to enhance instruction,* ed. S.J. Silverman and C.D. Ennis, 81–100. Champaign, IL: Human Kinetics.

Part IV

The *Curriculum*

10

Developing Your Curriculum

> **Individual commitment to a group effort makes a team work.**
>
> — *Anonymous*

Unit Outcomes
1. What will students
   Know?
2. What will students
   be able to do?

Cassandra and Desmond joined the physical education faculty at Gateway High School (grades 9 through 12) over the summer. During the first meeting of the physical education department, the chairperson announced that the department would revise its physical education curriculum during the year. Cassandra and Desmond were surprised by the reaction of some of the teachers. Sam and Tina, who both had been with the department for 15 years, remarked that it was about time. They looked forward to updating the document, although they did not cheerfully anticipate spending the time that would be required to do it. Jim, who had also been with the department for 15 years, shook his head with disgust at the announcement. Then he blurted out, "That is such a waste of time. We bust our tails to put in writing a pie-in-the-sky program that will never happen. And then all that hard work just sits on a shelf in the department office and in the principal's office collecting dust. In fact, I've seen a curriculum used as a doorstop! We won't use it and no one cares about it." Simone, a veteran of 6 years, added, "I agree. It's a lot of work for nothing. We forget what we write, and most of us do our own thing anyway, so what's the point?" Cassandra and Desmond turned to each other in wonder about how the process of developing curriculum would unfold in their new department.

Learning Objectives

After reading this chapter you will be able to

- define curriculum,
- explain the steps to curriculum development,
- explain the importance of an interaction agreement and ground rules,
- describe several curriculum models,
- examine your own value orientations,
- consider your philosophy of physical education, and
- articulate your commitment to the curriculum development process.

Key Terms and Phrases

Curriculum
Dynamic
Dynamic process
Interaction agreement
Surgeon General's Report on Physical Activity and Health
Value orientations
Scope
Breadth
Depth
Sequence
Multiactivity model
BU-HA-GOO
Sports education model
Social responsibility model
Fitness model
Lifelong physical activity model

Curriculum is a difficult word to define because its meaning is so complex. Generally, **curriculum** is a program of study often presented as a document, or "curriculum guide." Lambert (1996, 149) defined it as the means to the end for attaining predetermined learner outcomes. Comprehensively, it is an articulation of department, school, or district philosophy, a planned sequence of learner outcomes, developmentally appropriate units of instruction, methods for effective teaching, and a means for ongoing assessment of student learning and program effectiveness. Chapters 7 and 8 presented information on effective teaching, which should be planned in a curriculum, and chapters 11 and 12 will present pieces that go into a curriculum. We summarized our philosophy of secondary school curricula in chapter 1 with the Diamond Conceptual Framework. We believe that the main purpose of any secondary school physical education curriculum should be to guide students in the process of becoming physically active for the rest of their lives.

Used properly, a curriculum guide serves teachers in organizing and promoting student learning. Misunderstood or ignored, a curriculum guide may be regarded as pie in the sky, as Jim said, or a program document that is never used, as Simone sharply pointed out. As a result, a curriculum guide may be filed out of sight, placed on a shelf somewhere to collect dust, or used as a doorstop. We have even seen a curriculum placed under a computer monitor to raise the screen higher. Unfortunately, many teachers express poor sentiments about curriculum and perpetuate myths about its usefulness. Table 10.1 lists some of these curriculum myths and some facts for comparison.

Because the written curriculum guide is the direct result of people's hard work, we should look at it as having two parts: process and product. The process involved in curriculum is **dynamic,** or changing and evolving. This **dynamic process** brings concerned individuals together to discuss and create a physical education program based on student and teacher needs. Through the process, people produce the product, a curriculum document, and use it to guide the second and third stages of the curriculum process, called program implementation and assessment. The three stages of this process—development, implementation, and assessment—are ongoing. When physical educators reach the assessment stage, they determine what is effective in the curriculum and what is not. They use this information to redevelop or refine the curriculum before implementing it again. The whole process completes a cycle as illustrated in figure 10.1. Because the curriculum process is dynamic, we like to view the cycle as a spiral to give physical educators the sense of moving forward in developing improved curriculum that better serves student needs.

Understanding the steps involved in the dynamic process of curriculum development will lead to effective program development and enhanced student learning. In the following section we will explore the dynamic process of curriculum development.

Table 10.1 Curriculum Myths and Facts

Curriculum myths	Curriculum facts
Curriculum is	Curriculum is
◆ an unusable document,	◆ a program of study,
◆ a dust collector,	◆ a dynamic process (always evolving),
◆ grading on dress, participation, and attendance,	◆ guided by learner outcomes,
◆ a collection of activities guided by teacher likes and expertise,	◆ a guide for instruction and assessment,
◆ a lot of teacher time and effort for nothing, and	◆ developmentally appropriate,
◆ a task to be completed for administration.	◆ experienced daily by the student, and
	◆ both visible and hidden.

Modified from Dianne Wilson-Graham at the fall conference planning committee, 1995 California Alliance for Health, Physical Education, Recreation and Dance.

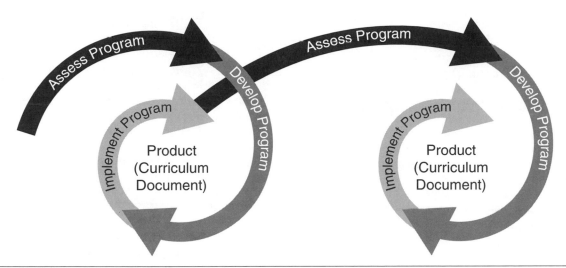

Figure 10.1 The curriculum process is a dynamic cycle that requires constant refining to better serve student needs.

Purpose

Use the Web to explore bulletin boards and chat rooms to determine reliable sources of assistance with curriculum development.

Resource and Procedure

Become familiar with the different e-mail threads, bulletin boards, and chat room postings that physical educators use for dispensing information and suggestions for curriculum development. Assess Web sites for their reliability and timeliness of responses. The best time to assess different sources is when you do *not* need help. Observe the sources for at least two weeks to assess their value. How timely are posts and responses? Are the various threads of conversation focused? How professional are the responses? Who are the primary respondents and what are their organizations?

Dynamic Process of Curriculum Development

Constructing an effective secondary physical education curriculum is like building a house. It begins with an idea. The party building the house comes together and shares ideas about what is important in the house and how to build it. Individual ideas and beliefs emerge from each person's value orientations about what is important in a house. In building a curriculum, physical educators share their values and beliefs as they discuss what is important in a physical education program. Soon, the group building the house or the physical education program comes to a consensus on what is important. They transform ideas into a blueprint or a plan of action for building a curriculum. A great deal of thought goes into the development of the blueprint. After all, when building a house, the builder considers personal needs, building goals, zoning laws, and available resources like money, land, and building supplies. When building a curriculum, teachers must consider national standards and guidelines, the GET ACTIVE FOR LIFE factors (presented in chapter 1), student needs, teacher expertise, attainable goals, and available facilities, equipment, and resources. After creating the blueprint, teachers begin the task of implementing the curriculum. Curriculum guides represent the blueprint for building quality secondary physical education programs. You and your curriculum development committee are indeed the homeowners of your program. Together you can design your curricular blueprint by following several important steps:

1. Select a curriculum committee or team
2. Create open lines of communication
3. Facilitate curriculum team meetings
4. Prepare the curriculum team for action
5. Examine curriculum team value orienta-tions
6. Develop a philosophy of physical education
7. Establish program goals
8. Determine an appropriate curriculum model
9. Develop a scope and sequence

10. Develop units of study

11. Implement the curriculum

12. Assess and revise, revise, revise

Select a Curriculum Committee or Team

The first step to curriculum development is establishing a curriculum committee or curriculum team. Core members of the curriculum team will be you and members of your physical education department. Remember, you and your colleagues have a stake in the quality of the program. You should invite several individuals from outside the physical education department to serve on the curriculum team. These individuals may be parents, students, and other school professionals with expertise in diverse student populations (Wuest 1994). For instance, an adapted physical educator serving on the curriculum committee would represent the needs of students with disabilities. A school professional working with students who speak English as a second language (ESL) would assist with identifying effective instructional strategies for students with language barriers. An instructional technology teacher would help identify interactive technologies for use in the gymnasium. A student member would offer a learner's perspective, and a parent would bring in points of view from home.

Beyond School Walls

As your mind searches the high school corridors for individuals who might serve on the physical education curriculum team, take a turn and wander out the main door, across the parking lot, onto the main street, and into the school district. Consider inviting elementary and middle school physical educators to join your curriculum team. Work to knock down the walls of programmatic isolation that exist in many districts so that you can build powerful curricular lines of communication across all grade levels. Working with elementary (if available) and middle school physical educators would add important information to your curricular efforts. You and your department would hear the curricular concerns and suggestions from teachers in those grade levels. You would learn more about the goals, objectives, and units offered to students in elementary and middle school. At the same time, you and members of your high school physical education department would share your curricular concerns and suggestions with elementary and middle school physical educators. For instance, you may share the Diamond Conceptual Framework with them. When you assemble a diverse group of people, a variety of professional knowledge and opinion will be present. At times, discussion may become lively, if not heated. These interactions will likely have a positive influence on the program at each grade level and create a more developmentally appropriate physical education curriculum for grades K–12 (Mohnsen 1997). This sort of dialogue is exactly what we promote in chapter 1, where we discussed the need for articulation among the three levels—elementary, middle, and high school. Communication and assurance that you are building on previous learning is essential if you want to build programs that encourage lifetime participation in physical activity.

Choosing a Representative Group for the Committee

Obviously, you cannot include the entire professional staff, student body, and parental community on the department curriculum team. The curriculum team should not exceed 12 members. When selecting curriculum team members, you should try to have representation from

- many aspects of the high school community and
- all levels of physical education, when possible.

Figure 10.2 illustrates potential members of a curriculum team. Acquiring members from outside your department may be difficult at times. Know that you may engage in the curriculum process with only the physical educators from your department. In the best-case scenario, however, you would involve members from outside the department as well as from outside the school.

Create Open Lines of Communication

Mike and Lisa have been working together for four years. They get along well. On Fridays they often join each other and friends for food and fun at a local restaurant. Four weeks ago their principal asked their department to revise their high school curriculum to make it more current with the state framework and the national physical education standards. Their department of three embraced the challenge enthusiastically and invited others—teachers, parents, and students—to join them. The curriculum team now included seven members. During their fifth meeting, the curriculum team engaged in a heated argument about what students should be learning in the 10th grade. Mike and Lisa were on opposing sides of the argument. As the discussion escalated, Mike and Lisa exchanged personal remarks. Both left the meeting angry and hurt. The next school day, neither one could talk

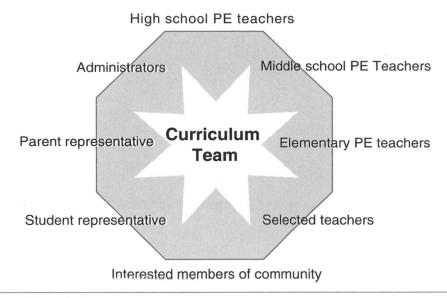

High school PE teachers

Administrators

Middle school PE Teachers

Parent representative

Curriculum Team

Elementary PE teachers

Student representative

Selected teachers

Interested members of community

Figure 10.2 Potential curriculum team members.

to the other. At the next meeting, neither contributed much to the discussion, and they avoided interacting with each other. During the whole curriculum development process they rarely spoke, and when they did they were again at odds. Their professional relationship turned negative, and their friendship turned cold. All of this may have been avoided or effectively resolved if the group had established an interaction agreement in the beginning of the process.

Once people have joined the physical education curriculum team, its members should consciously decide how they will work together. Maintaining open lines of communication throughout the entire process is crucial to the success of developing the curriculum. In committee settings, people often fail to set up procedures to maintain open communication. Establishing an interaction agreement among team members enables individuals on the committee to get along, even during lively discussions and heated debates.

An **interaction agreement** is a contract developed by group members. The contract describes how members agree to interact with one another during meetings, disagreements, and committee work. After the team members agree to the contract, they each sign it and maintain a copy in their records. In the event that a team member acts rudely, does not do his or her work, or becomes involved in a conflict with another member or members, the team uses the interaction agreement to remind members of their responsibilities, to resolve conflicts, and to maintain open communication.

Creating an interaction agreement is easy. First, present the idea to the curriculum team. Some members may find the idea silly. Ask them to humor you and participate seriously anyway. Next, ask the team to brainstorm a list of behaviors they expect of themselves and others while engaging in committee work. One way to do this is to separate the brainstorming exercise into several categories such as active listening, respectful speaking, team commitments, and conflict resolution. A sentence stem can help generate ideas under each of these categories. After completion of the brainstorming activity (figure 10.3), have the curriculum team condense the list under each category. Then format the list as a contract for each member to sign. Hold on to the original and provide copies for each team member (figure 10.4).

Facilitate Curriculum Team Meetings

After team members have opened lines of communication and produced an interaction agreement, they should think about how to run productive curriculum team meetings. Chances are that meetings will occur during lunchtime, a prep period, or after school for an hour before members have to run to other obligations like coaching, other committees, and families. On occasion, meetings will take place during staff in-service days or before staff members return to school at the end of the summer vacation. In other words, time will be short and available at irregular intervals. You must use your time wisely when running meetings. Developing facilitation skills will help you and your colleagues run effective meetings so that members do not feel as if they are wasting their time.

If you are serving as the chairperson or the facilitator, you must first determine a meeting purpose. We know that three purposes (outcome goals) for having curriculum team meetings are to develop (1) a curriculum guide, (2) an implementation strategy, and (3) a program assessment plan. So each meeting must have an agenda that

Active listening:

When I speak, I'd appreciate it if people would listen by

looking at me,

letting me finish before they speak, and

ending side conversations and paying attention to me.

Respectful speaking:

I find it to be important for people to _____ when they speak.

own their own thoughts

not pass judgment

speak for themselves and not for others

be concise and clear

watch the amount of time they take

Team commitments:

As a member of this curriculum team, I promise to

volunteer for written tasks,

complete tasks in a timely fashion,

attend all meetings,

be on time for all meetings,

come prepared to all meetings, and

contribute to group discussion.

Conflict resolution:

To avoid conflicts, I promise to

agree that committee members will disagree from time to time,

not pass judgment on people's ideas, concerns, and suggestions, and

refrain from putting others down with negative comments.

To resolve conflicts, I promise to

work to solve the conflict,

tell my side of the story using "I" messages,

listen to the other person's side of the story without interrupting,

restate what the problem is for the other person,

suggest possible solutions,

listen to the other person's suggestions for solution, and

work with the other person to agree on a solution.

Figure 10.3 Interaction agreement brainstorming activity.

Bear Valley High School

Physical Education Curriculum Team

Interaction Agreement

As a member of the Sierra Nevada High School Physical Education Curriculum Team, I promise to uphold the following behaviors in order to promote positive interaction and open communication with my colleagues:

- Be on time and attend all meetings
- Come prepared to all meetings
- Volunteer for curriculum tasks
- Complete tasks in a timely fashion
- Contribute to group discussions
- Listen to people speaking by giving my undivided attention
- Allow people to finish speaking before I speak
- Speak for myself, and without judgment
- Be concise and clear when I speak
- Be careful not to hog airtime while speaking
- Agree to disagree
- Work to solve the conflict by:
    telling my side of the story using "I" messages
    listening to the other person's side of the story without interrupting
    restating what the problem is for the other person
    suggesting possible solutions
    listening to the other person's suggestions for solution
    working with the other person to agree on a solution

signature	date	signature	date
signature	date	signature	date
signature	date	signature	date
signature	date	signature	date

Figure 10.4 A sample interaction agreement.

keeps your team on course and sailing toward one of those outcomes. In the first meeting of the curriculum team, you stated the purpose of convening the group and established open lines of communication. Now that you have done that, you will need to consider the purpose of each meeting that follows. As a chairperson or facilitator, you must make sure that your group helps define the purpose of each meeting. So relax; the responsibility for determining each meeting purpose is not yours alone.

Common Meeting Purposes

Meetings have many purposes. Determining the primary purpose of your curriculum team meetings will help everyone stay on task and achieve the goals set for that day. Initial curriculum team meetings might focus on the following: team building, informing and planning, and value orientations. As time passes and the team delves into the curriculum development process, meetings may focus on problem solving, decision making, and analyzing. Figure 10.5 lists the most common meeting purposes (Sibbet 1999).

Setting Meeting Goals

Now that you have determined the purpose of the next meeting, you should set desired meeting goals. Ask yourself the question, "What should we leave today's meeting with?" Sibbet (1999) identifies two types of desired outcomes: a product and knowledge. Products include written lists, plans, decisions, and agreements. Knowledge typically falls into two categories: awareness and understanding. Written notes of meetings help everyone remember what people said and what the group decided, and the notes create a document trail that will be helpful later.

Affiliating	Informing
Analyzing	Mediating
Celebrating	Planning
Conciliating	Problem solving
Decision making	Socializing
Enrolling	Team building
Evaluating	Tracking

Figure 10.5   Common meeting purposes.

You should prepare copies of these notes, called meeting minutes, and give them to team members before the next meeting.

Determining How the Team Will Make Decisions

Everyone must feel involved in the curriculum development process. The greater the commitment of team members, the greater the possibility of implementing the curriculum as planned. Have the team develop a clear way to make important decisions. Like an interaction agreement, a decision-making process should let everyone know what to expect. A clear decision-making process also builds greater support for final decisions. Because we are looking for the highest level of involvement, we recommend consensus as a means for making decisions. Having a consensus means that everyone agrees, but agreement doesn't require that everyone be ecstatic about an idea or strategy. Agreement does mean, however, that everyone is willing to live with the decision and will not sabotage it later. To see if you have consensus on an item, simply ask members to show a thumbs up, thumbs down, or in the middle. If all thumbs are up or in the middle, you have a consensus. People who place their thumbs in the middle are willing to live with the decision, which combined with thumbs up produces consensus. If members place their thumbs down, they disagree and are unable to live with the decision. More discussion will be necessary to reach consensus.

Consensus lends itself to the greatest member commitment. At times, consensus may be difficult to attain. When the curriculum team has exhausted efforts to attain consensus and a stalemate persists, we suggest that you use a majority vote. When voting on a difficult issue is necessary, we strongly recommend using an anonymous ballot, not a show of hands. A majority vote determines the decision, and those whose vote is in the minority agree to live with and support the results.

Agenda Setting

Every meeting should have an agenda displayed on chart paper, whiteboard, or chalkboard and accompanied with a handout. An agenda is a visible map of the meeting that tells members what to expect and helps to establish meeting flow. With a visible agenda, the team can manage its time more effectively. An agenda, when displayed, is a wonderful tool that the chairperson or facilitator can use to bring the group back on task when they wander off.

Purpose

Use e-mail to set up an effective system for introducing agenda items and sharing support materials with committee meeting participants.

Resource and Procedure

As the committee is forming, extend the capabilities of your meetings by setting up virtual meeting possibilities that don't require everyone to meet at the same time and place. Physical education teachers have varied activities and are busy with other responsibilities such as coaching and supervising after-school events. E-mail has the potential for agenda setting and assigning tasks and roles before face-to-face meetings. In your contract include a commitment statement for all of the members to use e-mail for meeting certain needs and goals. It should be easy to convince members to participate in e-mailing sessions by demonstrating live meetings that are focused on brainstorming, discussion, and consensus-building activities. It may also result in fewer live meetings.

An agenda should state the purpose of the meeting and have a clear beginning and end. Figure 10.6 is an example of an agenda. Keep the number of items on your agenda to no more than seven. If you have too many items, chances are you will not get to all of them and members will feel rushed and frustrated. A better method is to prioritize meeting items and save those that do not need immediate action or discussion for the next meeting. The last item on the agenda should always be setting agenda for the next meeting. Here, the group helps you determine items to include at the next meeting, tasks that need to be completed before the next meeting and who will do them, and when and where the next meeting will be.

Prepare the Curriculum Team for Action

The individuals selected for the curriculum team may come with varying levels of curricular knowledge and experiences. You should make the effort to provide members of the team with an overview of the curriculum process explained earlier. Pre-paring the team would be an excellent purpose and agenda for one or several curriculum team meetings.

The overview should include reference to and information about current national and state educational reform issues, educational goals, and national, state, and district physical education standards (Mohnsen 1997). To give you an idea of what we mean, we have included some information about the *Surgeon General's Report on Physical Activity and Health* (National Center for Chronic Disease Prevention and Health Promotion 1996), Goals 2000: Educate America Act, *Moving Into the Future: National Standards for Physical Education* (National Association for Sport and Physical Education [NASPE] 1995), and *Healthy People 2010* (U.S. Department of Health and Human Services 2000).

Surgeon General's Report

When the **Surgeon General's Report on Physical Activity and Health** came out in July of 1996, many physical educators and health professionals around the country rejoiced. The surgeon general's report confirmed what we knew all along—physical activity improves our health. The report went on to declare physical inactivity a health risk and make it clear that a sedentary lifestyle was directly related to higher rates of mortality and higher incidences of coronary heart disease, hypertension, colon cancer, and diabetes mellitus. The report strongly recommended regular moderate to vigorous physical activity as a means to improve health, add years to life, and combat the onset of disease and depression.

Reported findings, as mentioned in chapter 3, showed that only 40% of American adults are physically active on a regular basis. Twenty-five percent of American adults are not active at all. Nearly half of American youth ages 12 through 21 are not vigorously active on a regular basis, and youth involvement in physical activity declines drastically through adolescence.

Youth move from active lifestyles to more inactive lifestyles as they mature and enter adulthood. Recent studies have shown that physical activity programs at school, work, and health care sites have had a positive effect on people's health and well-being. Unfortunately, we have seen a drastic decline in daily enrollment in public school physical education classes. During the 1991 academic year, 42% of all high school students were enrolled in physical education. In 1995, that number had dropped to 25%.

Meeting purpose: Determine department philosophy on high school physical education

I. Review agenda.

  A. Make sure everyone reviews the agenda and is in agreement with it.

  B. If an someone wants to add an item, add it to the end of the meeting.

II. Review meeting minutes from the previous meeting.

  A. Ask if the previous meeting minutes are accurate.

  B. Note any necessary changes.

III. Determine department philosophy on high school physical education.

  A. Share examples of other department philosophy statements.

  B. Examine contemporary literature to help fuel thinking.

  C. Determine a strategy for developing a department philosophy.

  D. Begin strategy with discussion.

IV. Determine tasks for next meeting.

  A. Decide who will do what.

  B. Determine next meeting time.

V. Determine next meeting agenda.

VI. Adjourn.

Figure 10.6   Sample meeting agenda.

 As discussed in detail in chapter 3, the surgeon general's report strongly recommends that "all children and adults set a long term goal to accumulate at least 30 minutes or more of moderate intensity physical activity on most, or preferably all, days of the week." You should use the most recent surgeon general's recommendations, along with the NASPE standards, the GET ACTIVE FOR LIFE factors, and other guidelines related to physical activity promotion, to inform the development of your curriculum. Physical education curricula must address the health risk of inactivity and the inactivity of American youth by focusing on the outcome of lifelong participation in physical activity (National Center for Chronic Disease Prevention and Health Promotion 1996).

Goals 2000: Educate America Act

In working to improve our physical education programs, we should note that the whole world of education is changing too. The Goals 2000: Educate America Act was passed as Public Law 103-227 in 1994 (figure 10.7). The act provided our nation with plans for reforming and improving schools. By including physical education, the act boosted the credibility of physical educators among their colleagues and communities. The act is comprehensive, including areas such as school readiness, school completion, student achievement, citizenship, math and science, adult literacy, lifelong learning, safe schools, alcohol and drug-free schools, teacher preparation and professional development, and parental participation.

We are members of the educational community (Mohnsen 1997) and need to continue to make connections between physical education and other areas of education. Awareness and understanding of educational goals and current issues in education will help us prepare students for the future by providing them with the best learning opportunities available.

Moving Into the Future: National Standards for Physical Education

When the Goals 2000: Educate America Act passed in 1994, the move for national standards became law. The National Education Standards Improvement Council (NESIC) was established to work with appropriate organizations in determining criteria for subject matter content standards. The NESIC also had other responsibilities:

By the year 2000

1. all children in America will start school ready to learn;

2. high school graduation rate will increase to at least 90%;

3. the drop-out rate will be reduced dramatically;

4. the gap in high school graduation rates between American students from minority backgrounds and their nonminority counterparts will be eliminated;

5. all students leaving grades 4, 8, and 12 will demonstrate competency over challenging subject matter;

6. all students will be involved in activities that promote and demonstrate good citizenship, good health, community service, and personal responsibility;

7. all students will have access to physical education and health to ensure that they are healthy and fit;

8. every school in the United States will be free of drugs, violence, and the unauthorized presence of firearms and alcohol and will offer a disciplined environment conducive to learning; and

9. every school will promote partnerships that will increase parental involvement and participation in promoting social, emotional, and academic growth of children.

Figure 10.7 The Goals 2000: Educate America Act was passed as law in 1994.

1. To ensure that standards are internationally competitive,

2. To ensure that standards reflect the best knowledge about teaching and learning, and

3. To ensure that standards have been developed through a broad-based, open adoption process (NASPE 1995).

Based on these criteria, standards would become the cornerstones for all subject matter. The national standards for physical education are cornerstones for us, and we need to use them to develop our curricula.

The writers of the physical education national standards created two types of standards: content standards and performance standards. Content standards refer to what students should know and be able to do. Performance standards state how well students should be able to do each content standard. Chapter 1 presented the seven NASPE content standards. We believe that you will find the physical education standards a valuable tool while developing your curriculum. All physical educators should know and use these standards. Together with the other guiding lights for our profession (presented in chapter 1), they should guide your program.

Healthy People 2010

The document *Healthy People 2010* is a statement of the national systematic approach to health improvement. We examined it briefly in chapter 1, but will go into more detail here. *Healthy People 2010* includes two goals (U.S. Department of Health and Human Services 2000):

1. To increase the quality and years of healthy life, and

2. Eliminate health disparities among segments of the population, including the differences that occur by gender, race and ethnicity, education, income, disability, geographic location, and sexual orientation.

The document describes a systematic approach composed of four critical elements: goals, objectives, determinants of health, and health status. *Healthy People 2010* works to achieve its goals through the implementation and monitoring of 467 objectives in 28 focus areas. Many of the objectives are designed to reduce or eliminate poor health (U.S. Department of Health and Human Services 2000).

Your curriculum team will be particularly interested in objective 19, nutrition and overweight, and objective 22, physical activity and fitness.

Physical activity and fitness

Healthy People 2010 recognizes the importance of physical activity in maintaining good health. The following objectives were selected to measure progress among adolescents and adults:

- To increase the proportion of adolescents who engage in vigorous physical activity that promotes cardiorespiratory fitness three or more days per week for 20 or more minutes per occasion
- To increase the proportion of adults who engage regularly, preferably daily, in moderate physical activity for at least 30 minutes per day

Overweight and obesity

According to the U.S. Department of Health and Human Services (2000), a higher body weight is associated with a higher death rate on average. Overweight and obesity contribute to many preventable causes of death. In the past 40 years, the number of overweight children, adolescents, and adults has increased. Overweight and obesity not only tax the health of the individual but also cost the nation. In 1995, medical expenses and lost productivity at work attributed to obesity cost the country an estimated $99 billion (U.S. Department of Health and Human Services 2000). Overweight and obesity objectives include the following:

- To reduce the proportion of children and adolescents who are overweight or obese
- To reduce the proportion of adults who are obese

Along with healthy diet, regular moderate to vigorous physical activity has been recommended to help achieve these objectives.

Besides national documents, you should collect your state and school district physical education standards, if they have them. For instance, the state of California published *Physical Education Framework* in 1994 (California Department of Education 1994), which described three goals for grades K–12: motor skill and knowledge, social development, and personal development. This document is comprehensive and developmentally appropriate. Physical educators across California use it to guide their curriculum development and program assessment. Check to see whether your state and school district have physical education frameworks or standards.

Examine Curriculum Team Value Orientations

Even people who are well informed about educational reform and standards for physical education may not be able to come together and agree on curriculum design and curriculum content. The reason for this may be that all curriculum team members hold certain values and beliefs that reflect their priorities about student needs, student interests, program goals, management strategies, instructional strategies, and assessment needs (Ennis 1994, 1992a, b). These values and beliefs have been termed **value orientations** (Ennis 1992a). Five value orientations appear to compete for priority among teachers (Ennis 1994, 165): disciplinary mastery, learning process, self-actualization, ecological integration, and social responsibility (Ennis and Chen 1995). Examination of one's value orientations is critical. After curriculum team members have clearly identified the meaning of each value orientation, they can identify the one or several that best represent their own values and beliefs about teaching physical education. Understanding value orientations and their influence on curricular decisions will aid team members in their discussions and help them understand their similar and different beliefs. To help you with your examination, we will briefly explain each value orientation.

Disciplinary Mastery

Disciplinary mastery implies that students will learn the body of knowledge considered the traditional core of a particular discipline such as biomechanics or exercise physiology. In physical education, this often translates to skill knowledge and skill performance (Ennis 1994; Rink 2002). Students are often encouraged to learn to perform a motor skill, sport skill, or fitness component. Individuals with a disciplinary mastery value orientation may emphasize direct-style teaching such as Mosston and Ashworth's (1994) command and practice styles (we called these styles direct and teacher feedback in chapter 8). This orientation is common because teacher education programs tend to emphasize motor-skill acquisition, skill knowledge, discipline knowledge, and skill performance (Ennis 1992a).

Learning Process

The learning process builds on the knowledge and performance competencies acquired during disciplinary mastery. Here, educators provide opportunities for learners to apply their new knowledge and skill to problem-solving activities. "In classes taught with this orientation, students 'learn how to learn' new facts by applying prior knowledge to new problems" (Ennis 1992b, 319). This value orientation often lends itself to more interactive forms of teaching. Teachers give students more independence and responsibility so that they can actively engage in problem solving.

Disciplinary mastery and the learning process maintain a knowledge-based and performance-based focus. These value orientations are embedded in the cognitive and psychomotor domains. Self-actualization, ecological integration, and social responsibility shift the focus more to the affective domain.

Self-Actualization

Self-actualization is defined as the pursuit of one's fullest potential (Maslow 1954). Self-actualization as a value orientation is based on the work of Rogers and Maslow (Allen and Santrock 1993). Both of these humanistic psychologists referred to human potential as the centerpiece in their work to understand human behavior. Self-actualization shifts the curricular emphasis from a knowledge and performance base to an affective one. The focus becomes improving students' positive self-esteem. "Learning is guided toward self understanding with an emphasis on student autonomy, self direction, and responsibility as valued outcomes" (Ennis 1992b, 319).

Ecological Integration

Ecological integration is an orientation in which students determine their personal relevance by integrating their own needs and interests into a larger social and natural world. They search for personal knowledge and use that knowledge to change their lives and direct their futures. The discovery and creation of meaning is central to ecological integration. Students are expected to develop meaning for subject matter based on their interactions with subject matter, environment, and others. Doing this demands not only the search for individual self-actualization but also positive socialization among others. Here, the process of learning is as important as learning subject matter. Students learn to ask and examine critical questions. Overall, this value orientation views the individual as an integral part of his or her environment (Ennis 1992b).

Social Reconstruction–Social Responsibility

This orientation emphasizes social justice and equality and promotes citizenship, social skills, and respect for others. Teachers for social reconstruction–social responsibility encourage their students to get along with one another, respect one another, and examine social inequities of the school and the world. For example, students may look into the inequities that exist in physical education, health, and sport. After students identify inequities, teachers would have them explore strategies for changing inequities to more fair practices (Ennis 1994). In physical education, Griffin (1985) described sexist behaviors in co-ed classes and then identified strategies for promoting sex equity. A teacher who values social responsibility will promote curricular goals to enhance student prosocial behavior (Ennis 1994). Students will have opportunity to get to know one another, demonstrate respect, practice how to get along, learn to resolve or manage conflicts, and practice cooperation through group work. Physical education content serves as the catalyst through which students practice and develop prosocial behaviors. Hellison's (1995) model of responsibility (chapter 9) includes a good example of a teacher who demonstrates a social responsibility value orientation. He teaches social responsibility through basketball to inner city youth in Chicago. Youth learn to examine their behavior using five levels of responsibility. We will examine his approach more closely when we discuss the social responsibility curriculum model.

Value orientations are easily categorized for the purpose of this section. Determining your value orientation is complex and dynamic. Ennis and Chen (1995) have developed a value orientation inventory (VOI) that they have used in many studies to determine value orientations of physical educators teaching in public schools. For the purpose of the curriculum development process, you need not complete the VOI, but you should understand the kinds of value orientations that exist. Understanding your values and beliefs and those of your colleagues will help you communicate more effectively during the curriculum development stages.

Now that you have read the descriptions for each value orientation, you may find that you identify with one, two, or all types listed. You can certainly value aspects from one or several categories. You may also find that your beliefs change over time as you gather more information and gain experience. Use the descriptions of these value orientations on the worksheet (figure 10.8) with your curriculum team to fuel open discussions during team meetings. These discussions may help the team determine more clearly a program philosophy.

Develop a Philosophy of Physical Education

Now that you and your curriculum team have wrestled with value orientations and have a better understanding of where each of you stands in terms of what students should learn in physical education, you must put together a curriculum team philosophy. People tend to cringe

---

Value orientation worksheet

In the space, rank each value orientation as it fits your belief and value system about physical education. Five will be the highest rank and one the lowest. There is no right or wrong answer. You also may find that how you rank these value orientations changes over time. The purpose of this worksheet is to familiarize you with value orientations; understand that they influence your curricular decisions, and become aware of your own value orientations. Once you have an idea of where you stand, use this information to explore department/district philosophy and curriculum development with your colleagues.

Disciplinary Mastery   1   2   3   4   5

Students gain a proficiency in fundamental movement, skill, sport, and fitness activities. They will have a cognitive understanding of the rules, strategies, and principles associated with the activity and with improved performance. Students also demonstrate an appreciation for these activities. The focus is on knowledge and competence.

Learning Process   1   2   3   4   5

The focus here is on students learning how to learn movement, sport, and fitness subject matter. They also learn how to use this information to improve performance and solve problems. The emphasis is learning how to learn and how to apply what has been learned.

Self-Actualization   1   2   3   4   5

Students gain proficiency at working independently. They become more and more self-directed and responsible for their own learning. They are strongly encouraged to learn about themselves and on their own. The focus is both individuality and independence.

Ecological Integration   1   2   3   4   5

The world is run by larger systems. In this model, students focus on their relevance to self and to the world. They learn how to integrate their own needs and interests with the larger social and natural world. They focus on personal meaning and integration with balance into the world around them.

Social Reconstruction/Responsibility   1   2   3   4   5

Students learn how to be positive with themselves as well as with others. They learn to get along with others in a respectful and meaningful way. They work to tolerate and accept difference among people. They learn social rules and norms for personal conduct. They also learn to examine critically these norms and question inequities in hopes of finding solutions. The focus is positive social interactions and prosocial behavior in hopes of positively changing the environment around them.

Figure 10.8 By using a value orientation worksheet, curriculum development team members can discover the values held by different people in the department and help the group better arrive at a program philosophy.

when they have to write a philosophy statement. After reflecting on what you and others believe to be important, a philosophy statement should be the next logical step. You should be able to develop it easily. The difficulty for your team may be coming to a consensus about which philosophy will best represent the curriculum team and the physical education program. We strongly encourage you to consider the information in chapter 1 as you develop your philosophy statement. We believe that all secondary physical education curricula should focus on helping students become movers for life. We also believe that achieving this goal is possible even if a variety of different value orientations are represented on your curriculum team. By using the Diamond Conceptual Framework, team members can express and represent a variety of value orientations while working toward this worthy goal.

One exercise that helps people reflect and structure their thoughts about a philosophy of physical education is writing metaphors. If you listen carefully to others speak, you will find that people often use metaphors to describe or explain a point of view. Metaphors help us organize our thoughts and express them in ways that others may easily understand (Bie 1994; Hutchinson and Johnson 1993–94; Johnson and Hutchinson 1998). Ask members of your team to write a metaphor for physical education.

Your Turn ▶ ▶ ▶

Explore the metaphors that you have for physical education. Complete the following sentence stem: "Physical education as . . ." Some colleagues may describe physical education as a garden and the teacher as the gardener. Others have described it as a three-ring circus with the teacher as the ringmaster. How does your metaphor represent your philosophy of physical education?

After you and your teammates have described your metaphors for physical education, discuss them carefully. Compare them and find commonalities. You are looking for similarities in your beliefs about the purpose of physical education. After you have listed the similarities, you and your team will be able to draft a philosophy of physical education.

If you and your curriculum team are not enthusiastic about creating metaphors, you may want to focus your attention on the following questions to help you develop a philosophy statement.

1. What is the purpose of physical education? (You already know how we feel about this question and why we feel that way.)
2. How does the purpose of physical education relate to education in general?
3. Should learning be student centered or teacher directed? Why?
4. What is the role of the physical educator in the learning process?

Philosophy statements tend to be brief. Your curriculum team should create a philosophy statement that includes your common beliefs about physical education. Having common values is important because your philosophy statement will serve as the basis for action in your curriculum.

Establish Program Goals

The philosophy statement reflects the curriculum team's beliefs about student needs and student learning. The team must always keep student needs at the forefront of their thinking. You may want to survey students and other teachers about student needs. After you have collected this information, let it inform your decisions regarding program goals.

After the team members have agreed on the philosophy statement, the next step is to determine program goals. Program goals state what students will learn in your physical education program. An effective way to determine content standards is to complete another sentence stem: "After students graduate from our program, they will know and be able to do the following . . ." You should even do this by grade level. In other words, you should complete this sentence stem: "When students graduate from the ninth grade, they will know and be able to do the following . . ." Completing these sentence stems helps you formulate your exit outcomes. After your team has determined exit outcomes, then you must address the question of how students will acquire knowledge and skills. NASPE's seven content standards along with standards from your state or school district may help inform the writing of your outcome or program goals.

You can use the Diamond Conceptual Framework presented in chapter 1 to frame your curriculum decisions, including your program goals. Remember that the diamond's backbone is the national standards and other guidelines for physical education, as well as the GET ACTIVE FOR LIFE factors. Together, these guiding lights should help us make the major decisions for our curriculum, including developing program goals, which will guide the adoption of one or more curriculum models that we will use to build a scope and sequence of learning experiences.

Determine an Appropriate Curriculum Model

Many curriculum models are available. Each model represents a specific value orientation and philosophy, and each emphasizes particular student outcomes. You should select a curriculum model carefully. You and your curriculum committee should strive to find a model that best represents student needs and your philosophy and program goals.

Curriculum development teams may be tempted to take an eclectic approach by choosing important characteristics from several curriculum models. We do not recommend this approach. Selecting important characteristics from several models weakens your curriculum design and limits the depth of your program. Choosing one curriculum model enables your team to focus on program goals. If you find it difficult to select one model, we recommend that you use a combination of no more than two models. For instance, a curriculum team may decide that the social responsibility and fitness models would best fit student needs. These models, then, would be the foundation on which you would establish the scope and sequence of content.

Develop a Scope and Sequence

Determining the physical education content and learning activities that will enable students to achieve desired outcomes is the next step in curriculum development. Two questions guide this step:

1. What will students learn (scope)?
2. In what order will they learn it (sequence)?

Cassandra and Desmond's department struggled through sharing their value orientations, developing a philosophy, and determining program goals. The department came to a consensus that they would like to help students learn to get along with others and prepare students to be physically active for life. Cassandra and Desmond thought that a social responsibility model complemented by a model that emphasized helping students be physically active for life would be appropriate for guiding their program development. Jim and Simone had doubts about that idea. They felt that working with just one or two models would limit what activities they would be able to do with their students. They wanted to pursue a different activity unit with students about every three weeks and encourage their students to sample many activities (and probably not have time to master any). The department chair understood the dilemma and worked with the department to come to a consensus. After much discussion, Jim and Simone were still not convinced but agreed (thumbs to the middle) that they could live with the two models and try to implement them without sabotaging the effort. Cassandra and Desmond talked about the agreement after the meeting. They were happy to get somewhere but weren't convinced that Jim and Simone would be able to stick to the agreement. Cassandra and Desmond decided to work with Jim and Simone outside the meetings to convince them of the value of the department's approach.

Scope

What will students learn? **Scope** refers to the physical education content that students will be learning. Content depends on program goals and selected curriculum models. For instance, if your curriculum team has established a program goal such as "Students will demonstrate proficiency in a lifetime activity," chances are your team has selected the lifetime activity model as its guiding source. Content in this program, then, would include opportunities to learn a number of lifetime activities, such as in-line skating, bicycling, fitness walking, and orienteering.

Issues of scope go beyond content selection. For instance, your curriculum team will wrestle with breadth and depth of content. **Breadth** of content refers to the amount of content to be covered. For example, in the common use of the multiactivity model, breadth means exposure to a large number of activities and sports, the sort of content that Jim and Simone advocate. **Depth** means a more comprehensive study of a sport or activity, allowing students to develop competence and mastery. If a program has a lot of breadth, students will learn only the basics of a particular sport or activity, and they will only briefly practice the skills. On the other hand, if your curricular team values depth more than breadth, students will have opportunities to learn more than the fundamentals, and they will practice to a point of greater understanding and skill. Therefore, if one of your program goals is to have students demonstrate proficiency in a lifetime activity, you will probably adopt depth over breadth.

Sequence

The order in which you arrange physical education content is **sequence**. The basis of order in curriculum is to provide students with a progression and continuity of activity. In other words, your curriculum team must determine the order in which teachers will teach activity units during the school year. If you are working on a district level, sequence will include an ordered progression of skills and knowledge across grade levels. Sequence also depends on program goals and the curriculum model.

Develop Units of Study

After you have determined the scope and sequence, the next step is to develop the units of study. Each member of your physical education department and each physical education member of your curriculum team should develop units that align with the program goals and program philosophy that the team just established. Physical educators should take the time necessary to complete each step of unit development, which includes the following components (see chapter 11 for more information):

1. Unit goals
2. Scope and sequence of content to be covered in unit (block plan)
3. Lesson plans
4. Unit evaluation strategies

Implement the Curriculum

When curriculum teams reach the point at which they must implement or change a curriculum, the task can feel overwhelming to everyone. Our advice is to start small, to implement only small parts of the newly designed curriculum at one time. You will ensure greater success of curriculum changes if you implement doable pieces. As you implement small parts of the curriculum, like several units, you can evaluate them and revise them as you proceed. Some departments or curriculum teams review the curriculum and then outline a way to phase in the changes over a period of one to three years. This work takes place during curriculum meetings. As the curriculum team determines strategies for implementation, they may assign team members different tasks.

After Cassandra and Desmond's department finally agreed on curricular changes, they determined their strategy for implementation. They decided to pilot one new unit over a six-week period. Cassandra volunteered for the job to implement a volleyball unit. She would implement the unit with a focus on social responsibility and fitness. The chair of the department used curriculum team meetings to help Cassandra develop instructional strategies and to discuss her progress. The department learned from this six-week pilot. When the unit was over, the curriculum team analyzed the unit and suggested changes. Department members then had six weeks to revise and modify one of their own units. After the second unit, all team members would implement one unit that they taught. Their units would reflect the department philosophy, program goals, and the social responsibility and lifelong physical activity models.

Assess Then Revise, Revise, Revise

Back at the beginning of the chapter we talked about how much effort goes into creating a curriculum guide that might subsequently be placed on a shelf or used as a prop for a computer monitor. We guarantee the same will happen to your curriculum guide unless you work hard to keep the dynamic process alive. The best way to keep the guide from collecting dust is to refer to it often as you work to implement it into your program. Constantly evaluating its effectiveness and revising areas that need improvement will also help keep it alive. You can use numerous techniques and strategies for program assessment, or you can devise your own assessment techniques. Assessment and revisions take place in the context of team meetings. The department or the curriculum team must stay involved in each step of the process. You may choose to meet less frequently, but teachers should not make assessments and revisions in isolation. A collegial environment must persist.

Remember that curriculum assessment may focus on a number of categories. As you assess each of the following categories, ask yourself what your strengths are and what you need to improve.

- Alignment to national, state, or local standards
- Student needs
- Student learning and student achievement
- Teacher effectiveness
- Facilities
- Equipment
- Resources

Selected Curriculum Models for Secondary Physical Education

Teachers use many curriculum models in physical education. In this section, we will briefly review several that we promote and encourage our teachers to use: multiactivity, sports education, social responsibility, fitness, and lifelong physical activity. We will also express our beliefs about which models complement the purpose of physical education, which is to encourage adolescents to be physically active for life.

Multiactivity Model

The **multiactivity model** is popular in secondary physical education programs. The primary purpose of this model is to expose students to a variety of physical activity and sport. Teachers also strive to keep students physically active using this model. Activity units typically run two to three weeks (Hellison and Templin 1991). Instruction and practice time usually occur in the first two to three days. A week or more of game or tournament play follows.

We are critical of the multiactivity model for several reasons. First, the short units typically assigned to this model do not allow for much learning or improvement of motor skills and sport skills. Second, units tend to be the same from year to year. Students in the 10th grade often receive the same content in a flag football unit that they did in the 9th grade and will again in the 11th and 12th grades. As a result, students miss opportunities to deepen their understanding of and improve their skills for flag football and other activities.

Teachers tend to think that this model prevents students from becoming bored. Our experience and observation show otherwise. We have found that both students and teachers become bored with the multiactivity model because time is too short to learn much more than the fundamentals. When teachers become bored with teaching, they are more likely to engage in roll-out-the-ball behavior. Teachers' expectations about student learning diminish too. Teachers become satisfied with keeping students busy, happy, and good (Placek 1983). Hutchinson calls this behavior **BU-HA-GOO** teaching. Avoid becoming a BU-HA-GOO teacher.

When teachers roll out the ball and do not guide learning, many students are likely to lose interest in class. When we observe a multiactivity model in action, most of the highly skilled students appear to be enjoying game play, while those with average or lesser skills cut class, sit on the sidelines, hide behind the bleachers, or go through the (slow) motions of game play.

Modifications to this model will make it more effective. The first change would be to lengthen activity units from two or three weeks to four to eight weeks. Of course, longer units decrease the number of activities offered per year. Although the number of units per year decreases, the use of different units for each grade level will preserve the multiactivity approach (Hellison and Templin 1991). A second change would be to alter the educational focus of the units. Game and tournament play would take a backseat to skill and concept practice. Teachers would organize classes to maximize student participation in skill practice. Students would rarely engage in large groups for game and tournament play.

We introduced Sam in the opening scenario. He was excited to participate in the curriculum process. For years, he worked to modify the multiactivity model in his classes. Each fall he teaches a four-week unit in soccer in which he has his students concentrate on improving their soccer skills. Students in his classes can test or self-select a skills contract. In this contract, students rate their skill level in soccer at the beginning of class. Next, they determine doable goals for improvement over the four weeks. After they sign contracts, Sam works to provide opportunities for instruction and practice that help all students meet their goals. He also monitors their progress. Opportunities for practice include game play. Sam calls this purposeful game play, meaning that game play will have a specific focus like dodging or making passes to open spaces. Purposeful game play always happens in small groups. Sam doesn't allow his class to play 11 players on a side. He knows that few students would touch the ball. Instead, he has students playing 2, 3, 4, and 5 on a side. Sam feels that this modification enhances student learning. He certainly isn't a BU-HA-GOO teacher. He has modified the common use of multiactivity to make it more meaningful for students.

Sports Education Model

The **sports education model** (Siedentop 1994) is an activity-based model focused on teaching students to become sports literate. Using physical activity and sport, physical educators help students learn to become good sportspeople who engage in fair play and honesty, to be competitors who respect their opponents and play by the rules. Another feature of this model is that it provides opportunities for students to participate in a number of roles associated with sport. For instance, students may be players, coaches, equipment managers, general managers, officials, statisticians, and media. This model is appropriate for a number of team, dual, and individual sports at all levels.

To use this model effectively, however, the teacher must do a lot of preparation and planning. We have seen this model end up with teachers rolling out the ball and students engaging in unethical play and poor behavior. The physical educator must work hard to implement this model with knowledge and commitment to fair play and inclusion. This model can be placed into the Diamond Conceptual Framework to promote lifelong physical activity.

Social Responsibility Model

The **social responsibility model** is a humanistic model that de-emphasizes motor-skill development in favor of personal development such as self-control, self-motivation, self-responsibility, respect for others, and genuine caring for others. Hellison (1995) has developed an effective social responsibility model. He believes that it is important to help students learn appropriate social behavior and help them apply those behaviors to situations outside the gymnasium. Chapter 9 is an overview of the social responsibility model. This model serves well both to establish a positive learning environment and to promote lifelong physical activity in the Diamond Conceptual Framework.

Fitness Model

Improving and maintaining physical fitness for a lifetime is the primary goal of the **fitness model.** As we previously established, the surgeon general's report (National Center for Chronic Disease Prevention and Health Promotion 1996) stated clearly that physical inactivity is a health risk for all people in the United States. We also know that children and adolescents today carry more body fat than did children of 20 and 30 years ago (Corbin 1994). Not only that, but youth become less active as they grow older (National Center for Chronic Disease Prevention and Health Promotion 1996). This reality is very different from the two guidelines established for improving the rate of participation in physical activity by adolescents: (1) adolescents should be active daily or nearly daily as part of their lifestyles, and (2) adolescents should engage each week in three or more sessions of physical activity persisting for 20 minutes or more with moderate to vigorous levels of exertion (Bungum, Jackson, and Weiller 1998).

The fitness-for-life curriculum model does not replace the need for motor-skill development in physical education. With fitness and fitness concepts as the primary focus, motor-skill practice, physical activities, and game play are used to achieve fitness goals. Five hierarchical objectives guide the development of a fitness curriculum (Corbin 1994).

Step 1. Exercise: Students learn the proper ways to engage in the five components of fitness.

Step 2. Achieving fitness: Students learn to set realistic personal fitness goals for improving and maintaining levels of physical fitness.

Step 3. Learning physical activities: Students learn about appropriate physical activities that they can use to enhance fitness levels. They then select personal activities of interest and evaluate how well these activities will benefit fitness.

Step 4. Self-assessment: Students examine their own fitness and interpret their findings.

Step 5. Problem solving and decision making: After students evaluate their own fitness levels, they are required to set up an appropriate personal fitness program. They analyze fitness and program information to become critical and informed consumers.

Although the fitness model received wide support in the past, many prominent experts on fitness have abandoned the belief that physical education can or should make students fit (Corbin 2002). We explained in chapter 3 that the more logical approach to lifelong fitness is to focus on physical activity instead of fitness. The lifelong physical activity model does just that.

Lifelong Physical Activity Model

The primary goal of the **lifelong physical activity model** is to help students find physical activities they like and will do for the remainder of their lives. This model provides an opportunity for students to focus on physical activity and sports they enjoy and to become more skilled at them through practice. We embrace this model in our Diamond Conceptual Framework. We believe it is important to help students who are preparing for graduation and adult life to learn the skills and concepts they need to be physically active for the rest of their lives.

When we think about it, the idea of lifelong physical activity makes sense. Friends are often available during school years to play pickup games of basketball, football, or soccer. But as people grow older, friends may become less available as they take on more responsibilities with family and work or begin to experience ailments that prevent them from participating in team sports. On the other hand, jogging, climbing, skating, walking, bicycling, hiking, swimming, doing aerobics, weightlifting, skiing, snowboarding, surfing, and many other individual activities don't require the commitment of several friends. People can do these activities by themselves. Dual sports like tennis and racquetball stand a better chance of becoming lifetime activities because a person needs only one other person to do them. Activities such as basketball can be easily modified for play by one or two people. Helping students develop competence and confidence in a number of lifetime activities may help keep them physically active for the rest of their lives. In chapter 3, we explained in detail the concept of lifetime activities and asked a series of questions that you should consider when deciding what is a lifetime activity. Do you remember the questions? If not, review that section of chapter 3.

Besides becoming skillful in a number of lifetime activities, students must develop self-confidence for activities (self-efficacy) and self-esteem if they are to acquire lifelong activity habits. Self-management and problem-solving skills should also be major components of the lifelong activity model. When students have successful experiences in physical education classes and learn to take healthy risks with confidence, then during their adult lives they may be more willing to try new activities that grab their interest, like yoga, kayaking, step aerobics, Pilates, cardio kick boxing, and others.

You may have understood by now that this is the curriculum model best suited for the Diamond Conceptual Framework. We believe that it best addresses the concerns about physical activity levels in the United States, as expressed earlier in this chapter and in chapters 1 and 3. We have infused this book with the diamond icon in the margin because we want you to understand how all ideas should connect back to the ultimate purpose: to guide students in the process of becoming physically active for the rest of their lives.

Summary

Curriculum development is composed of two parts: process and product. You and your colleagues should convene a curriculum team to help navigate the process and develop the product, your curriculum guide. The process is dynamic and made up of three stages: planning, implementing, and assessing. A curriculum team consists of members from your department as well as members from your school. When possible, the curriculum team should open up the process to the district and invite participation by physical educators from other schools and grade levels. The curriculum development process comprises 12 steps. Initial steps focus on team building, establishing lines of communication, and setting up a decision-making process. Team members then spend time sharing value orientations and devising a program philosophy. A program philosophy serves as a foundation to program goals, exit outcomes, curriculum models, and eventually the scope and sequence for physical activity units. After a guide is in place, the team implements the curriculum and keeps the document alive by referring to it often and revising it when necessary. Changes should be phased in over time so that physical educators can assess their effectiveness. A reasonable implementation schedule keeps teachers from feeling overwhelmed and burning out. Assessment is key to determining program curriculum effectiveness. Assessment should be ongoing and provide information about curriculum changes. That information helps maintain the momentum of the curriculum process. Effective curricula are those whose keepers continually assess, revise, and implement, thus remaining actively engaged in their profession.

Checking for Understanding ▶▶▶

◆ What do we mean by curriculum as a dynamic process?

◆ How will you facilitate the curriculum process at your school?

◆ What does it mean to prepare your curriculum team for action?

◆ Why are value orientations important to the curriculum process?

◆ Which curriculum model do you identify with most and why?

◆ How will you collect information on student needs and use that information to guide your curriculum development?

For Reflection and Discussion ▶▶▶

◆ Your physical education department comprises four teachers. One holds the value orientation of discipline mastery, one believes in learning process, and two lean strongly toward social reconstruction–social responsibility. As you engage in the curriculum development process, how will you lead your department to a consensus about what is important in physical education?

◆ Examine curriculum models in depth and then determine the benefits and limitations of each. Present this information to simulated department meetings.

◆ How can you ensure that all members of your department have bought in to the curriculum changes? How will you know that members of your department will just do their own thing after they return to the classroom?

References

Allen, L., and J.W. Santrock. 1993. *Psychology: The contexts of behavior.* Madison, WI: Brown and Benchmark.

Bie, B.I. 1994. A preservice physical education teacher's metaphors for teaching: Learning from a difficult student. Doctoral diss., Florida State University.

Bungum, T.J., A.W. Jackson, and K.H. Weiller. 1998. One mile run performance and body mass index in Asian and Pacific Islander youth: Passing rates for the FITNESSGRAM. *Research Quarterly for Exercise and Sport* 69(1):89–93.

California Department of Education. 1994. *Physical education framework for California public school kindergarten through grade twelve.* Sacramento, CA: California Department of Education.

Corbin, C.B. 1994. The fitness curriculum: Climbing the stairway to lifetime fitness. In *Health and Fitness through physical education,* ed. R.R. Pate and R.C. Hohn, 55–66. Champaign, IL: Human Kinetics.

Corbin, C.B. 2002. Physical activity for everyone: What every physical educator should know about promoting lifelong physical activity. *Journal of Teaching in Physical Education* 21(2):128–144.

Ennis, C.D. 1992a. Curriculum theory as practiced: Case studies of operationalized value orientations. *Journal of Teaching in Physical Education* 11:358–375.

Ennis, C.D. 1992b. The influence of value orientations in curriculum decision making. *Quest* 44(3):317–329.

Ennis, C.D. 1994. Urban secondary teachers value orientations: Delineating curricular goals for social responsibility. *Journal of Teaching in Physical Education* 13:163–179.

Ennis, C.D., and A. Chen. 1995. Teachers' value orientations in urban and rural school settings. *Research Quarterly for Exercise and Sport* 66(1):41–50.

Griffin, P.S. 1985. Teachers' perceptions of and responses to sex equity problems in a middle school physical education program. *Research Quarterly for Exercise and Sport* 56:103–110.

Hellison, D.R. 1995. *Teaching responsibility through physical activity.* Champaign, IL: Human Kinetics.

Hellison, D.R., and T.J. Templin. 1991. *A reflective approach to teaching physical education.* Champaign, IL: Human Kinetics.

Hutchinson, G.E., and B. Johnson. 1993–94. Teaching as a career: Examining high school students' perspectives. *Action in Teacher Education* 15(4):61–67.

Johnson, B., and G. Hutchinson. 1998. The private universe of future teachers. *Issues in teacher education* 7(1):63–81.

Lambert, L. 1996. Goals and outcomes. In *Student learning in physical education: Applying research to enhance instruction,* ed. S. Silverman and C. Ennis. Champaign, IL: Human Kinetics.

Maslow, A.H. 1954. *Motivation and personality.* New York: Harper & Row.

Mohnsen, B.S. 1997. *Teaching middle school physical education: A blueprint for developing an exemplary program.* Champaign, IL: Human Kinetics.

Mosston, M., and S. Ashworth. 1994. *Teaching physical education.* 4th ed. New York: Macmillan.

National Association for Sport and Physical Education (NASPE). 1995. *Moving into the future: National standards for physical education.* St. Louis: Mosby.

National Center for Chronic Disease Prevention and Health Promotion. 1996. *Surgeon general's report on physical activity and health.* Washington, DC: U.S. Government Printing Office.

Placek, J. 1983. Conceptions of success in teaching: Busy, happy and good? In *Teaching in physical education,* ed. T. Templin and J. Olson, 46–56. Champaign, IL: Human Kinetics.

Rink, J.F.. 2002. *Teaching physical education for learning.* 4th ed. Boston: WCB McGraw-Hill.

Sibbet, D. 1999. *Graphic facilitation: A quick reference guide.* San Francisco: Grove Consultants International.

Siedentop, D. 1994. *Sport education: Quality PE through positive sport experiences.* Champaign, IL: Human Kinetics.

U.S. Department of Health and Human Services. 2000. *Healthy people 2010: Understanding and improving health.* 2nd ed. Washington, DC: U.S. Government Printing Office.

Wuest, D., and B. Lombardo. 1994. *Curriculum and instruction: The secondary school physical education experience.* St. Louis: Mosby.

Suggested Readings

Ediger, M. 1996. Sequence and scope in the curriculum. *Education* 117(1):58–60.

Melograno, V.J. 1996. *Designing the physical education curriculum.* 3rd ed. Champaign, IL: Human Kinetics.

Mohnsen, B.S. 1998. *Concepts of physical education: What every student needs to know.* Reston, VA: National Association for Sport and Physical Education.

Pate, R.E., and R.C. Hohn. 1994. *Health and fitness through physical education.* Champaign, IL: Human Kinetics.

Stillwell, J.L., and C.E. Willgoose. 1997. *The physical education curriculum.* 5th ed. Boston: Allyn & Bacon.

Yudkowsky, R., and A. Tekian. 1998. A model workshop in curriculum development. *Medical Teachers* 20(3):258–260.

Planning Units and Lessons

> Our plans miscarry because they have no aim.
> When a man does not know what harbor he is making for,
> no wind is the right wind.
>
> — *Seneca (4 B.C.-A.D. 65)*

When she was hired at Woodbridge High School, Alison knew she would be working with teachers who did things differently from what her cooperating teacher did and from what she had learned in college. But she didn't think it would be as bad as this. Her colleagues didn't seem to plan their lessons. The units were announced a week or two before they began, so there was not much evidence that the units were planned either. Yet one routine was definitely in place. Every physical education lesson would start with the same calisthenics, which the students seemed to despise. Three classes would warm up in the gym together, led by Carl, who had been at the school forever. The routine consisted of jumping jacks, toe touches, windmills, and so on—all activities that Alison thought were boring and useless. It irritated her that this routine was eating up 10 valuable teaching minutes of each lesson. Alison thought about her cooperating teacher at the other high school in town. She wished there had been an opening there. *Oh, well,* she thought. *I'm here now, and I'll just have to make the best of the situation.* At least she was free to plan her own lessons after the warm-up routine. She could easily modify the unit and lesson plans she had created in her classes in college because she had them stored on her computer at home. She was glad her teachers in college had made her do all that work. That made it easier now that she had so many other issues to deal with.

Learning Objectives

After reading this chapter thoroughly and discussing the issues in class, you should be able to

- explain the planning-implementation-assessment-reflection circle,
- explain the purpose of a unit plan,
- list the main components of a unit plan,
- list the four learning domains in physical education,
- use the national standards and guidelines and the GET ACTIVE FOR LIFE factors (from chapter 1) to examine the appropriateness of an objective for a unit,
- explain the purpose of a scope and sequence time frame,
- explain the purpose of planning lessons in detail,
- list the contents of a good lesson plan,
- examine the appropriateness of an objective for a lesson,
- describe a proper warm-up in physical education, and
- list and define the NBA/WNBA "rules" for stretching in physical education.

Key Terms and Phrases

Unit plan

Goals

Objectives

Learning domains: cognitive, affective, psychomotor, health-related fitness

Lesson plans

Learning activities

Variations

Challenges

Warm-up

Instant activities

NBA/WNBA "rules" for stretching

By the time you sit down to plan your units, you will be familiar with the NASPE standards (chapter 1), other national guidelines for physical education (chapter 1), the Diamond Conceptual Framework (chapter 1), the GET ACTIVE FOR LIFE factors (chapter 1), different curriculum models (chapter 10), effective teaching strategies (chapter 7), and different teaching styles (chapter 8). These factors should guide your planning every step of the way. Planning your physical education units and lessons is like drawing out on a road map where you want to go. Your destination is the "physically educated student" (NASPE 1995). You will know that you are going in the right direction through your assessment of student learning. Assessment becomes your compass, the tool you use to check if you're going in the right direction. Ultimately, you would use assessment to see if you have reached your destination. We have chosen to cover planning and assessment in two chapters, although the two go hand in hand. We have split up these intertwined subjects because we feel that the subjects will be easier to grasp and remember separately. Some overlapping and cross-referencing, however, will occur in this and the following chapter (chapter 12), which covers assessment and grading.

This chapter will take you through the details of planning a unit and a lesson. You may ask yourself whether teachers really plan this way. The answer is that excellent teachers plan in detail. After reflecting on how a lesson or unit went, they make changes for the next time. Experienced teachers may not have to write down everything because the details are in their heads. Their lesson plans may look incomplete compared with the ones we teach you to write in this chapter. But you have to remember an important thing—that we are teaching you how to do this from square one. We know how easy it is for a beginning teacher to forget to provide variations or cues, or to talk too long. With a detailed lesson plan, these points will be at your fingertips during your lesson. Likewise, planning the unit in detail allows you to practice all the important elements in writing. If you use detailed written plans for your units and lessons in your first years of teaching, the details will become part of your teaching. With experience, you may not need to write everything down. So that is one reason for detailed written plans. The other reason, for now, is that your professors and your cooperating teachers cannot read your mind. If they are to help you become a better teacher, they need to know what you know and are able to

do. The only practical way to show them this is through detailed lesson and unit planning.

Thorough plans, written down and saved on a computer so that you can easily revise them, are necessary for anyone learning to teach, and they are extremely helpful for beginning teachers. When you put your plans on paper, you must think through more details than you would otherwise. As you plan, you should constantly ask yourself if you are including the kinds of activities that will help *all* your students reach the objectives of the lesson and unit. You will find the answer to this question by using a variety of assessment tools described in chapter 12. The answer should affect your subsequent plans. It's a circle of planning, assessment, reflection, planning, implementation, assessment, and reflection (figure 11.1).

This chapter will discuss the importance of planning and reflection for your units and lessons. You will learn the components of a lesson and a unit plan. At the end of this chapter, we will discuss the warm-up and stretching in more detail because our experiences tell us that the need for change in this area is great, even with otherwise stellar teachers.

Planning the Unit

A **unit plan** helps the teacher determine specific student outcomes, develop a scope and sequence for particular activities, and organize meaningful learning experiences for students. The unit plan

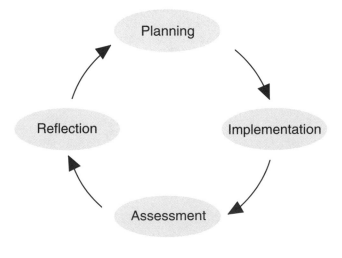

Figure 11.1 The planning-implementation-assessment-reflection circle.

is a comprehensive collection of work from various sources and your own imagination. You should assemble it in a way that you can easily remove and replace pages, perhaps in a binder (figure 11.2). The unit plan contains all the information you would need to teach a particular sport or activity. Everything from equipment needed and safety considerations to lesson plans and student handouts would be conveniently located in this binder. By organizing this information neatly, you will save time in finding the materials you need for a unit. If you also save the unit plan electronically, you can easily make changes to any part and readily produce copies of lesson plans and students' task sheets.

Contents of the Unit Plan

There are many "correct" ways to make a unit plan. Certain components, however, are included in most unit plans, such as a cover page; table of contents; intended grade level; copies of state and/or national standards for the grade level; student goals and objectives for the unit; list of equipment, facilities, and instructional materials needed; safety considerations; rules, scoring, etiquette, or special considerations for the activity; brief history and background information; a list and definition of skills and concepts to be taught; a scope and sequence time frame; lesson plans; practical approaches to student assessment; and an appendix with extra information. This may sound like an extensive set of components that will require a lot of work, and it will. But once you have completed a unit plan for each activity, you have everything you need in one binder. Later all you have to do is update the information as necessary and change lesson plans and assessments that didn't work the way you thought they would. Figure 11.3 lists the information that most unit plans include.

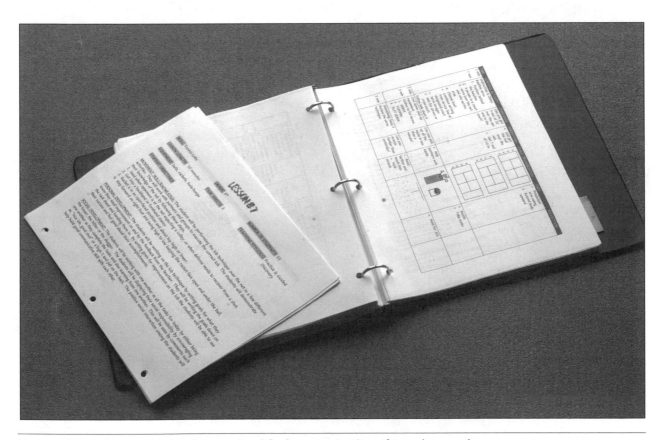

Figure 11.2 A lesson plan binder can simplify the organization of your lesson plans.

When Alison took the job at Woodbridge High School, she didn't know at first how useful her old unit plans from college would be. She'll never forget how she spent the last few nights before each one was due. She drank too much coffee, that's for sure. But when she started her job, she was glad she had made her unit plans detailed enough so that she could use them now. With a few changes here and there, she could use all the information! Best of all, the hard work it took to learn how to write detailed but concise objectives and explanations was paying off now when she had to write lesson plans all the time. Alison knew that learning how to write unit and lesson plans had made her transition into teaching much easier.

Unit Goals and Objectives

Many of the items on the unit plan list are self-explanatory, so we will not spend time on them in this book. Other items, however, require attention. Two of these are unit **goals** and **objectives**. Writing goals and objectives that are clear and attainable is not an easy task. Two NASPE publications, *Concepts of Physical Education: What Every Student Needs to Know,* and *Moving Into the Future: National Standards for Physical Education,* provide guidelines for what students should know and be able to do at each grade level. Depending on the curriculum model you've chosen, the amount of time you have to teach your students, the quality of their previous physical education experiences, and other special needs, these standards may be attainable. If not, they can serve as

---

Unit plan

Cover page and table of contents should be well organized and easy to follow. Use tabs for sections.

General information should be stated on a separate page and include

- grade level to be taught and length of unit,
- number of classes per week,
- length of time for each class,
- a copy of your state's standards or goals for the grade level, and
- a copy of the NASPE benchmarks and content standards for the grade level.

Student objectives for skills and concepts for the unit should be clearly stated and include objectives for each learning domain:

- psychomotor (skills),
- cognitive (knowledge),
- affective (social qualities, self-concept, attitudes), and
- health-related fitness.

Include a complete list of

- equipment and facilities needed,
- instructional materials needed, and
- safety considerations.

Include the following items:

- Rules and scoring, etiquette, and special considerations for the activity
- Brief history and background information of the sport or activity
- List and definition of all skills and concepts to be taught
- Scope and sequence time frame, including skills, concepts, and teaching styles to be used
- Lesson plans for the whole unit (include all task and criteria sheets)
- Practical approaches to student assessment for lessons and units
- Appendix that includes all class handouts and references used

Figure 11.3 Guidelines for unit plans for physical education.

broad guidelines when you plan your units. In either case, these NASPE publications and other guidelines can help you write your own unit goals and objectives. So before you start developing your unit goals and objectives, you should examine the appropriate sections of

 • the NASPE standards,
 • your state's standards or guidelines, and
 • your school district's or department's standards or guidelines.

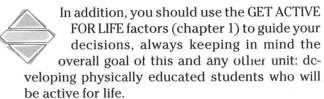 In addition, you should use the GET ACTIVE FOR LIFE factors (chapter 1) to guide your decisions, always keeping in mind the overall goal of this and any other unit: developing physically educated students who will be active for life.

The terms *goal* and *objective* have somewhat different meanings. A goal is a desired outcome; something you hope will happen as a result of your unit. An objective is something you can measure. For example, your goal for a unit on tennis could be to create in students the desire to play tennis for the rest of their lives. The goal for your in-line skating unit is to have your students find ways to incorporate this healthy activity into their busy schedules. These goals can be difficult to assess. Objectives, on the other hand, should be easy to assess. An objective for your tennis unit could be "By the end of the unit, the students will be able to explain three good cues for the forehand, backhand, volley, lob, and serve." An objective of your in-line skating unit could be "Students will learn to stop using at least three different techniques." You can assess these objectives using a variety of different methods. In chapter 12, we'll give you examples of several techniques.

Unit objectives should be simple. Ask yourself these two questions: "What do I want my students to know and be able to do when this unit is over? How will I know that they have reached the objective?" Each objective is then specific and includes criteria that you will use in your assessments to see if the students learned what you wanted them to learn.

Your unit plan should include objectives for all the **learning domains: cognitive, affective, psychomotor,** and **health-related fitness.** Although you have probably learned about the domains in a different course, we provide in table 11.1 a summary of each of them for your review.

In many states and school districts, and even in some departments, the main goals for the physical education curriculum cover these learning domains. Well thought-out goals and objectives will include all four learning domains. You do not need to have an objective for each domain for every lesson, but you should cover all the domains in each unit. For example, in the in-line skating unit mentioned earlier, you may write an affective domain objective like this: "Students will demonstrate positive encouragement to each other throughout the unit. This will be evident, when they are working with a partner or in small groups, by verbal communication such as 'You're improving!' and nonverbal messages like high fives, pats on the back, and so on." In the tennis unit, teachers may choose a cognitive domain objective like the following: "Students will be able to set realistic goals for themselves for any given tennis task and reach their goal for that task about 80% of the time." Because success boosts self-efficacy and self-image, the previous objective would cover the affective domain as well.

The last example shows that unit objectives need not specify what each student will be able to do. As discussed in earlier chapters, students' skill levels will vary considerably in any given unit, so it would be futile to write specific objectives that you know many of your students will be unable to reach. Especially for psychomotor objectives, specific objectives lack relevance because learning how to do a skill correctly takes time, probably more time than you have available in your unit. Individualizing your unit objectives by using goal setting (see chapter 7) is a way to help each student experience success. Health-related fitness objectives should also allow for individualization because genetics and previous movement experiences significantly influence this domain, as they do the psychomotor domain. Cognitive and affective domain objectives, however, are more suited for generalizing to all students because these skills usually don't take as long to learn as movement skills do. Table 11.2 shows sample objectives for middle school step aerobics and high school golf units.

The key when you write objectives for your unit is to use specific performance objectives when you know that *all* your students will be able to reach them, and to use goal-setting objectives when you know students will vary in the time needed to attain them. Goal setting, a wonderful tool in learning, can increase motivation levels (see chapter 7). When students learn to set and work toward reaching their own goals, they learn a skill that will help them later in life when they want to learn an activity on their own. Goal setting can also be useful in many other aspects of your students' lives.

Table 11.1 Learning Domains and Appropriate Aims for Learning Objectives

Learning domain	What does it include?	Appropriate aims for learning objectives
Cognitive	• Knowledge • Comprehension • Application of knowledge • Analysis • Synthesis • Evaluation (Bloom, Englehart, Hill, Furst, and Krathwohl 1956)	Teach concepts and help students build on that knowledge. Teach higher-level thinking skills so that students can ultimately reach the evaluation level of the cognitive domain taxonomy.
Affective	• Attitudes toward physical activity • Social qualities including cooperation, fairness, and tolerance • Self-concept and self-efficacy	Teach appropriate ways to express feelings. Encourage appropriate ways to display social qualities and promote socially acceptable behaviors through your learning activities. Encourage realistic goal setting, evaluation, and adjustment to enhance self-efficacy and self-concept.
Psychomotor	• Fundamental motor skills: locomotor, nonlocomotor, and manipulative • Specialized motor skills • Skill-related physical fitness components: agility, balance, coordination, power, reaction time, and speed	Make sure that students have the fundamental skills necessary to move on to more specialized motor skills. Encourage skill development by providing enough quality practice using effective teaching techniques (chapter 7).
Health-related fitness	• Cardiorespiratory fitness • Muscular strength • Muscular endurance • Flexibility • Body composition	Encourage realistic goal setting, evaluation, and adjustment to help students work toward reaching their fullest potential in each category.

Table 11.2 Learning Domains and Appropriate Aims for Learning Objectives

Middle school unit objectives for step aerobics	High school unit objectives for golf
• **Psychomotor domain:** By the end of the four-week unit on step aerobics, students will be able to perform at least the following 12 steps with competency and to the rhythm of the music: basic, tap step, V-step, turn step, over-the-top, corner-to-corner with variations, the Charleston, carousel, L-step, around-the-world, I-step, and the U-turn. They will also be able to use these steps to create short routines in small groups.	• **Psychomotor domain:** By the end of this 10-week golf unit, students will be competent in a variety of skills that make up the game of golf. They will be able to set up correctly for the skills of driving, putting, chipping, and pitching. They will be able to perform at least the chip shot and the putt consistently (80% of the time) using correct form.
• **Cognitive domain:** By the end of the four-week unit on step aerobics, students will be able to list and explain the health benefits of regular participation in step aerobics. They will be able to describe how to properly warm up and cool down for a vigorous activity and how to stay in their target heart rate zone by controlling the intensity of step aerobics by the step height they choose. They will also be able to set personal, obtainable goals for success and improvement with step aerobics.	• **Cognitive domain:** By the end of this 10-week golf unit, students will be able to list at least three good cues that can help them improve further in driving, pitching, chipping, and putting. They will be able to analyze their own and peers' skills on videotape as well as create a plan for how to go about practicing to improve those skills. Students will be able to explain the health benefits of regularly walking 18 holes. They will be able to apply the main rules of the game, select the proper club for a shot, and use good basic strategy when playing 9 or 18 holes. Students will be able to set realistic goals for improving in this lifetime sport and design their own practice as they go through the stages of learning. They will be able to set goals that are challenging, obtainable, specific, and have a time frame (COST) so that they experience success while being challenged (about 80% success rate). They will also be able to discuss the origins of golf, the social etiquette, and how golf has become the popular sport it is today.
• **Affective domain:** By the end of the four-week unit on step aerobics, students will be able to express their appreciation for activities usually stereotyped as "girls' and boys' activities." They will be able to solve problems and cooperate with their peers through the creation of group step routines. For many students this is a high-risk activity, and they will be able to describe the feeling of accomplishment that comes from taking risks and learning to enjoy activities they might never have tried if not for physical education.	• **Affective domain:** By the end of the 10-week golf unit, students will be able to express their appreciation for the physical and mental challenges and benefits of golf. They will be able to cooperate with partners while working on tasks to reach individual goals. They will be able to give and receive appropriate feedback and encouragement, as well as expess appreciation for the history and social etiquette of golf.

(continued)

237

Table 11.2 *(continued)*	
Middle school unit objectives for step aerobics	**High school unit objectives for golf**
• **Health-related fitness domain:** Because this unit is only four weeks long, students may or may not experience improvement in any of the health-related fitness areas. But by using heart rate monitors, they will be able to determine how hard they have to work to get a beneficial cardiovascular workout from step aerobics.	• **Health-related fitness domain:** By setting individual goals for improvement, students should be able to see an increased level of upper-body muscular endurance and flexibility from this 10-week unit.

Your Turn ▶▶▶

♦ Do you remember any instances when goal setting helped you?

♦ What is an example of a cognitive domain unit goal for swimming?

♦ What is an example of an affective domain unit goal for basketball?

♦ What is an example of a psychomotor domain unit goal for swing dance?

♦ What is an example of a health-related fitness domain unit goal for rock climbing?

Scope and Sequence Time Frame

Another section of the unit plan that needs attention and explanation is the scope and sequence time frame, or block plan, as some teachers call it. Let's say you have determined the overall goals for your unit and are working on specific objectives you want your students to reach. The objectives represent the scope of the unit, what you want your students to learn. The sequence is the order in which you want your students to learn the skills and concepts outlined in your objectives.

Before you start creating your scope and sequence time frame, you need to develop your goals and objectives for the unit. You also may need to do background research in these areas:

♦ Your state's standards or goals for the grade level

♦ The NASPE standards for the grade level

♦ Required equipment and facilities

♦ Required instructional materials

♦ Safety considerations for the unit

♦ Applicable rules and scoring, etiquette, and/or special considerations for the activity

♦ Brief summary of the history and background of the sport or activity

♦ Skills and concepts to be taught in the unit

Writing a scope and sequence time frame gives you an overview of the unit before you start planning the individual lessons. The overview is a one- or two-page document, organized to show the number of lessons in a unit and the skills and concepts that you will cover in each lesson. In our examples, skills and concepts can cover all four domains of learning. The key is to make the plan for the scope and sequence a short overview. The details should be in the unit plan objectives and the lesson plans. Besides including the skills and concepts that students will learn, many teachers choose to include the teaching style they plan to use for each lesson in the scope and sequence time frame. Table 11.3 shows examples of scope and sequence time frames for high school.

Planning the Lesson

Once you have found the background information you need for the unit, written your unit goals and objectives, and developed your scope and sequence time frame, the next step is to create your **lesson plans.** Each lesson plan is a detailed account of what you plan to teach and how you plan to teach it. You should write objectives for all learning domains in which you want students to learn something in a particular lesson: psychomotor, cognitive, affective, and health-related fitness.

Lessons in physical education vary in length, number of meetings per week, number of students in the class, and so on. Some schools have the traditional 50-minute (or so) lessons, whereas others have gone to block scheduling, in which lessons last about one and a half hours. No matter how long your lessons are, the main components of a good lesson are relatively consistent. A model lesson would include a warm-up or instant activity, instruction and demonstration episodes, learning activities, a cool-down or closure, and an assessment (we will cover this last piece in chapter 12).

Realizing that you will probably never deal with a homogeneous group in a physical education class, planning for diversity is the only way to ensure that all your students have a chance to learn. Chapters 7 and 8 discussed different techniques that you can use to include students of all skill and ability levels. The main thing to remember is that you want all students to experience about 80% success with a task. That is how they get the most practice because they tend to stay on task. They are not getting bored, as they might with more success, or frustrated, as they might with less. Two excellent techniques to use to achieve this are teaching by invitation and intratask variation. Another way to accommodate a variety of skill levels is to use different teaching styles as variations. (Review chapters 7 and 8 if this seems unfamiliar to you.)

Writing a good lesson plan can be a time-consuming job, at least until you get the hang of it, so you should save your work on a computer or disk. Changing what didn't work is much easier than writing the whole lesson plan again. Your lesson plan should be easy to follow and well organized so that if necessary you can just glance at it during a lesson and know immediately what you had planned to do next. The plan should be detailed enough to show a substitute teacher exactly what to do. If you develop an easy-to-follow format on a computer, you can use it repeatedly. If you do a good job, you have completed the main formatting with the first lesson plan.

T'nT
Formatting the Lesson Plan

Using a word program such as Microsoft Word makes formatting your lesson plan a breeze. The first time you write a lesson plan, it may take a while to get it right, but after that you never have to worry about it again if you follow these steps:

1. Open an existing lesson plan on your computer.
2. Go to "Save as" (in Microsoft Word this appears under the file menu on the top menu bar).
3. Save your new lesson plan with a different name. For example, if your first one is called "STEP, D: basic, V, turn, over," save the next as "STEP, TF: V, turn, over, corners." (If you use an abbreviation system to indicate the teaching style and specific skills, you will be able to find the lesson plan faster when you need it, e.g., D = direct teaching and TF = teacher feedback style).
4. Your old lesson plan remains unchanged and you still have it saved. Now you can delete and change the information for your second lesson plan.

The format we use is simple and calls for limited knowledge about working with tables. If you don't know how to create a table in your word program, you should spend an hour or so to learn the basics. Figure 11.4 shows the format we use. We use the landscape view, which you can find under the file menu. This lets us use the paper sideways and allows for a more organized-looking lesson plan that uses less paper.

Table 11.3	Scope and Sequence Time Frame for an Eight-Week High School Unit on Golf			
Lesson 1	**Lesson 2**	**Lesson 3**	**Lesson 4**	**Lesson 5**
Skills and concepts: overview of golf history and growing popularity, the importance of the short game, set up and grip for putting **Teaching styles:** direct, teacher feedback	**Skills and concepts:** setup for putting, the putting grip and stroke, putting rules **Teaching styles:** teacher feedback, partner feedback	**Skills and concepts:** putting and how to practice, appropriate warm-up for golf, goal setting for increasing flexibility by the end of the unit **Teaching styles:** partner feedback, convergent discovery	**Skills and concepts:** chipping, setup, grip, review putting, chipping-related rules **Teaching styles:** teacher feedback, partner feedback	**Skills and concepts:** chipping swing, the clock approach, create a flexibility program to be used every day (when muscles are warm) for the rest of the unit **Teaching styles:** teacher feedback, partner feedback, divergent discovery
Lesson 6	**Lesson 7**	**Lesson 8**	**Lesson 9**	**Lesson 10**
Skills and concepts: chipping and putting, keeping the score low, related rules **Teaching styles:** partner feedback, self-feedback	**Skills and concepts:** pitching, grip, and setup, full swing, pitching-related rules **Teaching styles:** teacher feedback, partner feedback	**Skills and concepts:** pitching, full swing, related rules **Teaching style:** partner feedback	**Skills and concepts:** pitching, three-quarter swing, putting **Teaching styles:** partner feedback, self-feedback	**Skills and concepts:** pitching, varying the distance and swing, related rules, revisit flexibility goals **Teaching styles:** partner feedback, convergent discovery
Lesson 11	**Lesson 12**	**Lesson 13**	**Lesson 14**	**Lesson 15**
Skills and concepts: pitching, varying the distance and swing **Teaching styles:** partner feedback, self-feedback	**Skills and concepts:** pitching, varying the loft and distance **Teaching styles:** partner feedback, self-feedback	**Skills and concepts:** Authentic assessment: students create a chip and putt hole for classmates to play **Teaching style:** divergent discovery	**Skills and concepts:** pitching, chipping, and putting, strategy **Teaching styles:** divergent discovery, self-feedback	**Skills and concepts:** pitching, chipping, and putting, strategy, revisit flexibility goals **Teaching styles:** divergent discovery, self-feedback
Lesson 16	**Lesson 17**	**Lesson 18**	**Lesson 19**	**Lesson 20**
Skills and concepts: irons, full swing, selecting the right club, related rules **Teaching styles:** teacher feedback, partner feedback	**Skills and concepts:** irons, full swing, selecting the right club, related rules **Teaching styles:** partner feedback, convergent discovery	**Skills and concepts:** irons, full swing, selecting the right club **Teaching styles:** divergent discovery, self- or partner feedback (students' choice)	**Skills and concepts:** irons, full swing, selecting the right club **Teaching style:** self- or partner feedback (students' choice)	**Skills and concepts:** irons, pitching, chipping, and putting, review and strategy, related rules, revisit flexibility goals **Teaching styles:** self- or partner feedback (students' choice), divergent discovery

(continued)

Table 11.3 *(continued)*

	Lesson 21	Lesson 22	Lesson 23	Lesson 24	Lesson 25
W E E K 5	**Skills and concepts:** irons, pitching, chipping, and putting, review and strategy, related rules **Teaching styles:** partner or self-feedback (students' choice), divergent discovery	**Skills and concepts:** irons, pitching, chipping, and putting, review and strategy, related rules **Teaching style:** self-feedback	**Skills and concepts:** irons, pitching, chipping, and putting, review and strategy, health benefits of golf **Teaching styles:** self-feedback, divergent discovery	**Skills and concepts:** irons, pitching, chipping, and putting, review and strategy, health benefits of golf **Teaching style:** self-feedback	**Skills and concepts:** irons, pitching, chipping, and putting, review and strategy, fitness training for golf, revisit flexibility goals **Teaching styles:** self-feedback, divergent discovery
	Lesson 26	Lesson 27	Lesson 28	Lesson 29	Lesson 30
W E E K 6	**Skills and concepts:** driving, grip and setup, related rules **Teaching styles:** teacher feedback, partner feedback	**Skills and concepts:** driving, the laws of physics, related rules **Teaching styles:** convergent discovery, partner feedback	**Skills and concepts:** Authentic assessment: students create a hole (modified, short game) for classmates to play **Teaching style:** divergent discovery	**Skills and concepts:** driving, chipping, strategies for practice at all stages of learning **Teaching styles:** convergent discovery, partner or self-feedback (students' choice)	**Skills and concepts:** driving, pitching, strategies for practice at all stages of learning, revisit flexibility goals **Teaching styles:** divergent discovery, partner or self-feedback (students' choice)
	Lesson 31	Lesson 32	Lesson 33	Lesson 34	Lesson 35
W E E K 7	**Skills and concepts:** review putting, pitching, and long irons, overcoming barriers to playing golf **Teaching styles:** divergent discovery, partner feedback	**Skills and concepts:** driving, chipping, and putting, the Stableford handicap system **Teaching styles:** convergent discovery, partner feedback	**Skills and concepts:** pitching, putting, and long iron shots, the Stableford handicap system **Teaching style:** partner feedback	**Skills and concepts:** driving, chipping, and putting, the Stableford handicap system **Teaching styles:** self- or partner feedback (students' choice)	**Skills and concepts:** putting together all the previous skills, scoring, selecting the right club (modified golf course), revisit flexibility goals **Teaching styles:** divergent discovery, self-feedback
	Lesson 36	Lesson 37	Lesson 38	Lesson 39	Lesson 40
W E E K 8	**Skills and concepts:** putting together all the previous skills, scoring, selecting the right club (modified golf course), related rules **Teaching styles:** self- or partner feedback (students' choice)	**Skills and concepts:** putting together all the previous skills, scoring, selecting the right club (modified golf course), related rules **Teaching styles:** divergent discovery, self-feedback	**Skills and concepts:** putting together all the previous skills, selected rules, strategy (field trip to public golf course) **Teaching style:** self-feedback	**Assessment:** traditional skills test (psychomotor domain), written test on rules of golf (cognitive domain), confidence in abilities rating scale (affective domain), health-related fitness flexibility test	**Assessment:** authentic assessment tasks (psychomotor, cognitive, and affective domains): Groups create a 3-5 minute video teaching their parents the basics of specified golf skills

Activity: _____   Lesson # in sequence: _____   Name: _____

Lesson length: _____   Number of students: _____

Grade level: _____   Equipment needed: _____

Teaching style(s): _____   Number of task sheet(s) included: _____

Student objectives, the "learnable pieces":

For each learning domain below, describe what you want your students to learn as a result of *this lesson*. Also describe how you will know if they **are able to do it** (in other words, how will you assess their learning for this lesson? Be specific, but as brief as possible, when you develop your objectives.

◆ **Psychomotor domain:** Describe the skill(s), or parts of a skill, the students will learn in *this lesson*? Describe what they will be able to do if they are successful.

◆ **Affective domain:** Describe how *this lesson* will contribute to learning in areas of the affective domain (for example, cooperation, social skills, self-image, self-efficacy, or behaviors related to attitude, such as trying one's best and working to achieve goals). Describe what students will be able to do if they are successful.

◆ **Cognitive domain:** Describe the concepts or problem-solving skills students will learn from *this lesson*. Describe what they will be able to do if they are successful.

Time	Learning activities	Variations	Challenges	Class organization	Cues	Reflection
Show here how many minutes are planned per activity.	In this column, describe each learning activity in detail so that it is clear to someone else what you are doing. Make a separate row for each new learning activity. Your lesson activities should reflect all your lesson objectives.	In this column, describe variations you have planned to make sure all students can experience success and feel challenged. Provide at least one easier and one harder variation per learning activity or task.	In this column, describe challenges you can use to make skill practice more enjoyable and motivating. Use at least one per activity.	In this column, draw Xs and Os to show how you will position yourself and your students for each learning activity.	In this column, write the cues for each skill you are teaching.	Use this space for immediate reflection after teaching *this lesson*.

Figure 11.4 Sample lesson plan format with basic instructions.

Contents of the Lesson Plan

Although lessons plan can take many forms, detailed ones usually include general information (equipment needed, grade level, number of students), learning objectives, teaching style or styles used, description of learning activities, cues, challenges, variations, class organization, and a space to record immediate reflection after the lesson. As you plan in detail, it is a challenge to be brief and clear. But putting together a short, coherent document is necessary if you want to use the plan during the lesson to remind you of the sequence and focus of the lesson. Lengthy objectives and explanations of learning activities would fill the document, making it difficult for you to use the plan as a reminder while teaching.

General Information

Start your lesson plan by stating the skills and concepts you will teach, the grade level for which the lesson is intended, the equipment you need, the facility you will use, your teaching style or styles, the number of students, and the lesson length. You should include this helpful information because you probably will make changes to the lesson plan in the future.

Learning Objectives, The Learnable Pieces

This section of your lesson plan should state exactly what you want your students to know or be able to do as a result of the lesson. The principles for writing good lesson objectives are much the same as for unit objectives. Objectives should be

- short,
- clear, by using observable verbs to describe the outcome, and
- attainable in one lesson.

Lesson objectives are sometimes more difficult to write than unit plan objectives because it is hard to say what students will be able to learn in one lesson. Until you gain experience, however, you will have to use an educated guess based on your needs assessment (see chapter 12) or previous knowledge of the students or similar groups. Then you have to decide what the learnable pieces of your lesson are. What do you want all students to know or be able to do after *this* lesson is over? You may want them to learn two cues for chipping in golf, or maybe you want them to be able

to show what the V-step looks like in step aerobics. If you keep the lesson objectives to the point, you can more easily communicate these learnable pieces to your students. You will also be able to assess more readily whether they really learned them. Students should know what you expect them to learn in each lesson. Your job is not only to create the learning objectives and design learning activities that lead to this learning but also to let your students know exactly what your objectives are. This will help them focus on the learnable pieces. Consequently, they will learn more.

As you write learning objectives for each learning domain you plan to cover, remember to make them clear and attainable. Certain things we teach in physical education take a long time to learn, especially some motor skills. The golf swing, for example, can take a lifetime to master. Expecting your students to become proficient in many skills and activities in a physical education program is unrealistic. The NASPE standards state that our goal should be to help students become competent in many, and proficient in a few, movement forms (NASPE 1995). Using the Diamond Conceptual Framework, in which students gradually focus on a few activities of their choice, they may become proficient in two to four activities by the time they leave high school. Likewise, it is unrealistic that students will develop significant health-related fitness from your lessons unless this is your only focus. Remember from chapter 3 that fitness is the product that comes about when people participate in sufficient physical activity. Physical activity is the process that leads them to fitness achievements. Teaching your students the concepts and skills they need to become active for the rest of their lives should be your focus. This means that your lessons may not include specific health-related fitness objectives. But you can and should use goal setting to help students achieve individual health-related fitness goals over the course of a unit or semester.

For the lesson objectives to be attainable, they must be specific to concepts, cues, or components of skills. If you constantly focus on the question "Can all my students learn this today if they just try?" you will probably write objectives for your lessons that represent learnable pieces. Table 11.4 lists sample lesson objectives for middle and high school.

Table 11.4 Sample Lesson Objectives for Middle and High School for a Variety of Activities	
Sample middle school lesson objectives	**Sample high school lesson objectives**
Affective domain: Students will set realistic goals for how many steps they will learn and remember in step aerobics. They will write in their journals about how confident they feel about their ability to do steps as a result of accomplishing their goals.	Affective domain: Students will be able to work cooperatively with group members to achieve success as they create a dance routine. They will show appreciation for individual differences by working together in teams to problem solve and complete two elements of a challenge course.
Psychomotor domain: Students will be able to demonstrate how to put on a rock-climbing harness according to cues given.	Psychomotor domain: Students will be able to demonstrate the stance for the golf drive according to cues given.
Cognitive domain: Students will be able to calculate their target heart rate zone using a worksheet and a calculator.	Cognitive domain: Students will be able to list three cues for a jump shot (basketball).

Your Turn ▶▶▶

♦ In which sports, activities, or skills would you say you achieved proficiency through your K–12 physical education program? (Do not include your extracurricular activities such as playing on the school's soccer team.)

♦ From your experience, do you think many students are able to become proficient in any sports or activities through their K–12 physical education programs? Why or why not?

In the next chapter we will discuss how to assess whether your students learned what you said they were going to learn in a lesson. This process, called lesson assessment, is usually a short informal or formal means of figuring out whether the learning activities led to attaining the objectives.

Learning Activities

The next step in lesson planning is to develop and write down the **learning activities** you will use to get students to reach the objectives. You should describe the learning activities in detail, but again you want to be clear and concise so that your lesson plan is easy to use. Explain exactly what you want to happen. If you are playing a game, explain the game and the rules or refer to where you can find the rules in your unit plan. If you have students work in groups, explain how they will form the groups. All the details need to be there, but don't be wordy. You can apply the KISS principle (from chapter 7) here: keep it short and simple. When you use task or criteria sheets, you don't have to be redundant. Attach the task or criteria sheet to your lesson plan and refer to it in the learning activity column.

Learning activities should take up most of your lesson because, when learning a new skill or a new concept, students need practice. How much practice they get and how well you organize that practice relates directly to how much they will learn (see chapter 7).

You must develop learning activities that will help students reach the objectives of the lesson. The learning activities should include variations to ensure success for students of all ability and skill levels. Remember the 80% success rule (from chapter 7). If students are about 80% successful with a task, they will learn more because they will not become bored or frustrated. They will stay on task longer and thus get more practice.

In chapter 7, we discussed in detail the best ways to free up more time for learning activities, including cutting down on teacher talk, making efficient transitions, and reducing student waiting time. All students should be involved in the task actively or cognitively at all times. Waiting in line for a turn is unnecessary in most instances, as well as an ineffective use of learning time. Students become bored when waiting, which can lead to off-task behavior. You can get around obstacles such as not having enough equipment for all students if you are creative and use a variety of teaching styles (see chapter 8). Remember that more waiting leads to fewer practice opportunities, which in turn means less learning.

The instant activity or warm-up should be described in the learning activity column. We have devoted a whole section at the end of this chapter to appropriate warm-ups, so we will skip the details here. Include your instructions, demonstrations, and planned managerial tasks in the learning activity column. Remember the KISS principle. The more time you spend talking and managing, the less time students have to learn.

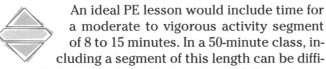

An ideal PE lesson would include time for a moderate to vigorous activity segment of 8 to 15 minutes. In a 50-minute class, including a segment of this length can be difficult if you want students to learn skills and concepts for activities as well. In schools that use block scheduling, classes last longer than one hour, so it should be easy to work in a 15-minute activity portion. You can work this segment into the unit in a natural way. For example, in an in-line skating unit, each lesson can have a period in which students practice the skills that they have learned so far. While they are working on their skills continuously for at least 10 minutes, the objective can be to have their heart rate in their target zone (60–80% of max) for most of that time. The problem-solving and self-monitoring skills involved in a learning activity such as this can easily transfer to the students' activities outside of class. But this must be taught. Students can learn what it takes to get their heart rates in the target zone for a particular activity and how to keep it there for a specified length of time. Heart rate monitors become a useful tool for teaching these concepts.

Another learning activity that you need to plan is the cool-down or closure. After vigorous activity, a cool-down should bring students' heart rates gradually back to resting levels. This usually takes about two to three minutes of slow movement, such as walking. If the intensity level for the lesson has been moderate to low, a cool-down like this may be unnecessary, but you may choose to work on flexibility while you do your closure. To save valuable minutes, you can have your students stretch while you review with them the important points of the lesson or do a lesson as-sessment (see chapter 12). Integrating a review or assessment with stretching is easier once you have taught your students proper stretching techniques. In any case, no matter when you stretch in your lesson you should follow a few simple rules. We have summarized these in the last section of this chapter.

In a separate column (see figure 11.4), note the approximate time you have planned for the learning activities, instructions, demonstrations, and management. Remember the rule of thumb that teacher talking should not exceed a minute or two at one time (see chapter 7). Also, planning too many activities is better than not planning enough, so plan for each item to take a little less time than you think it really requires. If your goal is for students to learn, you should not worry about not finishing all your planned activities. You can always use your great ideas in another lesson.

Variations

To maximize the opportunities for all your students to learn, you should use the inclusion approach to teaching (see chapter 8). This means that you have to plan **variations** for each of the learning activities. Use a separate column in your lesson plan format for variations. For each learning activity, you should have at least two variations, one easier and one harder. For example, if the main learning activity is practicing the volleyball serve over the net, some easier variations would be to practice serving against the wall, practice serving over a line on the wall, or practice serving using a beach ball. A harder variation would be to serve over the net and try to land the ball inside a hoop or to knock over bowling pins with the serve. Students could also be at different distances from the wall or net, or you could slant the net so that it is higher on one side. Developing variations for most learning activities is easy if you keep in mind all the variables within the learning activity: equipment type and size, distance, height, skill combinations, targets, speed, and obstacles. In addition, as we mentioned in chapter 8, you can use teaching styles as variations.

Challenges

As mentioned before, if the students are successful with a task about 80% of the time, they are less likely to become bored or frustrated (Graham 2001). Some students, however, still prefer games and fun to any type of skill practice. You can use **challenges** to turn just about any activity into a purposeful game. Purposeful game play is critical to skill and performance development. You want to provide learners with a *focus* during challenges and opportunities for competition. For example, at the end of a team handball unit many teachers have students engage in round-robin tournament play. As a result, when students play they focus on winning and losing. Attention to skills and strategies tends to go by the wayside. In purposeful game play, the physical educator either sets goals for improved play, such as a focus on give-and-go passing in team handball, or helps students focus on aspects of *their* game that need improvement (see ideas about purposeful play in the examples of convergent and divergent discovery teaching styles in chapter 8). Purposeful competition can occur between partners or small groups, or a student can compete with herself if she prefers. In a tennis lesson in which students have the choice of rallying with a partner to practice their forehand and backhand ground strokes, the challenge could be "How many successful forehand and backhand strokes can you hit in a row?" or "Can you beat your score?" Partners can keep cooperative score, or each student can keep score for himself. More competitive students may choose to compete with a partner to see who can hit the most successful forehands.

Goal setting is another way to use challenges. The students can set their own goals for the activity and try to reach them. An example of a goal-setting challenge for a self-defense lesson would be "Set a goal for how many perfect high blocks you can do in this activity." In a fitness part of a lesson in which the students work on abdominal crunches, a goal-setting challenge would be "Set a goal for how long you can do crunches continuously without stopping. Remember that you have to stay with the beat of the music." Goal setting is discussed in more detail in chapter 7. Always remember to consider the COST of goals. They should be Challenging, Obtainable, Specific, and include a Time frame.

When Alison was first learning about variations and challenges in college, she got the two confused. She was able to keep the two concepts straight after one of her classmates told her to think about the variations as changing certain *elements* of a task to allow for success and the challenges as a way to make the task more fun or interesting without changing the task itself. Although the two seemed to overlap somewhat at times, eventually she got the idea. Creating variations and challenges is now easy for her but only because she has practiced a lot!

Class Organization

In the class organization column of your lesson plan, a drawing (done by hand or by using the drawing tools in your word program if you want to save it on your computer) of what the classroom looks like for each activity is useful (figure 11.5). This can be an X and O or stick figure drawing; you don't have to be an artist. During a lesson a quick look at your drawing in the lesson plan will remind you how you had planned to set up your classroom or gym for a specific activity.

Cues

Because cues are so important to student learning, the next column of your lesson plan is probably one of your most important ones. For each activity write down four to six cues and plan on using them only one or two at a time. Use short cues that are easy to remember (see chapter 7 for more on how to create good cues). Tell your students the cues during the instructional episode or during the demonstration. If you are using the teacher feedback style, use the cues to give feedback that is useful for learning. Feedback that is congruent with the cues you gave is most effective. If you use a teaching style in which students give themselves or each other feedback, put the cues on their task sheets so that they become the criteria. But remind them that they should focus on only one or two cues at a time.

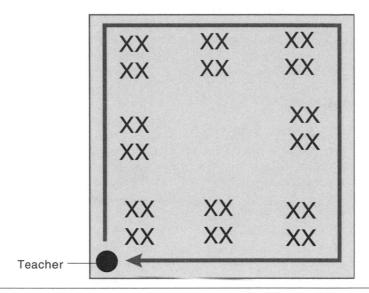

Figure 11.5 A simple sketch of how you want the classroom organized can be helpful when creating your lesson plan.

Purpose

Use technology to develop information and resources about activities that can be used for teaching, demonstration, and feedback.

Resource and Procedure

Visit Web sites devoted to the various activities (such as golf, step aerobics, in-line skating, tennis, and martial arts) that you will include in your curriculum. Certain sites contain demonstrations, learning cues, and teaching techniques for particular activities. Experts often develop these sites, which can be a rich resource for teaching. For example, at the Web site **www.turnstep.com** you will find an explanation and criteria for most steps used in step aerobics. There is even an animated demonstration for each step. No one can be an expert on every activity. Search for and use the resources that are available, but be a critical consumer (see chapter 18)!

Developing or finding good cues (see chapter 7) can be difficult, but once you have found or created them you can use them again and again. Good cues don't wear out.

Reflection

On your lesson plan make a separate column or use the space on the back to write down reminders for future lessons. Immediate reflection of what worked and what you need to change can be especially helpful for a begin-

ning teacher. You forget those ideas quickly, and by writing them down you can avoid making the same mistake several times. Remember that the lesson plan is just that, a plan. Sometimes things don't go exactly as planned, and that's OK. A student-centered teacher does not let a lesson plan dictate the lesson but instead uses the lesson plan as a guide to make the learning experience the best it can be for all students. The teacher then reflects on what went well, ponders what didn't go as planned, and makes changes for next time.

Your Turn ►►►

♦ What are the main questions you should ask yourself when you reflect on your lesson?

♦ If a lesson does not go at all as you planned it, how would you avoid beating yourself up about it? What would help you refocus for the next lesson?

Warm-Up or Instant Activity

Like Alison's colleagues in our opening scenario, many teachers start their classes with a set **warm-up** routine, which often causes students to become bored and unmotivated. Other teachers vary their warm-ups or use **instant activities** to get the students moving immediately as they enter the classroom or gym. Warm-up or instant activities work best if they get the blood pumping and relate to the rest of the activities for the day. The purpose of the warm-up is to warm and loosen the muscles gradually to get ready for the learning activities.

"Tried and True" Techniques?

Many of the chapters in this book have emphasized the importance of enjoyment in physical education. If students do not enjoy what they are doing, or at least do not see the usefulness of the activities, you will find it harder to guide them through the process of becoming physically active and healthy for a lifetime. So, if you start your lessons in a way that turns students off, they will be less likely to be excited about the content of the main lesson. "But don't they have to warm up and stretch?" you may ask. The answer is "No, not necessarily." In this section, we will shed light on the use of traditional warm-ups in physical education classes and provide safe, effective, and enjoyable alternatives to the "tried and true" techniques.

Starting the Lesson

When students come to physical education class they expect to be moving. Many students look forward to using their bodies in physical activities after sitting at their desks for hours. Yet many teachers start their physical education classes with 5 to 10 minutes of taking roll and then 5 to 10 minutes of boring calisthenics. Even in classes taught by well-meaning teachers, students can get the wrong idea about what's to come and develop a negative attitude toward the lesson and the activities. Starting physical education classes immediately with an energizing, enjoyable physical activity gives students the right idea: "You came here to move, and you're going to enjoy learning something new today!"

Warming Up

A warm-up is important if you have any moderate to strenuous activities planned for your lesson. The content and length of the warm-up would depend on the intensity of the activities that follow. People commonly ask a series of questions about the warm-up:

- What should a warm-up consist of?
- Do you have to stretch during the warm-up?
- Is jogging a good warm-up?
- How long should the warm-up be?

The answers to these questions depend on what you're doing in the rest of the lesson. The overall purpose of a warm-up is to prepare the body for subsequent movements by gradually warming up the appropriate muscles (figure 11.6). By using continuous, rhythmic movements (for example, progressing from walking to skipping to jogging), the body makes the transition from being almost completely inactive to being very active. This gradual, progressive method of getting the body moving reduces the risk of injuries because it increases the temperature in the muscles, making them more pliable and less susceptible to injury (Knudson 1998). If you are teaching a lesson on putting in golf, the risk of injuring a muscle will not be great simply because the putting movement does not require much muscular action. On the other hand, if you are teaching the full golf swing, it will be important to warm up the muscles involved to prevent students from pulling a muscle in the trunk, back, or shoulder region.

A warm-up should progress from slower to faster movements, causing the temperature in the body to rise slightly. The average increase in body temperature during a 10-minute warm-up has been reported to be around 1 to 2 degrees Fahrenheit, or 0.6 to 1 degree Celsius (Knudson 1998). Although this increase is sufficient to help the body shift into moderate to vigorous activity, it may not be sufficient to continue with stretching to increase flexibility. Later in this chapter, we will discuss in detail the issues related to stretching during the warm-up.

Activities that get the blood pumping and gradually warm up the whole body work well for many movements you may teach. These activities should be continuous and rhythmic, which means that the students must keep their bodies moving. The activities should also be "rehearsing" the most important movements to come.

Instant Activities

Instant activities are short, quickly organized, easy-to-explain activities that students can begin immediately upon entering the gym, court, or field. Besides starting your classes quickly, these activities can be a useful warm-up for activities to come, especially if they consist of continuous, rhythmic movements and include rehearsal movements. The instant activity you choose would depend on the activities that would follow. For example, if the main activity for the lesson is team handball, the instant activity can be a minigame of keep-away.

Figure 11.6 Proper stretching is important to prepare the muscles for activity.

In small groups, all students would be involved in the game the whole time. The key would be getting them to keep their feet moving throughout the activity. The students should gradually increase the intensity from a walk to a jog but should not sprint in the warm-up.

Alison went to her state Alliance for Health, Physical Education, Recreation and Dance conference about eight months into her first year at Woodbridge High. She tried to persuade her colleagues to go with her but had no luck. A few of them, however, asked her to bring home some good ideas, and she took that request to heart. She attended a session called "Instant Activities for Middle and High School," which dealt with ideas for enjoyable, safe, and effective warm-ups. The session refreshed her memory about many ideas she had learned in her college courses, and she was reminded to check **www.pecentral.com** for new ideas. When she returned to school she made copies of the handout from the session and put one in each of her colleagues' mailboxes with a suggestion that they discuss their warm-up routine at the next department meeting. She knew that Carl would probably see red, but she hoped that the others would support her gentle efforts to reform a stale teaching method.

Another example is a tag game as the warm-up–instant activity for a golf lesson. Tag games must not involve elimination because that would prevent many students from warming up. So this instant-activity tag game should involve several taggers (about a quarter of the class) and the stipulation that a student when tagged would make five full golf swing movements (without a club) before being free to move around again. You would ask students to move their feet continuously, first by walking, then by skipping, and finally by jogging. Taggers would switch every minute or so. Students would have their feet still only when they do the imaginary golf swings.

Although instant activities must be quick and easy to explain, you can obviously spend more time one day to teach an instant activity that you plan to use often in the future. You can easily modify instant activities to fit the unit. All it takes is a little imagination and perhaps some ideas from students, colleagues, or Web sites such as PE Central (**www.pecentral.com**).

Rehearsal Movements

An important purpose of the warm-up is to prepare the muscles for action. When demands are placed on the body, it adapts in a specific manner. We call this the specific adaptation to imposed demands (SAID) principle of fitness. Rehearsal moves simulate the main actions in skills of a later activity, but they are less intense.

Both of the previous examples involve rehearsal movements. The instant activity for team handball was the small-group keep-away game. The game includes passing, catching, walking, sliding, and jogging. All these movements occur in team handball, but the students perform them in a less intense fashion in the warm-up–instant activity. The instant activity for golf included a rehearsal move of the golf swing. After being tagged, the students must do a full swing five times before they are free. This full swing, without a club or ball, should be performed at lower intensity than the full swing that the student will practice later in the class. The purpose of having many taggers in this instant activity for golf would be to make sure that students get tagged often and thus perform rehearsal movements many times. You switch taggers often for the same reason. The taggers need their fair share of rehearsal movements, in this instance, the golf swing. In these examples, the instant activities serve as games that accomplish the main objectives of a warm-up and send the message that "We're going to learn and have fun today!"

Stretching in the Warm-Up

Many teachers incorporate stretching into their warm-up routines, but some experts question the usefulness of this practice (Knudson 1998). Do you really have to stretch during the warm-up? If so, why? This section will look at the two sides of this issue and conclude with a recommendation that weighs the pros and cons for the average physical education class.

Proponents of stretching refer to studies that have found that proper stretching after a warm-up period reduces the risk of injury (Knudson 1999). In a 50-minute lesson, however, the physical education teacher will be hard pressed to follow the recommendations for stretching during the warm-up unless all he wants to accomplish is to get the students warmed up. These recommendations include warming up the muscles for 15 to 20 minutes before stretching; using slow, static stretches; avoiding bouncing because it can increase risk of injury; stopping before feeling pain; holding each stretch for 15 to 20 seconds; stretching each muscle group three to five times; and stretching agonist and antagonist muscles equally to avoid flexibility imbalance (Knudson 1998).

Opponents of stretching during the warm-up question the belief that static stretching increases muscle temperature and prevents the risk of soft-tissue injuries during a workout (Knudson 1999). They claim that it is the continuous, rhythmic movements in the warm-up, not the stretching, that increases body temperature slightly and reduces the risk of injuries to soft tissue. Opponents say static stretching during the warm-up will not help to reach the goal of a permanent increase in flexibility. To increase flexibility permanently, the muscles have to be properly warmed up. Tissue temperatures of at least 103 degrees Fahrenheit (39.4 degrees Celsius) are necessary before static stretching of each muscle three to five times for 15 to 20 seconds will permanently increase flexibility. Tissue does not reach this temperature in a 5- to 10-minute warm-up, although it may at the end of the workout if the activity is vigorous enough. Those who question the usefulness of stretching during the warm-up say that if the goal is increased flexibility, stretching should occur at the end of the workout. In any case, stretching must be done properly, as described in the previous paragraph.

Alison knew that Carl would have a problem with the idea of changing their traditional warm-up routine. He had led this routine for as long as anyone could remember. She didn't really know what was the worst part of it: the stretching of muscles that were not warm, the inappropriate stretches, or the wasted time. She wondered how someone who seemed to be so concerned with success in his coaching endeavors could be so ignorant of the discoveries in this area over the last decade.

After some weeks of gentle pressure from other colleagues, Carl agreed to let Alison lead the warm-up her way for one lesson. He wasn't happy about it, and he communicated clearly that he knew she'd have no success. To Alison's delight, however, the students were thrilled to get out of doing the calisthenics. They were in a basketball unit, and Alison had them play a keep-away game for their instant activity. She did not have them stretch during the warm-up, so the classes were ready for the rest of the lesson after only five minutes. She wanted to suggest that her colleagues take roll during the instant activity, but she didn't want to push her luck. Besides, to do that they would need to know their students' names, and although that was rule number one for good teaching in her book, she knew that some of her colleagues knew only the names of the star athletes and the troublemakers. *One step at a time,* she thought. *Maybe there is a reason I am here after all. Maybe this place will end up OK with my help.*

When a physical education teacher designs a lesson, the issues of safety and using time wisely become important factors (see chapter 7). If a teacher were to follow the recommendations of the research for proper stretching during the warm-up, he would not have time for much else. On the other hand, if he chooses to go with the recommendations of the professionals that question the usefulness of stretching in the warm-up, he can concentrate on providing a useful, proper warm-up that may still go a long way in reducing the risk of injury. Whether the physical education class includes light, moderate, or vigorous physical activity, the issue becomes one of using the precious minutes in a way that benefits students. The fact that researchers arrive at different conclusions about the importance of warm-up stretches raises enough questions about the usefulness of stretching in the warm-up that the benefits of gaining extra time for learning activities may outweigh the risk of cutting it. For longer periods of intense activities (such as for elite athletes) the recommendation may be different. Time may not be a crucial issue, and there may be enough of it to spend 20 to 25 minutes on a proper warm-up that includes appropriate and useful stretching. Regardless of when you choose to work on flexibility, you must consider some important issues, or "rules," which we present next.

NBA/WNBA Rules for Stretching

Based on the reviews of the research on stretching, Himberg and Knudson (2002) developed the **NBA/WNBA "rules" for stretching** in physical education classes. The mnemonic helps us remember these principles: Never Bounce, Always Warm, Not Boring, and Appropriate.

Never Bounce

No matter when you have your students stretch, you should always use static, not ballistic, stretching to reduce risk of injury. Students should hold each stretch for 15 to 30 seconds and perform three to five repetitions for each muscle group to increase flexibility.

Always Warm

As discussed earlier, muscles must be properly warmed up before stretching. This too helps avoid injuries. Muscles are normally warm enough to stretch when they have been continuously active for at least 15 to 20 minutes.

Not Boring

Stretching need not seem boring and useless. To make stretching enjoyable and to save time, multitask it! You can have students stretch while you give instructions, as you review the main concepts of the lesson, or while you assess what they have learned. You can also work stretches into natural pauses in the learning activities, as long as students are properly warmed up.

Appropriate

The last rule concerns using only appropriate stretches. You have probably learned what these are in your exercise physiology class. If not, here is a list of things to remember:

- Avoid any stretch that puts unnecessary strain on the knee joint.
- Avoid any stretch that puts unnecessary strain on the back.
- Avoid any stretch that puts unnecessary strain on the neck.

As a professional you are responsible for keeping up on issues such as safe stretches. By using NBA/WNBA rules for stretching, summarized in figure 11.7, in your physical education classes, you will avoid wasting time in this area.

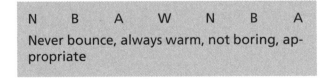

N   B   A   W   N   B   A
Never bounce, always warm, not boring, appropriate

Figure 11.7 A summary of the NBA/WNBA rules for stretching.

Purpose

Use video to assess students' stretching techniques as well as provide personal feedback and instruction to correct irregular techniques.

Resource and Procedure

Use a video camera to tape students stretching. Set the camera far away from the students to achieve a wide angle that allows you to catch all the "action." You will review the tape to spot irregularities from the stretching criteria. You should notice and correct any incorrect techniques as soon as possible because they could lead to eventual problems or injuries. It is particularly useful to show individual students how their techniques vary from the others who do it correctly. Take time to respond directly to those students in private to avoid any embarrassment.

Summary

This chapter took you through the process of planning a unit and appropriate lessons for physical education. You should plan units and lessons with one question in mind: how does this help my students become physically educated and active for life? When planning a unit, you should cover all four learning domains. When planning a lesson, it should be obvious which of the learning domains you are targeting that day. Lesson and unit objectives should be clear. When you plan, always ask yourself what exactly it is that you want the students to know or be able to do. To maximize students' opportunity for learning, variations should be a standard part of your lesson plan. The learning activities should be appropriate, and you should plan for students always to be actively involved in the lesson. Use challenges to motivate students. Warm-ups should be purposeful and should not normally include stretching. All stretching should follow the NBA/WNBA rules. Using the planning-implementation-assessment-reflection circle will help you plan appropriate and useful units and lessons.

Checking for Understanding ▶▶▶

- What is meant by the planning-implementation-assessment-reflection circle?
- What is the purpose of a unit plan?
- Can you list the main components of a unit plan?
- What are the four learning domains in physical education?
- Using the national standards and guidelines and the GET ACTIVE FOR LIFE factors (from chapter 1) as your guide, can you determine the appropriateness of an objective for a unit?
- What is the purpose of a scope and sequence time frame?
- Why should teachers plan their lessons in detail?
- What are the contents of a good lesson plan?
- Can you examine the appropriateness of an objective for a lesson?
- What is a proper warm-up in physical education?
- Is it necessary to stretch during the warm-up in most lessons?
- Can you define the NBA/WNBA rules for stretching in physical education?

For Reflection and Discussion ▶▶▶

- Thinking back on your secondary school physical education experiences, can you remember any teachers who seemed to have carefully planned lessons that had a purpose?
- Can you remember any teachers who did not seem to plan or planned with no clear purpose?
- If you were observing a teacher at a local high school, would you be able to tell if she had planned her lesson in detail? How?
- What do you feel are the most important reasons to plan your units and lessons in detail?
- What role do you feel unit and lesson planning plays in ensuring a quality physical education program?
- What were the warm-up routines like in your middle and high school programs?

References

Bloom, B., M. Englehart, W. Hill, E. Furst, and D. Krathwohl. 1956. *Taxonomy of educational objectives: The classification of educational goals. Handbook I: Cognitive domain.* New York: Longmans, Green.

Graham, G. 2001. *Teaching children physical education, becoming a master teacher.* 2nd ed. Champaign, IL: Human Kinetics.

Himberg, C., and D. Knudson. 2002. The NBA/WNBA Rules for Stretching. *Strategies* 15(3):23–26.

Knudson, D. 1998. Stretching: Science to practice. *Journal of Physical Education, Recreation and Dance* 69(3):38-42.

Knudson, D. 1999. Stretching during warm-up: Do we have enough evidence? *Journal of Physical Education, Recreation and Dance* 70(7):24–27, 51.

NASPE. 1995. *Moving Into the Future: National Standards for Physical Education.* St. Louis: Mosby.

Chapter 12

Assessment and Grading

"Will you please tell me which way I ought to go from here?"
"That depends a great deal on where you want to get to," said the Cat.
"I don't care much where," said Alice.
"Then it doesn't matter which way you go," said the Cat.

— *from* Alice in Wonderland *by Lewis Carroll (1832-1898)*

"**W**here are we headed with our physical education program?" Dr. Eli Jansen, principal of Birch Point Middle School, asked the four physical education teachers sitting across from her desk. They were having their monthly update conference, something she did with all her academic departments. "Our fitness scores are among the lowest in the state, and you told me last month that your focus is not on fitness, but on physical activity promotion. What are our students learning in physical education? Do you have any evidence that what you are doing is working?" she asked. The four teachers, Linda, Stian, Craig, and Dana, looked at each other. None of them really knew how they could produce evidence that what they were doing in the PE program was working. Yet they *knew* that their students were learning. Without waiting for an answer, Dr. Jansen told them what she wanted to have happen. "I have signed all of us up for a two-day in-service on physical education assessment," she said. "I have already arranged for subs, and you will have nothing to worry about other than learning how to show evidence that your students are learning in PE." Seeing their somewhat defensive expressions she added, "I know that we have worked hard in the last two years to make this program good, and you all deserve credit for that. But we need to make sure we can show parents that their kids are not wasting their time in physical education. I think this workshop will be a good start, and I will be expecting an assessment and grading plan to be developed within the next two months."

◆ Learning Objectives

After reading this chapter thoroughly and discussing the issues in class, you should be able to

- explain the purpose of student assessment,
- describe the current trends in the area of assessment,
- define traditional assessment,
- define alternative and authentic assessment,
- explain the difference between unit assessment and lesson assessment,
- explain the relationship between objectives and assessment,
- give examples of alternative and traditional assessments for a unit,
- give examples of alternative and traditional assessments for a lesson,
- define exit slip,
- explain the concepts of validity and reliability,
- explain the difference between intrarater and interrater reliability in alternative assessment, and
- explain the issues to consider when you decide how to grade your students in physical education.

◆ Key Terms and Phrases

Assessment
Traditional assessment
Alternative assessment
Authentic assessment
Unit assessment
Needs assessment
Lesson assessment
Exit slip
Reliability
Intrarater reliability
Interrater reliability
Validity
Grading

As a physical education teacher, you should ask yourself where you want to go with your physical education program and how you will know if you are on the right course to reach that destination. A physical education program without proper assessment built in is like a ship sailing the Atlantic Ocean without a compass or other navigational equipment. If the captain doesn't care where the ship ends up, it doesn't really matter that no equipment is on board. But if the passengers and crew think that the ship is heading for Amsterdam, the captain had better make sure that navigational equipment is on board and that someone knows how to use it. If the ship is your physical education curriculum, if the passengers and crew are your students, and if the captain is you, the physical education teacher, then the navigational equipment would be your assessments. The destination port would be your ultimate goal (i.e., helping your students become active for the rest of their lives), and the ports where you dock your ship along the way would be your objectives. Without regularly assessing your students' learning and progress, your PE ship could be heading anywhere. And if you've decided that you're heading toward the goal of helping all your students become active for life, you must regularly check the status of your ship. Are your students learning the things they need to know to become active adults? Will they become proficient in a few and competent in many skills and activities in which they can participate for most of their lives? Do they understand the most important concepts, such as how to be physically active in their community and how to create and modify a regular exercise plan that they will adhere to? Do they understand that learning new skills takes time and that all people go through the stages of learning? Do they feel confident in their ability to perform skills and activities that are beneficial to their health and wellness? These questions are important, and the only way to find the answers is through **assessment.**

Without assessment you have no way to know for sure if what you are doing in your curriculum is worthwhile. Eyeballing students' performance in class is not enough. Feeling that you're doing a good job may not convince your administrators, parents, and the community that your program is needed and that what you are doing is beneficial and important. Not all physical educators are as lucky as those in our opening scenario. Linda, Stian, Dana, and Craig have a principal who cares about physical education. She is trying to help solve the problem before it gets out of hand, before parents say, "Stop wasting our kids' time."

Assessment is a necessity in any program that has goals and objectives, and a program without goals and objectives is not a program worth keeping. Your goals and objectives should be congruent with the national standards for physical education (NASPE 1995), other national guidelines, the GET ACTIVE FOR LIFE factors, and your state framework or standards (see chapter 1). Your assessments will help you determine if you are heading in the right direction and if your students are really learning what you meant to teach them. In other words, the assessments become your navigational tools as you sail the physical education seas on your curriculum ship with your student passengers.

This chapter will present an overview of how to assess and grade your students. We will present two main types of student assessment: traditional and alternative/authentic. Entire books and courses focus on assessment, as well they should. NASPE has recently (Lambert 1999, Mitchell and Oslin 1999, Melograno 2000, O'Sullivan and Henninger 2000) published a K–12 assessment series that covers a variety of assessment topics for elementary and secondary schools. This series would be a useful addition to any teacher's library. For the purposes of this book, we offer a summary of student assessment for lessons and units. We also tackle the controversial issue of grading, a topic that books and courses on assessment, measurement, and evaluation often do not address.

Assessment Today

Many teachers use eyeballing to assess student progress in a unit or lesson. Some have become experts at this informal type of assessment. But in today's educational climate this method is not good enough. We need proof of what our students have learned. We need to assess student learning in each lesson and for each unit if we want to make sure we are reaching our objectives. If you have set objectives that are in line with national and state standards for physical education, and your assessments show that students are reaching those objectives, then you can assume that your part of the program is successful, that you are doing well as a teacher. If your whole PE department has similar results, you probably have a good program, but you must document your success. The best way to document success in teaching is through evidence of student learning.

Accountability

Accountability has been an education buzzword for a while now. In general, what that has meant for teachers is that they are encouraged, and often required, to prove that their students are learning in their classes. In a variety of subjects the accountability trend has resulted in selection of standardized tests that are supposed to indicate what students know as a result of a year's curriculum. Many critics condemn this trend toward standardized testing in education. They claim, among other things, that standardized tests take too much time and do not assess important higher-level learning. Critics also assert that standardized tests do not account for societal inequities such as socioeconomic status, parents' level of education, and the unique challenges of students who are English language learners (English is their second language).

Accountability should not mean simply using standardized tests. In physical education, standardized tests usually mean fitness tests, with the FITNESSGRAM and the Presidential fitness test being the most common. Neither of these tests alone would provide a good indication of what your students have learned in your physical education classes. But they could serve as a tool for assessing progress in one of the four domains of learning in physical education—health-related fitness. Beyond that, it would be deceiving to use the fitness test as an indicator of student learning in physical education.

The following paragraphs will present the two main types of assessment that you can use as a way to monitor student learning and progress in each of the four domains. These two main types are usually referred to as traditional and alternative assessment.

Traditional Assessment Defined

Traditional assessment tools are widely used in education. We usually think of traditional assessment as specific tests that measure characteristics that are more or less narrowly defined. This kind of assessment usually assesses only one learning domain at a time. Traditional tests in the cognitive domain include written standardized tests and other kinds of written tests that use multiple choice, short answer, fill-in-the blanks, true-false, matching, and essay questions. In the psychomotor domain, skills tests are considered traditional. For the health-related fitness domain,

fitness tests are a traditional type. Examples of traditional tests for the affective domain would include surveys of students' attitudes toward an activity or a self-concept rating scale. These kinds of tests have been criticized for being artificial in nature and for not challenging students to problem solve and use higher-level thinking skills. Most educators see a need for traditional tests, but the trend is to use them alongside alternative assessments to gain more information about student progress and learning.

Alternative Assessment Defined

Alternative assessments tend to be more holistic in nature than traditional assessments and frequently ask the students to solve real-world problems. The term **authentic assessment** is often used

Purpose

Introduce students to basic video techniques to help them with authentic assessment assignments.

Resource and Procedure

Students who are given video production assignments without guidance often are disappointed with the finished product. This is because they compare their projects to television programs that are professionally done with large budgets and experienced staff. Students involved in creating and taping alternative assessment skits could benefit from some basic video shooting and production techniques. The basic and most important concept with video production involves the viewer's ability to see and hear the production. This includes focusing on longer steady shots and avoiding zooms, tilts, and pans. Have students focus on recording the action from a steady position rather than moving with the camera. Staying close to the action and using wide angle lenses produce a feeling of steadiness even when the photographer is inexperienced. Ample lighting is another key principle. Have students plan outside shooting when possible to take advantage of the sunlight, but make sure they avoid shooting directly into the light. Make sure proper audio recording devices are available. If limited to just the microphone on the camera, make sure the actors are reasonably close to the microphone. Finally, let them have fun and be creative.

synonymously with alternative assessment, but it is a little more narrowly defined to include only assessments that focus on solving real-world problems in a context that is as authentic as possible. We will use the term *alternative assessment* and include authentic assessment examples under the broader umbrella term. Alternative assessments include several characteristics:

- The tasks are meaningful and often simulate real-world tasks or problems.

- Criteria are used to score the assessment and are presented to the students in advance. In other words, the students know what is expected of them. These criteria come in the form of a rubric, criteria sheets, or checklists (we will explain later in the chapter how to write these).

- The assessments focus as much on the process as on the product.

- The assessment becomes an integral part of the instruction and can blend in to the point where the assessment is really a learning activity. For example, teaching styles (see chapter 8) such as divergent discovery, partner feedback, and self-feedback can easily serve as alternative assessments.

- The assessments focus on higher-level thinking skills and problem solving.

- The teacher becomes an ally in the assessment process, not an adversary. He can be a guide on the side and help the students express how much they really know and are able to do.

- The students enjoy these assessments more and tend to spend more time to do them well.

- The final product is often showcased publicly, which makes accountability an important issue for students.

Alternative assessment examples include creating videos, bulletin boards, skits, and portfolios; writing journals and letters; conducting interviews; observing and analyzing peers; performing self-assessment; and much more (figure 12.1). The NASPE standards (1995) and the NASPE assessment series (Lambert 1999, Mitchell and Oslin 1999, Melograno 2000, O'Sullivan and Henninger 2000) include many examples of alternative assessments.

Figure 12.1 Teachers need to meet to discuss what assessment methods they want to use in evaluating the students in their program.

Purpose

Use video to assess students' learning of cues for physical activities.

Resource and Procedure

Select students to be reporters and have them interview other students in the class on the correct performance of skills. The students should demonstrate as well as describe the cues used during the skill. This may be a particularly useful activity to do during inclement weather or "plan B" days that interrupt scheduled class activities. View the interviews and assess for learning and retention of skills and cues. Refer to **www.videomaker.com/scripts/index.cfm** for a comprehensive guide to video production from beginner level to professional.

Alternative assessments can be individual, partner, or group tasks (figure 12.2). The main thing to remember when you conduct an alternative assessment is to have some kind of record. For example, if you have your students create and act out a skit about how to be more active, you should videotape the skit so that you can more easily assess and score it. Seeing the skit one time may not give you enough information to determine the deserving level on your rubric. In addition, we have found that students put more effort into the assessment when they are videotaped and they usually enjoy seeing the result of their work.

Figure 12.2 Alternative assessments deal with real-world problems and can be individual, partner, or group tasks.

Unit Assessment

As we discussed in the beginning of the chapter, teachers today can no longer justify eyeballing student learning, no matter how good they are at observing. Administrators, parents, politicians, and others now demand proof. School funding is often tied to assessment results. Many controversial issues surround the new wave of accountability in the public schools, but most teachers probably agree that the image of physical education needs a boost. Proving that students are learning valuable skills and concepts that will help them become active for the rest of their lives can only help.

Proof of learning is generated by assessment. In physical education, **unit assessment** typically comes toward the end of a unit. Conducting an assessment in the beginning of a unit, however, can help you see where you should begin. With a new unit you probably don't know the knowledge and skill level of your students. A **needs assessment** would help you figure this out. A needs assessment can also be used as a starting point to facilitate goal setting (chapter 7). The unit objectives should determine what you should be assessing. In other words, unless your assessment is congruent with the objectives, you lose the purpose of both. The two main categories of assessments, traditional and alternative, can be used for both pre- and postassessment as well as any assessment you choose to do in the middle of the unit.

Traditional Approaches to Unit Assessment

Traditional assessments usually ask students to reproduce a skill (psychomotor domain), express attitudes or feelings (affective domain), show knowledge or comprehension (cognitive domain), or perform tests that establish their fitness level (health-related fitness domain). These kinds of tests usually separate components and assess them individually. For example, a traditional skills test (psychomotor domain) for soccer would ask students to demonstrate one skill at a time, such as a pass, dribbling, or a kick for accuracy. Although some skills tests do a better job of examining the whole activity, traditional tests still ask students to reproduce rather than create and produce one or more skills.

For the affective domain the most common traditional tests consist of attitude and self-concept surveys. Traditional measurement and evaluation textbooks include many examples. These kinds of assessments can be useful, but are limited in assessing student learning.

As mentioned earlier, traditional health-related fitness domain tests usually take the form of some kind of fitness test. Some fitness tests are definitely better than others. Many states require the use of specific fitness tests, so the teacher has no choice. No matter which fitness test a teacher uses, she must administer it in an appropriate manner. This means making sure that students are not tested in the spotlight, that test results are kept private unless the student wants to share them, and that grading is based on goal setting rather than scores (more on this later).

Teachers can find some helpful hints about how to use fitness tests appropriately at the Concerned Adults and Students for Physical Education Reform Web site: **www.helpcasper.org**.

For the cognitive domain the traditional test usually takes the form of a written test of knowledge or comprehension. Multiple choice, true-false, and short-answer tests are common (see figure 12.3) for a reason. Teachers find these tests easy to produce and a breeze to grade. But many teachers are concerned that these tests do not tell the whole story. They know that they are testing the lowest forms of cognitive functioning—knowledge and comprehension. Higher-level thinking and problem-solving skills such as application, analysis, synthe-

sis, and evaluation are not easy to assess in these kinds of tests. For the same reason many teachers do not like standardized cognitive tests. To tap into the higher levels of the cognitive domain taxonomy (Bloom 1956), tests must take a more holistic approach and require problem solving and higher-level thinking (table 12.1).

Alternative Approaches to Unit Assessment

Alternative assessments ask students to create and produce rather than reproduce skills and knowledge. They tend to be more holistic in their approach, which means that they demand higher-level thinking by students. Alternative assessments are often done in groups or pairs so that the cooperation becomes part of the assessment (affective domain). In an alternative assessment task, students may be asked to produce an aerobics routine, create a video that will help their parents learn to swing the golf club correctly, create a brochure that will encourage sixth graders to join an after-school activity program, develop a program for improving in-line skating skills, keep a journal of exercise and dietary habits for a month and then analyze it, or create and videotape a commercial that shows the importance of physical activity. All these examples ask students to do more than just reproduce an answer on a test. Many teachers feel that alternative assessments show more accurately what students have learned than traditional tests do. The assessment is seen as part of the learning process as well.

Rubrics

Earlier in the chapter we mentioned that alternative assessment tasks require teachers to present the criteria for the task in advance. This usually takes the form of a rubric. There are many kinds of rubrics and no laws about how to make them, but teachers should follow some general guidelines (Lund 1999):

- Describe what a perfect response looks like (top level).
- Describe what a minimally acceptable response looks like (middle level).
- Describe what an unacceptable response looks like (bottom level).
- Add more "in-between" levels if needed.
- Be specific, but leave some wiggle room (doing this becomes easier with experience).
- Make the rubric holistic or use several specific sub-rubrics and checklists, depending on the task.
- Test your rubric with some students and expect to revise it.

Tennis test

1. What is tennis terminology for 0–4 points (what are the points called)?

   0 points = _____

   1 point = _____

   2 points = _____

   3 points = _____

   4 points = _____

2. In a tennis match, if the score is 40–40, what is the tie called?

3. When do players change sides of the court in a tennis match?

4. Name two tiebreaker systems used in tennis.

5. If the ball is on the line, is it in or out?

6. If a ball in play bounces off the net, is it good?

7. What are two good cues for the forehand ground stroke?

8. What are two good cues for the backhand ground stroke?

9. When would you use a volley?

10. When would you use a lob?

Figure 12.3   Written comprehension tests are a form of traditional assessment (cognitive domain).

Table 12.1   Sample Ideas for Assessment of the Different Levels of the Cognitive Domain Taxonomy

Level of the taxonomy	Action verbs (Hastad and Lacy 1998)	Sample assessment focuses
Evaluation	Judge, interpret, criticize, justify, appraise, defend	Appraise the value of various memberships at local, public, and private golf courses. Justify using golf as a way to stay in shape.
Synthesis	Create, invent, plan, formulate, devise, design	Create a lesson to teach a third grader how to throw and catch. Plan a two-week vacation that will provide enough physical activity to satisfy the CDC guidelines for a teenager.
Analysis	Analyze, identify, examine, illustrate, point out, diagram	Point out the health-enhancing aspects of rock climbing.
Application	Apply, develop, solve, use, prepare, produce, organize	Develop helpful new cues for three swing moves: the pretzel, the cuddle, and skin-the-cat.
Comprehension	Summarize, defend, predict, infer, estimate, distinguish	Explain the differences between moderate and vigorous physical activities.
Knowledge	List, name, state, select, match, label, recall, define	Define each area of health-related fitness. List cues for the tennis serve.

Those are just some of the guidelines for developing alternative assessment rubrics. A useful publication to read and keep as a reference is *Creating Rubrics for Physical Education* (Lund 1999). Creating alternative assessment tasks and rubrics can be a challenge, but it becomes easier and more fun as you see how much your students enjoy this form of assessment.

Figure 12.4 shows an example of an alternative assessment task for a rock-climbing unit, and figure 12.5 shows its corresponding rubric.

Your Turn ▶▶▶

◆ What are other examples of unit assessment focuses in table 12.1?

◆ Did any of your teachers use alternative assessments when you were in school? If so, in which subjects? How did you like it?

◆ Do alternative assessments appeal to you? Why or why not?

◆ What are the drawbacks to using only traditional assessments?

◆ Do you see any downsides to using only alternative assessments? Explain.

At first Linda, Stian, Dana, and Craig were a little troubled by their principal's pointed suggestions about assessing their physical education program. But in discussing it over lunch the next day, they agreed to ignore the method (the principal was known for being a little pushy, but then she also *did* get things done) and focus on the message. All four of them knew that they needed to find ways to prove that their students were learning. They agreed that their department had come a long way, and they prided themselves on the fact that their students, for the most part, were excited about physical education and seemed to learn a lot. After talking about their program, they all looked forward to the workshop on assessment. They had been told that the presenter was a well-known assessment expert in physical education. She had written several articles for the *Journal of Physical Education, Recreation and Dance* on alternative assessment and was the author of one of the books in the NASPE assessment series. The principal didn't do anything halfway.

Note: This task can be done in middle or high school with slight variations in criteria. Small groups, pairs, or individuals can do the assignment. The example uses groups.

Rock-climbing assessment task

One of your neighbors heard that you have had a unit on rock climbing in physical education. He's always wanted to learn how to climb, and a friend has said she'll learn with him. They have enrolled in a rock-climbing class at the local recreation center, but they don't want to look like total fools the first day, so they need your help. Create

◆ a 4- or 5-minute video or
◆ a 4- or 5-page brochure

in which you

◆ explain the most important safety issues in rock climbing,
◆ give good cues for climbing technique, and
◆ give hints for good strategy.

You have 50 minutes to plan your content and either practice and make the videotape or make your brochure.

Start planning at one of the planning stations.

◆ If you are making the video, go to the video station when you are ready to videotape.
◆ If you are making the brochure, go to the brochure station to get your supplies when you are ready to make your brochure.

Your group will be assessed and graded according to the rubric.

Figure 12.4   Alternative assessment task for a rock-climbing unit.

Rubric for rock-climbing assessment task

Level 4—Masterpiece!

Your brochure or video is extremely helpful for your neighbor and his friend. You do an excellent job of explaining the most important safety issues in rock climbing. You give at least three great cues for climbing technique and two helpful hints for good strategy, and these are clear and easy to understand from your explanations and demonstrations. Your group cooperates well through the process of making the video or brochure. Everyone in your group contributes to the product.

Level 3—Good work!

Your brochure or video is helpful for your neighbor and his friend. You do a nice job of explaining the most important safety issues in rock climbing. You give at least two good cues for climbing technique and include a hint for good strategy. Your group cooperates well through most of the process of making the video or brochure.

Level 2—Somewhat helpful; needs improvement.

Your brochure or video is somewhat helpful for your neighbor and his friend. You explain some of the most important safety issues in rock climbing. You give fewer than three cues for climbing technique and strategy, or some of the cues you use are not very helpful. Your lack of good cooperation may be the reason why your product needs improvement. You may choose to redo your work on your own time by this date: _____

Level 1—Not helpful; do over.

Your brochure or video is not helpful for your neighbor and his friend. You explain few or no safety issues in rock climbing, and you give no cues for climbing technique and strategy, or the cues you use are not helpful. Your lack of group cooperation may be the reason that you need to redo your product. You must redo your work on your own time by this date: _____

Figure 12.5 Sample rubric for rock-climbing alternative assessment task.

Lesson Assessment

How will you know if students have learned what you hoped they would in your physical education lesson? If your objectives for each lesson are clear and concise, a **lesson assessment** will permit you to determine rather easily whether students have grasped some of the concepts, skills, or cues. Although you can assess all the domains in a lesson or a unit, you should remember that improving their health-related fitness or learning to perform a skill correctly (psychomotor domain) takes time, often much more time than what you have available to spend with your students. In one lesson, however, they can learn key components of a skill, performance cues, and concepts related to the skill.

If your lesson objectives are realistic, they focus on what students can learn in one lesson, the "learnable piece." Lesson assessments help you see if the students reached your objectives. They can take the form of traditional or alternative as-

sessments but can be more informal and formative. This means that the information is as much for the students to understand how they are doing as it is for you to see what they know and are able to do.

Traditional and Alternative Approaches to Lesson Assessment

As in unit assessment, you have choices of traditional and alternative assessments in a lesson. Alternative assessments often take more time than traditional assessments. When you have only three to five minutes for assessment as the students are stretching or relaxing at the end of the class, using a holistic approach may be difficult. But you could have the students evaluate their performance for the day, write a paragraph in their physical education journals, or discuss with a partner why they did or didn't reach their goals for the day (figure 12.6). Traditional forms of assessment are easy to administer quickly. One method is to use **exit slips**, small pieces of paper that students

Figure 12.6 Having your class write in their journals while stretching at the end of a class period is a good use of class time and an ideal opportunity for students to reflect on their experiences.

hand in as they leave class. Exit slips are similar to quick review quizzes. For example, the teacher could ask students to write down the two cues they remember from the team handball pass or two rules they remember from the lesson on Ultimate Frisbee. As the teacher collects the exit slips he can easily see who has paid attention in class and who has learned at least what is being assessed. Again, we can't emphasize enough that what you test has to be something you taught. In addition, remember that students may need lots of practice to learn the concepts or skills that you will assess.

Lesson Assessment Examples

Let's take some of the lesson objective examples from table 11.5 in chapter 11 and give you some ideas of how to assess them in the same lesson. One way to assess the lesson objective "Students will learn how to put on a rock-climbing harness correctly" would be to have a checklist with criteria and let students assess each other's success in pairs. Instead of your deciding whether each student is successful, the students do so with help from the criteria sheet. This way they learn through the assessment process, and although you oversee the exercise you spend less time with the assessment. The students then hand in the checklist for accountability. Can students cheat? Sure. But because you

oversee the process, cheating is less likely. Moreover, if students have learned what you taught, none would feel the need to cheat. The preceding is an example of an alternative assessment.

Another lesson objective, "Students will set a realistic goal for how many steps they will learn and remember in step aerobics," could be assessed simply by asking students on an exit slip what their goal was and how many steps they remember. This would be a formative traditional assessment. Students could then show a partner how many steps they remember, and the partner would attest that the number of steps remembered was correct.

If you wanted to assess whether students had reached the objective "Students will learn how to set up for the golf drive," you could ask them for three key cues for the drive setup on an exit slip. This would also be a formative traditional assessment. And if you wanted to assess quickly whether students reached the objective "Students will work in groups to create a line dance routine and learn to work cooperatively to achieve success," you could ask them to write in their journals for five minutes about how well the group cooperated. Another option here would be to give the journal entry as a homework assignment. This would be an example of an alternative assessment if you had communicated criteria in advance.

All these examples are reasonably simple, and most require less than five minutes. If quick assessments at the end of each lesson become routine, you may find that students focus on reaching the objectives for the lesson. But remember that you must clearly communicate the objectives to the students at the start of the period so that they know what to focus on throughout the lesson.

The process of assessing student learning and holding students accountable for what they learn in every lesson is not automatic. The teacher must plan and be consistent. Although the principles of unit and lesson assessment are the same, lesson assessment obviously needs to be simpler and more informal because of time constraints. The lesson objectives should determine what you will assess at the end of the lesson. Again, your lesson assessment must be congruent with the lesson objectives, or you lose the purpose of both.

Your Turn ▶▶▶

- Create a lesson objective for swimming and a corresponding exit slip question.
- Create a lesson objective for volleyball and a corresponding exit slip question.
- Why is knowing the criteria in advance important in alternative assessments?
- Why is it important to make sure that you teach what you will be assessing?

At the assessment workshop Linda, Stian, Craig, and Dana learned a variety of useful methods for assessing their students' learning. Nothing they learned was really difficult to grasp. But they all knew that the challenge would be to get into the habit of using what they were learning. They decided to start building an assessment bank on the office computer immediately. The presenter had encouraged them to borrow ideas from others, so Dana scanned the examples from the workshop handouts into the computer early the following morning. It was a start. The assessment report was due to the principal in less than two months, and they wanted it to be good. They would also have to devise a new grading system. They could no longer justify the subjective assignment of grades that they had used in the past. But with all their newfound knowledge from the workshop, they knew that creating a fair grading system based on student learning would not be as hard as they had previously thought it would be.

Important Issues for Any Type of Assessment

You want to be confident that the assessments you use will provide credible evidence of your students' performance and learning. To accomplish this, assessments must be valid and reliable.

Validity is the idea that an assessment measures what it proposed to measure. For example, if we say that we are going to assess students' ability to create a physical activity program for a friend, it would not be sufficient to use a multiple-choice test on the importance of physical activity. That test may be OK for another purpose, but it would not be a careful assessment of what we intended to measure—the ability to create a program.

Reliability refers to the consistency and objectivity of an assessment. If you give the same assessment to a student twice within a relatively short period of time, she should score about the same (assuming no new learning has taken place). This is called test-retest reliability.

Alternative assessments include two kinds of reliability: intrarater and interrater. **Intrarater reliability** refers to the consistency of one rater in scoring a task. If you score a task today and redo it a week from now, will you give it the same score? **Interrater reliability** is the consistency among a group of scorers. If you and your colleagues score 10 tasks, do you give the same scores to the same students at least 80% of the time? Training the raters and keeping the criteria somewhat specific can ensure both interrater and intrarater reliability. The more specific your rubrics or criteria sheets, the more reliable your alternative assessments. This specificity makes it easier to be objective when scoring, whether you have one (intrarater reliability) or several (interrater reliability) scorers. Too much specificity, however, will penalize creativity and thus take away from one of the main benefits of alternative assessment. The key is to find a balance.

Traditional tests that you find in textbooks are usually tested for reliability and validity through one of a variety of methods. Alternative assessments, on the other hand, are often not tested for validity and reliability because many of these assessments are homemade. Part of the advantage of alternative assessments is that you tailor them to fit your specific needs. The nature of many alternative assessments makes them appear to be more valid (face validity) because they are more true to the real world. The NASPE standards (1995) suggest that teachers run their homemade traditional or alternative assessments through a couple of easy tests to make sure that they will be good indicators of student learning and performance. The standards offer these main points.

* To ensure validity, follow these steps:
  - Define exactly what you will be assessing (for example, students' knowledge of the rules of tennis; or students' knowledge of the cues for the heel stop, the A-frame turn, and the spin stop in in-line skating; or students' performance of these skills).
  - Design an assessment that measures the concepts or skills you have defined.

If you can show that what you said you were going to assess is really what you are assessing, you have obtained content-related evidence for validity. You should be able to show a logical connection among your objectives, your list of what you will assess, and your assessment.

* To ensure reliability, follow these steps:
  - Define your scoring criteria as clearly and specifically as you can without sacrificing your students' ability to be creative.
  - Pilot test your rubric or criteria sheet to see if you can score a performance consistently. You can do this by scoring a handful of assessment responses, wait a few days, and then score them again using the same rubric or criteria sheet. If your scores are consistent, your rubric or criteria sheet is fine. If your scores vary, you would want to make some changes.
  - Train any other raters you may use so that all of you are consistent and use the criteria sheet or rubric the same way.

Remember, most traditional tests that you find in textbooks, such as a variety of skill tests and fitness tests, have already been tested for validity and reliability. If you use one of these , you should closely follow the instructions for the specific test to ensure reliability.

Grading Your Students in Physical Education

Teachers often determine grades in physical education by noting how often students dress out, observing how well they participate, and interpreting their attitude. Although these issues are important, they should not be the basis for **grading** in physical education. Imagine a math teacher grading her students on whether they brought pencils and paper to class and how she thought they felt about the subject matter. Bringing proper equipment to class (or being willing to use loaners when you forget) and showing basic respect for the teacher and fellow students by following instructions should be prerequisites for being allowed to participate in class, not a basis for evaluating performance. In all subjects, student learning, achievement, and performance should determine grades. If teachers continue to determine students' grades based on behaviors that have little to do with learning, physical education will continue to suffer from the image of being unimportant. If, on the other hand, teachers can help parents, administrators, and politicians understand that what they teach is important, we may yet save our prestige-deprived profession. But that means we have to believe that what we teach is important—yes, important enough to assess and to base students' grades on that assessment (figure 12.7).

Criteria Versus Goal Setting

Some teachers set criteria for their students to reach to obtain a certain grade, whereas others emphasize goal setting by teaching them to set obtainable goals and basing part of the grade on whether or not they reached those goals. The goals must be both attainable and challenging if students are to reach higher and learn more. Setting goals is a process that we have to teach (see chapter 7).

The goal-setting approach has several advantages. It allows for individual differences in ability and adheres to the inclusion approach to teaching (chapter 8). Genes, body type, fitness level, and previous movement experience all play important roles in determining who will excel in what activity, but goal setting reduces the effect of these factors in the evaluation process. If we teach students to set their own attainable goals, hold them accountable for making modifications when necessary, and challenge them to reach those goals, learning takes center stage. This way both learning and assessment become individualized, or student centered. This method is different from grading on improvement, which is simply looking at an increase from one assessment to the next. The improvement approach is unfair to the higher-skilled students because they have less room for improvement than do the lower-skilled students. Assessment based on goal setting works for all the domains, but it is especially important in the

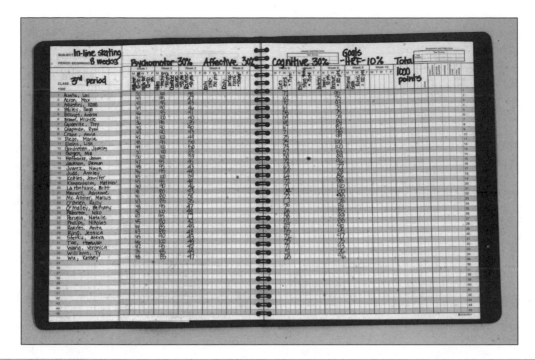

Figure 12.7 Student learning, achievement, and performance must be the main focus in assessing students if physical education is to remain worthwhile.

psychomotor and health-related fitness areas because learning and improving can take more time in those domains.

Purpose

Use e-mail to record student goals as well as set up a mechanism for students to track their progress toward their goals.

Resource and Procedure

Have students provide you with e-mail addresses and have them send their goals for the unit. Make sure students who do not have access to computers at home know how they can get an e-mail account and access their e-mail in the school library or computer lab. You may also want to require them to provide weekly updates on their progress toward reaching their goals. Make sure that they send a copy of their e-mail message to themselves. One of the nice things about e-mail is the built-in tracking system that stores messages with dates and times. The students can refer to their messages as they progress through their goal pursuits. Be sure to provide regular responses of encouragement by sending e-mail messages back to your students.

Weighting Each Domain

You should think carefully about all aspects of grading in physical education, including how you choose to weight each learning domain. There is no correct answer here, but we will discuss some of the pertinent issues.

First, if you use criterion grading, remember that physical education is different from many other subjects because we deal with all four learning domains. The psychomotor and health-related fitness domains bring up a couple of difficult questions:

- How much of an effect do previous movement experiences and genetics have on students' abilities in these domains?
- Can you provide enough learning time in your class to allow *all* students the opportunity to reach your criteria?

We believe that grading in these domains should be based on goal setting. This method allows for a more inclusive learning environment in which you challenge all your students to improve from where they started. If they have already reached their potential (such as in a health-related fitness test component like the mile run), maintaining that level can be a worthy goal.

The affective domain can be hard to get a handle on when it comes to grading issues. If you grade students on their attitudes, as expressed in attitudinal surveys, you can be sure that students will tell you what they think you want to hear so that they will receive a good grade. In this domain you should instead focus on behaviors that reflect affective domain issues:

- Assess fair play by observing students' behavior in games. A rubric or criteria sheet is useful for this kind of assessment.

- Assess cooperation by using a rubric or criteria sheet for group or partner assignments.

- Assess attitudes by behaviors such as dressing for activity (barring a valid excuse), participating in all activities, willingly trying new activities, being on time, staying on task, and showing evidence of effort in all activities. A rubric or criteria sheet would be a useful tool for assessing this area.

- Assess acceptance of differences by behaviors such as willingness to work with anyone in the class and volunteering to help others when needed.

Those examples should give the idea of how you can avoid just eyeballing it when you assess the affective domain.

The cognitive domain is probably the easiest to assess and grade. When you cover any concept in your class, you can assess it with a variety of traditional and alternative assessments. Many of the examples earlier in the chapter were appropriate for the cognitive domain. This area of physical education is more like other subjects. You can grade students on how much they have studied and grasped because the playing field is more even for every student. Some students, of course, will not grasp concepts as quickly as others do, but chances are that no concept you teach in your physical education class will go completely over anyone's head. That is, if you really teach it.

So now we ask the big question again: how should you weight each domain when grading your students in physical education? Our guiding lights (chapter 1) do not tell us directly. Although they emphasize the importance of each domain, what shines through as the main message is that physical education should help students become active for the rest of their lives. From the GET ACTIVE FOR LIFE factors (chapter 1) we know that self-efficacy is important. Self-efficacy belongs in the affective domain, but learning in the psychomotor domain directly influences it. People feel better about their ability to perform an activity after they learn how to do it. Another important factor is learning *how* to be physically active in the community. At first this appears to be a purely cognitive issue, but you have to tie it to learning the skills needed to be active in the programs that are available. Likewise, learning how to solve problems and use the self-management skills needed to squeeze physical activity into a busy schedule are important concepts that students must learn, but with that they also have to learn skills in activities that they are likely to be able to participate in when they become bogged down with life's responsibilities. We could give more examples of how the domains overlap when it comes to addressing the GET ACTIVE FOR LIFE factors, but you probably get the point. The weighting issue is not clear cut. We are not going to tell you that you should weight each domain equally, or that you should weight one this much and another that much. But in examining the issues in chapters 1 and 3, you will note that adolescents' current fitness levels do not automatically carry over into adulthood. How fit they are today does not predict how active they will be in the future. This finding suggests that we may want to place less emphasis on the health-related fitness domain when we grade students in physical education. That doesn't mean that you de-emphasize the health-related fitness domain in aspects other than grading. Chapter 3 shows a need for improved health-related fitness in adolescents, but you don't have to weight this domain as heavily as the other three when you devise your grading system.

We urge you to critically reexamine the guiding lights and the GET ACTIVE FOR LIFE factors when you develop your grading system. If you follow the general guidelines for assessment provided in this chapter, you will do OK as long as you don't overemphasize (assign more than 40% to) any of the four domains. All are important and deserve consideration. Your grading system should be an accurate representation of what your students are learning in your program. As long as you teach according to the national standards and guidelines, consider the GET ACTIVE FOR LIFE factors when you develop your curriculum, and assess your students' learning based on what you taught them, you should do well.

Although developing a new grading system was not difficult, it took a lot of discussion to arrive at one they all could agree on. Stian thought that they should weight the affective domain heavier than the others, and Linda favored the psychomotor domain. Dana and Craig both argued that the cognitive domain deserved top priority in their new grading system. They all had good justifications for their arguments. As the discussion progressed, they all backed up their opinions by citing the NASPE standards, their state framework, and other important guidelines for physical education. The only thing they agreed on was to de-emphasize the health-related fitness domain in their grading. They would continue to provide opportunities for their students to improve their cardiovascular fitness, muscular strength and endurance, and flexibility and body composition, but they would assign only 10% of the total grade to that domain. The grade for that 10% would be based on students achieving the goals they had set and revised throughout the semester.

Discussion continued about the remaining 90%. After agreeing to do more reading and discussing, they met a week later to complete their assessment report for the principal. The report had to include their new grading policy, so they had to reach a compromise. A few cups of coffee later, they arrived at the solution. They would weight each of the remaining domains 30%. Dressing out and students' attitudes would be included in the daily affective domain rubric that Stian would be in charge of developing. Students would now have to participate to earn the daily available points for the various domains throughout the unit.

The assessment and grading plan was one they could all live with, and the four physical educators were proud of what they handed to their principal—on time and with a thank-you note for the little push they had needed to address this important issue.

Summary

Appropriate unit and lesson assessment will help you find out what your students are learning in your physical education classes and whether your program is headed in the desired direction. For each domain of learning you can use traditional and alternative methods to assess student learning in your units and lessons. Assessment tools should be reliable and valid. Assessment and grading should be a process, not a one-shot deal. Assessment is time consuming, but if you make it part of the learning experience it will serve many purposes. Besides giving you the documentation you need to show that students are learning valuable skills and concepts in your classes, assessment can also can give students a chance to learn even more. We stated in the previous chapter that planning and assessment go hand in hand. Many of the examples we have used in this chapter for alternative assessment are difficult to distinguish from learning activities.

Checking for Understanding ▶▶▶

- What is the purpose of student assessment in physical education?
- What are the current trends in assessment?
- What is traditional assessment?
- What is alternative assessment?
- How do unit and lesson assessments differ?
- What is the relationship between objectives and assessment?
- What is an example of an alternative unit assessment?
- What is an example of a traditional unit assessment?
- What is an example of an alternative lesson assessment?
- What is an example of a traditional lesson assessment?
- How would you use an exit slip?
- How can you tell if an assessment is valid?
- How can you tell if an assessment is reliable?
- What are some major issues to consider when you decide how to grade your students in physical education?

For Reflection and Discussion ▶▶▶

- How do you think parents would react if an English teacher in middle or high school had the following grading policy: "If you try your best every day and bring your books, you get an A"?
- How would they react to a similar grading policy in physical education: "You dress, you play, you get an A"?
- Why do you suppose most parents would react in different ways to the previous scenarios?
- What could you do to change parents' perception of physical education and the way that their children earn their grades in the subject?

References

Bloom, B. 1956. *Taxonomy of educational objectives: The classification of educational goals.* New York: Longmans, Green.

Hastad, D., and A. Lacy. 1998. *Measurement and evaluation in physical education and exercise science.* 3rd ed. Needham Heights. MA: Allyn & Bacon.

Lambert, L. 1999. *Standards-based assessment of student learning.* Reston, VA: NASPE.

Lund, J. 1999. *Creating rubrics for physical education.* Reston, VA: NASPE.

Melograno, V. 2000. *Portfolio assessment for K–12 physical education.* Reston, VA: NASPE.

Mitchell, S., and J. Oslin. 1999. *Assessment in games teaching.* Reston, VA: NASPE.

National Association for Sports and Physical Education (NASPE). 1995. *Moving into the future: National standards for physical education.* St. Louis: Mosby.

O'Sullivan, M., and M. Henninger. 2000. *Assessing student responsibility and teamwork.* Reston, VA: NASPE.

Suggested Readings

Herman, J., P. Aschbacher, and L. Winters. 1992. *A practical guide to alternative assessment.* Alexandria, VA: Association for Supervision and Curriculum Development.

Chapter 13

Be Ready for the Unexpected

There are risks and costs to a program of action, but they are far less than the long-range risks and costs of comfortable inaction.

— *John F. Kennedy*

On a rainy day in March, in normally sunny Yolo City, California, 90 students from three classes had to squeeze into Yolo High School's small gym for fifth- and sixth-period physical education. The three teachers, Diane, Troy, and Fran, got ready to do the old standby for the rainy-day lesson, a game of knockout in the gym. Students would get in lines and shoot once at the basketball hoop. They would get back in line if they made it. If they missed, they would sit down. Troy had just attended a session at the California Association for Health, Physical Education, Recreation and Dance conference, and he told Diane and Fran that he felt badly about what they were doing. "We're not teaching anything," he said, "and worse, we're playing a game that uses elimination. The students who need the shooting practice the most are eliminated first. Besides, many of the students miss on purpose right away so they can sit down and talk to their friends." "That may be true," said Diane, "but what else can we do with 90 kids in the gym?" Fran, who had been the department leader in the reforms toward developmentally appropriate practices in their school, was pleased to hear the comments and suggested that they call a department meeting to discuss the rainy-day issue and devise a better solution. "After all, "she said, "none of us really enjoy the rainy days. It seems that we just try to keep the students busy until the bell rings, and that's not why we became teachers."

◆ Learning Objectives

After reading this chapter thoroughly and discussing the issues in class, you should be able to

- list at least four circumstances that could interfere with your regularly scheduled lesson plans,

- explain why teachers should have a plan B ready for the days when circumstances interfere with plan A,

- describe two ways to be better prepared when you must use plan B, and

- list and describe at least five different ideas for plan B lessons when you have to share a gym or have very little space.

◆ Key Terms and Phrases

Unforeseen circumstances
Plan B
Inclement weather
Preparedness

You will have days when your well-thought-out plans for your lessons fall apart because of **unforeseen circumstances.** Most schools do not have sufficient facilities for all purposes. The physical education teachers' classroom, because it is the largest facility, is usually the one that is pressed into service for activities of all sorts. Some teachers, like the ones described in our opening scenario, use days when plan A will not work as excuses not to teach. That is not acceptable. Part of a teacher's job is to be prepared for the unexpected. Ideally, you would be able to modify your existing lesson plan when the unexpected happens. We realize that this can be impossible in many situations, especially when three or more classes must share a gym.

This chapter will give you some ideas for what you can do when you have to use **plan B.** The main message is to be ready for anything that may cause you to lose gym space temporarily. By anticipating and planning for these unforeseen circumstances, you will be ready for the unexpected. A teacher who plans can usually avoid becoming a babysitter.

The Unexpected

Teachers get bumped out of the gym and have to share space temporarily for a variety of reasons. Poor weather, assemblies, picture days, and health screenings are events that commonly require physical education teachers to work together and share available space.

Rain, especially unseasonable, unexpected rain, creates a problem for physical education teachers and students in climates where the curriculum is based on using outdoor fields and courts for teaching. Of course, snow, wind, cold, and heat can cause the same problem. The situation described in our opening scenario is common in climates where school districts count on good weather for most of the school year. Schools in these areas often have limited indoor facilities available for physical education classes. So sharing a gym on a rainy day in Arizona, California, or Texas is the norm, not the exception. In climates where it is common to plan for one or several classes to use outdoor facilities on a regular basis, **inclement weather** leads to the need for immediate adjustments of the lesson and unit plans. When teachers are forced to share indoor facilities, three or more classes may have to be in one

gym at one time. The teachers in the scenario had a backup plan for lessons on such days, but they realize that their plan is a weak effort to keep the students under control until the bell rings. On rainy days their role switched from teacher to babysitter.

Purpose

Select and use weather sources to keep track of weather conditions that may cause you to alter planned activities.

Resource and Procedure

When weather may affect planned activities, you must think ahead and be prepared for alternative activities. When you have outside activities planned, make it a habit to check weather sources for short-term and extended forecasts. Although local television news is a typical source, the Weather Channel on cable provides constant updates. In addition, various weather Web sites are provided by news organizations. Also try the National Weather Service home page at **www.nws. noaa.gov** for information. (Crossing your fingers wouldn't hurt either.)

Because the gym or multipurpose room (common replacement for a gym in many middle schools) is the largest indoor gathering facility at the school site, the facility will at times be needed for special occasions such as assemblies, school pictures, health screenings, and other events. Although physical education teachers should receive notice of plans to use their classroom sufficiently far in advance that they can make alternate arrangements, this does not always occur. Of course, part of a teacher's job is to educate her administrators, when necessary, about the importance of her subject matter. This task may take time in schools where physical education has been low on the totem pole for a long time. With respect comes consideration for subject matter and student learning. Advance warning of plans to use the physical education facilities will follow. Regardless of the circumstances, the teacher must plan backups so that students can learn skills and concepts that will help them become active for the rest of their lives.

So what can teachers do to provide students with a meaningful learning experience if they have to squeeze three classes into a small gym? The answer is simple: Be prepared and plan for the unexpected. The time-consuming part is coming up with enough ideas to avoid being repetitive in prolonged plan B situations.

Be Prepared

When the unexpected occurs, **preparedness** is the key. By having 10 lesson plans ready for unforeseen circumstances or a cramped gym, you are prepared for 10 out-of-routine days. If conditions force you to use plan B more often than that, you can rotate through the plan B lessons again. These plans, of course, should follow the same guiding lights (chapter 1) as other lesson plans. Although they may be outside the planned unit, these alternate plans should still follow the Diamond Conceptual Framework we discussed in chapter 1. With creativity and collaboration, teachers have found ways to use these out-of-the-ordinary days to help them reach the NASPE benchmarks and their state guidelines or standards. It really comes down to how you think about it. Even if you're teaching in a hallway, there is a concept or skill you can teach.

Of course, to make the implementation of these plan B lesson plans easier, you must cooperate with your colleagues when planning and let students know up front what your routines or protocols will be for plan B days.

Cooperate With Colleagues

Some physical education departments do a lot of cooperative lesson and unit planning. In other departments, collaborative planning is a rarity. Obviously, if poor weather forces three or more teachers to share a small gym, they all have to adapt, and the best solution will probably be to cooperate in planning for these occasions. If all affected teachers plan the out-of-the-ordinary lessons, implementation will be much smoother. Imagine the alternative: Three teachers, each with 30 to 40 students, trying to implement a different rainy-day lesson plan in a gym with no dividers. Even if each lesson plan were a good one, the result would be highly distracted students, at best. If you sit down and focus your discussion on how to make sure that your students will learn something that will help them become physically educated people, you will be able to find solutions to even the most difficult situations. This coopera-

tive effort would have to include a plan for protocols as well as lesson content.

Routines and Protocols

Just as you need routines and protocols to make your regularly planned lessons run smoothly (as we discussed in chapter 7), you need routines and protocols to help you when unforeseen circumstances crop up. Students should know the routines for these kinds of days. For example, they should know that if it rains, snows, or is over 100 degrees outside, they will share the gym with two other classes, with the three teachers team teaching. Students will also need to know and practice the protocols for such days. What do they do when they enter the gym? If they normally perform an instant activity, do they do one with the whole group of 90 students? How will they get information on what to do in class? Will they go to you, their teacher, or will an instructional segment be geared to the whole group? If you normally take roll while your students participate in a warm-up or instant activity, will you do that in another way on those days? If students have answers to these questions before the situation arises and they practice the protocols, you will waste less time and have more time for learning and activity.

Out-of-the-Ordinary Lesson Ideas

When an unforeseen circumstance prevents you from going with your regularly scheduled lesson plan, you may find it difficult to be creative on the spot and ensure that the students are learning and working toward overall unit or yearly goals and objectives. What we're suggesting here is that you plan before you are caught by surprise. When the unforeseen happens, you are ready to go with your plan B. As discussed earlier, your plans should be a cooperative effort by all affected teachers. In other words, if you have to share the gym on a rainy day with three other teachers, four of you should be creating these plan B lessons together.

The following sections present a variety of ideas for days when inclement weather or other unforeseen circumstances interfere with your regularly planned lesson. The ideas are useful for both middle and high school physical education. All the ideas work toward the overall goal of guiding students in the process of becoming physically active and healthy for a lifetime. We feel that all students should be actively involved in learning activities on rainy days, just as they are on all other days. Obviously, there are many different ways to go about this, but these ideas can get you started and possibly trigger other ideas that you can share with your colleagues.

> **F**ran was eager to lead the department meeting when they discussed their rainy-day routine. She started out by asking her colleagues how they felt about the students playing knockout or just sitting around. Troy said he felt bad about it after attending the conference. "What the presenter was saying fits us so well," he said. "It made me feel like I accept that my job is babysitting rather than teaching on rainy days, and I don't like that feeling." Diane said she understood how he felt but that having 90 students in the gym at the same time left her mind blank as far as ideas for how to change things. Then she suddenly remembered when a class from the local university had come out to do some teaching practice several years ago. A winter storm had come through the area, and she had called the professor to cancel because of the shared-gym situation. But the professor had persuaded her to let his students teach anyway. "They have plan B ready," he had said. The lesson went well, with only a few complaints from the students who enjoyed their sitting-around time. After the college students had completed the lesson, several students commented on what a great workout they got from the fitness stations. This all happened before Troy and Fran were hired, so Diane shared the story with them. It was a place to start.

Fitness Stations

One way to fit health-related fitness objectives into your school year is to use every unforeseen circumstance day as a fitness day. When you have many students, stations are the way to go. To make a fitness-stations lesson work with 100 students in one gym, however, you must be extremely well prepared and organized. Making a large poster for each station that describes the particular exercise is a good idea. This can be a lot of work, but if you do it well, you will not have to do it again unless the status of an exercise changes (i.e., it becomes contraindicated). The best way to make sure your posters have a long life is to laminate them.

How many exercises do you need? If you have about 100 students you could put them in groups of 4 to 6. You could have 20 stations spread all around the gym, using all the available space (figure 13.1). All stations do not have to be different. By having 10 different stations, each repeated once, and rotating students every 2 to 3 minutes, your students would be unlikely to do many of the stations more than once in a 50-minute lesson. Remember to do a proper warm-up and cool-down and to use the NBA/WNBA rules for stretching (see chapter 11).

What should the stations include? Any health-related fitness exercise that focuses on muscular strength, muscular endurance, flexibility, or cardiovascular endurance would be suitable, as long as it would fit in the space provided. Figure 13.2 offers some suggestions for health-related fitness station posters. The posters should include the information that students need to be successful at that station.

Your Turn ▶ ▶ ▶

- Do you think it would help if the teachers created drawings to go along with the instructions for the posters in figure 13.2? Explain.
- How would fitness stations help a student reach the goal of becoming a physically educated person?

You can use a variety of teaching styles with the fitness stations (for a review of teaching styles see chapter 8). As always, you should observe the inclusion premise. Students are at different levels of fitness, and they need to participate at their own level to be motivated and successful. You should offer variations through choices of levels on the posters, as in figure 13.2, or on the criteria sheets if you provide them.

Teacher feedback style would allow the teachers involved to move around the gym and provide feedback to students. If you decided to use partner feedback style, you could have one of the partners provide feedback, following the criteria on the poster or on a criteria sheet, while the other performs the exercise. The limitation of that style would be that each student would be physically active only half the time. This could be desirable, however, for fitness activities that require a resting

Figure 13.1 Use posters to guide students on what to do at a variety of fitness stations in your gym.

period between sets. Partner feedback style could also be an option for students at lower fitness levels who need more rest between activities.

Self-feedback would be a natural style to use with fitness stations, as students would check their form or fitness level on a criteria sheet. Students could use the sheets later for examples when they write in their physical education journals or create their own fitness programs.

Convergent and divergent discovery teaching styles could also work well with fitness stations. Which one you use would depend on whether you want your students to discover one correct solution to a problem (convergent discovery) or several possible solutions (divergent discovery). Simply by varying the teaching styles, you could use fitness stations many times before the students ever tired of them.

As with any other fitness activity, music makes the workout more enjoyable. If the students have participated in choosing the music, they tend to enjoy it even more. Besides explaining and demonstrating the stations the first few times you use them, you should make sure that the students understand why the particular fitness exercises are important. You can reinforce your oral explanation by including the information on the posters as in figure 13.2.

Your Turn ▶▶▶

- What are some other ideas for fitness stations?
- Could you have students help create fitness stations or another plan B activity as homework? How would you go about that?

Concept Days

If you ask physical education teachers to name the most challenging space they have had to teach a class in, they may give answers such as the hallway or the locker room. With planning and a little creativity, however, even a hallway lesson can be purposeful. If you want to cover concepts in your curriculum that may be too complicated to incorporate into regular lessons that focus on physical activity, you could have some of your unforeseen-circumstance days become "concept days." A class focusing primarily on concepts may not require a gym, so this kind of lesson could be an alternative for teachers who have to use cramped space such as the hall or the locker room. Keep in mind that students don't learn much from a lecture, especially

Jump-rope station

Objective: To improve cardiovascular endurance

Equipment needed: One jump rope per student

Task: Jump rope to the beat of the music. You may do double jumps or single jumps, depending on your level of fitness. You should try hard not to stop. Instead, jump at a slower pace if you become tired.

Why: Cardiovascular endurance is important for overall health and can help prevent cardiovascular disease, stress, high blood pressure, obesity, and certain forms of cancer. In addition, it may improve your mood!

Biceps curls station

Objective: To improve muscular endurance in the biceps

Equipment needed: Use one resistance band. The bands vary in degree of resistance. You may choose which color to use: green is easiest, blue is in the middle, and gray is hardest.

Task: Step on one end of the elastic band with your right foot. Hold the other end of the band in your right hand. Your right elbow should be touching the right side of your torso. Pull the band toward your biceps with a firm wrist; release slowly. You should adjust the tightness of the band so that it does not flap or jerk your arm. Alternate right and left arms on every 10 to 20 curls (depending on how fast you become tired).

Why: Upper-body endurance is important for everyday tasks such as lifting and carrying.

Sit-up station

Objective: To improve endurance in the abdominal muscles

Equipment needed: One exercise mat per student

Task: Lie on your back with your feet flat on the mat. Put your hands behind your head or neck for support. Keep a fist-sized space between your chin and chest. Keep your elbows out so that you do not pull on your neck. Do the sit-ups to the beat of the music. Take a rest when you need to, but start again as soon as you can.

Why: Abdominal endurance is important in maintaining proper posture and avoiding back pain.

Keep-away station

Objective: To improve cardiovascular endurance

Equipment needed: One ball per group. The four cones mark the borders.

Task: Form two teams quickly by the first letter of your last name. The half with letters closest to Z form one team, and the half with letters closest to A form the other team. This should take no more than 20 seconds. One team starts with the ball. The activity includes no scoring. The object is to try to keep the ball away from your opponents. You must pass the ball continuously. You can hold it a maximum of 3 seconds and take a maximum of two steps when you have the ball. When a pass is intercepted, the game continues with the other team trying to keep away. Move your feet at all times.

Why: Cardiovascular endurance is important for overall health and can help prevent cardiovascular disease, stress, high blood pressure, obesity, and certain forms of cancer. In addition, it may improve your mood!

(continued)

Figure 13.2   Suggestions for health-related fitness station posters.

Shoulders, arms, back, and legs station

Objective: To improve endurance in a variety of muscles in the upper and lower body

Equipment needed: Use one resistance band. The bands vary in degree of resistance. You may choose which color to use: green is easiest, blue is in the middle, and gray is hardest.

Task: Stand with your feet about double shoulder-width apart. Hold one end of the band in each hand. Reach your arms over your head and slowly pull the band down and outward behind your head. At the same time you should lower your body by bending your knees, keeping your back straight and up. You should go as far down as you can but stop before your knees block the view of your feet. Then slowly come back up to starting position. Do three to five slow sets of 10 to 15 repetitions and rest 5 to 20 seconds between sets (depending on how fast you become tired).

Why: Muscular endurance is important for many everyday tasks. In addition, exercises like these tone your body and make you look stronger and more fit.

The square

Objective: To improve cardiovascular endurance

Task: Travel around the square performing one of the movements written on the index card. You may choose between the three movements on the card each time you pass a new cone.

Why: Cardiovascular endurance is important for overall health and can help prevent cardiovascular disease, stress, high blood pressure, obesity, and certain forms of cancer. In addition, it helps your brain work better!

Setup instructions to the teacher: This station forms a square around several other stations. Use four cones to mark the square, which should be at least 100 feet on each side. Each cone has an index card displaying three different movement forms. The movements can include skipping, hopping, jumping, galloping, running, walking, sliding, and leaping. Movements can include additional directions such as backward, zigzag, fast, slow, and high, middle, and low levels.

Figure 13.2 (continued)

because physical education is not typically conducted in lecture format. Students expect activity in physical education, so you should use activity in some form, even if it's not physical activity. Group work, problem solving, discussions, and debates are good ways to get concepts across to students. In schools where a spirit of cooperation exists among the faculty, teachers often help each other with ideas to get students excited about topics and ready to participate in activities that stimulate the mind and develop social skills.

The teaching styles that focus on discovery learning are ideal for teaching concepts (chapter 8). Teachers often use convergent discovery if they have a concept with one correct answer, or "one truth," that they want students to discover in small groups, with a partner, or individually. If they want students to find multiple solutions to a problem, or discover several "truths," they may use divergent discovery. We have found that students respond well to problem solving in groups in physical education, perhaps

because they are comfortable with working in groups in our classes (figure 13.3).

An ideal divergent discovery activity for a concept day would be to have students create their own exercise programs. Obviously, each person could develop many possible solutions, so the best teaching style for this activity would be divergent discovery. The students can work alone, with a partner, or even in small groups for this project. This activity could take several class periods to complete, depending on how in-depth the teacher wants the students to go. Students could complete the program during the next concept day or days, or they could take it home and finish it as part of their homework.

You should set clear criteria for your students in an activity like this one. If students know exactly what you want them to produce, they are less likely to "finish" early and goof around. In addition, if students understand that the program is supposed to be authentic, one that you expect

Figure 13.3 Students enjoy working together to solve problems in physical education classes.

them to use, they will be more likely to make it realistic.

Many teachers strive to collaborate across disciplines. This activity would be an ideal one to integrate with subjects such as health, science, math, English, or even a word-processing or desktop-publishing class. A finished product with high-quality content is more useful if it is well organized and put together in a way that makes it easy to use during physical activity.

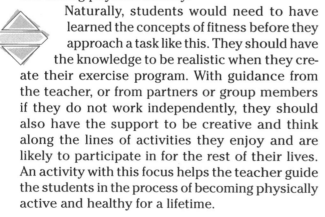 Naturally, students would need to have learned the concepts of fitness before they approach a task like this. They should have the knowledge to be realistic when they create their exercise program. With guidance from the teacher, or from partners or group members if they do not work independently, they should also have the support to be creative and think along the lines of activities they enjoy and are likely to participate in for the rest of their lives. An activity with this focus helps the teacher guide the students in the process of becoming physically active and healthy for a lifetime.

Dance Review

 Another activity for unforeseen-circumstance days is to review the dances that students have learned in earlier dance

units, even in previous years. Every middle and high school physical education program should include dance because many of the dance forms are activities that people can participate in and gain health benefits from throughout their lives. Dance, perhaps the most social form of exercise in today's society, can be an individual, partner, or group activity. Many adults, however, are reluctant to participate in dance because they feel they don't have the skills to avoid looking clumsy. By teaching students the basics of a variety of dance forms in middle school and then offering dance as a choice in high school, students are more likely to gain enough self-efficacy for dance to continue with it as they grow older.

In middle and high school programs, unforeseen-circumstance days can provide wonderful opportunities to review dance skills (figure 13.4). Having three or four classes in a gym at one time need not be a problem if the students participate in the same dances. For example, ballroom dances such as the swing, cha-cha, and salsa use different music, but with all students reviewing the same dance at the same time, you need only one stereo system. You can fit a large crowd into one gym for a dance lesson.

The important thing, again, is for teachers to plan. For example, at the high school level, students who are in the gym on a rainy day may be a

Figure 13.4   When weather forces class indoors, reviewing dance skills can be a worthwhile option for students.

mix of 9th, 10th, and 11th graders. These students will probably have learned different dances, and those who hadn't learned a particular dance before wouldn't be reviewing it. If the high school has an extensive elective program, some students may not have taken dance since middle school. In that case the high school teachers would need to check with the middle school teachers to decide what dances to review.

You can, of course, choose to teach new dances on these days. Folk dances, line dances, and ballroom dances can all be taught to large crowds in a relatively small space, although it may be difficult to see and hear the instructor, which makes it harder to learn. Proper planning, using all teachers effectively, using criteria sheets, and frequently rotating students' location in the gym can help immensely in a crowded dance environment.

Cardio Workouts and Aerobics

With so many different types of aerobics today, most students will probably find a type that they like. Low- and high-impact aerobic dance, step aerobics, cardio kick boxing, and funk are just some of the types currently taught at health clubs all over the world. Teachers of middle and high school physical education incorporate a variety of aerobics in their classes and programs, although they are not necessarily trained as aerobics instructors. The most important point in teaching these kinds of group exercises is always to put the students' safety first.

Many teachers use the help of aerobics professionals by using videotape and TV screens. This is a great way to incorporate aerobics into your program, especially on days when you use plan B. Using a TV instructor doesn't mean that the teacher should not teach. In fact, by using a videotape instructor, the teacher is available to help students in class by giving feedback, one-on-one instructions, and demonstrations (figure 13.5). The teacher can, and should, move around the room to help and encourage the students as well as to provide variations when needed if the instructor on the tape does not do this.

T'nT

Purpose

Make sure that fitness tapes used as alternative activities are reviewed for learning appropriateness as well as to alert you to the need for additional support.

Resource and Procedure

Make it a priority to review all preproduced fitness video tapes that you consider including in your physical education class. When reviewing, play the tape on the same VCR and in the same room that it will be played during class. This will enable you to determine whether the visuals and audio can be received from various spots in the room. In addition, preproduced fitness tapes often do not accommodate various fitness levels. If this is the case, you will need to actively provide variations. Remember that your goal is to have everyone succeed; a video that appears to be too advanced for certain students should be augmented with teacher-led examples and variations.

Create a Routine

A wonderful creative divergent discovery activity for unforeseen-circumstance days is having students create their own dance or aerobics routine. Students can work in groups of four to eight (depending on number of students and the size of the gym) to create a routine lasting one to two minutes. They practice the routine and prepare to show it to the rest of the class that day or during another class period (maybe on the next rainy day). An alternative to a live performance is videotape. Students could tape themselves and then show the videotape to the class later. The tape would also be available to show to parents, other teachers, and other students. Students tend to put more time and energy into a creation if they know that it will be shown publicly. Our experience is that the embarrassment factor is smaller when they work in groups and videotape themselves, as opposed to working alone and having the teacher do the videotaping.

The routine should consist of movements that the students already know, either from class or from another source. The teacher may require students to include certain movements (for example: one pivot turn, one jumping jack, one elbow to knee step, and one step touch). Requiring

Figure 13.5   Teachers should provide personal feedback to students when using a videotape in class.

the inclusion of certain steps often helps students get started, and they start feeling comfortable adding their personal touches to the creation. If students can choose their music, they may enjoy the activity even more. They can practice to other music as long as the beat is about the same.

Our experience with this task has shown that students of all ages, from elementary to college level, enjoy the creativity involved in this task. They also like showing off the finished result if they've had enough time to practice. We have also learned that some students feel more comfortable when we don't call it dance and if we allow them to use equipment for their creation. We've had groups create wonderful routines using basketballs, tennis rackets, hoops, boxing gloves, and jump ropes. Students who say they hate dance created many of these great routines. We believe it is helpful to have a variety of equipment available for students to use and to avoid calling the routine a dance. Figure 13.6 is an example for creating a routine.

Purpose

Have your students create and develop exercise programs for the purpose of producing a fitness guide that can be given to students' family members.

Resource and Procedure

An alternative physical education experience involves having your students create their own exercise programs for adults. The finished programs could be created in a word-processing document and produced in a variety of forms such as a printed guide, posted on your school's physical education Web site, or created in poster form and prominently displayed during a parent school night. The nice thing about the printed guides is that they can be bound, and students can present them to their parents or guardians as a holiday or birthday present. What a wonderful way to get parental support for your program!

Create a routine

Objective: You will create a one- to two-minute long movement routine to music. You will work cooperatively in groups and use steps and movements you learned in class and from other sources.

Task: Get in groups of four or five. Create a movement routine to music that lasts one to two minutes. You should include at least five of the movements listed below. You may include any other movements or steps, as long as you stay in the space provided (and as long as they are not disrespectful). You can also use one piece of equipment each, choosing from what is available: hoops, jump ropes, basketballs, tennis rackets, or hockey sticks. Be creative in the way that you use the equipment in your routine. You may also choose your own music from the selection next to the stereo. After you have created your routine, practice until you feel ready to be videotaped. When you are ready to videotape, go to an open videotape station and record your performance.

Your routine must include at least five of the following movements:

- Pivot turn
- Grapevine
- V-step
- Knee raise
- Knee twist
- Squat
- Front kick
- Side kick
- Shuffle
- Slide
- Jump shot

Note to teacher: You may want to assign groups and divide the equipment. The size of the groups depends on the available space and the total number of students in that space. You may also want to have the students perform live to the class or for the parents at a PE show.

Figure 13.6 Sample "create a routine" task sheet.

Assessment Days

Unforeseen-circumstance days are always good for conducting general assessments. If you really want to know if students learned a concept, assess them weeks or months after they supposedly learned it. As discussed in chapter 12, however, you should use this kind of surprise assessment to evaluate your program and overall teaching effectiveness rather than for grading purposes.

Authentic or alternative assessment tasks take a holistic approach and are excellent to use for program assessment. These kinds of tasks should be meaningful to the students. The tasks should represent real-life experiences by asking the students to create, produce, perform, devise, or design something. Authentic or alternative assessment tasks are perfect for group work because the purpose is not only to assess but also to have the students learn something in the process. You become a guide on the side, helping the students get the most out of the learning and assessment experience. Authentic assessment tasks require rubrics, which serve as a specific guide to what you expect from the students for the task and how you will evaluate them. Rubrics can be time consuming to write, but once you create a task and a rubric to go with it, you can easily make adjustments later to improve both the task and the rubric (for examples of authentic and alternative assessment tasks, see chapter 12).

An alternative/authentic assessment task can take several class periods to complete, so you can either have the students finish it as part of their homework or continue the task on the next unforseen-circumstance day. Depending on the specific task you devise, an alternative/authentic assessment can be a meaningful learning experience when you deal with large crowds in a small space. These kinds of tasks are best when they are as close to real life as possible, so public display, presentation, or performance of the work can help make them seem more authentic. Two of the earlier examples, "Create a routine" and "Create your own exercise program," could include a public display or presentation. If the students perform their routine to the class, to another crowd, or on videotape to be shown later, "Create a routine" could be an authentic experience. The "Create your own exercise program" activity could involve a public display at a parent-teacher-student night at the school to show what the students have learned in physical education. A variation of that task would be to have students write programs for their parents, siblings, a teacher, or a friend and present the program to that audience.

Diane, Fran, and Troy brainstormed with the rest of their colleagues to develop more ideas for lesson plans that they could use on rainy days. The exciting aspect of this was that they were talking about all kinds of issues related to their curriculum. They agreed to start with a rotation of fitness stations and to modify their plans as needed. Fran was keyed up! For once, the push had not come from her. Diane rose to the occasion and called the professor who had brought his class that rainy day years ago. She was able to get a copy of the fitness stations they had used. The professor even offered to have some of his students develop laminated fitness station posters. They were off to a good start. Now they just had to persuade the students to understand and accept the change. Fran didn't think this would be too hard, as long as they kept the new lessons purposeful and fun. "Why don't we have our students help us gather fun and appropriate music for our fitness days?" she suggested to her colleagues. "What is appropriate?" asked Troy. Fran smiled. The momentum was building. They were talking about major changes here, and she knew this was just the start.

Summary

Teachers are responsible for *teaching* their students, not only when the lessons go as planned but also when the unexpected happens. Being bumped out of your teaching space because of inclement weather, school assemblies, or band practice should not be an excuse to roll out the ball just to keep students busy until the bell rings. Modifying your existing lesson plan would be best, but when that's impossible you can use some of the ideas in this chapter to help you plan for the unexpected. These ideas include concept days, fitness days, creating routines, reviewing dances, and assessment days. With a plan in place for unforeseen circumstances, a teacher will always be prepared, and students will always have an opportunity to learn and develop into physically educated people.

Checking for Understanding ▶▶▶

- ◆ What are some of the unforeseen circumstances that could interfere with your regularly scheduled lesson plans in physical education?

- ◆ Why should teachers have a plan B ready for the days when unforeseen circumstances interfere with their scheduled lesson plan?

- ◆ What are two ways you can be better prepared when you must use plan B?

- ◆ Can you list and describe at least five different ideas for plan B lessons?

For Reflection and Discussion ▶▶▶

- ◆ What other learning activities could you use when unforeseen circumstances force you to share space or send you into the hallways to teach?

- ◆ How do you think parents, administrators, and other colleagues view physical education teachers when they let their students sit around or play games like knockout?

- ◆ How can physical education teachers make sure that administrators and other teachers treat their subject matter as important when it comes to planning for use of the school's facilities?

- ◆ How will you avoid falling into the trap of treating unforeseen circumstances as excuses not to teach?

Suggested Readings

MASSPEC. 1998. *Appropriate practices for high school physical education.* Reston, VA: NASPE.

MASSPEC. 1995. *Appropriate practices for middle school physical education.* Reston, VA: NASPE.

NASPE. 1995. *Moving into the future: National standards for physical education.* St. Louis: Mosby.

U.S. Department of Health and Human Services. 1996. *Physical activity and health: A report of the surgeon general.* Atlanta: U.S. Department of Health and Human Services, Centers for Disease Control and Prevention, National Center for Chronic Disease Prevention and Health Promotion.

U.S. Department of Health and Human Services. 1997. *Promoting lifelong physical activity: At-a-glance.* CDC Guidelines for Schools and Community Programs. Atlanta: U.S. Department of Health and Human Services, Centers for Disease Control and Prevention, National Center for Chronic Disease Prevention and Health Promotion.

Part V

The Setting

14

Challenges and Roles of the Teacher-Coach

> Happiness and misery are both found in teaching physical education. The determining balance is struck day by day, year by year, within that tight little society called the school, and that noisy microcosm called the gymnasium.
>
> — *Larry Locke,* The Ecology of the Gymnasium: What the Tourists Never See *(1974)*

One evening in late July, Frank was grocery shopping with his family. With every turn of an aisle, it seemed that someone recognized him and asked how the team was doing. Frank was gracious as he explained that it would be a rebuilding year because he had lost eight players to graduation the previous spring. His admirers chuckled and told Frank they were not worried because he had built state champions on several occasions. Frank smiled and rejoined his wife and son.

Frank has been the head football coach at Central High School for the past 10 years. In that time he has taken four teams to the state championship, where they won first place three times and second once. He knows this year will be tougher because he will be working to replace eight excellent seniors. He also knows that solid younger players are moving up the ranks. It should be another good season.

Frank has known and loved the game of football all his life. He decided in junior high school that he would become a physical education teacher and football coach so that he could stay involved with the game. He has been teaching and coaching for 15 years. He is proud of the fact that he was able to move up to head coach in only 5 years.

When preseason starts in August, Frank lives and breathes football until December. Each day requires him to review game films, examine stats, meet with his staff, plan practice, and conduct practice. He spends 30 to 40 hours a week coaching football. Add that to his daily teaching schedule, and he works an average of 67 to 77 hours a week during the fall. He is happy that his wife understands the need for this large time commitment; he only hopes his son does too.

Frank loves his job but sometimes feels badly for the students in his physical education classes. He knows he doesn't put the same amount of energy into his teaching as he does his coaching. During football season he basically walks into each class and wings it. He figures as long as he keeps the kids busy and involved in games (Bu-Ha-Goo), he is doing OK. But, as we said, on occasion he feels badly.

◆ Learning Objectives

After reading this chapter you will

- ◆ examine your biography,
- ◆ determine the attractors and facilitators that influenced your decision to become a physical education teacher,
- ◆ define role conflict and role strain,
- ◆ explain teacher-coach role conflict and strategies for coping,
- ◆ describe the spectrum of workplace conditions that exist in schools,
- ◆ list other roles a physical education teacher may take on at work, and
- ◆ explain moonlighting and the need for it.

◆ Key Terms and Phrases

Teacher socialization
Apprenticeship of observation
Attractors
Facilitators
Marginalized
Teacher-coach role conflict
Role strain
Moonlighting

Many physical educators teach and coach in the way that Frank does. Many prospective physical educators enter teacher preparation programs with the desire to continue their affiliation with sports and become high school coaches and physical education teachers. When these prospective teachers hit the job market, they find that many school administrators seem more interested in what they can coach rather than what they can teach. There seems to be a cultural assumption that if you teach physical education, you are more interested in coaching. Think about it. When others ask you about what you do and you say that you're studying physical education, they tend to smile and ask, "What do you coach?" You hear many physical educators referred to as "Coach" by students, colleagues, parents, and staff, whether they coach sport teams or not. This cultural assumption creates a context in which physical educators feel torn between the responsibilities of coaching and teaching. We will examine the issue in this chapter. We will begin with a historical overview of physical education to explain how athletics became so closely tied to physical education. Then we will take a critical look at teacher socialization and the multiple roles and challenges of the teacher-coach.

Historical Overview of Physical Education and Athletics

In the late 1800s the purpose of school physical education programs was to improve the health of students through lessons of hygiene and physiology (Figone 1994a). High school sport teams were not part of the school curriculum. Teams were organized after school and coached mostly by students. As the popularity of sport increased, the pattern of organization in public schools changed. By the early 1900s more school boards and administrators accepted school sport programs and turned the responsibility over to the physical education departments (Sage 1989).

The role of physical educator grew to include the role of coach between 1906 and 1939. According to Lewis (1969) as quoted by Figone (1994a), the role of physical educator and coach evolved from 1906 to 1916 during a movement called "athletics are educational." As the popularity of sport grew, health and fitness goals and curricula began to take a backseat. The dual roles of physical educator and coach were consummated from 1917 to 1939 during the age of "sports for all." The philosophy of physical education shifted. Curriculum was now sports-based and included intramural and varsity athletics. Health and fitness goals that were once the centerpiece of physical education programs were demoted to secondary positions.

Control of interscholastic athletics was turned over to schools to monitor rules and control abuses of high school sports (Figone 1994a). As the organization of school athletics grew, physical education departments became known as physical education and athletics departments. With the merger of the two, physical education department heads also served as athletic directors.

The marriage of physical education and athletics changed teacher preparation programs at four-year institutions. Teachers-to-be were taught to be teachers and coaches. Sound familiar? Principals and superintendents hired physical educators who could coach and run the athletic program. The practice is still prevalent today.

Physical education and athletics may have merged in context and perception, but their purposes are different. In athletics, the purpose of competition is to gain respect. When a team performs well and wins, all involved acquire respect. The players earn respect; the coaches earn respect; the school and community earn respect (Figone 1994a). "American high school athletics is unlike any others in the world. There is a great deal of public interest in the teams, large crowds attend some contests, and community spirit and reputation often are linked to teams' performances" (Sage 1987, 252). This remains true today as we witness continued community involvement in high school athletics (figure 14.1).

Figure 14.1   Communities across America pack venues to watch their local high school teams play sports.

Your Turn ▶▶▶

♦ Take a moment to remember your hometown. Describe the importance of high school athletics to the school community and the local community. Recall the physical educators whom you had in high school. Were they coaches? If yes, what sports did they coach?

♦ Review local newspapers and news media for an entire week or month. Pay particular attention to the coverage of high school sports. What did you discover? Do all sports receive equal coverage? Why or why not? Do boys' and girls' sports receive equal coverage? Why or why not?

Respect may be a social skill practiced and developed in physical education classes, but it does not represent the purpose of physical education. The purpose of physical education is to help students improve sport skills, expand social skills, and find benefit and enjoyment in physical activity so that they will continue to participate in physical activity for a lifetime. Improvement in these areas increases a student's self-esteem, but it doesn't earn respect from an entire community. Physical education is not perceived as a subject of importance among administrators, teachers, students, or parents (Stroot, Collier, O'Sullivan, and England 1994). It is easy to see why coaches hired as full-time teachers in physical education or other subjects feel stress about their roles and how they spend their professional time.

Teacher Socialization

To understand better the dual role of a physical educator-coach and the role conflict that may exist, we must examine three aspects of **teacher socialization**: teacher recruitment into physical education, attitudes about physical education, and physical educators' world of work. Teacher socialization is the process by which individuals acquire the knowledge, values, beliefs, attitudes, and skills that are essential to teaching physical education. When reading the following paragraphs, reflect on how your experiences and beliefs parallel or differ from the findings in teacher socialization research. In other words, examine your socialization into teaching and coaching using Buschner's (2001) *Physical Educator's Biography Survey* (figure 14.2).

Your Turn ▶▶▶

◆ What does your biography tell you?

◆ How has your biography influenced your beliefs about teaching and coaching?

Teacher Recruitment

Remember back when you were in high school? At times you probably watched your teachers and thought to yourself, *How hard could teaching be? I could do that with my eyes closed. Heck, I've watched teachers do their work since preschool.* In some ways you are right. You have engaged in a process called **apprenticeship of observation** (Lortie 1975). It means that for many years you have watched and learned about how teachers do their work. Review the biography survey you just filled out and read about your sports background. Look at the number of years that you have been involved in organized sport and activity; this experience adds to your apprenticeship of observation. By watching and learning over the years, you formed beliefs, values, and ideas about teaching that helped to attract you to a career of teaching physical education (Hutchinson 1993).

Attractors are perceptions, thoughts, and beliefs that people find appealing about teaching. Back in 1975 Lortie conducted a large study with teachers and found that people were attracted to teaching for five reasons:

1. Interpersonal—a desire to work with young people
2. Service—an opportunity to contribute to society by working with youth
3. Continuation—a need to remain in the school environment
4. Time compatibility—attractive work schedule, that is, summers off
5. Material benefits—steady job and benefits

Research on teacher socialization in physical education determined that many prospective physical educators were active sport participants and athletes and wished to continue their involvement in sports (Dodds et al. 1992; Doolittle, Dodds, and Placek 1993; Hutchinson 1993; Stroot et al. 1994). This attractor would fall under Lortie's (1975) continuation theme. Prospective physical education teachers who wished to teach at the secondary level expressed the desire to coach one or more sports. According to the information on your survey, what is your career goal? What attracted you to a career of teaching physical education and coaching sports?

Facilitators are the significant people in your life who influenced your perceptions and decisions to become a physical education teacher and

Personal Information

Date: _____   Name: _____

Age: _____   M _____ F _____   Frosh _____ Soph _____ JR _____ Grad _____

Parent(s)/Guardian(s) occupation

Parent/Guardian: _____   Occupation: _____

Parent/Guardian: _____   Occupation: _____

Sports Background

1. List the interscholastic sports (JV and Varsity) that you played in high school.

2. List any club or intramural sports that you played in high school.

3. List any intercollegiate sports (junior college and/or university) that you have played.

4. List any club or intramural sports (junior college and/or university) that you have played.

5. List any community recreational sports/leagues that you have played in in the past five years.

6. List key nonschool participation in the past five years. For example: road races, bike races, time trials, triathlons, dance performances, golf/tennis tournaments, bodybuilding or martial arts competitions.

7. List roles in which you have been involved in sport/physical activity other than as a participant. For example, officiating, coaching, scorer, timer, equipment manager, team manager, athletic trainer.

8. List any leisure activities that you have participated in with friends/family that were *not* part of a formal program. For example: pickup games, shooting hoops, aerobics classes, lifting weights, jogging, walking, playing tennis on weekends.

9. Have you worked with disabled youth and/or adults? If so, please discuss the activities and types of disabilities.

10. Do you have disabilities or deficiencies that may challenge or limit you from performing and teaching in physical education? If so, please discuss.

11. Looking back at your school years, what would you say was the main purpose of the physical education program in . . .

    Elementary school:

    Middle school:

    High school:

(continued)

Figure 14.2 Physical educator's biography survey.

Career Choice

12. At this time, what level of teaching physical education interests you the most? Please rank your top three choices as 1, 2, and 3.

_____ Teach elementary physical education

_____ Teach middle school/junior high school physical education

_____ Teach high school physical education

_____ Coach middle school/junior high sports

_____ Coach high school sports

_____ Teach adapted physical education

_____ Other: _____

13. What attracted you to a career in physical education and why?

14. Who served as mentor(s) to you and the main person(s) by whom you became interested in physical education?

Reprinted from C. Buschner, *Physical educator's biography survey.*

Figure 14.2   *(continued)*

coach. Significant people may include fathers, mothers, siblings, peers, physical education teachers, and coaches (Dodds et al. 1992; Hutchinson 1993; Pooley 1972; Steen 1985). Who are the facilitators in your life and how did they influence your decision to pursue a career in physical education and coaching?

Frank played football all through his youth. He began with a Pop Warner league and played all the way through college, finishing his playing days as a cornerback for a Division II school. Frank loved his high school coach, who not only taught him and his teammates a lot about football but also modeled and valued virtues like integrity, honesty, respect, and fair play. Frank wanted to be like his coach (facilitator), who also taught physical education, and he wanted to continue his association and love for football (attractor). It made perfect sense that Frank became a physical educator and coach.

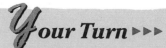

Your Turn ▶▶▶

Using the information from Buschner's (2001) *Physical Educator's Biography Survey,* write a two-page biography of your experience and the attractors and facilitators that were influential in your decision to pursue a career in physical education. Share this biography with classmates and note similarities and differences. What meaning do you make of your findings?

Attitudes About Physical Education

Studies have been conducted on student attitudes about physical education (Silverman and Subramaniam 1999). These attitudes affect how we, as physical educators, perceive our work. Speaking from personal experience, we have heard students, parents, teachers, and administrators tell us for years that they believe physical education is important. They believe it should help students become more fit, learn and develop a repertoire of sport skills, and learn social skills like cooperation and teamwork. In the same breath, students, parents, teachers, and administrators have told us that physical education is not as important as more academic subjects like English, math, and science. In the ranking of subject matter, physical education often appears at the lower end of the spectrum.

A number of contextual behaviors demonstrate that most people do believe physical education to be an important subject. For instance, it is common for events like taking school pictures, disseminating yearbooks, and health screening to be conducted during physical education classes. School assemblies are often scheduled in the gym during physical education classes, sometimes without warning (see chapter 13). These kinds of contextual behaviors send messages to the school community that physical education is not an important subject. If this occurs in your school, you may consider working with your principal for alternative times and places to schedule special events.

Purpose

Use technology to create a handout that communicates the differences between your expectations for achievement as a teacher and as a coach.

Resource and Procedure

If the public seems to be confused on coaching and teaching roles, it may be useful for you to brainstorm and develop a list highlighting the differences in focus, participation, expectations, and behavior between the two roles. It may be an eye-opening exercise for you and help reinforce your teaching and coaching philosophy. You can have a completed list professionally designed in a word-processing document, print it, and copy it as handouts and include it in your orientation package that students take home to their parents. The list could also be reproduced as a poster and displayed outside your office door.

Let us return to student and parent attitudes about physical education. A study by Tannehill et al. (1994) reported that student attitudes about physical education were not overly supportive. Physical education did not rank high among school subject areas. The researchers further explained that student attitudes toward physical education influence their willingness to participate fully in classes. They suggested that creating an environment that fosters respect and fairness where students feel as if they have a voice and choice will develop more positive attitudes toward physical education. Better attitudes may improve student participation in class. Better attitudes may also improve student participation in physical activity.

Tannehill et al. (1994) found that parents viewed the main purpose of school as academic with a focus on intellectual development. Therefore, they did not view physical education classes as critical to their child's success. Some parents recall hating "gym" because of negative experiences. Others simply believe that physical education is nothing more than recess (Stroot et al. 1994, 356) or supervised game play (figure 14.3).

> *Parents think PE is an easy A. I'll get phone calls from parents who say: "How can my son be doing poorly? He is there and he dresses out." They don't think physical education is important. To them, it's just like it was when they went to school, a glorified recreational period where students have fun and get an A."*
> —Linda Allen, Physical Educator, Chico High School

Parents did believe, however, in the importance of physical fitness, and they thought that health and fitness should be a primary purpose of physical education classes.

Figure 14.3 Physical education programs need to make parents aware that classes are more than just glorified recess.

F rank noted that parents and students never asked him about his physical education classes. He smiled when he imagined a world where parents in the grocery store would ask him about his football team and then ask genuine questions about the quality of the physical education program. But Frank was troubled because he realized that the physical education program had the potential to have a positive effect on the health and well-being of every student at Central High, whereas the varsity football team included just 32 student-athletes.

Workplace Conditions

Your beliefs and ideas coupled with people's attitudes about physical education and workplace conditions affect how you make sense of your work as a physical education teacher and coach. Workplace conditions include all aspects of work that influence job performance.

People often mention facilities and equipment as part of workplace conditions. Physical educators find that facilities range from poor to excellent depending on the school. Over the years, we've met physical educators who work in an urban setting with facilities that include only a small gym and a hard-top area. At the other end of the spectrum,

we've met physical educators who work in a suburban setting with abundant field space, two gymnasiums, a pool, and a weight room. The amount and quality of equipment varies as well. Some schools have high-quality equipment for every student in class, whereas others possess a limited quantity of well-worn equipment. Class size, weather, and school events require physical educators to improvise teaching stations and equipment needs more often than other teachers in the school do (Fejgin, Ephraty, and Ben-Sira 1995, 66) (see chapter 13).

Limited equipment, inadequate facilities, students who want to be doing something else, and lack of support from students, parents, teachers, and administrators create working conditions in which physical educators feel **marginalized,** on the fringe of school curricula (Stroot et al. 1994). Marginalization can lead to social isolation of physical educators because principals, teachers, counselors, and others do not feel it necessary to involve physical education teachers in decisions concerning students and school organization (Fejgin et al. 1995, 66). We see this when physical educators are not invited to participate on student IEP committees (see chapter 6). We also see this with academic teaming, a concept in which students are scheduled for physical education during a certain period so that English, math, science, and social studies teachers can meet to plan an integrated program. Further research regarding quality of work life of physical educators (Stroot et al. 1994, 360) found that physical educators

- received little respect from other adults,
- had few professional interactions with members of their school,
- did not always have an opportunity to exercise their knowledge and abilities about physical activities because the multiactivity model (chapter 10) rarely allowed them to teach anything other than beginning levels of skills,
- exercised important decisions only in their classrooms because colleagues often held differing philosophical views, and
- received little recognition, respect, or support for their role as physical educators.

Workplace conditions are far from ideal. Physical educators who are aware of the realities of workplace conditions and student attitudes are better prepared to make a difference. Consideration of these realities helps us understand why physical educators experience role conflict and often decide to spend more energy in coaching their sport teams.

Teacher-Coach Role Conflict

The **teacher-coach role conflict** is defined as "the experience of role stress and role strain due to the conflicting multiple demands of teaching and coaching" (Sage 1989, 217–218). Figone (1994a) defines **role strain** as "subjective feelings of frustration, tension or anxiety that are associated with low quality work, low job satisfaction, absenteeism, and quitting." In the case of the physical educator and coach, he or she will either fall short of the job expectations for both positions or spend more time with one, usually the one that carries more external rewards, coaching.

Multiple Role Demands of the Teacher

Much of the teacher-coach role conflict boils down to the issue of time. Teachers' schedules often include five or six classes each day with one "prep," or free, period. Their days typically begin 20 minutes before the first bell. For many secondary physical educators the beginning of school may be around 7:30 A.M. Lunch may range from 20 to 60 minutes. The final bell of the day rings about seven hours after the first one, so many physical educators complete their class responsibilities by 3:00 P.M.

If we estimate average class size as 32, physical educators will see and work with 160 to 192 students per day. Unfortunately, the reality at many schools is that an average class size will exceed 40. Class periods range from 45 to 55 minutes in length. Class rotation is often rapid, with only 5 to 7 minutes between periods.

Teaching is more than simply handling a class schedule. As you know, teaching responsibilities include determining student needs, planning lessons, supervising locker rooms and locks, taking attendance, implementing lessons, giving feedback to students, reflecting on lesson implementation, assessing student achievement, managing equipment, and dealing with behavior issues.

Many physical educators have administrative duties too. Those responsibilities require time. For example, the physical education department at one middle school in our county is responsible for moving traffic through the parking lot when students are dropped off in the morning and picked up in the afternoon. Some physical educators monitor the locker room during lunch period or supervise other areas on campus during lunch. Of course, someone must perform administrative

tasks. Principals and teachers often work a rotating schedule so that individuals are not stuck with one administrative task for the entire year. In other places, physical educators consistently receive administrative duties because they are perceived as effective disciplinarians.

Physical educators must also serve on committees and attend meetings. You remember from chapter 6 that physical educators serve on IEP committees to assist students with special needs. They also serve on a number of other committees. Committee work and meetings require time. Typically, meetings take place after school, making attendance nearly impossible for physical educators who are coaching after-school sport teams. Therefore, teacher-coaches may be unable to serve on committees effectively.

Interrole Conflict

The physical educator's day is packed (figure 14.4). After a fast-paced school day, the teacher-coach

Figure 14.4 The roles of a physical education teacher/coach are numerous and can require many extra hours to get tasks done.

trades class rosters for team rosters and heads out for two to four hours of team practice. Responsibilities of coaching can be just as demanding as those of teaching. In many cases teacher-coaches find their coaching responsibilities more demanding because of pressure from the school and community to develop successful teams. Frank is in that situation because he heads up a highly successful football program.

Coaches are responsible for student-athletes, coaching staffs, planning and conducting practices, viewing game tapes, repairing and ordering equipment, ordering uniforms, writing recommendations for student-athletes, and more. In situations where there is not an athletic director, coaches schedule games, meets, and matches and perform related tasks like arranging transportation and hiring officials.

Individuals in roles as teachers and coaches experience pressure to meet the demands of both positions (figure 14.5). Role strain often occurs. Physical educators experiencing role strain will feel either that they don't meet the expectations of either position or that they spend more time in one than the other. Two coaches remark to each point (Sage 1989):

> *"It's just like having two jobs instead of one to put in the same time period. . . . I always feel like I just don't have time to do what I really want to do in either [teaching or coaching]."*

> *"The biggest conflict that I have . . . is the time. . . . If I'm honest with myself, it's the classroom that gets shortchanged more than the coaching and that is I may not come prepared on a certain day, as prepared as I would if I didn't have the coaching responsibilities."*

Other Roles

Many physical educators coach sport teams and thus confront the teacher-coach role conflict. Many school administrators and teachers expect physical educators to coach. Therefore, it is common for physical educators to be hired for teaching with an expectation that they will coach some of the school's largest and most popular sport teams such as football, field hockey, basketball, volleyball, softball, and baseball. Teaching and coaching may be the most discussed role conflict, but it is not the only one.

Multiple preparations may contribute to the sense of overload, role conflict, and role strain. Multiple preparations may occur in several ways. As a physical educator you may have several different kinds of classes to teach each day. For instance, your schedule may include two ninth grade classes, two sophomore classes, one junior class, and one senior class, totaling six class periods. The two ninth grade classes may be scheduled for cooperative games, the sophomore classes may

Figure 14.5 PE teachers who also coach often experience role conflict, and their students may struggle to make sense of the dual roles as well.

be engaged in biomechanics, the junior class may have fitness, and the seniors may be learning in-line skating. You have four content areas to prepare, an undertaking that will take some planning on your part.

Multiple preparations may also include preparation in other subject areas. Many physical educators teach several sections of physical education and several sections of another subject. For example, you may find yourself with four sections of physical education and two or three sections of math. Each class requires careful planning. Planning for different content areas may overburden your schedule and create feelings of frustration. Careful time management is essential.

As we mentioned in previous paragraphs, physical educators will be asked to assume a number of administrative duties such as parking lot duty, lunch duty, and study hall supervision (see figure 14.6 for a more detailed list).

Teachers may perform other tasks as well. A number of school committees are central to school programs and curricula. Teachers are often ex-

pected to serve, representing themselves and their departments. Physical educators who coach have difficulty finding time to serve on committees. Some teacher-coaches serve anyway, adding to their sense of work overload and further squeezing their time. Other physical educators may not coach at all, but they serve on a number of school committees. A few examples of school committees are the following:

- Curriculum
- Site council
- IEPs
- Facilities management
- Yearbook
- Development (fund-raising and grant writing)
- Professional development

Many schools are now using academic teaming, in which teachers from several subject areas form a team and plan integrated units. The purpose of integrated curriculum is to help students learn and

---

Locker-room supervision

Parking lot supervision

Lunch duty

Study hall supervision

Equipment maintenence

Equipment ordering

Emergency supervisor

Assembly supervision

Present at Open House and Back to School nights

Special events supervision like dances, proms, field trips

Sporting event assistant
- running the 30-second clock
- timing
- announcing athletic contests
- scoring
- chain gang in football
- statisticians

Coordinate and maintain soda machines in the locker rooms

Attend special events like games

Conduct parent–student conferences

Write grants

Present at administrative and committee meetings

Monitor special education students and file reports

Join committees and attend meetings
- school site council
- instructional council
- academic teams
- parent club
- booster club
- grants committee
- healthy kids committee
- sunshine committee
- union representatives
- peer assistant review committee
- master teacher (mentor)
- beginning teacher supervision and assessment

Figure 14.6 List of teacher administrative duties.

understand the interconnections of all subject matter (Barth and Mitchell 1992; Placek and O'Sullivan 1997). The method recognizes that the world is not made up of compartments that separate reading, writing, math, history, geography, science, art, music, and physical education. All subject matter is connected. When we take time to help students understand these connections, they find more meaning in what they learn and more application of what they learn to their lives. Over the past two decades much of the integrated curriculum effort has centered on the core courses: math, language arts, science, and social studies (Placek and O'Sullivan 1997).

Purpose

Use technology to enrich a physical education experience by incorporating other subject matter such as geography, history, and math.

Resource and Procedure

Have students use pedometers to keep track of the miles the entire physical education class accumulates through working out during class. Explore possibilities of teaming with a geography teacher who may be interested in using the same information to chart a geographic trip that each week can correspond with the amount of miles. (For longer trips you can make 1 mile equal 100 miles.) Students can keep track of their progress in geography class and report on points of interest on the trip. Advancing toward your goal can be a significant motivating factor for your students. A final destination theme party can be planned for the day you reach your destination (maybe a lawn party at the gates of the White House). Be creative and aware of other interdisciplinary possibilities for your classes.

The physical educators with whom we work report that teachers on academic teams are typically rewarded with smaller class sizes and a shared preparation period with their team members. Because class size reduction means that students must be relocated somewhere, they are often scheduled into physical education classes. Shared preparation periods for several teachers mean that students must be placed somewhere.

Our teachers report that they are placed in an extra section of physical education. For our physical educators, academic teaming has meant larger class sizes in physical education. Does this mean that the idea of integrated curriculum is not a good one for physical education? Certainly not.

Physical educators can contribute significantly to integrated curricula. More physical educators are approaching their principals and curriculum committees and presenting sound arguments about why physical education should be an integral member of all academic teams. Placek and O'Sullivan (1997) point out that physical educators have written extensively about how physical education can help students learn subject matter like math, reading, writing, science, history, geography, and social studies. We need to continue this effort and work harder at truly integrating across disciplines. Placek and O'Sullivan (1997) also point out that physical educators have written little about how we can integrate physical education content into other subject matter. The challenge today for physical educators is to demonstrate how we can integrate physical education content into other subject areas and vice versa. We must realize our potential and become involved in integrated curriculum. Are you ready for this challenge?

Your Turn ▶▶▶

Examine area physical education programs. Determine if these programs are involved with integrated curriculum or interdisciplinary curriculum. If they are, describe how the physical education teachers work with other teachers to integrate diverse subject content.

Moonlighting

Believe it or not, some physical educators work other jobs to supplement their income. Some do so to make ends meet and continue to live to a certain standard. Others take on additional employment as a means to grow and learn, and they enjoy it. Working at a job outside the primary place of employment is called **moonlighting.**

Teachers, including physical educators, have been moonlighting for years. A teacher may moonlight by holding additional employment outside the school district during the school year or by working during holidays and school vacations, such as spring break and summer vacation (Williams 1993).

In an interview study with secondary physical educators conducted by Williams (1993), two themes that relate to other roles emerged from participant data about moonlighting. The researcher identified these as life-cycle squeeze and pushed out of teaching. Life-cycle squeeze refers to the financial squeeze that occurs during one's lifetime. The financial squeeze may include things such as buying a house, having a baby, supporting kids in college, buying a new car, and unexpected medical bills. When financial resources run low, individuals often seek additional employment. Although additional employment rarely brings in a great deal of money, it increases the disposable income available to pay bills.

Williams described the second theme, pushed out of teaching, as teachers seeking other jobs to distance themselves from the negative aspects of teaching. The negative aspects of teaching may lead physical educators to find teaching unsatisfying and somewhat of a dead-end profession. Consequently, these individuals seek extra jobs and compensation outside of teaching (Williams 1993, 69). For some physical educators, coping with the marginalization of physical education in the school curricula is difficult. It is difficult to remain positive when it feels like the rest of the school doesn't take you seriously.

I always live with the stigma, that "What are you?" "A teacher." "What do you teach?" "Physical education." The stigma, that you can't do anything else. So I had to prove to myself that there's other things out there that I can do besides teach and coach and work with kids. . . . I had to prove to myself that there are other things out there [I could do]. (Williams, 1993, 69)

Your Turn ▶▶▶

- How will you prepare for the negative attitudes that exist about physical education?
- How will you combat the urge to seek other employment?
- Interview secondary physical educators about moonlighting and ask about their reasons for doing it or not doing it.

To this point, we have defined other roles to mean other school roles and responsibilities or employment outside the school district. We haven't discussed physical educators' personal lives. At this point, you may be wondering, "What personal life?" Good question. All of us have lives outside school. For good health and well-being, we must strive to find a balance between work and private life. Most of us have several personal roles outside work, such as spouse, significant other, mother, father, brother, sister, aunt, uncle, friend, and others. These roles demand quality time. You will find yourself negotiating time with significant people in your life as you try to make your relationships with partner, family, and friends successful.

Strategies for Coping With Multiple Roles

Chances are good that you will take on roles other than teaching physical education while you work at the secondary level. If you find that you feel stressed, frustrated, or anxious because you cannot carry out all your job responsibilities, you may be suffering role strain. Role strain may cause you to commit to some responsibilities, like coaching, and withdraw from other responsibilities, like teaching, to manage time better. When you have to choose where to commit your time, some aspect of your job will suffer. If you suffer from role strain, we recommend the following:

- State the primary reason that you were hired for the job.
- List the multiple roles and responsibilities you have, including roles outside school (that is, family and moonlighting).
- State reasons for your involvement in each role. Answer these questions: Do you have to be involved in a role? Do you want to be involved in a role? Are you hired to perform a role?
- Determine roles that you can eliminate from your list.
- Identify responsibilities from roles that you can delegate to others or drop because they are not essential.
- Review your weekly schedule, decide how much time you are willing to spend in each role, and commit to that.
- Be prepared to drop some roles and responsibilities that are not essential to your work or personal life.

Summary

Being overloaded with responsibilities and having limited time can lead to role strain. In this circumstance, physical educators will make choices about how to spend their time. Many teacher-coaches choose to pursue coaching and let their teaching slide (Chu 1981). Some coaches decide to commit to coaching and withdraw from teaching so that they can continue their role as coaches. They may have to make this choice because they are rehired for their coaching positions based on their win-loss records. Many more coaches choose to commit their time to coaching because of their love for a certain sport and their desire to continue their participation with it. They simply choose to spend their time coaching. They find the rewards and recognition greater in coaching than in teaching. As one teacher-coach put it, "No one around here knows or cares what I do in the classroom, but the community, administration, and students are behind my teams" (Sage 1989, 264).

Regardless of whether role strain comes from teaching and coaching, teaching and committees, teaching and moonlighting, or teaching and personal life, people make choices about where to commit their time based on where they feel they can be most effective and appreciated for what they do. While teaching, look critically at all the roles you choose to take on. Where will you choose to spend your time?

Checking for Understanding ▶▶▶

- ◆ What was the purpose of school physical education in the 1800s?
- ◆ What was the "athletics is educational" movement of the early 1900s? How did it influence school physical education?
- ◆ Define teacher socialization.
- ◆ What is apprenticeship of observation? How did it affect you?
- ◆ What are attractors and facilitators in teacher socialization?
- ◆ Describe why physical educators may feel marginalized in the school setting.
- ◆ Define teacher-coach role conflict.
- ◆ What is moonlighting and why do some physical educators do it?

For Reflection and Discussion ▶▶▶

- ◆ Think of a time when you experienced a sense of role conflict. Discuss why you felt conflict and how you resolved it.
- ◆ How do the purposes of athletics and physical education differ? What effect do these purposes have on each program, respectively?
- ◆ Interview several physical educators and find out about the multiple roles they hold as teachers and how they cope with them.
- ◆ Visit one or two secondary schools and describe the workplace conditions for physical educators.

References

Barth, P., and R. Mitchell. 1992. *Smart start: Elementary education for the 21st century.* Golden, CO: North American Press.

Buschner, C. 2001. *Physical educator's biography survey.* Unpublished manuscript. Chico, CA: CSU, Chico.

Chu, D. 1981. Origins of teacher/coach role conflict: A reaction to Massengale's paper. In *Sociology of sport: Diverse perspectives,* ed. S. Greendorfer and A. Yiannakis, 158–163. Westpoint, NY: Leisure Press.

Dodds, P., J. Placek, S. Doolittle, K. Pinkham, T. Ratliffe, and P. Portman. 1992. Teacher/coach recruits: Background profiles, occupational decision factors, and comparisons with recruits into other physical education occupations. *Journal of Teaching in Physical Education* 11:161–176.

Doolittle, S., P. Dodds, and J.H. Placek. 1993. Persistences of beliefs about teaching during formal training of preservice teachers. In *Socialization in physical education* (monograph), ed. S. Stroot. *Journal of Teaching in Physical Education* 12:355–365.

Fejgin, N., N. Ephraty, and D. Ben-Sira. 1995. Work environment and burnout of physical education teachers. *Journal of Teaching in Physical Education* 15(1):64–77.

Figone, A.J. 1994a. Teacher-coach role conflict: Its impact on students and student-athletes. *Physical Educator* 51(1):29–35.

Hutchinson, G.E. 1993. Prospective teachers perspectives on teaching physical education: An interview study on the recruitment phase of teacher socialization. *Journal of Teaching in Physical Education* 12(4):344–354.

Lortie, D. 1975. *Schoolteacher.* Chicago: University of Chicago Press.

Placek, J., and M. O'Sullivan. 1997. The many faces of integrated physical education. *Journal of Physical Education, Recreation and Dance* 68(1):20–24.

Pooley, J.C. 1972. Professional socialization: A model of the pre-training phase applicable to physical education students. *Quest* 18:57–66.

Sage, G.H. 1987. The social world of high school athletic coaches: Multiple role demands and their consequences. *Sociology of Sport Journal* 4:213–228.

Sage, G.H. 1989. The social world of high school athletic coaches: Multiple role demands and their consequences. In *Socialization into physical education: Learning to teach,* ed. Thomas J. Templin and Paul G. Schempp, 251–269. Dubuque, IA: WCB Brown & Benchmark Press.

Silverman, S., and P.R. Subramaniam. 1999. Student attitude toward physical education and physical activity: A review of measurement issues and outcomes. *Journal of Teaching in Physical Education* 18(1):97–125.

Steen, T.B. 1985. Teacher socialization in physical education during early training experiences: A qualitative study. Paper presented at the annual meeting of AAHPERD, Atlanta.

Stroot, S.A., C. Collier, M. O'Sullivan, and K. England. 1994. Contextual hoops and hurdles: Workplace conditions in secondary physical education. *Journal of Teaching in Physical Education* 13(4):342–360.

Tannehill, D., J-E. Romar, M. O'Sullivan, K. England, and D. Rosenberg. 1994. Attitudes toward physical education: Their impact on how physical education teachers make sense of their work. *Journal of Teaching in Physical Education* 13(4):406–420.

Williams, J. 1993. Teacher moonlighting: Interviews with physical educators. *Journal of Teaching in Physical Education* 13(1):62–77.

Suggested Readings

Figone, A.J. 1994b. Origins of the teacher-coach role: Idealism, convenience, and unworkability. *Physical Educator* 51(3):148–157.

Kosa, Boonsong. 1990. Teacher-coach burnout and coping strategies. *Physical Educator* 47(3):153–159.

Pastore, D.L., and D.J. Kuga. 1993. High school coaches of women's teams: An evaluation of burnout levels. *Physical Educator* 50(3):126–135.

Staffo, D.F. 1992. Clarifying physical education teacher-coach responsibilities: A self-analysis guide for those in dual roles. *Physical Educator* 49(1):52–57.

Chapter **15**

Legal Issues Associated With Teaching Physical Education

Experience is a hard teacher because she gives the test first, the lesson afterward.

— *Vernon Law, baseball pitcher*

Gabriella is teaching a unit on in-line skating at Castle Rock High School. She has been diligent in preparing her students on safety issues, including showing a safety videotape provided by a skate manufacturer. She has developed safety procedures, policies, and required equipment for in-line skating class activities and posted them outside both the boys' and girls' locker rooms. As she is gathering her class one day, two students not enrolled in her class distract her attention when they engage in a fistfight in the courtyard. While separating the students, she tells her class to begin their follow-the-leader skating activity on the outdoor basketball courts. After resolving the fight, Gabriella skates over to catch up with her students. To her dismay, one of her students has fallen and apparently broken his wrist. She notices that he was not wearing appropriate equipment. When she reports the incident to her principal, he says that they should probably eliminate in-line skating activities from the curriculum. The principal thinks that these activities put the school at risk for liability suits. Gabriella is disheartened by the news because she has worked hard to get the activities into her physical education classes. She too is concerned about personal legal ramifications of this incident. Is it inevitable that she will have to drop higher-risk activities such as in-line skating from her program?

What effect will legal considerations have on including lifelong physical activities that carry higher risk for injury in your physical education curriculum?

Learning Objectives

After reading this chapter thoroughly and discussing the issues in class, you should be able to

- explain what constitutes liability within teaching physical education,
- explain why physical education by its very nature can put teachers at risk,
- explain differences between acts of commission and omission in teaching physical education,
- describe situations in which physical education teachers are at risk for behaving in a negligent manner,
- list and explain each of the five conditions typically cited in negligence cases,
- describe why legal problems become more likely when you implement a new curriculum with experimental activities into your program,
- explain how national standards and practices can be a significant source of protection when implementing a new curriculum with experimental activities,
- explain how teachers can minimize parental fears associated with alarming phrases and language that exist on standard parental consent forms,
- describe willful and wanton conduct of a physical education teacher,
- explain the likely consequence if a teacher is found guilty of willful and wanton conduct, and
- describe instances in which practices such as name calling, inappropriate touching, exercise as punishment, and gender-segregated classes can be interpreted in court as negligent and as willful and wanton behavior.

Key Terms and Phrases

Liability
Acts of omission
Acts of commission
Negligence
First aid
Preexisting conditions
Parental consent
Willful and wanton conduct
Sexual harassment
Exercise as punishment
Title IX

One of the major challenges of the teaching profession concerns the relationship between offering rewarding experiences to your students and providing a safe environment that limits the possibility that they will be harmed. The issue of legal liability is never far from the mind of teachers as they practice their trade. The number of lawsuits in physical education has grown at an astonishing rate over the last few decades. This comes as no surprise considering the ever-increasing number of lawsuits in business and everyday life. Because of the nature of activities in physical education, students are at risk for physical injuries. Uninformed and unaware teachers can put their students at greater risk for injury while putting themselves at more risk for personal and professional sanctions. Note also that physical education classes are typically larger than other classes. It stands to reason that the greater the number of people involved in physical activity, the harder it will be to monitor the activity for possible risks and the more likely it is that accidents will occur. Schools and school districts face greater risk of losing financial resources and public trust. Unfortunately, those losses can result even if litigation issues are resolved favorably for the schools.

The purpose of this chapter is to inform you of key issues concerning legal liability associated with teaching physical education. We will provide brief summaries of case studies to personalize and illustrate relevant legal issues, and we will offer concrete suggestions for safe activities, supervision, equipment, and facilities that maximize learning while limiting legal risks.

Purpose

Use technology to provide assistance and ideas pertaining to new legal issues that affect the teaching of physical education.

Resource and Procedure

Select Web resources for the purpose of keeping up on legal issues associated with school settings. In addition to popular journals and newspapers, Lexus-Nexus databases can be accessed for articles published in law review journals. Once in the database, type "physical education" in the online search engines provided. Remember that in legal matters ignorance may not be a defense. Most important, you may be able to learn from others' mistakes.

Liability

Generally, a teacher is considered to have **liability** because he or she is legally bound and obligated to make good on any loss or damage that occurs in the performance of teaching duties. The fact that you have been hired as a physical education teacher means that you possess knowledge, skill, and experience consistent with other similar physical education professionals. You are expected to know and demonstrate safe practices that do not put your students in high-risk situations. You are also expected to be actively involved in supervision of students, equipment, and facilities. Finally, you are expected to engage students with appropriate interaction and communication consistent with the standards of professional physical education teachers. You should also know that liability concerns both acts of omission and acts of commission.

Real World Case Study 1

A student broke her leg during a soccer game in physical education class when another player slid in to her, breaking both bones in her lower leg. She claimed that she was required to participate in coeducational full-contact soccer and was not given proper protective equipment. Her parents, on her behalf, filed a $50,000 claim against the school district for negligence. The student's injury resulted in surgery, hospital care, and long-term care. Her family is seeking the money as compensation for her injury as well as for "loss of enjoyment of life." The school superintendent has filed a denial of the claim, following the recommendation of the district's insurance company.

(*Milwaukee Journal,* May 8, 2001)

Your Turn ▶ ▶ ▶

- ◆ Do you believe that the student has a legitimate case for suing the district?
- ◆ What preventive measures could you take as a physical education teacher to minimize the possibility of a similar event occurring in your classes?

Acts of Omission

Acts of omission are actions you have purposefully omitted that in some way led to a situation with negative consequences. The actions would be deemed significant and necessary to ensure the carrying out of professional duties. Let's say that you are teaching a class in the gymnasium on a hot early September day. Your class is doing volleyball activities. You quietly step out, leaving the class unsupervised, to grab a soft drink from the machine near your office. You come back to find the students gathered around a boy who has passed out because of dehydration. He has suffered a head injury due to the fall. The action that now puts you at risk was not your going to get the soft drink; it was your not doing something, mainly your not being there physically to supervise your students during the activity. You willfully omitted one of the responsibilities associated with and expected of professional physical education teachers. That omission could put you at legal risk.

Acts of Commission

Acts of commission are actions you committed that in some way led to a situation with negative consequences. These actions would be considered significant yet unnecessary and inappropriate for a professional. Let's take the same example as before. You return with your soft drink and notice the same boy in the same condition. Starting to panic, you threaten all the other students with physical harm if any of them reports to the principal that you had left the gymnasium during the class. By threatening your students with bodily harm, you have acted in a way that was clearly beyond what is expected of a professional physical education teacher. One can also assume that a professional with experience knows the difference between appropriate and inappropriate actions. Willfully choosing to act in an inappropriate way could constitute an act of commission and put you at legal risk.

Negligence

Typically, lawsuits arising from injuries sustained during physical education class involve a teacher's showing **negligence** in failing to avoid conditions that led to the injury or in failing to provide adequate care once a condition has been established that results in the injury. Again, the issue concerns what a professional physical education teacher should know concerning safe procedures, appropriate activities, and supervision skills. Acting in a way contrary to professional standards, without providing sound reasons for those actions, can be shown to be negligent behavior. If harm or injury occurs as a direct result of the failure of the teacher to act in a professional way, the teacher can be found negligent.

According to Wuest and Lombardo (1994) negligent behavior in physical education typically occurs in the following conditions:

1. Supervision
2. Instruction
3. Classroom environment
4. First-aid emergencies
5. Transportation

Gabriella knows that other schools have been able to include in-line skating curriculum in their schools despite the risks involved. Maybe if she could find out how the other schools went about setting up an environment that stressed safety and minimized potential legal issues, she could persuade her principal to allow her to continue with the activity. Gabriella went on the Internet and found a NASPE list serv where she could post questions. She hoped that other physical education teachers would read her questions and post successful ideas back to her. Her "SOS" included the following message: "Help! I have set up an in-line skating lesson unit and my students love it. Yesterday one of my students had an accident, and now my principal is not sure he can support such a potentially hazardous activity. I know other schools have been able to set up similar programs. Are there any suggestions out there to help me?" When she checked back to the list serv over the weekend, she was pleased to see seven replies to her question. The responses included ideas for conducting safe practices during instruction, suggestions for setting up student peer review sessions in which students ensure that their partners are wearing all the safety equipment correctly, and helpful hints for establishing an environment for the teaching of in-line skating. One of the best responses came from a professor who teaches in the physical education teacher education program at a university. He said he had just conducted a study and published an article about the successful implementation of in-line skating into high school curriculum. He said he would send her a copy of the article. Gabriella now believed that she had ideas and success stories to present to her principal that would alleviate his concerns about the activity.

Conditions for Negligence

Your attention to each of the five conditions for negligence listed earlier will help you avoid negligence suits should accidents occur. We cannot stress enough how important it is to follow the procedures and practices addressed by the guidelines of national organizations. In the unfortunate event of a lawsuit, evidence of following acceptable professional guidelines will go a long way in your defense. We believe that a holistic physical education practice based on the content and philosophy of this book will lead to effective, worthwhile, and safe physical education, which will in turn reduce the incidence of situations in which negligence can be claimed.

Real World Case Study 2

A student was changing his clothes in the locker room following a physical education class when a pack of gum and candy fell out of his pocket. Two classmates reached down, took the items, and ran out of the locker room. The student attempted to run after them in his socks and slipped on the ceramic tile floor, injuring his elbow. The injured student sued the district, alleging that lack of proper supervision by the physical education teacher led to the proximate cause of injury. The teacher testified that although teacher supervision is required until all students are out of the locker room, he had been called out of the room to meet with another student at the time of the incident.

(*Your School and the Law,* November 7, 2000)

Your Turn ▶ ▶ ▶

◆ Do you believe that this example could commonly occur at schools?

◆ As a physical education teacher, how could you lessen the possibility that this would happen to you?

◆ Why do you think the boy's suit centered on lack of supervision by the physical education teacher?

◆ What would you do if you were called out of the room in a similar situation?

Supervision

We know that good education begins with actively involved teachers constantly assessing their students. The major focus of assessment is ensuring that students are properly and safely executing activities (figure 15.1). Assessment includes a system to monitor students for signs of overexertion, physical ailments, sickness, and potential dangers. It stands to reason that lacking physical proximity to your students would put you in a position difficult to defend should something arise. Rolling out the ball and then permitting unsupervised physical education is not only poor practice but also implies a lack of understanding of teacher responsibility.

Supervision is an active, ongoing process. Just because everything and everyone in the class appear to be in order does not mean that problems cannot suddenly occur. An experienced, focused teacher actively supervising a class is also looking for clues or indicators that may precede a dangerous result. Examples include students getting off task, lacking purpose in their movements, and goofing off. As the saying goes, an ounce of prevention is worth a pound of cure, and a teacher can head off potential problems by getting students back on task.

In the case of sudden accidents or unavoidable occurrences, active supervision can be the difference in limiting damage. Remember that negligence can include failing to act sufficiently and properly in the event of an accident. Failing to supervise properly and not being in close proximity can lead to situations in which you may not be able to provide first-aid assistance. In the worst-case scenario, that could be the difference between life and death. We cannot overstate the importance of supervision of the class (figure 15.2). In instances when you have to leave the class, a qualified replacement must supervise in your absence.

Finally, another good approach that teachers practice is educating and encouraging students to supervise one another during challenging activities. This method is not a substitute for your supervision, but by having more eyes monitoring the environment, you have evidence that you are stressing safety in your class and you are more likely to become aware of problems at an early stage. You can easily incorporate this method into the partner feedback teaching style discussed in chapter 8.

Figure 15.1 Teachers need to consistently supervise their classes in a focused manner that ensures safety and encourages learning how to perform skills properly.

Figure 15.2 Proper supervision, particularly in risky activities, is essential for all physical educators to emphasize.

Instruction

Negligence often becomes an issue when students suffer injuries that result from improper or insufficient instruction necessary to complete activities. Physical activities such as tumbling, rock climbing, and judo require movement that can put the body in serious danger if improperly performed. Incorporating a teaching style that identifies skills needed and students who lack those skills is not only good teaching practice but also important to the issue of liability. Using an appropriate teaching style is especially relevant when students perform activities in which they may be unable to judge their personal capability. Lack of proper instruction negatively affects student confidence and efficacy, which in turn can result in improper performance leading to injury. Obviously, you would not ask your students to attempt something far beyond their immediate capability, especially when the results could be harmful. A teacher cannot expect students to figure out proper movement and positioning on their own. This point is particularly relevant in high-exertion activities that require proper balance and weight distribution. Because some adolescent learners possess enough strength to experiment with

Real World Case Study 3

At a Catholic school, a student and his classmates were assembling to start physical education class at a staircase leading to an outside door. The physical education teacher instructed the students to run up the stairs, across a landing, and down another flight of stairs to the first of two doors that led to the parking lot. After completing the run, a student pushed the first door back into the direction of a classmate without warning. As that student put his hands up to stop the door, he put his hand through the glass, resulting in injuries to his hand and wrist. The student and his parents sued the diocese for negligent supervision resulting in the injury. The parents raised the issue that the student's physical education teacher should have been stationed at the doorway. A trial court dismissed the action, and the parents appealed to the New York Supreme Court.

The appellate division ruled that the trial court had erred in dismissing the parents' claim of negligent supervision. The court noted that schools have a duty to supervise students under their care and that schools are liable when injuries could have been reasonably foreseen and ultimately remedied with proper and adequate supervision. The case was returned to trial court to consider the negligent supervision charge.

(*School Violence Alert*, February 7, 2001)

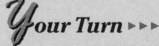

Your Turn ▸ ▸ ▸

◆ Do you agree with the trial court's initial decision or the supreme court's decision to uphold the parents appeal?

◆ What do you believe is meant by the court's ruling that schools are liable when injuries could have been reasonably foreseen?

◆ In this case could you as the physical education instructor reasonably foresee problems associated with the learning environment?

difficult maneuvers, dangerous results can occur if they do not receive proper instruction.

Besides teaching skill movements, teachers need to provide proper instruction to ensure correct application of protocols and procedures for setting up, using, and returning equipment. Chapter 6 presents ways of communicating procedures and protocol expectations to your students. In putting these procedures and protocols together before presentation to the students, you should be sure that they are consistent with the manufacturer's recommendations for equipment use and the company's safety cues for handling equipment (figure 15.3). Let's look at the example of a lesson plan on rock climbing. Students must use equipment to scale a wall successfully. If you have not properly instructed and tested your students, the potential for serious injury increases.

Equipment of various sizes may have maximum height and weight limits. Students who learn something incorrectly can harm themselves. Improper setting up of equipment can cause students to harm others. When giving safety instructions, state them in simple terms. You can never speak too simply when you discuss safety. You should state objectives clearly, emphasize them, and reinforce them visually for future reference by the students. Students will thus be aware of the precautions they need to take when performing activities in physical education class. Informed students know what is acceptable and what is not acceptable, so the responsibility is on them to act in an appropriate manner. Proper safety training reduces the likelihood of injuries and helps protect you against charges of negligence.

Figure 15.3 Make sure that students understand how to properly use equipment using your classroom guidelines as well as the manufacturer's guidelines.

Real World Case Study 4

On the fourth day of participating in a skating unit, a student fell and broke his wrist while roller skating. At the time of the injury he was not wearing protective gear. The student and his parents filed suit against the school seeking damages for his injury. The school district brought a motion raising sovereign immunity as a defense to the action. The trial court sided with the district, saying that the school and teacher were immune from liability. The student and his parents appealed to the state court of appeals. Although the court found that the teacher's failure to require students to wear protective gear during the skating lessons in physical education class might have been negligent conduct, it did not constitute reckless behavior. The court therefore ruled that the teacher was immune from a student injury suit.

A substantial component of the deciding factor in the case involved the fact that the teacher informed students and parents about the roller and in-line skating curriculum. In addition, the teacher required the class to view a video that addressed topics including safety and maneuverability skills. He had also given the class a written skating test in which the injured student had received a perfect score. Safety procedures had also been reviewed each class period. The court decided that the teacher's omission in requiring protective gear could not be construed as reckless or malicious and be-cause most activities in physical education require risks, "public policy demands that school districts offer physical education classes as the benefits of fitness and healthy recreation habits outweigh whatever occasional and usually minor injuries that may occur." Because the student's suit did not prove reckless behavior, the claim was barred by immunity.

(*Managing School Business,* August 10, 2000)

Your Turn ▸▸▸

- What do you think was the main reason the court did not find the teacher's behavior reckless or malicious?

- Why do you believe the teacher's actions of getting parental consent forms and providing safety procedures outweighed apparent negligent conduct by the teacher?

- Do you agree or disagree with the court's decision that public policy demands that school districts offer physical education classes despite the usually minor injuries that are likely to occur? Why or why not?

- Do you believe that the decision would have been different if the court deemed that a particular physical education activity was not beneficial to fitness and was not healthy recreation?

Classroom Environment

The physical education teacher is solely responsible for being vigilant and aware of potential dangerous conditions involved in the setup of the classroom environment. Most physical education teachers conduct classroom activities on fields and in gymnasiums that serve several purposes. Thus the classroom environment can be radically different from day to day. Say, for example, that a dance was held in the gym the night before a class. Because of some spillage, certain areas on the floor sustained damaged and pose a risk for certain classroom activities. You should be aware of changes in conditions that may require you to modify your activities for that day. Your action could range from merely informing students of the restricted areas to having to find alternative space for class. In some cases the fact that your classroom areas involve extracurricular activities over which you have little or no control should be protection against liability. But that protection may be limited because you are still responsible in the role of supervisor and teacher for being aware of changes to your classroom environment that may endanger your students.

Purpose

Use technology to develop multimedia designed to provide students with consistent instruction and reinforcement for safety procedures.

Resource and Procedure

In addition to instructing students on safety procedures, you should make multimedia artifacts that can be displayed and referred to throughout the school year. At times you will need to show that all students have been given proper instruction on procedures and safety issues associated with your class. To make sure that all areas have been covered consistently with each class, you can make a brief safety video similar to the ones that airlines use. Show the video to the class at a designated time. In addition, you can give students a handout of the items covered. This handout should include the same information covered in the video and, if possible, should include pictures and graphics from the video. Finally, a copy of the handout should be close by during class for easy reference for students who do not seem to be following safety procedures. Ultimately you want to show that all students were made aware of proper procedures during class.

Many injuries occur when students are attempting to avoid cracks in the pavement and debris while performing an activity. Imagine teaching a lesson unit in in-line skating on outdoor tennis courts. Assume that you gave proper instruction, required students to wear all the equipment recommended by the manufacturer, and checked that the equipment was working properly (figure 15.4). You have them play an instant-activity game of high-five tag. Students begin to fall while trying to avoid debris that is blowing around the area. Obviously, you cannot control the wind, and the swirling debris could be interpreted as resulting from an "act of God" and beyond the control of the teacher. But let's say that you are notorious for having a disorderly teaching environment. Besides reflecting negatively on your professionalism, your practices are more likely to create unsafe conditions. The lack of care synonymous with and symptomatic of your program puts you at risk of negligence.

The best way of dealing with the environment is to be so keyed in to your activities that you are aware of how even subtle changes can affect student safety.

Figure 15.4 Teachers should always be vigilant about preventive maintenance on the equipment they use.

Consider, for example, the setup design you use for positioning your students during activities. You should give students sufficient personal space so that they can move without endangering or impeding the movements of others. You know that where you place students is not always where they end up, so active supervision is again a key component.

Finally, the condition of equipment also changes. The reality in many schools is that students must often use older equipment that has been repaired. You should be aware of manufacturer warranties with equipment and know that attempts to repair or rebuild equipment from other parts may affect the manufacturer's liability. Using altered equipment that malfunctions can have serious effects on school liability in the event of an injury. In addition, students should use equipment only in the manner for which it was designed. All equipment should include the attached original warning labels and operational instructions. Students should be familiar with both content and proper procedures. You should immediately stop any activity in which students are using equipment improperly or inappropriately. In the end, how consistently and actively you take charge of your teaching environment will go a long way in establishing your efforts to ensure a safe learning place. Accidents will still arise, but you will know that you have done your best to anticipate problems, properly instruct students, and follow equipment specifications and guidelines. Evidence of all three will be your best defense against charges of liability in the event of an injury.

Real World Case Study 5

A student was injured in a physical education class when she slid into third base while playing softball. Her parents claimed that the injury took place when she slid because of unsafe playing conditions and because the teacher did not inform her that she should not slide. The parents provided expert testimony that the playing field was unsafe. The state supreme court ruled that although the girl had not been warned that year, the school provided sufficient evidence to show that she had been warned in previous years. The student had attended the school for three years. In addition, the court ruled that she assumed the risk of injury when she slid. The court sided with the school, saying that although the districts have a duty to supervise students adequately, they can be held liable only when the injury was foreseeable and they failed to supervise the student adequately. In addition, the court ruled that districts are not ensurers of student safety and did not violate any specific standards or customs.

(*Your School and the Law*, 2000)

Your Turn ▸ ▸ ▸

* How do you think the school showed sufficient evidence that the student had been warned in previous years?
* What evidence would you consider credible to show that she had been warned?
* Do you believe the findings of the case would have been different if she had not been warned about the hazards of sliding?
* How might the situation differ if the teacher had instructed students to slide in a safe manner?

First-Aid Emergencies

The nature and philosophy of physical education mean that students will be physically moving. People are more at risk when they are active, so it is logical that accidents resulting in injury are more likely to happen in physical education classes than in other classes. When incidents occur the physical education teacher's liability issue takes on new meaning. A professional physical education teacher should be able to offer appropriate assistance in a calm, cool manner. Lawsuits often arise over the behavior of the teacher after the accident occurs. You should understand that even the best physical education teachers encounter injuries with their students. Sadly, in such cases, improper first-aid assistance can worsen an already grave situation and in a worst-case scenario lead to serious conditions or even death.

First aid is defined as treatment for injury or sudden illness before the injured person has access to hospital care or a treatment facility (figure 15.5). The laws concerning first-aid assistance reflect the notion that you are providing help, often under extreme situations, with the intent of providing immediate comfort and stability for the victim. Physical education teachers must have training in first-aid procedures and practices and should possess proper and current first-aid certificates. Proper training will ensure that you possess current knowledge on what to do and what not to do. Physical education teachers have been liable for doing too much, such as attempting to move a seriously injured student. When additional injuries or further complications arise from inappropriate actions on the part of the teacher, liability can be established.

Figure 15.5 Teachers need to be prepared to help students who are hurt.

Besides knowing first-aid procedures and practices and possessing certification, you should have class procedures in place in the event of emergency. You should meet with school officials and health staff to develop or clarify a clear, identifiable list of steps that you will follow. School policies may differ, so we cannot offer a clear set that would be sufficient for every school. Once those procedures have been developed, you should incorporate them into your class objectives so that all students will be aware of and be able to follow procedures. Remember that time is valuable during an emergency. The speed with which you can deliver first aid when needed is of the highest importance. The time you spend directing students away from the injured person and providing students with instructions during the emergency is time wasted and an obstacle to your providing assistance. Placed where you teach classes, a poster that visually represents the procedures can be helpful (figure 15.6). The poster should include appropriate contact names and phone numbers. During an emergency we often have difficulty recalling appropriate steps of a procedure.

The poster is a convenient reference for students who are unaware or unsure of the proper steps. Referring students to the poster can serve to get them out of the way and clear space for you to assist the injured or ailing student. You should know these procedures cold so that you can focus on providing assessment and assistance rather than figuring out what to do. Again, your best defense during first aid is professional knowledge, preparation, and procedure.

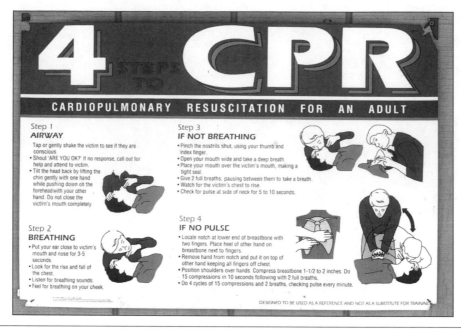

Figure 15.6 Displaying a poster of your emergency procedures can help you and others think clearly in a crisis situation to make the right decisions.

Purpose

Use technology to find and display emergency first-aid procedures that anyone can follow in the event of an emergency.

Resource and Procedure

You can download information on proper first-aid procedures from reputable sites endorsed by the American Heart Association, the Centers for Disease Control and Prevention, and the Red Cross. These procedures provide task aids that should be printed out, laminated, and prominently displayed in areas where physical activities are conducted. Personalize materials by adding local contacts and relevant phone numbers. Visit **www.depts. washington.edu/learncpr** for illustrated guides that can be downloaded and distributed.

After you have resolved an incident at the scene, you must write a detailed report covering who, what, where, when, why, and how. Include a brief summary of lesson objectives, student instruction, and preparation for the particular activity procedures. Your report should include any action you took. Write as objectively as possible. By committing fresh thoughts to paper, you will be less likely to have to recall and reconstruct events long after they occur. Remember to be specific and clear. No one expects you to be able to see all, hear all, and know all. In addition, reasonable people will assume that with all your duties as a focused active teacher, you may not have seen the circumstances that led up to the accident. Send the report to the appropriate school administrators, who may ultimately use it as evidence in a liability case. Be clear, precise, and honest in your recollections.

Finally, it is vital to be aware of students' **preexisting conditions**, which may direct your action when you provide first aid. Conditions such as epilepsy or diabetes may require that additional equipment and supplies be on hand. The beginning of the school year is the best time to acquaint yourself with particular health issues. You should handle these issues confidentially and without calling attention to other students.

Purpose

Use technology to generate a timely, detailed report and provide evidence of the time elapsed between an incident and your written recollection of events.

Resource and Procedure

Use your computer word-processing program to provide a detailed report of an incident. Be as specific as possible and list in simple sentences what you witnessed and heard during the incident. When you complete the report, send an e-mail of the report to yourself. Every e-mail includes a record of the time and date it was sent. This functions as evidence of how quickly the written report follows the actual event. Your recollections will appear more credible if they closely follow the time of the actual incident.

Transportation

Although not necessarily a component of all physical education classes, transporting students to and from class activities taking place outside the school premises can be a liability concern for physical education teachers. Again, your best protection is to follow school policies, procedures, and practices in every instance. Policies will surely include requiring all students to bring in school and district parental consent forms. Although you will be tempted to let a student who has mistakenly forgotten to return the form to make the trip anyway, by doing so you will be putting yourself and your school in a virtual indefensible position should anything happen to that student. A good approach is to have students return parental consent forms at least a week before the trip so that you can remind those who have not returned signed forms of the consequences. Teenagers have no problems remembering complex video game codes, rap lyrics, and movie show times. The responsibility for returning the permission slip rests entirely with them. If volunteers will be driving, proper rules of eligibility, insurance, and restrictions must be determined through relevant documents beforehand. This is a particular problem in secondary schools. Many students drive to and from school, but school or district policies could forbid them from transporting fellow students during a regular scheduled school activity. If traveling to an off-campus site will be a regular occurrence for a class, explore the rules and regulations about using a one-time parental consent form for regularly scheduled activities. Impromptu classroom excursions, no matter how popular with students, are never feasible. Finally, students with special needs must also have transportation and accessible equipment to accommodate them on trips. You must observe school or district rules, regulations, and procedures at all times.

New Curricula Risks

This book has offered many suggestions for exploring new ways and alternative approaches to teaching physical education. The challenge of offering new curricula becomes clear. New activities may lead you into uncharted waters in terms of possible dangers, liabilities, and unexpected outcomes. In-line skating provides an excellent illustration of this challenge. As in-line skating has become popular as a fitness activity, it has become apparent that including it in a curriculum that stresses lifelong activities would be appropriate. Early adopters of in-line skating in physical education programs, however, faced a host of problems because the public lacked experience with the activity in a physical education setting. Besides the obvious physical risks associated with the activity, issues such as safe and proper skates versus nonconforming skates, communicable disease issues associated with sharing helmets, and requirements for safety equipment all had the potential to affect teacher liability.

Imagine what the early innovators who attempted to modernize physical education activities had to endure with issues working against the new activity. Newer activities by their nature don't come equipped with easy-to-follow adoption procedures. One is always at risk of leaving out significant considerations until after the fact. Although a trial-and-error process will make steady progress, few physical education teachers want to jeopardize their careers by making errors that they can never recover from. When taking your program into uncharted waters, some pointers can help you design alternative activities consistent with previous activities in both objectives and safety. A commonsense approach based on professional standards and guidelines will give you confidence that your newly adopted activities are exciting, effective, and, most important, safe for your students.

A commonsense approach includes identifying potential physical limitations and danger, preparing properly, offering instruction on dos and don'ts, adhering strictly to the rules, preventing continued unsafe practice during a particular activity, and being present and aware at all times during activities. In addition, adding a new activity requires constant assessment and awareness of required equipment and facilities. The teacher must develop creative alternatives, which may include modifying or eliminating potential dangerous components to an activity. An example is to play roller hockey in a noncontact mode using foam rubber balls. Attempts to address the potential hazards at the design phase will go a long way in ensuring successful implementation of the new activity into the program.

 Finally, be aware of the national standards and practices prescribed by national organizations like NASPE and AAHPERD, Web sites such as PE Central designed by physi-

cal educators to share successes with similar implementation activities, and professional list servers. With a variety of credible resources at your disposal, you will be able to show that your new activity is based on sensible practices and standards, not some experimental, half-baked idea. You should share your successes with other professionals in the field so that more schools can benefit from exciting, innovative activities. Figure 15.7 provides a list of situations that you should avoid to decrease potential litigation.

Your Turn ▶▶▶

What new curriculum activities would you like to add to your physical education program? What sorts of liabilities would you have to consider?

Real World Case Study 6

A 17-year-old boy was taking part in a physical education class in which students were required to take part in a running session or an in-line skating session. The boy suffered injuries while in-line skating in the class. The boy and his father sued the school district for injuries, alleging that the skates provided were of an experimental design with the brake mechanism situated at the toe of the boot instead of at the heel as in more traditional models. The suit also alleged that students were not offered any additional safety equipment. As the boy attempted to roll around the wooden floor, he fell and broke two bones in his right leg.

The complaint alleged negligence on the school district's part for failing to provide the necessary safety equipment for in-line skating, such as helmets, shin guards, wrist guards, knee guards, and elbow pads. The suit also alleged willful and wanton misconduct for failing to provide necessary equipment and measures for the activity.

The school district moved to dismiss the suit by claiming it was immune from liability. A trial court granted the dismissal. The plaintiffs appealed to the state supreme court. The state reversed the trial court's dismissal of the plaintiff's suit, citing that school districts cannot be immune from liability in instances in which it has been shown that the district failed its independent duty to provide appropriate safety equipment to students. Thus, the suit dismissal was overturned, and the plaintiffs were allowed to proceed with their lawsuit against the district.

(*Chicago Daily Law Bulletin,* March 13, 2001)

Your Turn ▶▶▶

Who do you believe will ultimately win the lawsuit? Why? What message can physical education teachers take from this example?

The following list includes situations raised by plaintiff and defense lawyers in court cases as examples of negligence on the part of physical education teachers. To decrease the likelihood of being involved in litigation and, more important, to ensure students' safety, you may want to avoid the following:

- Not properly supervising locker room and facilities
- Leaving activity room doors open and unsupervised
- Giving your keys to students
- Having students move equipment that they cannot handle easily
- Permitting horseplay
- Placing a student in the role of sole supervisor in class
- Not establishing safety rules before class activity
- Not becoming involved in resolving conflict
- Neglecting to warm up students properly before activity
- Physically overextending a student
- Ignoring prescribed curriculum
- Bypassing fundamental skills
- Not continually updating and reviewing a safety checklist
- Not having a checklist
- Not having an emergency plan
- Permitting activity on a wet, slippery floor
- Not providing special attention to students with special needs
- Leaving unnecessary equipment in the way during activity
- Permitting students to wear inappropriate shoes or attire
- Using correct equipment improperly
- Participating in improper areas
- Using an inadequately lighted class area
- Hiring unqualified personnel
- Not informing proper school personnel of first-aid procedures
- Not maintaining written records of objectives, incident reports, and so on
- Not posting safety rules in conspicuous places
- Failing to check equipment on a regular basis
- Testing students' ability before teaching necessary skills
- Permitting inappropriate running and jumping in hazardous conditions
- Not maintaining awareness of legal issues

Figure 15.7 Situations to avoid to decrease potential litigation.

Adapted from R. Borkowski, 1986.

Gabriella's principal decided that if she put all the safety suggestions from the list serv in place, she could continue to teach the in-line skating unit. Although parents had signed a generic physical education consent form, he thought it would be best if she could develop one specific to the in-line skating activity so that parents could decide if they wanted their children to participate. He also suggested that she include, with the parental consent form, a brief description of the safety mechanisms she put in place to minimize accidents. Students who had parental permission for skating could participate.

Figure 15.8   Parents and legal guardians sign consent forms provided by physical education teachers.

Parental Consent

When students are involved in physical education classes, they assume a certain amount of risk. The risk, however, must be normal and reasonable. When conditions may add to the risk, the teacher must distribute **parental consent** forms and waivers. A parent or legal guardian must sign the forms and return them to the school (figure 15.8). Obtaining parental or legal guardian consent can at times be problematic for the physical education teacher who attempts to incorporate new ideas and activities into the class. Standard consent forms typically include alarming language. Documents may say that participating in an activity "may cause serious injury," "may increase the likelihood of catching communicable diseases," or "may cause death."

Normally, parents are familiar with the nature and language of these consent forms and will sign them. But in some instances parents or guardians may be concerned about the language of the form. They may have serious reservations about signing such a document. Am I signing away all legal rights to hold the school responsible if something horrible and unexpected should occur? Why does PE class include these dangerous new activities? Why is the school putting my children at risk?

In such cases, direct communication with concerned parents can alleviate the problem. You might provide reluctant parents a clear list of the objectives and benefits of the proposed activity. In addition, you could explain that you have anticipated potential problems and developed specific solutions to ensure safety. Finally, include a description of all the safety issues and describe the procedures you will use to instruct, direct, and test students.

In the case of an entirely new activity with new potential dangers, you may want to include with the consent form to parents a brief letter communicating the potential outcomes, benefits, and procedures. The letter will help parents understand why you are introducing the activity into the curriculum. Accompanying the letter should be a clear set of rules and procedures that your students can refer to at home with their parents. By providing this information you are explaining your rationale for offering a new activity as well as showing commitment and care for their children.

One last point is that students regularly bring home consent forms with similar alarming language when participating in extracurricular activities. Adopt a similar approach with your students by taking time to motivate and excite your students about the new activities they'll be involved in during the semester. They will be more likely to take the consent forms home, make sure that their parents read and sign them, and return them so that they can participate.

Willful and Wanton Conduct

Issues presented so far in the chapter have focused particularly on negligence and circum-

Purpose

Use technology to create an electronic spreadsheet that contains your students' health-related issues that can be accessed quickly when needed.

Resource and Procedure

Use a spreadsheet that you have created for student attendance, and include a section for notes concerning preexisting conditions, medication information, and previous injuries. You can keep copies of this information on your home computer, your office computer, and on a palm PC. You should safeguard this information so that students do not have access to it. You need to have this information on students' health status so that you can provide assistance in the event of an accident. Students may not always be conscious or fully aware to provide you with this important information.

stances in which physical education teachers may find themselves at risk. **Willful and wanton conduct** is a more serious situation in which it is proven that unjustifiable actions were taken deliberately and with intent to cause harm. When injuries occur because of negligence on the part of the teacher, some states require the plaintiff (person suing) to show an additional charge of willful and wanton conduct to collect damages. In dealing with legal issues it is wise to be aware of the rules and statutes that govern the state in which you teach. The school or district should have guidelines that describe your rights and liabilities. Although willful and wanton conditions carry a higher standard of proof, you could find yourself in a position of having to defend against those charges. Although issues of liability vary from state to state, it is consistent that actions determined to be willful and wanton, that is, carried out with malicious intent toward students, will produce dire results for a teacher, perhaps ending a career and causing financial ruin.

Additional Areas of Liability

Although issues covered earlier in the chapter concerning negligence can be clearly stated, interpretation and perceptions of events sometimes differ

considerably. What a teacher might consider a slight indiscretion and lack of good judgment, a student and parents might believe to be a hazardous level of willful and wanton conduct. The discrepancy often occurs because of a lack of understanding and communication between teacher and student. A professional teacher should be aware of potentially dangerous situations and should have the foresight to cut them off before they escalate into an unfortunate situation for all parties.

Teacher-student relationships can cause misunderstandings that escalate into legal problems. Parents have the right to expect a learning environment to be free of excessive personal attacks toward their children and without physical and mental abuse. Parents (and lawyers) readily understand when problems result directly from negative stereotyping and unwanted comments. In addition, they are keenly aware of situations that teachers may attempt to cause injury to the student and go beyond the limits of instruction or classroom management. A professional teacher does not refer to a student with obvious physical limitations as "glasses," "nerd," "fat Freddy," or "book worm."

Certain inappropriate practices have become more dangerous because professional organizations are clear in their published opposition to such behavior. A physical education teacher having to present a defense for inappropriate practices is in a difficult position. Teachers have lost their jobs for similar actions. One such example involved a teacher who consistently and repeatedly referred to a student short of stature as "midget" in front of other students. They began to use the same name when ridiculing the student. The teacher's behavior was found to be "perverse and outrageous, and clearly indicated a pattern of abuse" (*School Violence Alert* 2001, 1). His teaching credentials were permanently revoked. In other instances, abuse directed at students was determined to be the catalyst to devastating subsequent actions by students and was considered contributory to injury. These cases may be extreme, but student behaviors ranging from withdrawal to confrontations can create situations that quickly careen out of control.

Sexual Harassment and Misconduct Issues

Physical education teachers are often involved in providing instruction that requires them to guide students physically through correct procedures to complete a movement. To demonstrate a pick and roll in a basketball unit, you have to show a student physically how far out the hip should be in setting a legal pick. You put your hands on the student's waist and adjust the position to provide appropriate feedback. Because of the growing number of instances in which charges of inappropriate touching have been proven, a teacher should be extremely vigilant in touching students only for the purpose of direct and focused instruction (figure 15.9). Words and actions should be completely consistent with the instruction and objectives. Comments that can be construed as unwanted and sexual in nature are inappropriate and can be considered **sexual harassment.** Instructional verbal cues such as, "Hold me like you hold your boyfriend" are embarrassing and intimidating for the student. Consistent with most laws, a secondary physical education teacher is in a position of power implied by the position and is not allowed to engage in or advance the notion of sexual contact with a student, even if the student is above the age of consent. Teachers should always be clear about their purpose and intent when engaging a student in physical contact during instruction.

Exercise As Punishment

In chapter 1 we explained that using **exercise as punishment** to extinguish negative behavior is inappropriate when the purpose of teaching physical education is to promote lifelong physical activity among teenagers. National standards and guidelines for the profes-

Figure 15.9 Teachers should provide focused instruction when touching students and be aware of the potential for students to misconstrue their touches.

sion and the Centers for Disease Control have published directives calling for the elimination of those practices. Some states have developed laws that prohibit or limit corporal punishment in schools. According to a former California attorney general, certain forms of using exercise as punishment clearly fall under the definition of corporal punishment. The best way to avoid potential for damaging situations is to steer clear of them in the first place. The legal issues in this matter may be open to interpretation, but in judgment cases, judges and jurors make interpretations all the time. When they agree with your interpretation you win; when they don't you lose. When exercise as punishment causes students to exceed safe levels of physical exertion, the issue is less ambiguous. Teachers have been found liable in those kinds of cases because inappropriate practices deemed to have no place in meeting class objectives contributed to the student's injury.

Your Turn ▸▸▸

- ◆ Do you agree with the California attorney general's assertion that exercise as punishment in some cases would constitute corporal punishment? Why or why not?

- ◆ Describe activities that would constitute corporal punishment.

- ◆ Where would you go to determine if a state in which you will work has sentiments similar to those of California?

Title IX

Although issues concerning **Title IX** are far reaching and beyond the scope of this chapter, physical education teachers should be aware of the potential illegalities of conducting gender-segregated physical education classes in public schools. Although in a substantial number of cases Title IX is being ignored for a variety of well-intentioned reasons, the fact remains that should you find yourself involved in an action concerning your practices, well-intentioned reasons may not be enough to protect you against action. In the case of Title IX application in physical education class, teachers should be aware of the principles listed in figure 15.10. These principles are particularly relevant in the context of liability issues presented in the chapter.

Purpose

Use technology to provide assistance, ideas, and caution from other physical educators when introducing new physical activities into your curriculum.

Resource and Procedure

When adopting new activities, always research Web sites, listservs, and electronic bulletin boards for any cautions and problem-avoidance techniques. Introducing new and innovative ideas is a rewarding and creative experience; however, it also increases the potential for new problems that you may be unaware of. Physical education sites dedicated to professional development offer support. But remember that support is a two-way street. As your new activities become successful, make sure you spread the word and offer details about your successful strategies when others in the field make similar requests for help.

Summary

Legal issues continue to be front and center in education. Because of the nature of their instruction and the physical activities performed by students, physical education teachers find themselves at risk for certain liabilities. Using clear, commonsense approaches to your curriculum design, delivery, procedures, and practices can help you avoid legal problems. Making sure that your curriculum meets national professional standards and guidelines is a good start. Accidents can happen, and risks are implied when performing tasks in physical education class. As long as your intent is to provide safe, challenging, and rewarding activities that meet standard learning objectives, and if you have proper procedures in place for offering first aid after an incident occurs, you can be confident that others will construe your actions as being careful, reasonable, and professional.

Title IX covers a broad spectrum of education and resources in the United States. Physical education is only a small portion of the law. Further, a common misconception about Title IX is that it applies only to athletics. As good physical educators know, the purpose of a school's athletic program is very different from the purpose of its physical education program. The following are the basic principles, in plain language, of Title IX as they apply to physical education.

1. Physical education classes may not be conducted separately, nor participation required or refused, on the basis of sex.

2. Students may be grouped by ability, as assessed by objective standards, within classes or activities. Such groupings may result in groups composed of one or predominantly one sex.

3. Students may be separated by sex within classes for participation in wrestling, boxing, rugby, ice hockey, football, and other sports when the major purpose of activity involves body contact. Baseball and softball are not considered contact sports and are not included in this definition.

4. When a single standard for skill measurement is used, and this adversely impacts on one sex, different standards, without gender bias, must be used. For example, dividing an eighth grade class for a track and field unit by having students successfully broad jump two meters, might result in boys (or the tall students) surpassing the requirement, while many girls (or shorter students) might not. Challenging students to jump a percentage of their own height might be more equitable. Following instruction and practice, measurement improvement might also be an objective criteria (as would using personal goal setting).

Figure 15.10 Title IX principles for physical education.

Adapted, by permission, from S. Wikgren, 1995, "Coeducational physical education: Seeking quality and equity for all students," *Teaching Middle School Physical Education* 14:1-5.

Checking for Understanding ▸▸▸

♦ What is an example of a teacher's being liable for an accident when teaching physical education class?

♦ Why should physical education teachers be especially prepared for being sued by students?

♦ What is the difference between acts of commission and acts of omission as they pertain to teaching physical education?

♦ What is an example of teacher negligence in a physical education class?

♦ What are the five conditions most often cited in negligence cases involving physical education?

♦ What is the major reason that your legal risk will increase when adopting new curricula and experimental activities into your program?

♦ What resource will offer the best legal protection when adopting new curricula with experimental activities into your program?

♦ What should teachers include with their parental consent forms to alleviate parents' concern about allowing their children to engage in new activities?

♦ What actions must the plaintiff show when attempting to prove willful and wanton conduct on the part of a teacher?

♦ What is the most likely outcome for a teacher who has been found guilty of willful and wanton conduct during class?

♦ How could exercise as punishment be used in a liability case alleging willful and wanton conduct on the part of the physical education teacher?

References

Chicago Daily Law Bulletin. 2001. [Online], March 13. Available: Lexis-Nexis.

Teacher's failure to require safety gear is 'negligent,' not 'reckless.' 2000. *Managing School Business.* 5:11

Milwaukee Journal. 2001. [Online], May 8. Available: Lexis-Nexis.

School Violence Alert. 2001. LRP Publications [Online], 7(12). Available: Lexis-Nexis.

Wuest, D.A., and B. Lombardo. 1994. *Curriculum and instruction: The secondary school physical education experience.* St Louis: Mosby.

Student assumed risk in softball participation, district not liable. *Your School and the Law.* 2000. LRP Publications [Online], 31:15. Available: Lexis-Nexis. [August 1, 2001.]

Suggested Readings

Daugherty, N., D. Auxter, A. Goldberger, and G. Heinzmann. 1994. *Sport, physical activity, and the law.* Champaign, IL: Human Kinetics.

Sawyer, T. 1999. Title IX. *Journal of Physical Education, Recreation and Dance* 70(4):9–10.

Sawyer, T. 2001. Negligent transmission of communicable disease. *Journal of Physical Education, Recreation and Dance* 72(9):8.

Sawyer, T. 2001. Adequate equipment and supervision. *Journal of Physical Education, Recreation and Dance* 72(8):11–12.

Sawyer, T. 2001. Supervision: Willful and wanton misconduct. *Journal of Physical Education, Recreation and Dance* 72(7):9–10.

Sawyer, T. 2001. Teacher-student sexual harassment. *Journal of Physical Education, Recreation and Dance* 72(5):10–11.

Sutliff, M. 1996. The duty to provide proper supervision. *Teaching Secondary Physical Education* 2(1):8–9.

Sutliff, M. 1996. Physical educators and products liability. *Teaching Secondary Physical Education* 2(4):8–9.

Chapter 16

Designing Your Physical Activity Center

> Argue for your limitations, and sure enough they're yours.
>
> — *Richard Bach*

Edgar is a secondary physical education teacher in a large urban area. He has worked hard to add new alternative physical activity units into his class. He is particularly proud of the climbing wall he constructed with help from donations of time, materials, and money from members of the local community. One problem with the class is keeping track of all the equipment needed, including ropes, harnesses, clasps, and hooks. Items are constantly being lost or

326

switched between students, and Edgar spends a lot of time trying to piece together necessary equipment. He realizes that he has little control over equipment distribution, usage, and collection. His current procedure of having students gather equipment from a box before class and assemble it themselves is causing too many students to be unprepared for class. In addition, he has no tracking system in place for identifying and removing defective equipment. At the start of nearly every class period, some students appear to be unprepared and frustrated. Once class is in session, however, the students enjoy the activity. Some students are reluctant to give up the activity at the end of class. They run late and throw their equipment loosely back in the box, creating problems for the next class. This vicious circle causes equipment to be discarded before its time. Edgar is reluctant to go back to the community for funds to replace equipment because he does not believe the public will support a cause they have little connection with. Edgar knows that it is time to make a change.

How can Edgar improve his equipment-handling policy to ensure that students will collect, use, and return equipment so that it is ready for the next class? Can he set up a system to monitor equipment better? How can he involve community members on an ongoing basis?

◆ Learning Objectives

After reading this chapter you will be able to
- explain the benefits associated with involving community partnerships with your physical education program,
- list and explain the elements associated with any successful design process,
- describe the process of adopting design principles into equipment management strategies for physical education,
- describe the process of adopting design principles into facility management,
- describe how to deal effectively with resistance to implementing change in equipment management,
- explain issues associated with teaching in an area used for a variety of purposes besides physical education activities,
- describe the position of the Centers for Disease Control on expanding your physical education program to include access and partnerships beyond regularly scheduled class activities,
- list beneficial activities and support systems in place to help expand your physical education program,
- list and describe steps associated with startup projects that have led directly to newly designed physical education programs that involve outside support, and
- describe how new communication technologies can be uniquely beneficial in providing support for design, implementation, and public awareness activities associated with physical education design.

◆ Key Terms and Phrases

Community partnership
Components of design
Equipment management
Facility management
Community involvement
Grant opportunities
Communication technologies
List servers
Class Web site

Physical education departments that lack insight, ingenuity, and partnership opportunities usually receive limited support and respect from the school, district, and community. Working in isolation, however, has its advantages. You may be effective in meeting your day-to-day short-term curriculum needs. You have a routine and a system that help you meet the incredible demands on your time. Your survival techniques are proven. Although you are able to stay only one step ahead of the next problem, you don't have to deal with the new concerns and challenges associated with change. But what if you begin to notice fundamental problems with continuing to operate the same way year after year? Part of the problem with ignoring the need to update and refresh your program is that you may not be meeting your students' fundamental needs. And if you are not achieving that, your objectives, no matter how worthy, are beyond reach.

Figure 16.1 School officials should encourage community use of facilities when school is not in session.

Implementing a Creative Instructional Design

Typical challenges to a static program are lack of appropriate facilities, equipment, funding, and support from colleagues, parents, and policy makers. According to those who follow physical education trends, programs throughout the country are under attack from outside forces for not being particularly useful, worthwhile, or necessary.

According to the Centers for Disease Control (U.S. Department of Health and Human Services 1999), physical education programs must develop a substantive relationship with the public to build a strong, dynamic **community partnership**. This partnership will serve everyone's interest because physical education efforts will reinforce community messages about the benefits of a physically active lifestyle. Communities have the resources and ability to unite organizations, legislatures, and businesses to assist school physical education programs by providing support and facilities (U.S. Department of Health and Human Services 1999). According to the International Life Sciences Insti-

tute (1999) parents play a vital role in successful physical education programs by engaging in activity with their children. School facilities should be inviting and accessible to families in the community when school is not in session (figure 16.1). But unifying schools, families, and communities does not occur without a great deal of effort.

An underlying theme throughout this chapter involves designing and managing a changing physical education environment based on your vision. The topic ranges from designing and managing your equipment and facilities more effectively to taking on the Herculean task of constructing a dynamic new physical activity learning center. You should know that any lasting change starts with an effective design approach. You will explore design ideas, ranging from minor alterations of day-to-day class functions to comprehensive changes and renovations to your program. Each design should include a planning component, a systematic approach, and creativity. Designs lacking one or more of these elements will often end up creating environments that result in poor situations.

Purpose

Use technology to set up a communication system among colleagues who use physical education facilities for other events.

Resource and Procedure

Encourage colleagues to send e-mail when requesting and setting up extracurricular events that involve the use of physical education facilities. Create a group titled "PE facilities," which includes all of the people who may need the information. Each time you need to send a message to everyone involved, just click on your group and the message will be sent to everyone. It is far better for you to receive messages that don't directly affect your classes than to miss one that does.

Edgar believes that a change in his physical education class must take place. He sat down and made a list of the problems associated with providing, tracking, and maintaining the equipment. He determined that the major problem was lack of a system that put sufficient responsibility on the students for handling equipment. He knew that he would need a creative approach to persuade students to buy into the system. Although the system would not address every problem with his class, he believed that by tackling issues, one at a time, he could accomplish an overall change.

Components of a Sound Design

To implement change successfully, you must apply **components of design**. The first element of design involves a planning component. Here you reflect on the areas lacking in your program, identify possible solutions, and determine the effort needed to accomplish the change. Second, you apply a systematic approach to provide all of the steps and organize actions within your design so that they occur in smooth, logical progression that you can easily assess throughout the process. Finally, you need creativity to free yourself from the psychological sets that you typically rely on when assessing and solving problems. Creativity includes brainstorming alternative approaches for your design for change. You should try to identify parties who may resist the change and identify reasons for their opposition. The greater the effort applied to design elements (planning, systematic approach, and creativity), the greater likelihood that permanent change will occur. In the end, none of us would attempt the design process unless it had great likelihood of resulting in positive and lasting change.

Designing Systems for Managing Equipment

According to many physical education teachers, **equipment management** can be a problem that interferes with more pressing issues. Lack of equipment can contribute to ineffective teaching situations, such as students waiting for turns. In contrast, if all students are engaged with appropriate equipment, they are likely to be actively involved with the learning activity, which leads to more practice time and more learning. Teaching with more equipment, however, offers challenges. Obviously, more equipment will need to be purchased. The teacher will need more time to hand out equipment and meet students' needs, so less time will be available for learning. Finally, with more equipment, the likelihood increases that equipment will be lost, stolen, or broken.

So, can we design an approach for effective distribution and return of activity equipment? Of course, no single solution will be successful in all class settings, but it is clear that a tailor-made design for equipment will increase time available for learning. Certain elements have been consistently successful in a variety of settings. One such element involves shifting the responsibility for equipment readiness to the students. We can easily identify as inefficient the process of a science teacher handing out books and microscopes at the beginning of every class. A similar strategy in teaching physical education is equally inefficient.

In one case, a teacher using heart rate monitors had to hand out all the units at the beginning of class and collect them at the end. The design problem was that the units had small pieces that could easily fall off and be lost. In addition, the teacher had to replace nonworking pieces at the beginning of the next class on a case-by-case basis. The time spent administering heart rate monitors often spilled over into the time scheduled for active learning. In addition, the teacher could not identify students who failed to return the equipment properly, and it was likely that the same students would mishandle new equipment the next day.

When you must hand out individual equipment, a color-coding or numbering system (in larger classes) may be effective in tracking equipment and identifying chronic perpetrators who may need remedial training in storing equipment after class. Students' names can appear on your sheet with corresponding numbers. The students will know their numbers and be responsible for the equipment with the corresponding number (figure 16.2). If you add this protocol to other class protocols, you will have effectively communicated expectations and acceptable standards. Thus, you have planned before the semester begins a system that appears logical and doable.

The last key is to make sure that you are creative at anticipating resistance to your new design. Clearly, a typical adolescent may not put forth the effort necessary to obtain and return equipment correctly. Requiring them to do that isn't anything personal. Students just need to understand that the system you put in place keeps the equipment accounted for and available to all students. Besides creating acceptable standards, you must be consistent from day one, pointing out any irregularities or deviations early in the school year and insisting that students correct the problem.

Many ingenious storage systems have been created. You should set the standard for how students store returned equipment. Eliminate all variations. Remember that you want students to model their behavior after your expectations, so choose one method, show them how to do it, and be consistent. When return policies lack clear, observable standards, students tend to throw equipment back in a pile, in various states of readiness for the next class. This situation is unfair to the next group of students.

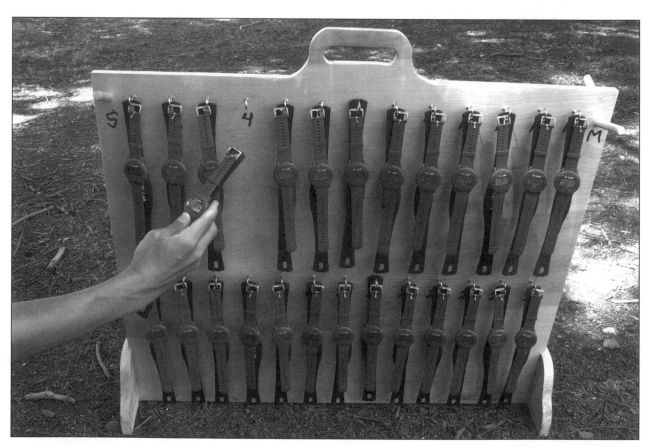

Figure 16.2   When you can match students with the equipment they use in class, it becomes easier to monitor the use of equipment.

The numbering system also helps you keep track of the normal wear and tear of each equipment item. This feature can be particularly useful when you have enough items that you can rotate equipment in and out of usage throughout the school year. Normally, you will receive a discounted price when you buy a large number of items, so if you can use your current set longer, you will make fewer purchases of more items at a greater discount.

Finally, in dealing with equipment management, use a realistic approach. Items will be broken, lost, or stolen over time, but by making students accountable for specific items, you will decrease the number of careless incidents that lead to depletion of equipment. You will at least know which student was responsible for not returning equipment properly. Students should not attempt major repair of equipment because doing so could lead to permanent damage and violation of equipment warranty agreements.

Your Turn ▶▶▶

- ◆ How was equipment distributed in your middle and high school years?

- ◆ As a student did you ever feel a sense of responsibility and ownership over a piece of equipment? Why or why not?

- ◆ How motivated are you to participate in activities when your equipment malfunctions or is in less than ideal shape?

Designing Systems for Managing Your Facilities

The major issue in **facility management** for physical education is having ample, safe space where students can learn and participate in fitness activities. In many schools the physical education teacher does not handle facility maintenance. Teachers must always be aware of the spacing and conditions needed for teaching specific activities, including giving specific attention to maximum occupancy postings in rooms. Large classes, with students moving at various speeds and engaged in various physical tasks, are often the norm for a physical education class. Teachers must provide instructions and protocols for operating in confined spaces and enforce them constantly. In addition, the floor of the activity room should be appropri-

ately marked for movement directions when necessary. The teacher is responsible for maintaining a clean fitness facility that communicates safety.

Safety can be compromised when the physical education facility is used for purposes other than physical education. The gymnasium is a classic example. Equipment may be in place for an afternoon volleyball match while you conduct class activities. Here, you must use your design approach of planning, being systematic, and being creative. The time to design around the problem is not at the start of a particular class. A curriculum design plan should include a schedule of events (time and date) that may affect planned activities. An effective approach would be to create a master schedule at the beginning of the semester and update it as new events pop up. This schedule should be placed where all physical education teachers can review it and update it with information. That way everyone has the same reference point for scheduling, and you are able to plan alternative or modified activities for that day. In addition, you will be able to give your students a heads-up beforehand and prepare them for the change in their activities. Finally, you will have an opportunity to remind them to stay away from equipment that has been set up for that day. Your goal is to prevent horseplay or injuries. The more prepared you are, the more prepared your students will be. And the earlier you can prepare them for changes caused by other scheduled events, the less distraction and disruption will occur in your class.

After designing a better system for equipment and experiencing success with it, Edgar wondered if he could use the same design approach to address other improvements to his program. His next list of problems pertained to persuading the community to become part of his program. He had not experienced much success when he had asked the local ice-skating rink to provide his students with ice time for a lesson unit involving skating. He realized that his typical routine was to ask for things from people who had little connection with the school or his program. He decided that his next mission was to design a system for strengthening the connection with the community by encouraging partnerships. Once the partnerships were in place, he believed that businesses and organizations would be more likely to offer assistance to his program. They would feel more connected to the program and might closely align Edgar's success with their own.

Designing Systems for Community Involvement

Developing **community involvement** with the schools may require a concerted effort on your part. To rally support in the community, you may have to be both the designer of change and an active promoter. One of your tasks would be to identify key members of community, business, and government who are willing to become participants and stakeholders in your effort. Expanding your program beyond the classroom offers clear benefits. According to the Centers for Disease Control, physical education teachers should "promote an environment in which school administrators, faculty, staff, students, and their families can readily participate in some form of physical activity in and out of school" (U.S. Department of Health and Human Services 1999). Physical environment in the schools should be supportive and inviting to the public. According to the International Life Sciences Institute (1999) the public agrees with this sentiment; 90% of parents surveyed said that they would use school facilities for their children's supervised educational and recreational activities in the summer if they were open. In addition, 96% of parents surveyed said they approved of using community volunteers to supervise educational and recreational activities.

Specific challenges are associated with extending school facilities to the community. In dealing with liability issues (see chapter 15) you must recognize that as more people use your facilities, the possibility for injuries increases. This is a special concern when community volunteers become active instructors and supervisors of physical activity. A community program should involve all community factions in drawing up policies and procedures for recreational activities outside school hours. Some teachers supervise after-school activities and set up workshops for after-school volunteers.

One thing is clear. The more opportunities and facilities that community members have to be active, the more likely it is that your students can build on concepts you are teaching them and have avenues available to them for lifelong fitness after they graduate. No matter how dedicated a physical education teacher may be, the challenges associated with changing the environment for school community relations is a task too involved for any one person

to take on. But the teacher who offers an exciting, successful physical education program involving numerous lifelong activities provides an example of the kind of program that community members can benefit from. A successful school program can also establish credibility and worth in the eyes of the public that could lead to continued or growing support for the program and the school.

Your Turn ▶▶▶

♦ What type of access did you have to your middle and high school facilities during school off hours?

♦ Did the school have any supervision mechanism in place?

♦ How important do you see your role as a teacher in setting up opportunities for community involvement with your facilities?

♦ What are the benefits of conducting health and fitness workshops that the public could attend?

♦ Whom would you need help from if you were to make your facilities more accessible to the community?

Creating Partnerships

A rich source of support for help with ongoing equipment and facility problems can be organization and corporate partnerships. You want to show potential outside sponsors how your physical education goals and objectives correspond to their organizational or corporate goals and objectives. Potential sponsors include not only shoe and equipment manufacturers and retailers but also organizations such as health clubs, community centers, municipal parks departments, and golf clubs. If you have evidence of strong activity and interests in your physical education programs from students, parents, teachers, staff, and community residents, you can approach outside resources with good likelihood of success.

Remember that relationships with the community and public schools are extremely important to local businesses. Their support for your program may range from donating disposable painting hats for your students to wear inside shared roller-skating helmets (an effective way of dealing with transmission of head lice from shared equipment) to providing you with facilities during certain off-hour times. These times would be available when most people are at work. What a treat it would be for students who have finished a lesson unit on golf to set up a school tournament (with fun creative prizes) at a local golf course. Companies that cater to the specialized physical activities that you are introducing gain clear benefits because they may gain future consumers. Although this type of sponsorship may take time and test your ability to persevere, people have achieved success in all parts of the country. Be persistent and diligent in your sponsorship building. Any help from companies, including merchandise discounts, used equipment, or discounted participation fees, should be promptly recognized publicly through direct letters of thanks from you and your students. In addition, you may want to show appreciation by informing news agencies through letters to the editor or by contacting local radio and television news assignment desks. These activities accomplish two objectives. First, you are showing proper appreciation for the support and making others aware of the opportunity to help. Second, you are publicizing an exciting new physical education program, achieved through the help of a significant partnership.

Exploring Grant Opportunities

Allow yourself to think beyond company involvement. Organizations may offer funding through **grant opportunities** if you can show that your goals and needs coincide with theirs. In 1993 Mainland High School was able to set up the Lifestyle Improvement and Fitness Enrichment (LIFE) Center through the collaborative efforts of government (Florida Department of Education) and private industry (Wood et al. 1995). State-of-the-art equipment and facilities were secured to create a center that improves cardiovascular fitness and promotes student adoption of a physically active lifestyle. In addition, a goal of adding more fitness technology into the center was addressed. The more people involved in your efforts, the more support you will have and the more long-term commitment you will generate for your program. Everyone likes to back a winner. Think of the objectives and topics presented in this book as potential talking points for generating interest in your program from the public and private sector.

Purpose

Use technology to provide access for outside funding sources to augment your physical education program.

Resource and Procedure

Outside sources are available for funding new educational programs. Link your program goals with far-reaching societal goals, such as getting teens to be more active, creating after-school fitness programs for at-risk students, or promoting antiviolence fitness activities for children and adolescents. Sites such as the Pew Charitable Trusts site at **www.pewtrusts.com/ideas** present current grant projects, calls for grant proposals, and helpful links for educators interested in pursuing outside funding (figure 16.3). More focused Web sources for physical education include **www.aahperd.org** and **pe.central.vt.edu.** The more information you have about the types of projects that are being funded, the more likely you are to submit a proposal that will be accepted.

Figure 16.3 Teachers can use the World Wide Web to search for activity and grant ideas to improve their programs.

Participants in the Mainland High School project made their dream become a reality in the form of a state-of-the-art, award-winning fitness center. They took several clear steps in the start-up phase to go from concept to concrete. If you want to emulate their success, follow these steps:

1. Start with a vision. You do not necessarily need a focused list of specific objectives, but you should develop a statement of desire to serve as a compass for future steps.

2. Share your vision. This is not a one-person operation. Bring in the school administration and other members of the physical education staff. If you are not able to enlist members who are naturally like-minded and sympathetic to the cause, you may need to revisit step 1.

3. Fund the vision. Start developing a fund-gathering approach that identifies partners and granting organizations that may be willing to back your vision with tangible support. You need to be extremely visible and creative in thanking those who support the project.

4. Communicate the vision. Now you are ready to build on the momentum from step 3. Public displays of thanks can be opportunities to inform the public about your successes and elicit more support.

5. Assess needs. You should develop your vision to include sound decisions about adapting the project to the needs of your particular situation. It makes no sense to grow a popular project beyond what would be manageable in terms of facilities, personnel, and equipment. Bigger is not always best, especially if it results in something that you are incapable of controlling.

The list was excerpted from a complete list provided by Wood, Fisher, Huth, and Graham, *Teaching High School Physical Education,* 1995, Human Kinetics, Champaign, Illinois.

After implementing his new design for community involvement, Edgar still found himself discouraged at times by unsuccessful attempts. On certain issues, he seemed to be hitting dead ends. He decided that he needed input from like-minded physical education teachers who were attempting to make changes. He had read list serv postings from his national organization in the past, but because he didn't relate to the topics he never paid much attention. He kept in touch with a friend from college who was teaching in another state. During a recent conversation with her, he mentioned the changes he was making to his program. She was impressed with his progress. Edgar also mentioned the roadblocks that he had run up against. She asked if he had checked the list serv and told him that she had seen a topic heading about effecting change to programs as well as one centering on community involvement. She suggested that he look at those areas because the postings and responses would likely be pertinent to his needs. His creativity came alive following the conversation.

Using Communication Technologies as Resources for New Design

The design of equipment, facility, and community innovations must be specific to the needs of each program. Fortunately, new **communication technologies** have made information about other programs more readily available than ever before. Knowledge is a powerful tool in designing solutions, and the growth of the Internet has created a vehicle for sharing ideas, successes, and resources. People are more willing to share. We do not have to tackle problems concerning facility sharing or equipment management alone. The

World Wide Web provides a lone physical education teacher with a vision and with powerful vehicles for implementing change.

Web sites such as the PE Central home page are changing the physical education profession by housing and providing materials, suggestions, products, curriculum assessment, funding sources, and strategies in all areas from preschool through high school. In the past, teachers experiencing problems could not easily connect with teachers who had designed successful solutions. Rule number one in designing solutions is not to reinvent the wheel. The knowledge-sharing revolution has played a large role in the unparalleled growth of the World Wide Web and Internet technologies.

PE Central home page
www.pecentral.org

In addition to sites set up as clearinghouses for curriculum development ideas, e-mail and **list servers** are valuable resources for equipment and facility management solutions. You can be reasonably sure that a program out there has successfully designed and implemented a solution to the problem you may now be facing. Likewise, if you have found something that worked well with your program, you should provide information on list servers and clearinghouse Web sites so that others may benefit. No physical education program is an island. A success at one school can be a catalyst for change throughout the profession.

Using Technology to Communicate Your Success

Finally, you want to make the public aware of the successful designs you have put into action to turn your physical education program into a purposeful and exciting experience for your students. A physical education **class Web site** could easily have a link from your school's home page (provided your school has one). Software allows relative programming novices to create and update Web page information. Your most valuable resource may be your students, some of whom are likely to be experienced in Web design and development. Visit

Web sites that you find particularly interesting and useful and analyze what components you like. A Web site should be accessible, visual, and easily navigated. People will never return to your site if they feel trapped and cannot leave easily. Simplicity in content and layout is the rule. Web sites such as dreamink (**www.dreamink.com**) provide design tips for creating successful sites. A worthwhile classroom activity is to have students brainstorm about how and why their class activities and experiences are preparing them to stay active for a lifetime. Besides developing content for your Web site with this exercise, you are assessing whether your students are recognizing your messages and efforts.

Web sites such as Web Design Guide (**www.dreamink.com**) provide design tips for creating your own successful Web sites. Web sites such as **www.videomaker.com** provide information about production techniques and issues.

Finally, the video equipment that you use for your effective learning and assessment example presented in chapter 2 can also be used for creating public service announcements, cable access programs, and video presentations for parent teacher organizations and chamber of commerce meetings. Your design efforts will likely go unrecognized in the community unless you vigorously tell your story. Simplicity is the rule with video vignettes. Develop a clear objective for your video vignettes, such as demonstrating how new activities in physical education class promote lifelong fitness activities. You might produce something as simple as a 30-second spot for local television and radio broadcasts. Another possibility is a longer program that could be shown on community cable access channels or presented at community meetings. Grants and support for community cable program development are often available at the local and national level, especially when issues center on education and promote public health issues. Sites such as **www.videomaker.com** cover topics ranging from beginning video production techniques to creating full professional broadcast productions.

Summary

Physical education programs continue to identify and address the need for change. Implementing ideas presented in this book requires changes not only in curriculum development, design, and delivery but also in day-to-day management of equipment, facilities, and public awareness and involvement. Change cannot take place without a strong and committed effort based on fundamental design principles. Although redesign efforts may at first appear to be overwhelming, support systems offer detailed descriptions of improvement projects, suggestions, and resources for new projects. Advancement in communication technologies allows instantaneous access to support and a vehicle for communicating physical education successes. Finally, community resources and support have provided other programs with substantial solutions to the challenges associated with facility and equipment management.

Checking for Understanding ►►►

- What direct benefits are associated with developing and strengthening community partnerships with your physical education program?

- What are the three basic components in a design process?

- What is the benefit of designing student responsibility for gathering, using, maintaining, and returning equipment?

- What design considerations can be adopted to help students accept changes associated with equipment management?

- How can learning be negatively impacted by having to teach in a multipurpose room?

- How can communication among physical education teachers, coaches, and other school officials who may have events scheduled in the same room be better coordinated?

- What is the position of the Centers for Disease Control and Prevention as it pertains to schools providing access and activities beyond the student body?

For Reflection and Discussion ►►►

- How can communication technologies be used in securing, maintaining, reinforcing, and communicating successful partnerships between community members and your physical education program?

- How can teachers prepare students to deal with changes in classroom facilities?

- What strategy could teachers use to convince outside business sources to get involved in sponsoring their physical education program?

- What visuals would you expect to be particularly effective in communicating successful partnerships in a promotional video or television news story? How would they be effective? How could you use those visuals in the future to recruit more potential partners?

References

International Life Sciences Institute. 1999. *Executive report.* As cited in U.S. Department of Health and Human Services, *Promoting physical activity: A guide for community action.* Champaign IL: Human Kinetics.

U.S. Department of Health and Human Services. 1999. *Promoting physical activity: A guide for community action.* Champaign, IL: Human Kinetics.

Wood, K., C. Fisher, T. Huth, and P. Graham. 1995. Opening the door to tomorrow's classroom. *Teaching High School Physical Education.* 1(1):1, 4–5, 8.

Suggested Readings

American Alliance for Health, Physical Education, Recreation and Dance. 1999. *Physical education for lifelong fitness: The Physical Best teacher's guide.* Champaign, IL: Human Kinetics.

Baker, K. 2001. Promoting your physical education program. *Journal of Physical Education, Recreation and Dance* 72(2):37–40.

Mitchell, M., and T.P. Cone. 2001. No gym? No problem! Maintaining quality physical education in alternative spaces. *Journal of Physical Education, Recreation and Dance* 72(5):25–29.

Potter, L. 1997. Getting the media on our side. *Education Digest* 62(5):22–24.

Part VI

The *Journey*

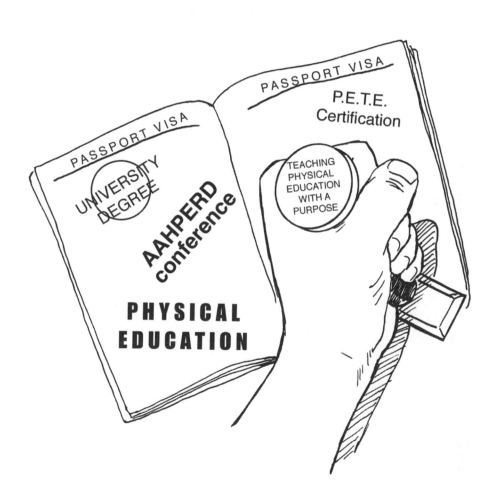

Chapter 17

Emerging as a Teacher Leader

The greatest problem in teaching is not how to get rid of the "deadwood," but how to create, sustain, and motivate good teachers.

— *Michael Fullan and Andrew Hargreaves (1996)*

Dave and Chuck are best friends. They have been teaching physical education at the same middle school for 10 years. Both men believe they have an ideal work situation. Their principal is knowledgeable about the physical education national standards and firmly supports their program. For instance, every hire she made in the department was for a full-time teacher. Each of the six teachers, three men and three women, is experienced and has a reputation of being innovative and current. Dave and Chuck think the world of their department because everyone gets along, listens to ideas, strives to be a good teacher, and works to bring innovative activities to the curriculum. Other teachers and parents support their program as well. Chuck believes that they enjoy this support because the department joined academic teams and promoted their program with the PTA two years ago.

A prestigious law firm in a neighboring town recently offered Dave's wife a job. Both are excited by the opportunities the job and move would create for their children, so they decided to relocate. Luckily, one of the middle schools in their new town had an opening for a physical education teacher. Dave applied, and he landed the job. Although the move was best for his wife and family, Dave knew that he would miss Chuck, the department, and the school. He and Chuck vowed to stay in touch, and they did. Mostly, they spoke on the telephone on Monday nights after football to go over game highlights, compare team statistics, and catch up on life.

After several conversations Chuck became concerned about Dave's work situation. Evidently, Dave found out quickly that his new principal did not support physical education. The staff kept largely to themselves. No one seemed openly friendly or willing to share ideas as they did at his old school. And the teachers in the physical education department were difficult to get along with. The department was made up of four physical educators. Three were full-time, one man and two women. The part-time person taught four sections of English and one section of physical education and was not available for locker-room supervision. It was a tough year for Dave. He told Chuck that he felt trapped. Although the move had been good for his family, he didn't enjoy going to work and he wondered how long he would last if things didn't change.

◆ Learning Objectives

After reading this chapter you will be able to

- describe the nature of teaching as it relates to overload, isolation, group think, and limited teacher roles;
- explain why it is important for physical educators to emerge as teacher leaders;
- define school culture;
- explain stakeholders and their influence on school culture;
- define a school microculture;
- explain the importance of power relationships;
- describe why a principal is key to school reform and change;
- examine the meaning of informal leadership roles;
- list several ideas for developing positive public relations and advocacy; and
- state several guidelines to keep in mind as you strive to become a teacher leader and change agent.

◆ Key Terms and Phrases

Overload
Isolation
Group think
School culture
Stakeholders
Power

ave and Chuck are fortunate to have each other to talk to about their teaching and their careers. Each year many educators have experiences like Dave's. New and veteran teachers alike take new positions with hopes of being part of a vibrant school community where students are important, teachers are valued, and learning is a high priority. This is the reality in many schools, but many other schools offer little support to students, student learning, and teacher collegiality. Taking a position at a different school is not the only way that a teacher might move from a supportive, vibrant learning community to an unsupported, stifled environment. Changes to administrative leadership and staff may cause such a change. Just thinking about this may be disturbing. Some teachers become frustrated by this reality and wonder what they can do to change it. In this chapter we will examine the issue more closely and explore ways to create positive change in schools to create vibrant learning communities.

Increasing Complexity of Teaching

The best way to begin to understand schools and the nature of change is to understand more clearly the complexity of teaching. In the last two decades, the nature of teaching has changed drastically. Teaching has become more complex in several ways.

National and state standards and numerous accountability measures have changed the complexion of teacher work. Many school districts and teachers have committed time and effort to improve student test scores, particularly in language arts and mathematics. When this happens, many administrators adjust school schedules by eliminating classes such as art, music, and physical education. Administrators have also cut minutes from class periods to free up time to work specifically on math and language arts. Some schools have asked homeroom teachers to spend their entire period teaching vocabulary, reading, or math skills. Numerous schools have provided teachers from all subjects with training about how to teach language arts and mathematics. We have visited schools where 10 minutes in the middle of the day is dedicated to reading regardless of the subject during that period—science, foreign language, or physical education. In many ways, find-

ing extra time to devote to these fundamental skills is admirable. The difficulties teachers have with these efforts are twofold. First, it takes time away from their own subject matter content, and second, many teachers must supervise and teach subject matter outside their area of expertise.

In a study by Fullan and Hargreaves (1996) teachers identified five problems that affect teaching and create barriers to educational change and reform:

1. Overload
2. Isolation
3. Group think
4. Limited teacher role
5. Poor solutions and shallow trends

We will use these five problems to discuss the increasing complexity of teaching physical education.

Overload

Teachers' responsibilities have changed a great deal in the last 15 to 20 years. As a result, teachers find themselves engaged in responsibilities they were never trained for. Several metaphors for teaching illustrate these responsibilities. First is teacher as teacher. The primary responsibility of teaching is helping students learn. Changes in teaching have included moving from a teacher-centered approach to a student-centered approach. In other words, teachers help students learn to take responsibility for their own learning. Teachers have moved away from the front of the classroom or gym. They have stepped out from behind the lectern and away from straight lines of calisthenics into learning activities that engage student thinking, initiative, and interaction. The teacher is no longer "the sage on the stage." Instead, she has become the "guide on the side."

A shift away from teacher-centered instruction requires retraining for many physical educators. Retraining, like learning a sport skill for the first time, takes time and patience. Student-centered instruction also requires thoughtful planning and preparation, and in some cases more planning and preparation. Unfortunately, school schedules do not give teachers ample preparation time, so many physical educators plan before and after school. Others plan in the evening and over the weekend. During instruction, teachers must supervise student learning. Gone are the days of supervised game play in which teachers break the class into two teams and watch them play. The stereotype of physical educators handing out equipment and then sitting back to watch kids play, read the paper, and eat a doughnut is fading into the gym floor. Effective teaching requires creative and interactive supervision. Effective teaching involves showing accountability for student learning. Interactive instructional styles are only part of teacher **overload.**

Large class size is another contributor to overload (figure 17.1). In California a governor's initiative has the goal to lower class sizes in elementary schools. Nationally, former President Clinton called for the reduction of class sizes. As a result many school districts are trying to lower class size in elementary classrooms. At the middle and high schools, administrators are striving to lower class size in subjects like English, math, and science. But many schools are overcrowded, and few new schools are being built. Therefore, a reduction in class size in one subject creates a bulging effect in another. Many students are rescheduled to peripheral courses (courses outside the academic core), such as art, music, industrial arts, and physical education. Imagine English and math classes with no more than 20 students while other classes have 30, 40, or more. We know firsthand that teachers with whom we work have anywhere from 40 to 65 students in their classes.

Indoor physical education facilities cannot accommodate large class sizes, so when large classes are forced indoors instruction is more difficult.

Although field space can accommodate large numbers, instructing large groups of students in open space is challenging. Let's not forget that most departments do not have enough equipment for a large number of students in one class. To ease the situation, one or two teacher aides may be assigned to large physical education classes. Aides are generally not trained in content and instruction, so their responsibilities are often limited to helping the teacher manage a large group.

The issue of overload doesn't stop here. The Education for All Handicapped Children Act (P.L. 94-142, 1975) and the Individuals With Disabilities Act (1995) clearly established that all children with special needs should be placed in regular classrooms unless, of course, their needs cannot be met there. Schools that comply with children with disabilities laws participate in full inclusion, integrating children with special needs into regular classrooms. Full inclusion is a positive, powerful approach to providing education to all students, yet it can create additional overload for teachers whose class size is already large.

Meeting the needs of all students is a primary goal of education. Physical educators strive to assess student ability and prepare lessons that will serve the needs of all students in class. Students with special needs receive the same dedication and service, and their needs vary in severity. Physical educators must work with the exceptional student to determine what modifications, if any, they must make with activities done in class.

Figure 17.1 Large class sizes can create problems for physical education teachers.

Students with disabilities usually work with a team of professionals who have developed an individualized education plan (IEP) (see chapter 6). This plan includes specific goals and objectives. The physical educator has a responsibility to work with the student to achieve the goals and objectives written for physical education. Working with exceptional students is highly rewarding. When several student IEPs are added to a class of 40 to 65 students, the physical educator must prepare well and work hard to help all students achieve learning objectives.

Most of the overload discussed so far has dealt with planning, preparation, and instruction of physical education. Teacher responsibilities outside class also contribute to overload. Many physical educators serve on academic teams and committees. Academic teaming requires time to plan with colleagues. Schools provide some planning time, but most planning will occur outside class, prep time, and school. Committees are another responsibility. Physical educators concerned with students will be active members of student IEP teams. Those teams will meet after school periodically to review students' progress. Physical educators will serve on other committees as well.

A teacher's responsibility doesn't end there. Many school-related functions require teacher or adult supervision (see chapter 14). Physical educators volunteer to chaperone dances, pep rallies, bake sales, car washes, spaghetti feeds, and pancake breakfasts.

Finally, many physical educators coach several sport teams each year. Coaching requires dedication, time, planning, and preparation. Many physical educators who coach spend from two to six hours after school conducting practices and attending games, meets, or matches. Many sport teams require time on one or two days of the weekend as well. Physical educators may find themselves having insufficient time to prepare for both their classes and their teams. This dilemma, known as the teacher-coach role conflict, adds to the sense of teacher overload (see chapter 14).

Isolation

Teaching has been called the lonely profession (Lortie 1975). It's lonely because teachers often work with students all day and never spend large blocks of time with colleagues. Teaching physical education can be lonely too. Being on your own all day may cause a feeling of **isolation.** Isolation is not always a bad thing, but it prevents you from sharing ideas, discussing concerns, and observing the styles of other teachers.

Many physical educators share an office with one, two, or three colleagues. They may banter here and there in passing. They may spend time with colleagues during department meetings, staff meetings, and lunch. Most physical educators have a heavy class schedule with one preparation period. They typically teach their classes by themselves. Between classes, they return to the department office to supervise the locker room and respond to student questions and requests for locker combinations, loaner clothes, and solutions to peer confrontations. As student interactions subside, teachers fill out attendance sheets or perform other administrative requests before making last-minute preparations for their next class. The day is fast paced. Teachers can become comfortable in the daily routine of working alone.

Isolation can breed conservatism and resistance to innovation in teaching (Lortie 1975). Isolation can lead teachers to be protective about their classes, territorial about their resources, and defensive to criticism and suggestions. Isolation can make it difficult for teachers to be open to observation and team teaching. Isolation can keep effective strategies and innovative ideas locked away with one teacher. At the same time, it can hide teacher incompetence and weakness. Isolation limits professional development. Physical educators accustomed to working alone may find it difficult to work with others on collaborative endeavors and programmatic changes. But isolation is a way of teaching that has been around for more than a hundred years. To understand it better, let's look at some of its causes.

Traditionally, schools are built and divided into compartments similar to the carton of eggs in your refrigerator. Each egg sits alone in a space separate from the others in the box. Classrooms and departments are arranged the same way in schools, giving rise to the description "egg-crate structure of schooling" (Lortie 1975). So by the very structure of the building, teachers are isolated from each other by classrooms. In many ways, physical educators are further isolated from the other parts of school. Physical education offices are divided by gender and located in the middle of the girls' and boys' locker rooms. Gymnasiums and athletic fields are usually located at one end of the school or even in a separate location such as across a parking lot, creek, road, or city block. Communication is difficult to maintain with other parts of the school and even within the department itself because gender responsibilities separate the teachers.

Fullan and Hargreaves (1996) offer a wonderful quotation regarding the issue of isolation: "The problem of isolation is a deep-seated one. Architecture often supports it. The timetable reinforces it. Overload sustains it. History legitimates it." Finding ways to relieve the isolation and privatism of teaching will lead to stronger student achievement. Yet breaking the wall of isolation and replacing it with collegiality doesn't guarantee positive results. What may emerge is the negative side of group think.

T'nT

Purpose

Use technology to actively create a vibrant network of physical education teachers and students and college professors to overcome feelings of isolation within the profession.

Resource and Procedure

Use e-mail technology to establish lines of communication with numerous professionals and soon-to-be professionals and thus overcome the isolation problem. When you visit professional conferences, networking becomes a major goal. Find like-minded physical education teachers and professors and students to share ideas, frustrations, and successes. Connecting with others for support is vital in the teaching profession. Create an e-mail group and maintain regular contact. Be aware that everyone is busy, so shorter direct messages are appreciated and more likely to be returned.

Group Think

Improvement strategies for program and school reform in the 1990s have encouraged us to work collaboratively with our colleagues (Goodlad 1994). You would think that when teachers work together to examine instruction, curriculum, student needs, facilities and equipment, and other issues, positive changes and programmatic reform would result. The answer is that it does, but not as often as we would like. Why have we not seen the expected results? Well, the answer is not simple.

One reason may stem from the realization that schools are not set up for collegial work. Recall the egg-crate structure of schools. Working alone, isolated from other teachers, is the norm. Isolation among teachers can breed defensiveness, distrust, and territoriality. Teachers seeking to break out of the egg crate and find ways to work collaboratively will have to learn how. Teachers who learn how to create collegial schools or professional communities in which learning is central to the vision of the school become powerful forces of change and school improvement. (Brandt 2000; Fullan and Hargreaves 1996; Senge et al. 2000). Other teachers may demonstrate contrived collegiality that works to maintain the status quo or even block innovation and creative solutions (Fullan and Hargreaves 1996).

The whole idea of **group think** can be either positive or negative. On the positive side, teachers who come together to share ideas and critically examine curriculum and instructional strategies will develop positive collaboration with one another. This type of positive group think often results in constructive changes to programs. Any changes that occur are purposeful, not change for change's sake. The opposite side of group think is a negative or destructive collaboration among colleagues. Teachers may come together to discuss why they don't need to look seriously at their teaching or the quality of their program. Teachers engaged in negative group think and group talk find ways to keep things the same. Negative group think is as powerful as positive group think. Teachers surrounded by negativity may find their ideas for innovation squashed or dismissed.

Through our experience in working with physical education departments, we have witnessed both positive and negative group think. Negative group think may look something like this. It is the beginning of the school year. The physical education department chair, Joel, is excited to bring the department together to talk about newly mandated state standards for physical education. After viewing the standards Joel realizes that the department is doing many things well. At the same time the department could improve a few things in the existing curriculum. Joel is determined to share his findings with the department and ask them to join him in examining areas of the curriculum that they can improve. Calling the meeting was the first difficult task. He had the distinct feeling that the teachers attended the meeting only because the principal had required all staff to attend an initial department meeting. Two of the seven teachers in the department, Barbara and Stephanie, arrived at the meeting on time and were comfortable with joining the department chair in working to improve the curriculum. Two others, Dion and Greg, arrived a few minutes late and seemed not to care one way or the other. Tom didn't make the meeting because he was tied up in football practice. The seventh member of the department, Ginny, arrived 30 minutes late. She was in a grouchy mood and demonstrated with strong body language that she did not want to be there and felt that the meeting was a waste of her time. As Joel introduced his findings and asked for department help, Ginny offered flippant remarks and was adamant that the effort would be a waste of time because nothing ever changes. She added freely that she was already over-worked and underpaid and didn't have time for one thing more. Dion and Greg used sarcasm to show their alliance with Ginny. Barbara and Stephanie sat quietly, hoping not to make waves. Quickly, Joel realized that his request had just been shot down and that any examination of the program would be contrived or sabotaged. This example of negative group think shows how nega-tive collegiality can block ideas and suggestions. You also notice the power and influence of one member of the group.

Now, switch channels and imagine a positive scenario. Jennifer and Mike spent two weeks over the summer at a physical education institute. They learned some exciting ways to improve class man-agement and instruction. Together, they asked their department chair if they could share some of what they learned at the department meeting scheduled for the first week of school. Their de-partment chair, Connie, was thrilled that Jennifer and Mike wanted to share information, so she placed them on the agenda. The other four mem-bers of the department attended the meeting in good spirits. It was evident that they all enjoyed seeing each other on their return from summer vacation. The meeting went smoothly. When Jen-nifer and Mike shared what they had learned, their colleagues asked many questions. All of them thought that they could use several of the man-agement techniques. As a department, they de-cided that they would like Jennifer and Mike to teach them the grading program they had learned at the institute. Connie immediately set up another meeting so that Jennifer and Mike could instruct everyone in the use of the new grading software. When the meeting ended and the department headed off to lunch together, they were still talk-ing about the possibilities of using various man-agement and instructional techniques in their classes. Collegiality in this department appears

genuine. The group encourages sharing and try-ing new things to improve their program.

Group think is powerful. Positive group think in departments and schools is a key to program im-provement and school reform. Positive group think doesn't mean that everyone gets along all the time. One of the most important rules of colle-gial discussion, as we pointed out in our discus-sion of the curriculum development process (chapter 6), is an agreement that individuals may disagree on occasion. When individuals offer var-ied opinions and perspectives, a group often has its most meaningful discussions.

As noted in the scenarios, an individual can powerfully influence a group, in either a positive or a negative way. Thus the individual teacher re-mains a significant force and can be a strong leader in bringing about school improvement.

Limited Teacher Role

Traditionally, the role of a physical education teacher has been described by a series of teacher tasks such as planning a class, setting up equip-ment, taking attendance, making announcements, leading warm-ups, teaching movement skills, or-ganizing skill practice, providing feedback, assess-ing student learning, and supervising game play. These tasks are essential to good teaching and student learning. But these traditional tasks de-scribe only what the teacher does in the class-room. We have come to understand that improv-ing and maintaining quality physical education programs requires the physical educator to step beyond these traditional tasks.

School improvement and school reform litera-ture recognize the need for teachers to be involved in the process from the beginning. This idea is dif-ferent from the philosophy of years ago when prin-cipals and other school administrators provided the leadership. We have learned that school im-provement led only by school administrators re-sults in what is called a top-down approach, a method that teachers often resist. They feel that administrators frequently miss the mark because they do not interact directly with students and student needs every day. Principals who collabo-rate with teachers create a more formidable team for effecting school improvement. Physical edu-cators who are able to step beyond the gym and engage in active leadership roles will help steer the physical education program and school to-ward positive improvement (figure 17.2).

Teacher leadership begins with you.

Teach developmentally appropriate physical education always.

Reflect on all aspects of your teaching.

Be willing to step outside your comfort zone and take risks.

Commit to professional growth and development.

Build professional relationships with students, parents, colleagues, administrators and community.

Utilize appropriate assessment tools for student learning and effective teaching.

"Push and support principals and other administrators to develop interactive professionalism" (Fullan and Hargreaves, 1996, 64).

"Refuse to mind your own business" (Hargreaves and Fullan, 1998, 92).

Expand your circle of influence through the relationships and bridges that you build with others.

Understand that Rome was not built in a day, and neither is a developmentally appropriate physical education program.

Learn from your mistakes and experiences.

Glean information from professional development opportunities, resources, and networks in order to stay current.

Find patience and be persistent!

Figure 17.2 Teacher leadership guidelines.

The physical educator who expands her role to become a teacher leader not only helps the program and school but also avoids falling prey to isolation. Remember, isolation separates the teacher from colleagues. Over time, isolation and the monotony of class routines can lull the best teacher into mediocrity. When this happens we see a physical educator who has done the same routine for 10, 20, or 30 years simply as a teacher with one year of experience 10, 20, or 30 times over (Fullan and Hargreaves 1996). Your biggest challenge will be to make sure this doesn't happen to you. One strategy is to break down isolation and step up to the plate as a teacher leader.

Poor Solutions and Shallow Trends

Overload, isolation, and group think—what else does a physical educator need to know about the complexity of teaching and school reform? Well, first we remind you that the information in the preceding paragraphs should not discourage you from becoming the most effective teacher you can possibly be. Second, we don't want this information to overwhelm your sense of ability to accomplish great things. Keep in mind that knowledge is

power. When you understand the nature of teaching and the culture of schools, chances are you will be more effective in devising useful strategies for effective instruction, curriculum development, and program improvement. Ultimately, you must do all these things to meet student needs and help them learn.

We now shift our discussion to the kinds of program and school improvement strategies that have been unsuccessful. This information will be helpful as you learn more about your department and school. History offers compelling lessons. From failed attempts we learn how to avoid making the same mistakes, and we generate thoughtful and innovative strategies.

It is probably safe to say that program or school improvement that doesn't involve the teachers will result in failure. We must find a way to mobilize physical educators to step beyond the gym and assume leadership roles as teachers. Physical educators who accept the challenge must be committed to improving teaching practices and programs. Let's face it—change will not occur if physical educators give lip service to new strategies. Teachers must be willing to incorporate proposals for change and improvement into their classes and programs.

Education reform is often locked into faddism and quick-fix solutions. When word gets out that a great program or curriculum guarantees improved student test scores or sizable improvement in student learning, schools are quick to buy and try the program. If the school fails to examine how the product will meet student needs or how the product would have to be modified to be useful to its students, failure often results. Schools must also look closely at the kind of training and practice teachers need to use the product successfully. For example, a few years ago the school district where we live decided to buy and try a brand new math program that had received rave reviews, although we were not sure it had been field tested extensively. The district spent a lot of money to buy the program for all the schools. Teachers did their best to try the program and found that it did not work at all. Students were not learning math fundamentals as quickly and solidly as they should have. As a result the program was nixed. The district spent five years to phase it out and replace it with curriculum that worked once before.

We have seen similar things happen with physical education programs. Many physical educators are in search of quick-fix activities that will keep kids busy, happy, and good (Placek 1983). If you remember from chapter 10, these kinds of teachers are known as BU-HA-GOO teachers. Some physical educators attend conference after conference collecting activities that they think their students will enjoy. Realistically, there is nothing wrong with this approach. We too learn and collect activities from teachers at conferences and meetings. The problem lies with the approach. If a teacher is merely looking for activities that will keep the kids BU-HA-GOO, then the teacher is not thinking about what students should be learning and why. If we think about program goals and objectives, then we go back to the idea of curriculum development. When you center everything on what students should be learning, then activities collected from conferences serve to complement the program. Unfortunately, many teachers become caught up in the routine of presenting one activity after another. Activities strung together with no thought of what students will learn from them are nothing more than activities. When this happens, it is easy to see why students and others have difficulty taking physical education seriously.

Given sufficient time and support to create the change, some plans for reform would work. Unfortunately, timelines for improvement and reform are often short and unrealistic. This circumstance often develops when policy makers, administrators, or legislators are impatient for positive results. People tend to underestimate the complexity of school and program problems. Problems must be identified and examined thoroughly before any plans for improvement can be designed. Once designed, proposals for improvement must be phased in. This process requires time, support, and resources. Many schools and departments reach the implementation phase but fail because money, resources, and support are not available. When this happens, it is no wonder that committed teachers withdraw from these sorts of endeavors and retreat to the comfort and isolation of their classes.

Steps for Creating Change

Teachers must guard against making a change just to be doing something. Movements for educational change or reform are not necessarily positive or warranted. Many teaching strategies and program practices are highly effective and should remain in place, not be cast aside. To illustrate this point, folklore often reveals stories about the wisdom people acquire with age and experience. When an elder person dies or is cast aside by his or her people, the people suffer the loss of the elder's wisdom. This event may be similar to losing an entire library (Fullan and Hargreaves 1996) or access to the Internet.

On many occasions change is imperative. You must learn how to examine teaching and curriculum critically to determine its effectiveness. You must learn when change is needed and when it is not. You also must teach others how to examine and analyze teaching and curriculum effectiveness. When you and your colleagues are informed, you can make good decisions about curriculum and instruction.

Let's return to the scenario in the beginning of the chapter. Dave's wife accepted a great position in a new town, and the family moved. Dave was fortunate to find a teaching position at a local middle school. The physical education department at his new school was different from the department at his old school. Dave was discouraged in his first year. His reports to his friend and former colleague Chuck included descriptions of a department with no direction or collegiality. Dave also complained that his new colleagues had no idea about student needs, program goals, or curriculum development. He was surrounded by teachers who believe that keeping kids busy, happy, and good (BU-HA-GOO) was the epitome of effective teaching. Dave was dejected. He wasn't sure how long he would last with BU-HA-GOO teachers.

Dave is in a difficult situation. His experience is similar to that of many physical educators. He has several choices. First, he can keep to himself and hide within the isolation provided by school structure. If he does this, he won't have to worry about the other teachers, and he can probably get away with doing what he knows is right in his own classes. Second, he can choose to leave the department. Perhaps he has a supplement credential in another subject, such as math. If so, he may be able to ask for more math sections to teach. He could quit his job and find another, but he may be unable to find a teaching position at another school in the district or at another school in the area. Third, Dave can study his situation and begin implementing steps for change in hopes of having a positive effect on his department and program. Dave has an adventurous spirit. He doesn't give up easily and loves a challenge. He decides to strive for change. Dave tried the steps outlined by the tenets of Action Research (Coghlan and Brannick 2001; Greenwood and Levin 1998; Stringer 1999) and was pleased by the results.

Step 1: Examining School Culture

Creating change within a school, department, or program is extremely difficult if you don't understand how it all works together. One step requires that you examine **school culture**. Find out how your school, department, and program operate. The goal is to understand how everyone in your school community interacts with one another. Examining school culture begins with information gathering. Your role is to be a detective, one who watches and pays close attention to the interactions, rules, norms, routines, decision-making processes, and politics of your school and community. As you do this, you will learn important lessons about school culture.

To understand school culture we look at the school as a complex whole, an organization that has its own set of knowledge, beliefs, philosophies, morals, values, routines, rules, norms, ceremonies, heroes, and informal understandings. You already have a great deal of experience with school culture. Think back to your years as a high school student. You were aware of cool fashion and popular kids. As a student you knew which teachers didn't mind if you strolled into class tardy and which teachers seemed to watch you closely, just hoping to catch you doing something wrong. Rallies, dances, and sporting events were important ceremonies. Some students emerged as heroes through their accomplishments in sports, drama, music, and art. Most students wore school colors at school events to show their school pride. All of this makes up school culture.

Students witness and participate in one aspect of school culture. As a teacher you experience school culture from another dimension, one that includes seeing how important decisions are made about school management and program delivery. What would school culture look like from a teacher's perspective? Well, it would include the items mentioned earlier—cool fashion, popular kids, daily routines, homeroom, bells sounding the beginning and end to periods. It would include teaching tasks, interactions with students, interactions with other teachers, and school events. In addition, teachers observe and participate in department, staff, and IEP meetings, as well as other committee meetings, so those events would be part of the school culture from the perspective of a teacher, as would various administrative tasks like completing attendance and tardy sheets.

Teachers make up one group of people active within a school culture. Active groups of people are called **stakeholders**. Stakeholders have an investment in what happens at school. Among the other stakeholders are students, parents, administrators, school staff, some agencies and businesses, and the surrounding community. Your examination of school culture should include an understanding of how all stakeholders participate in the operation of the school.

Interactions among stakeholders support school culture. Interactions, whether they are collaborative or confrontational, occur because stakeholders have established many formal and informal understandings about what it means to be at school. A formal understanding may be the physical education handbook that explains rules and criteria for grading student learning. An informal understanding may be that people walk forward on the right side of a hallway between periods. If you were to walk against the sea of students in the hallway, you would notice puzzled or unkind looks, and you would have physical difficulty moving forward and around the students. Another example of informal understanding might involve lunchtime in the teachers' room. Teachers probably take the same seats around the lunch table every day. If a substitute teacher were to take a regular teacher's chair, people might feel some tension for a moment. Depending on who the teachers are and how they handle change, the substitute teacher may catch some friendly ribbing, be asked to move, or feel momentary awkwardness in the room after sitting down.

School culture is the big picture, or the macroculture. Within this macroculture are microcultures, or smaller groups. The compartmentalized structure of schools enables the formation of some of these subcultures. For instance, many schools group teachers with similar training and expertise into departments. Therefore, if you teach physical education you are a member of the Physical Education Department. If you coach you are a member of the Athletic Department. If you teach one section of science, you are a member of the Science Department. Each department typically has a chairperson who serves as the department leader. Each department establishes its own set of rules, norms, philosophies, values, routines, ceremonies, heroes, and informal understandings, creating a complex microculture.

Microcultures may be formal groups like a department or a committee. Microcultures can also be groups of people who spend time together regularly. Teachers who eat lunch together every day in the teachers' room would qualify as a microculture. As a teacher you should pay close attention to microcultures in the school to begin to understand their relationship to power.

Your Turn ▶▶▶

- As a class, describe the culture of the classroom. How does this culture affect your behavior in class and outside class.
- Conduct an on-campus observation of a school culture at a local school. Once you have completed your observation, discuss the positive and negative aspects of this school culture, its influence on student learning, and its effect on the physical education program.

Step 2: Understanding Power Relationships

Sarason (1990) introduced the idea of power relationships in schools. He talks about two definitions of power. First, **power** is the control of, authority over, or influence over others. Another, less confrontational, definition of power is the "ability to act or produce an effect" (49). In the paragraphs that follow we will look at power relationships in schools using both definitions.

Traditionally, school management is hierarchical. Hierarchy illustrates power as an authority structure. Examples of control are state and federal legislation that mandates what happens in schools. Boards of education take control when they oversee the work of district offices. Superintendents of schools show authority in their management of school policy and procedures. Each school in a district has a leader, the principal, who demonstrates influence over teachers by carrying out the commands of the superintendent. The hierarchy continues. Principals manage the daily functions of schools with the help of one or more assistant principals. Department chairs carry forth the orders from the principal and lead their teachers. Teachers answer to department chairs. Teachers must climb this long chain of command one link at a time to state their concerns and suggestions. Teachers, even with all their training and expertise, are on the lowest rung of the traditional school hierarchy. Their voices often go unheard. Teachers, those closest to the students and more in touch with student needs, are seldom asked to contribute to important school decisions.

In many ways the traditional school hierarchy is not set up to treat teachers as professionals; instead, it is designed to regard teachers as hired help who are paid to carry out predetermined tasks (Sarason 1990). True professionals have command of a body of knowledge (like physical education and pedagogy) and control over the rendering of their services. Teachers will proudly acknowledge their subject matter expertise, but most will report that they don't have control over what and how they teach.

Reform efforts recognize that teacher expertise is underused. The creation of professional communities would allow better use of teacher expertise and would encourage teachers to continue to develop throughout their careers. Establishing professional communities in schools would break the isolation of teaching that we discussed earlier. Professional communities would encourage teachers to work together, share, learn, and provide leadership concerning student learning and welfare (Brandt 2000). School districts and principals are beginning to recognize the value and need for teacher expertise in making decisions about schooling.

A school stakeholder who has a great deal of power and influence in schools is the school principal. The principal can single-handedly create and sustain positive change or prevent change from taking place. Because the principal is key in any school reform, it is important to get to know your principal and determine if that person is an effective leader or not. An effective principal will be able to assist your efforts to make positive curriculum and instruction changes to your physical education program.

The experience of one of our students illustrates the point. After graduating a number of years ago, this student took a physical education position at a nearby middle school. The principal at that school was a go-getter. He hired her with the intention of helping her make changes in the physical education program to bring it in line with state standards. Our student friend and neophyte teacher was a go-getter herself. She rose to the challenge in a department of veteran teachers. That year was not easy for her, but with the principal's support she persuaded the department to make drastic changes to its curriculum. By her third year several veteran teachers had left. Innovative teachers willing to comply with state standards and work to improve the physical education program replaced them. Our ex-student would not have been as effective without the help of her principal. If this principal had not been at her school when she was hired, our guess is that our young colleague would have helped bring about program change but that accomplishing it would have taken longer. Keep power relationships in mind, particularly the power and influence of the principal, as you consider your role as a teacher leader and change agent.

In reform efforts, teachers are redefining themselves as teacher leaders and change agents by taking on informal leadership roles. Informal leadership roles are about stepping beyond the gym or classroom and into the school community. In these roles, teachers are becoming involved in making important school decisions and promoting quality curriculum. People in informal leadership roles can be highly effective. One doesn't have to be a department chairperson to be a leader. Many effective leaders provide leadership and guidance from the sideline.

Step 3: Assuming Informal Teacher Leadership Roles

Remember from the earlier scenario that Dave decided to stay with his new job and try to improve the physical education program. He spent much of his first year learning about the school culture and the nature of power relationships there. He wasn't asked to assume any formal leadership roles. He was comfortable with that because he believed he could be more effective as an informal leader.

Understanding the power of informal leadership roles, Dave started by modeling effective teaching strategies in his own classes. He shared with his colleagues management and instructional techniques that worked at his old school. For instance, at his old school, Dave's department kept track of student locks with easy-to-use computer software. So at his new school, Dave took his computer to his new office, placed it on his desk, and volunteered to take charge of locks for the boys' locker room. He entered all the lock numbers and combinations. His colleagues were amazed at the ease and efficiency of his lock management system. Soon the other teachers wanted to learn how to use the program. The women loaded it into their computer in the girls' locker room, so the department now tracks every lock with computers. The teachers are impressed with how well the computerized system works, and they want to learn about the program Dave uses for grading.

Dave is being a role model and sharing with his colleagues some effective computer programs. His new colleagues don't appear to be threatened by the changes Dave has made to managing locks and grading. Dave is serving as an informal leader. He has led by doing. As a result he is earning credibility and respect among his colleagues.

Dave also started modeling effective instructional techniques. At his new school, students line up in squads each period. Teachers stand in front of squads and take attendance. Student leaders take positions in the front of each class and lead their classmates through a routine of calisthenics. It looks sharp and sounds impressive as the students chant the school name and mascot to a four count. Dave questioned the value of these warm-ups. First, teachers were having students stretch before they engaged in any aerobic activity. Second, students went through the motion of exercise without much passion. Students were not held accountable for progress on these exercises. The routine took about 15 minutes, which cut Dave's teaching time in half.

Dave asked his colleagues if he could take his class directly to his teaching area where he would engage students in warm-ups that practiced the skills of the unit he was teaching. His colleagues responded with a firm no. They denied Dave's request because they had always done warm-ups as a group, with three classes together. They strongly believed that their method built school spirit and helped students bond. Dave was disappointed, but he respected their decision. Still, he was not about to give up. He would comply with the class routine but continue to inform the other teachers of the benefits of splitting into their classes after the changing bell. He would be patient and understand that time was on his side.

Informal leadership doesn't mean that you will always implement the change you think is important. Sometimes change will have to come later. In his situation Dave will have to learn more about school culture and the interactions among his department colleagues to find a way to persuade them to move from ineffective warm-up routines to ones that are more effective.

Step 4: P.R. and PE: Publicly Celebrating Our Work

The best people to advocate the importance of physical education are physical educators. We know first hand the positive benefits of daily physical activity in people's health. We can help the school community understand why learning motor skills and concepts improves a student physically, personally, socially, and academically. Positive public relations will help you secure your program in the school curriculum. Positive public relations will help you create positive attitudes and perceptions about your program among students, parents or guardians, teachers, and administrators. Positive P.R. will help everyone understand what students learn in physical education. Advocacy can dispel the myth that physical education is a peripheral subject in which tenured teachers get paid to supervise locker combinations and student pickup games. Unfortunately, few physical educators build strong public relations with their school communities.

We believe that advocating your program is an important part of teaching. In performing public relations, the teacher assumes an informal leadership role that enables her to step beyond the gym and into the school community. Here are a few steps that will help you learn how to promote your program and build positive public relations.

Physical Education Vision

Meet with the department and determine a vision for your physical education program. After agreeing on a vision, urge the department to follow the steps for building a quality daily physical education program grounded in the national standards.

Physical Education Brochure

Create a physical education brochure that includes your vision, goals, year block plan, assessment criteria, student dress code, and a code of student conduct. Send brochures home with all students at the beginning of each academic year.

Physical Education Newsletter

A newsletter can be a valuable communication tool. A physical education newsletter may tell parents what students have been learning during the last unit or quarter. A newsletter could include tips on good health and nutrition. Everyone loves to try new recipes, so you could include some of those. You may want to include information about physical activities for the whole family and tips about fitness. Newsletters are good forums for praising outstanding students and student work. Don't forget about the possibility of an on-line newsletter. Many districts have Web sites where students can find missed homework assignments and progress reports. Parents or guardians can catch up on the latest district news on these sites. Let people know what is going on in your program.

Bulletin Boards

Colorful bulletin boards with catchy phrases catch everyone's attention. Ask the principal for a large bulletin board that hangs in a busy place like the cafeteria, library, or outside the office. Every month or two, create an exciting bulletin board that reflects what students are learning in physical education. Bulletin boards are wonderful ways to communicate physical education content and events to students, other teachers, school staff, administrators, and parents.

One-on-One Interactions

Show students that you care about them. Be firm yet fair and show students you care about them first as a person. Talk to your students one-on-one (figure 17.3). Try hard to learn every student's name. Knowing students' names shows that you care. Call parents about their child's behavior, both good and poor. Show parents and guardians how much you care about their sons and daughters.

Back-to-School Night Presentations

At back-to-school night, prepare a short PowerPoint presentation. The PowerPoint slides (or overheads) should include highlights from your physical education brochure. Pictures speak a thousand words, so scan in pictures of your students enjoying and working hard in a number of your physical education units. A PowerPoint presentation will capture the attention of parents and guardians. They will learn about your program and perhaps realize that it differs from the one they experienced in high school.

Staff Meetings

One of the best ways to earn credibility on the staff is to invite other teachers over to your side of the school. Ask the principal to place your department on the agenda. At the meeting have teachers participate in a few developmentally appropriate and inclusive activities from your program. Many physical education teachers lead their colleagues through cooperative games, team-building activities, or adventure problem-solving activities. Physical educators find that their colleagues truly enjoy the activities and come to appreciate the value of physical education as a school subject.

Figure 17.3 Consistent one-on-one interaction is a good way to let your students know you care about them and their achievements.

Academic Teams

More physical education teachers are asking to be members of academic teams and participate in integrated curriculum (see chapter 14). Academic teams typically consist of a small group of teachers from core academic areas such as language arts, math, science, and history. These teachers collaborate to plan and provide students with a holistic approach to content. For instance, students may study the influence of the Roman Empire on Britain and contemporary Western culture. The English teacher would present students with British literature influenced by the Roman Empire. A mathematics teacher would team up with a physics teacher to tackle physical dilemmas of the period, such as the construction of aqueducts. The social studies teacher might have students investigate social issues in daily life. The history teacher would apply historical concepts and events to practical projects in the classroom. The integration of academic disciplines provides students with a comprehensive view of the influence of the Roman Empire on British history and contemporary Western culture.

A physical educator joining this team may contribute a unit on Roman games and their influence on British games and modern world games. Or the physical educator may examine the physical fitness and health of the Roman soldier and the British peasant and contrast their fitness and health to what we see in contemporary cultures. Academic teaming enables students to study content with breadth and depth across academic disciplines. Involvement on academic teams brings the physical educator an opportunity to contribute to holistic learning and advocate the importance of the physical education curriculum.

PE Shows

A physical education show is a special event that you might put on once or twice a year. The show would take place in the evening for about 90 minutes. Students from physical education classes would perform 5- or 10-minute routines before an audience of families, teachers, students, school staff, administrators, board of education members, and representatives of community agencies. Physical educators would have their classes develop performance routines based on the unit the class was studying. For instance, Mrs. Johnson's fourth-period basketball class would create a basketball routine in which all students performed the skills they learned in class. Mr. Washington's class would prepare a routine on the climbing wall. His students would demonstrate their skills in spotting, bouldering, and knot tying. PE shows bring individuals in the community together and offer positive public relations for physical education programs. A regional high school in western Massachusetts regularly drew a crowd of 500 to its annual PE shows.

Family Fun Nights

The purpose of family fun nights is to help families become active and learn more about health and the benefits of physical activity (figure 17.4). Family fun nights are typically held in the evening after dinner. Students bring their families to the gym or physical education fields, where they find other students set up in booths or stations. Families rotate from booth to booth or station to station trying activities that students are learning in physical education.

PE Homework Assignments

Assigning homework to students is a good way to engage them in physical activity outside school. You may decide to assign homework to the whole family, such as a walk after dinner. You should include health and fitness tips for the family on homework assignments.

PTA Meetings

Ask the president of your local PTA chapter if you can have time on the agenda at the next meeting to explain developmentally appropriate physical education and its importance to student health and well-being.

Press Releases

Every time something new or novel takes place in your physical education program, write a press release and send it to the local newspapers, radio stations, and television stations. Keep the public informed about the exciting things happening in your program.

Create a Web Page

As physical educators gain savvy about technology and the Internet, many create Web pages about their physical education programs. A Web page is another communication tool that enables you to keep the school community and public aware of your program development and improvement.

Figure 17.4   Family fun nights are a chance for community members to meet teachers and learn about healthy lifestyle choices.

Summary

You have probably heard the idea that a team is as strong as its weakest link. Let's apply this axiom to physical education programs. If we are to create effective and lasting change to the quality of physical education in schools, we must begin with each teacher and his or her classes. Individual teachers link together the department chain that makes up a physical education program.

As a physical educator and teacher leader you have the responsibility to confront and solve problems that affect student learning and teacher effectiveness such as overload, isolation, negative group think, and limited teacher roles. Schools and teachers can solve many of these issues by approaching the business of serving students as a professional community built on a foundation of collegiality and learning. Learning organizations, learning schools, learning departments, and learning individuals remain flexible and capable of changing with the times. Those who choose to stand still perpetuate mediocrity, ignorance, and incompetence.

As a teacher leader, you will come to understand the importance of school culture and power relationships as you navigate your way through each school year. Knowledge you acquire about how your school operates will assist you in building a quality physical education program that students, staff, and community respect. A strong, effective leader serving in the school principal's role will help. Be sure to make that person an ally and inform her or him of the importance of quality physical education programs.

Promoting your program is essential. Use a variety of public relations tactics but remember that public relations is futile unless you have a quality program to back it up. One of the best vehicles for promotion is word of mouth. Your students may be your best advocates.

Checking for Understanding ▶▶▶

- Describe the nature of teaching as it relates to overload, isolation, group think, and limited teacher roles.
- Explain why it is important that physical educators emerge as teacher leaders.
- Define school culture.
- Define stakeholders and explain how they influence school culture.
- Define a school microculture.
- Explain the importance of power relationships.
- State several guidelines to keep in mind as you strive to become a teacher.

For Reflection and Discussion ▶▶▶

- Describe why the principal is crucial to school reform and change.
- Examine the meaning of informal leadership roles.
- List several ideas for developing positive public relations and advocacy.

References

Brandt, R.S., ed. 2000. *Education in a new era: ASCD yearbook.* Alexandria, VA: Association for Supervision and Curriculum Development.

Coghlan, D., and T. Brannick. 2001. *Doing action research in your organization.* Thousand Oaks, CA: Sage.

Fullan, M., and A. Hargreaves. 1996. *What's worth fighting for in your school.* New York: Teacher's College Press.

Goodlad, J.I. 1994. *Educational renewal: Better teachers, better schools.* San Francisco: Jossey-Bass.

Greenwood, D.J., and M. Levin. 1998. *Introduction to action research: Social research for social change.* Thousand Oaks, CA: Sage.

Lortie, D. 1975. *Schoolteacher.* Chicago: University of Chicago Press.

Placek, J. 1983. Conceptions of success in teaching: Busy, happy and good? In *Teaching in physical education*, ed. T. Templin and J. Olson, 46–56. Champaign, IL: Human Kinetics.

Sarason, S.B. 1990. *The predictable failure of education reform: Can we change course before it's too late?* San Francisco: Jossey-Bass.

Senge, P., N. Cambron-McCabe, T. Lucas, B. Smith, J. Dutton, and A. Kleiner. 2000. *Schools that learn: A fifth discipline fieldbook for educators, parents, and everyone who cares about education.* New York: Doubleday.

Stringer, E.T. 1999. *Action research.* 2nd ed. Thousand Oaks, CA: Sage.

Suggested Readings

Day, C. 2000. Beyond transformational leadership. *Educational Leadership* 57(7):56–60.

Hargreaves, A., and D. Fink. 2000. The three dimensions of reform. *Educational Leadership* 57(7):30–35.

Hargreaves, A., and M. Fullan. 1998. *What's worth fighting for out there?* New York: Teacher's College Press.

Ward, P., ed. 1999. The Saber-tooth project: Curriculum and workplace reform in middle school physical education. *Journal of Teaching in Physical Education,* Monograph 18(4):379-489.

Wheatley, M.J. 1994. *Leadership and the new science.* San Francisco: Berrett-Koehler.

Chapter 18

Keeping Up to Date: Learner for Life

> There is no failure, except in no longer trying.
>
> — *Elbert Hubbard*

Jimika and Don recently graduated from a university with physical education teaching credentials. Both are excited to begin their careers. With teachers in high demand, both had secured full-time jobs teaching physical education before they walked across the stage to shake the hand of the university president.

The summer months passed quickly. Jimika and Don prepared for the first days of school and organized the materials they had developed while working on their credentials. The first year of school passed without incident for either of them. Our new teachers remained excited to be teaching physical education and coaching. They found that the unit plans they had developed at the university were useful. When they had to teach physical activities for which they had not developed a unit plan, other teachers in their department offered theirs. All was well in the physical education departments in which they taught.

One year of teaching turned into 5 years and then rolled into 15 years with what seemed like a blink of an eye. Jimika and Don remained in their current positions. Jimika seemed just as excited about teaching in year 15 as she did during her first year. Don, on the other hand, seemed tired and bored. Jimika found her students to be fun and challenging. She worked hard to know her students' needs and stay up with current trends in teaching physical education. Don stayed current with coaching baseball but felt that students in his classes were bored and lazy. What Don didn't realize was that he was teaching his first year 15 years in a row. He didn't work on improving his teaching or staying current the way Jimika did.

How can two graduates from the same program have such different experiences teaching physical education over the course of their careers?

Learning Objectives

After reading this chapter you will be able to

- explain what apprenticeship of observation means,
- give an overview of career development,
- list a variety of professional development opportunities,
- explain what being a critical consumer means, and
- discuss how you will be a learner for life.

Key Terms and Phrases

Career development
Apprenticeship of observation
Induction
In-service
Professional development
Critical consumer

You've almost finished the book, and now you can sit back to reflect on what you have learned. As you reflect, you can't help but wonder what tomorrow may bring. If you are a student you consider what life will be like as a physical education teacher. If you are already teaching, you wonder what life will be like in your classes tomorrow and the day after.

The previous chapters have focused on the issues we believe you should understand to be able to teach secondary physical education with the purpose of helping your students become active for life. We have given you information and ideas to help you develop into an excellent teacher. In this last chapter we will take it a step further and suggest ways that you can enjoy the journey of excellence by continuing to learn throughout your career.

Whether you are teaching today or in the near future, you probably can't help but think about the quality and longevity of your career. The significance and length of your teaching career will depend on many things, the most important of which is *you*.

Overview of the Career Process

Our hope is that you will strive to become an excellent teacher. As we stated in chapter 1, an excellent teacher is committed to be a learner for life. When you are a learner for life, you comprehend the need to stay current and the importance of change. Will you spend your career being enthusiastic about teaching challenges like Jimika is, or will your energy slowly wane as Don's did, transforming you from a thriving tree to deadwood? The choice is yours.

By recognizing the complexity of career development, you will be better able to understand why people like Jimika thrive and why those like Don burn out. Let's review some important aspects of **career development**.

Apprenticeship of Observation

We mentioned in chapter 14 that all of us spend many years in school watching teachers teach. This process is called **apprenticeship of observation.** By the time we reach physical education teacher education training programs, most of us think we have a good idea about what teachers do and how they do it. Many physical education recruits feel as if they know enough to begin teaching physical education without receiving college or university training.

Apprenticeship of observation may be helpful in recruiting individuals to teaching. Through direct observation for a number of years, teachers-to-be learn a great deal about the job. They develop beliefs, values, and attitudes about teaching, which follow them into college, credential programs, and teaching careers. Some of these beliefs, values, and attitudes may align with what we know about effective teaching and developmentally appropriate physical education. Others may not.

If prospective teachers carry the belief that everything they need to know about teaching they learned in grade school, high school, and college, then they will be less apt to adopt the learner-for-life approach to teaching. People who do not adopt the lifelong learning approach to teaching may find themselves teaching the same way for an entire career, as did our friend Don.

Induction Phase

After students graduate with their teaching credentials and accept a teaching position, they enter the **induction** phase of their careers. The induction phase typically comprises the first five years of teaching. This period is an important time. During the induction phase teachers receive on-the-job training. Many teachers decide during this time that teaching is not for them, and they move on to other types of work. For many others the on-the-job training received in the first five years of teaching further shapes career behavior.

In-Service Phase

The **in-service** phase covers the years spent teaching after the induction phase. During the in-service years physical educators have many opportunities for **professional development.** Professional development can occur in a variety of venues. Many physical educators more interested in coaching attend only coaching workshops and seminars. These activities are valuable and helpful for coaching sports, but coaching content often has limited application to developmentally appropriate practices in the classroom. Other physical educators spend much of their time attending workshops that offer 101 activities for keeping students busy, happy, and well behaved. These professional development opportunities are valuable only when physical educators reflect thoroughly on the appropriateness of the activities and how they relate to program, unit, and lesson goals and objectives.

Professional development opportunities must provide physical educators time to examine what they are learning and how it might affect their programs. We hope that physical educators who stay in the classroom will choose to become learners for life. Those who choose to learn will find available an abundance of professional development opportunities. The next sections provide an overview of those opportunities.

Your Turn ▶▶▶

♦ How do you think your apprenticeship of observation has affected your views on physical education?

♦ Can you describe teachers you've had in the past who seemed to tackle their teaching career as Jimika did?

♦ Can you describe teachers you've had in the past who seemed to tackle their teaching career as Don did?

♦ Why do you suppose so many teachers leave the profession during the first five years?

Change With the Times

Becoming a learner for life means that you are willing to take risks and change with the times. It takes courage to admit that what you are doing is not working as well as you'd like. You need courage to be open to new ideas. Although you can stay current in many different ways and choose from abundant opportunities, few physical education teachers put in the effort to seek them out. State conferences and workshops, in-service training sessions, on-line classes, continuing education classes, listservs, and certification programs are just some of the ways a teacher can get involved with the profession. The effort it takes is more than worth it. Teachers who take advantage of opportunities to stay current bring new ideas to their classrooms and stay excited about what they teach.

Purpose

Use technology to keep aware of new trends in popular teenage culture for the purpose of including relevant and appropriate activities in your existing program.

Resource and Procedure

Keep up to date on new trends in popular culture that may affect your students' physical activity choices, motivation for succeeding in physical education class, and possible teaching resources. Web search engines typically include "What's New," "What's Hot," and "What's Cool" buttons to provide Web surfers with the latest and most popular Web sites. You can bet your students are checking them out.

What are considered effective teaching methods may not change much during your career, but the content of your curriculum should change with the times. Many physical education teachers still teach the sports they learned in school. When planning their curriculum they do not consider the fact that young people today have different interests and opportunities than they did. When some older teachers were in school, activities like in-line skating, Ultimate Frisbee, step aerobics, cardio kick boxing, orienteering, and rock climbing were mostly unknown or not yet invented. Today, some of these activities are extremely popular among both children and adults. Did you know, for instance, that in-line skating is currently the world's fastest growing sport on wheels? Every time we go to the park to skate, we see people skating behind strollers or skating alongside their dogs. At our gym the step aerobics classes are always full. This activity was not even around 15 years ago! People who thought it was a fad were wrong. Now, instead of young girls in thongs and leg warmers, we see classes filled with women and men of all ages enjoying the challenge of following the instructor's complex routines. People's preferences for lifetime health-enhancing activities are changing, and if you want to help your students become active for life, you have to change with the times!

Jimika, in our opening scenario, used the opportunities available to her to keep up with advances in the field and stay current. After 15 years of teaching she's still feeling fresh. But changing with the times doesn't mean that you hop on any bandwagon that happens to rolling by. An excellent teacher will takes risks but will also be a **critical consumer.**

Be a Critical Consumer

Many of the professional development opportunities that come your way will be appropriate and meaningful to you and your program, but others will not. How will you know the difference? The first step is to check the credibility of the source. For example, if you would like to go to a workshop, investigate before you sign up. Find the answers to the following questions:

- Who are the presenters?
- What are their credentials?
- Are they promoting or selling a product or service?

Even state and national conferences offer sessions in which the presenter stands to gain from your participation. That doesn't mean that what they are saying or teaching won't be useful to you. Just keep in mind that some presenters are salespeople or company representatives. Then ask yourself these questions:

- How can the information help me reach my unit goals and objectives?
- How can the information help me align my objectives more closely with national standards?
- How will the information help me teach and encourage my students to become active for the rest of their lives?

You should ask these questions, of course, about any professional development opportunity you are evaluating. When you carefully examine the credibility of the sources and reflect on all the issues presented, you become a critical consumer. Your evaluation should be based on what you have learned from this book and from national guidelines about appropriate physical education practices, effective teaching, and sound curriculum development. If you haven't done so already, start practicing being a critical consumer today!

Ways to Keep Up to Date

Teachers today have so many opportunities to stay current in their profession that those who don't can offer no acceptable excuse. Even the excuse that one doesn't have enough time isn't acceptable because some professional development opportunities do not require the commitment of large blocks of time. Going to a state conference can be a three-day ordeal, but staying connected with other physical educators on a listserv is possible with the expenditure of only a few minutes a day. Checking in on **www.pecentral.com** a few times a week need not be a big time commitment either. On the other hand, taking a continuing education class may take weeks in the summer, or months if the class is spread out throughout the year. However, teachers who participate in any of these professional development opportunities find that the time is well worth it. The following paragraphs will explain some of the opportunities that are available to help you keep up to date.

Go to Conferences and Workshops

During the course of a year a variety of conferences and workshops will be offered in your state. These are great opportunities to learn what other teachers are doing in their programs. Your state AHPERD conference will include presentations by educators and professors from your state as well as other states and countries. Summer workshops are common in many states, as are weekend workshops. Remember that you can learn from disciplines other than your own. Don't limit yourself by traditional boundaries. Check out the possibilities and keep an open mind! Your state AHPERD office, county office of education, or school district will be able to help you find out about conferences and workshops in your area (figure 18.1).

Your Turn ▶▶▶

What are some examples of thinking out of the box when it comes to professional development opportunities like conferences and workshops?

Figure 18.1 No matter where you live, professional conferences and workshops are excellent places to enrich your teaching knowledge.

Network Through List Servers

Physical education teachers may be isolated from other teachers because of the location of their offices. This circumstance may make it more difficult for them to share ideas about teaching with colleagues throughout the day. But they need support and networking opportunities, too. Thankfully, with modern technology even the most physically remote teacher has ways to overcome isolation.

If you have a computer and Internet access you have a tool for networking and accessing new sources of information. Listservs have become an important way for teachers to communicate with professionals around the world. When you subscribe to a listserv you can read about the concerns and ideas of other teachers and participate in the discussions by writing responses or asking questions. Topics discussed on listservs range from effective teaching and curriculum issues to managing equipment and legal issues. You can subscribe to listservs by visiting **www.pecentral.com**.

Visit Web Sites

Credible professionals have put together several Web sites for physical educators. We find that the best way to find credible sites is to go through **www.pecentral.com**. PE Central offers an abundance of ideas and tips for lesson planning and effective teaching and keeps an up-to-date review of Web sites that can be helpful to your professional development. The professors and teachers who manage PE Central do their best to screen all content (including links to other Web sites) to make sure it is consistent with national guidelines and standards for appropriate physical education.

Read

A simple and inexpensive way to stay up to date is to subscribe to professional journals in physical education. Many are available, ranging from hands-on, practical journals to those presenting the latest research. AAHPERD (American Alliance for

Health, Physical Education, Recreation and Dance) offers several journals, and you can find information about each of them on their Web site, **www.aahperd.org**. The following is a non-exhaustive list of professional journals in physical education:

- *Journal of Physical Education, Recreation and Dance*
- *Strategies*
- *Teaching Elementary Physical Education*
- *Quest*
- *The Physical Educator*
- *Journal of Teaching Physical Education*

Work With Student Teachers

A wonderful way to stay current is to work with student teachers. By becoming a cooperating teacher you offer your expertise and services to future physical education teachers and have a chance to learn from them as well. They will come to you full of fresh ideas and knowledge from their university classes. If you decide to work with a student teacher, remember what it was like when you were in that situation. Keep an open mind but remember to be a critical consumer!

Become Involved

From networking with other professionals through the Internet to going to conferences and workshops, the variety of opportunities available in professional development is so substantial that we cannot cover them all in detail. We have listed more professional development opportunities in figure 18.2 so that you see can the range of possibilities. The main point is to become involved any way you can! Take advantage of the opportunities to become a learner for life!

- Conferences
- Workshops
- List servers
- Web sites
- Professional development consortia
- Action research
- Learning from other disciplines
- Observing other teachers
- Connecting with a mentor teacher
- National certifications
- Teacher-of-the-year competitions
- On-line classes
- Continuing education classes
- Advanced degree
- Journals
- Books
- Consultants

Figure 18.2 Professional development opportunities to help you stay up to date.

Summary

Becoming an excellent teacher is a lifetime process, a journey. By choosing the path of excellence, you decide to become a learner for life. During the various stages of your career you will find that different kinds of professional development will work for you. The main reason to stay current is to make sure that you can help your students become physically active for the rest of their lives. Many opportunities are available for teachers who want to keep up to date. No matter which ones you choose, you should always be a critical consumer.

Checking for Understanding ▶▶▶

◆ What is meant by apprenticeship of observation?

◆ How does a typical physical education teacher's career develop?

◆ Can you list at least 10 ways for a physical education teacher to stay up to date in the field?

For Reflection and Discussion ▶▶▶

◆ How will you avoid becoming part of the large percentage of teachers who leave teaching during the first five years?

◆ What will you do to avoid becoming deadwood?

◆ Of all the ways to keep up to date, which appeal to you most? Why?

◆ Have you ever attended a physical education professional conference? If so, what was it like?

◆ Why do you think it is important to continue learning throughout your career?

◆ How will you become a learner for life?

Suggested Readings

Chu, D. 1981. Origins of teacher/coach role conflict: A reaction to Massengale's paper. In *Sociology of sport: Diverse perspectives*, ed. S. Greendorfer and A. Yiannakis, 158–163. Westpoint, NY: Leisure Press.

Dodds, P., J. Placek, S. Doolittle, K. Pinkham, T. Ratliffe, and P. Portman. 1992. Teacher/coach recruits: Background profiles, occupational decision factors, and comparisons with recruits into other physical education occupations. *Journal of Teaching in Physical Education* 11:161–176.

Doolittle, S., P. Dodds, and J.H. Placek. 1993. Persistences of beliefs about teaching during formal training of preservice teachers. In *Socialization in physical education*, ed. S. Stroot, *Journal of Teaching in Physical Education*, Monograph 12:355–365.

Fejgin, N., N. Ephraty, and D. Ben Sira. 1995. Work environment and burnout of physical education teachers. *Journal of Teaching in Physical Education* 15(1):64–77.

Hutchinson, G.E. 1993. Prospective teachers perspectives on teaching physical education: An interview study on the recruitment phase of teacher socialization. *Journal of Teaching in Physical Education* 12(4):344–354.

Lortie, D. 1975. *Schoolteacher.* Chicago: University of Chicago Press.

Placek, J., and M. O'Sullivan. 1997. The many faces of integrated physical education. *Journal of Physical Education, Recreation and Dance* 68(1):20–24.

Pooley, J.C. 1972. Professional socialization: A model of the pre-training phase applicable to physical education students. *Quest* 18:57–66.

Senge, P., N. Cambron-McCabe, T. Lucas, B. Smith, J. Dutton, and A. Kleiner. 2000. *Schools that learn: A fifth discipline fieldbook for educators, parents, and everyone who cares about education.* New York: Doubleday.

Silverman, S., and P.R. Subramaniam. 1999. Student attitude toward physical education and physical activity: A review of measurement issues and outcomes. *Journal of Teaching in Physical Education* 18(1):97–125.

Steen, T.B. 1985. Teacher socialization in physical education during early training experiences: A qualitative study. Paper presented at the annual meeting of AAHPERD, Atlanta.

Stroot, S.A., C. Collier, M. O'Sullivan, and K. England. 1994. Contextual hoops and hurdles: Workplace conditions in secondary physical education. *Journal of Teaching in Physical Education* 13(4):342–360.

Tannehill, D., J-E. Romar, M. O'Sullivan, K. England, and D. Rosenberg. 1994. Attitudes toward physical education: Their impact on how physical education teachers make sense of their work. *Journal of Teaching in Physical Education* 13(4):406–420.

Index

About the Authors

Cathrine Himberg, PhD, has been teaching physical education teacher education at California State University at Chico since 1996. Every week she spends the equivalent of a school day in the public schools with her university students so that they can get the hands-on experience they need to become effective and reflective teachers. She is the founder and director of CASPER (Concerned Adults and Students for Physical Education Reform), an international advocacy organization for developmentally appropriate physical education.

She earned an MA with distinction in exercise physiology from California State University at Chico and a PhD in pedagogy (curriculum and instruction) from Virginia Tech in 1996.

Gayle E. Hutchinson, EdD, chairs the department of physical education and exercise science at California State University at Chico, where she helps prepare teachers who will provide quality physical education. She has taught middle and high school students and worked closely with physical educators since 1979. She earned her doctorate from the University of Massachusetts at Amherst and her master's degree from Columbia Teacher's college, both in curriculum and instruction.

As principal investigator and project director for the Northern California Physical Education Health Project, Dr. Hutchinson helped create a vision of schools as wellness communities. She also has assisted middle schools in developing curriculum and implementing programs that are in accordance with state and national standards.

John M. Roussell, PhD, teaches communication design at California State University at Chico. A professor and researcher in instructional technology since 1996, he focuses on effective adaptation of technology into learning situations. He earned his doctorate in curriculum and instruction from Virginia Tech, and his master's degree in instructional technology from California State University at Chico.

Dr. Roussell enjoyed a 20-year career as a professional radio and television broadcaster, producer, journalist, and consultant. He also has served as an assessment consultant of communication and instructional technologies for corporate training and K-12 education.